T0336461

ISLAMIC FINANCE

A Catalyst for Shared Prosperity?

GLOBAL REPORT ON ISLAMIC FINANCE

ISLAMIC FINANCE

A Catalyst for Shared Prosperity?

WORLD BANK GROUP

1 2 3 4 20 19 18 17

ISBN (paper): 978-1-4648-0926-2
eISBN (electronic): 978-1-4648-0927-9
DOI: 10.1596/978-1-4648-0926-2

Cover design: Critical Stages
Cover image: Yuriy Spodarenko. The Great Mosque of St. Petersburg, St. Petersburg, Russian Federation. Creative Commons Attribution-Share Alike 3.0 Unported

Library of Congress Cataloging-in-Publication Data has been applied for.

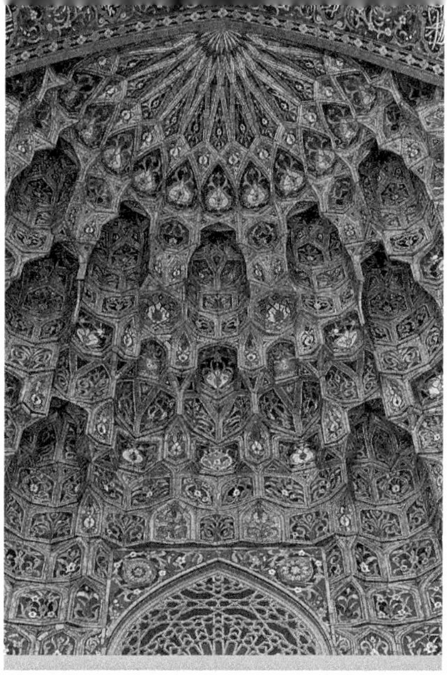

Contents

BOXES

FIGURES

TABLES

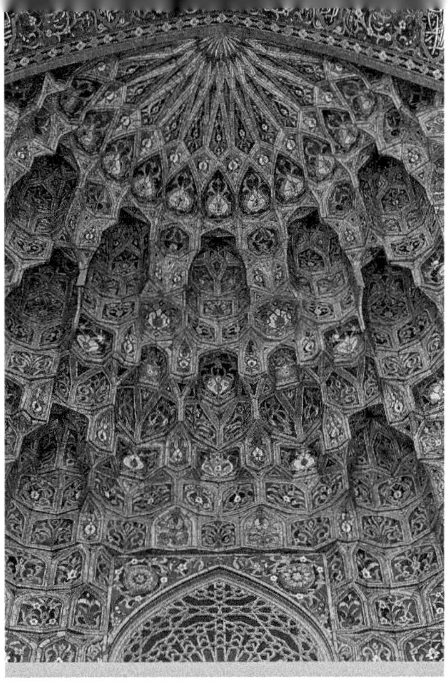

Foreword

Under a joint initiative of the Islamic Development Bank Group and the World Bank Group, the inaugural *Global Report on Islamic Finance* has been prepared with a focus on the widening disparity of global wealth and how Islamic finance can help in enhancing shared prosperity. This Report is timely, as world leaders have adopted the 2030 Agenda for Sustainable Development, which includes a set of Sustainable Development Goals (SDGs) to end poverty, fight inequality and injustice, and tackle climate change by 2030. The Islamic Development Bank Group, in its 2016–25 Strategic Plan, gives priority to inclusive and sustainable socioeconomic development among member-countries within its role in advancing Islamic finance globally.

Besides imposing social and environmental costs, severe inequality adversely affects economic growth and wealth creation. The question that needs to be addressed is how to minimize the disparity in wealth and enhance shared prosperity. Given its potential role in economic development, Islamic finance can contribute toward achieving these objectives. Accordingly, the joint initiative of the Islamic Development Bank Group and the World Bank Group provides detailed research under the general theme "Islamic Finance: A Catalyst for Shared Prosperity."

The *Global Report* provides a comprehensive overview of the existing status of various Islamic finance sectors and identifies major challenges hindering the growth of Islamic finance. It also identifies policy interventions and tools for policy makers to leverage the principles of Islamic finance in an effort to eradicate extreme poverty and work toward a more equitable distribution of wealth. The main message of the Report is that Islamic finance, built on a foundation of social and economic justice, can contribute to shared prosperity through the principles of inclusive participation and risk sharing.

The experts from both institutions who helped create this Report come with vast experience and technical knowledge and provide dual perspectives on finance, enabling readers to connect with the Islamic perspective of finance. The joint initiative highlights that there is a lot that we can learn from one another. We hope that this Report will be the beginning of a fruitful and productive collaboration among international and multilateral institutions to serve our global community.

Dr. Ahmed Mohamed Ali
President, Islamic Development Bank Group
September 2016

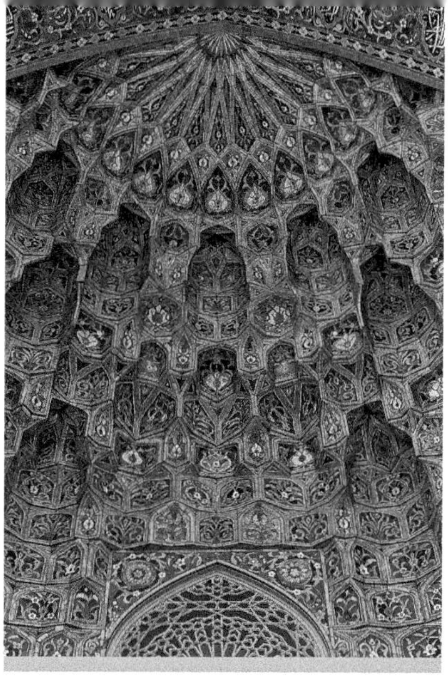

Acknowledgments

This Report was prepared as a joint initiative of the World Bank Group (WBG) and Islamic Development Bank Group (IDBG). The team was led by Azmi Omar, Director General of the Islamic Research and Training Institute (IRTI), IDBG, and Zamir Iqbal, Lead Financial Sector Specialist, Finance and Markets (F&M) Global Practice, World Bank. Special thanks are owed to Dawood Ashraf, Senior Researcher–Islamic Finance, IRTI, for his commitment and contributions, and for taking the lead at IRTI in preparation of this Report. We are also thankful to Abayomi Alawode, Head of Islamic Finance, Finance and Markets Global Practice, World Bank; Ahmed Fayed al-Gebali, Director, Islamic Development Bank (IDB); and Abdul Aziz Al-Hinai, former Vice President of Finance, IDB, for their support on this project.

The team would like to thank and acknowledge the contributions of the Advisory Committee, comprising Dr. Ishrat Husain, Chairman, Center of Excellence for Islamic Finance, Institute of Business Administration; Prof. Dr. Abbas Mirakhor, the International Centre for Education in Islamic Finance (INCEIF); and Dr. Ghiath Shabsigh, Assistant Director, Monetary and Capital Markets Department, International Monetary Fund (IMF), who guided the team with their wisdom, experience, and expertise. As advisers, they provided extensive feedback and comments throughout the conceptualization and review stages of the Report. Their comments helped the team enhance the content of earlier versions of the Report.

The team would also like to thank the peer reviewers, Alwaleed Fareed Alatabani, Lead Financial Sector Specialist, Finance and Markets Global Practice, East Asia and Pacific Region, World Bank; Muhammad Umar Chapra, Advisor to the Director General of IRTI, IDB; Ahmed Mohamed Tawfick Rostom, Senior Financial Sector Specialist, Finance and Markets Global Practice, South Asia Region, World Bank; and Sami Al-Suwailem, Head of Financial Product Development Centre, IDB, for their valuable comments and feedback, which enriched the Report.

The teams at IRTI and World Bank Global Islamic Finance Development Center are recognized for their commitment and efforts in writing, updating, editing, and assembling this Report. They were led by Dawood Ashraf (IDBG) and Nihat Gumus (World Bank Group). We thank all the team members from both institutions for their valuable expertise and contributions, including Ayse Nur Aydin, Financial Analyst; Mehmet Murat Cobanoglu,

Financial Sector Specialist; Nihat Gumus, Financial Sector Specialist; Rasim Mutlu, Research Assistant; Canan Ozkan, Financial Sector Specialist; and Mustafa Tasdemir, Financial Sector Specialist, all from the World Bank; and Tamsir Cham, Economist; Hylmun Izhar, Economist; Anis Ben Khedher, Information Technology Specialist, Mohammed Obaidullah, Senior Economist; Ousmane Seck, Senior Economist; Nasim Shah Shirazi, Lead Economist; Salman Ali Syed, Senior Economist; and Muhamed Zulkhibri, Senior Economist, all from IDB.

In addition, the team benefited greatly from discussions, valuable input, and constructive comments provided by Prof. Habib Ahmed, Durham University; Prof. Azam Shah, INCEIF; and Prof. Rodney Wilson, INCEIF, who served as consultants to the team for select chapters.

The team would also like to thank Prof. Obiyathulla Ismath Bacha, INCEIF; Sohail Jaffer, FWU-Group; Prof. Tariqullah Khan, Qatar Foundation; Dr. Shehab Marzban, Shekra; Prof. Abbas Mirakhor, INCEIF; and Prof. Philip Molyneux, Bangor University, for their valuable comments and feedback as external peer reviewers for select chapters.

Finally, we acknowledge the support of Liudmila Uvarova, Knowledge Management Officer, Finance and Markets Global Practice, World Bank; the World Bank publishing team; the IRTI publishing team; and Nancy Morrison, Editor, the Morrison Group, for her invaluable efforts in editing this Report.

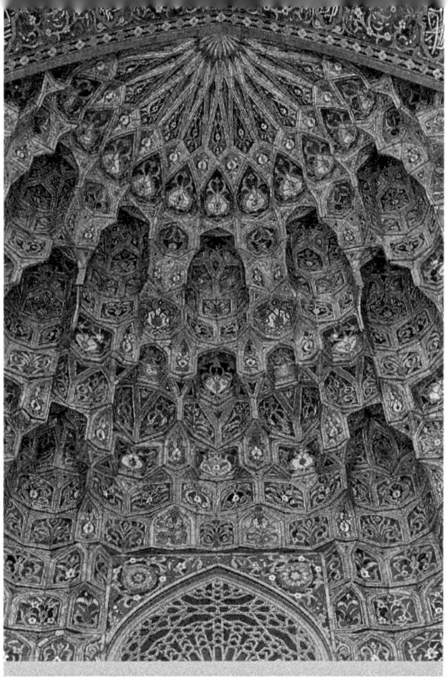

Glossary

Introduction

A lot of Islamic technical terms of Arabic origin have, over the last few decades, entered the dictionary of economics, banking, and finance in view of the rise and spread of Islamic economics, banking, and finance worldwide. It is not possible to collect them all and add them all to this glossary, however, the most important and most used ones are provided here.

A large number of the teachers, practitioners, researchers, and students interested in learning, practicing, or researching the subjects of Islamic economics, banking, and finance need to know the meanings of these technical terms and their proper usage. Therefore, this glossary has been prepared to facilitate their tasks. It provides broad, general, and precise explanations of the technical terms used in the literature of Islamic economics, banking, and finance. Because the terms were collected and compiled from various sources, it is difficult to recall or point out which term comes from which source. Our thanks and gratitude go to all of those from whom we benefited in compiling this glossary.

Notes

- Usually most of the terms used in this glossary are preceded by the article *al-*, meaning *the*. The articles are not used in this glossary, except when it is necessary to keep them, such as *al-ghunm bi al-ghurm* or *al-kharāj bi al-Damān*. Therefore, words like *al-'adl*, for example, are written just *'adl* without the *al-* article.
- Some Arabic words bearing the same meanings are pronounced differently. These are separated by a slash **/** as in the case of **عَرْبُون/عُرْبُون** *'arbūn/'urbūn,* meaning down payment.
- Both the singular and plural forms of some Arabic words are put in the same entry instead of in two entries. The plural forms are put between parentheses after the singular form, as in the case of عَالِم (عُلَمَاء) *'alim* (*'ulamā'*) meaning scholar(s).
- The terms used in this glossary are arranged alphabetically according to the second column on the left, titled "**Transliterated as.**"

Arabic original word	Transliterated as	English meanings
عَدْل	*'adl*	Justice, equity, fairness
عَفَاف	*'afāf*	Abstinence, satisfaction with the little one has
عَفْو	*'afw*	Surplus, which is over one's basic needs
عَهْد (عُهُود)	*'ahd ('uhūd)*	Covenant(s), treaty(ies)
عَالِم (عُلَمَاء)	*'alim ('ulamā')*	Scholar(s)
عَمِيل (عُمَلَاء)	*'amīl ('umalā')*	Customer(s)
عَامِل (عُمَّال)	*'āmil ('ummāl)*	Worker(s), manager(s), entrepreneur(s)
عَقَار (عَقَارَات)	*'aqār ('aqārāt)*	Immovable property(ies), building(s)
عَقْد (عُقُود)	*'aqd ('uqūd)*	Contract(s), agreement(s), bond(s)
عَقِيدة (عَقَائِد)	*'aqīdah ('aqā'id)*	Belief(s), creed(s), doctrine(s)
عَاقِلَة	*'āqilah*	Mutual solidarity between the members of a community to help those in need
عَقْل (عَقُول)	*'āql ('uqūl)*	Intellect(s), mind(s)
عَرْبُون/عُرْبُون	*'arbun/'urbūn*	Down payment
عَارِيَة	*'āriyah*	Loan of small items
عَيْب (عُيُوب)	*'ayb ('uyūb)*	Defect(s), fault(s)
عَيْن	*'ayn*	Tangible (physical) asset
عَيِّنَة	*'ayyinah*	Sample
أَجِير (أُجَرَاء)	*ajīr (ujara')*	Employee(s), worker(s)
أَجْر (أُجُور)	*ajr (ujūr)*	Salary(ies), wage(s), commission(s), compensation(s)
أَجْر الْمِثْل	*ajr al-mithl*	Prevalent similar wage
آخِرَة	*ākhirah*	Hereafter
أَخْلَاق	*akhlāq*	Ethics, morals
الغُنْم بِالْغُرْم	*al-ghunm bi al-ghurm*	Earning profit is legitimized by risk taking. Earning is subject to taking risk.
الْحَوْل	*al-ḥawl*	A year
الخَرَاج بِالضَّمَان	*al-kharāj bi al-damān*	Revenue is subject to liability
الْمُجَازفَة	*al-mujāzafah*	Speculation
أَمَان	*amān*	Security
أَمَانَة (أَمَانَات)	*amānah*	Trust, honesty, trustworthiness
أَمِين (أُمَنَاء)	*amīn (umana')*	Trustee(s), trustworthy, honest
أَمْر	*amr*	Order
أَرْض (أَرَاضِي)	*arḍ (arāḍi)*	Land(s)
أَصْل (أُصُول)	*aṣl (uṣūl)*	Origin(s)
أَصْنَاف	*asnaf*	Eligible beneficiaries
أَثَاث	*athath*	Furniture
آيَة (آيات)	*āyah (āyāt)*	Qur'anic verse(s)
بَرَكَة	*barakah*	Blessing
بَاطِل	*bāṭil*	Null, void, invalid
بَيْعُ المُرَابَحَة	*bay' al- murābaḥah*	Mark-up sale

Arabic original word	Transliterated as	English meanings
بَيْع (بُيُوْع)	*bay' (buyū')*	Sale(s)
بَيْعُ العُرْبُون	*bay' al-'urbūn*	Sale with down payment
بَيْع الدَّيْن	*bay' al-dayn*	Sale of debt
بَيْعُ الكَالِئ بالْكالِئ	*bay' al-kālī' bi-al-kālī'*	A sale in which both the delivery of the object of sale and the payment of its price are delayed. It is similar to a modern forward sale contract.
بَيْعُ السَّلَم	*bay' al-salam*	Sale in which payment is made in advance by the buyer and the delivery of goods is deferred by the seller
بَيْعُ الوَفَاء	*bay' al-wafa'*	Buy-back sale, sale and repurchase
بَيْع بالتَّقْسِيط	*bay' bi al-taqsīt*	Sale with installment payments
بَيْعُ بِالثَّمَن المُؤَجَّل	*bay' bi al-thaman al-ājil*	Credit sale or sale at deferred payment
بَيْعُ مُؤَجَّل	*bay' mu'ajjal*	Credit sale or sale at deferred payment
بَيْعُ العِينَة	*bay'-al-'inah*	Buying an object for cash then selling it to the same party for a higher price whose payment is deferred so that the purchase and sale of the object serve as a ruse for lending on interest
بَيْتُ المَال	*bayt al-māl*	Treasury
بِدْعة (بِدَع)	*bid'ah*	Innovation in Islamic rituals
دَعْوَة	*da'wah*	Claim, invitation
دَلِيل	*dalīl*	Proof, evidence, reason
ضَمَان	*ḍamān*	Guarantee
ضَرَر	*ḍarar*	Harm
ضَرُوْرَة	*ḍarūrah*	Necessity
ضَرُوْرِيَّات	*ḍarūrīyāt*	Basic needs
دَيْن (دُيُون)	*dayn (duyūn)*	Debt(s)
ذِمَّة (ذِمَم)	*dhimmah (dhimam)*	Liability(ies), responsibility(ies)
دِين	*dīn*	Religion
دِينَار	*dīnār*	Dinar (currency)
دِرْهَم	*dirham*	Dirham (currency)
دِيَّة	*diyyah*	Blood money (compensation)
دُعَاء	*du'ā*	Supplication
دُنْيَا	*dunya*	Life in this world
فَائِض (فَوَائِض)	*fā'id (fawa'id)*	Surplus(es), excess(es)
فَضْل	*fadl*	Excess, additional, surplus
فَضْل الله	*fadl-al-Allah*	The bounties bestowed by Almighty Allah
فَلَاح	*falāḥ*	Prosperity, success
فَقِيه (فُقَهَاء)	*faqīh (fuqaha')*	Jurist(s)
فَقِير (فُقَرَاء)	*faqir (fuqara')*	Poor person(s)
فَرْض (فَرَائِض)	*farḍ (farā'iḍ)*	Duty(ies)
فَرْض عَيْن	*farḍ 'ayn*	Compulsory duty on everyone
فَرْض كِفَايَة	*farḍ kifāyah*	Compulsory duty on everyone if nobody did it

Arabic original word	Transliterated as	English meanings
فَاسِد	*fāsid*	Void, invalid
فَسْخ	*faskh*	Terminate
فَتْوَىٰ (فَتَاوَىٰ)	*fatwa (fatāwá)*	Religious verdict(s) made by a *faqih*-competent *shari'ah* scholar
فِقْه	*fiqh*	Islamic jurisprudence
فِقْهُ المُعَامَلَات	*fiqh al-mu'āmalāt*	Jurisprudence of transactions
فِقْهِي	*fiqhī*	Juristic
فِطْرَة	*fitrah*	Law of nature
غَبْن /غُبْن	*ghabn/ghubn*	Misappropriation or defrauding others with respect to specifications of the goods and their prices
غَنِيمَة (غَنَائِم)	*ghanīmah (ghana'im)*	Spoils of war, booty(ies)
غَرَر	*gharar*	Excessive risk and uncertainty, ambiguity
غَرَر فَاحِش	*gharar fāḥish*	Excessive risk
غَرَر يَسِير	*gharar yasīr*	Minor risk
غَارِم – غَارِمِين	*ghārim (ghārimīn)*	Indebted, bankrupt
غَصْب	*ghaṣb*	Taking by force, possess unlawfully
غَاصِب	*ghāṣib*	Violator
غِشّ	*ghishsh*	Deception, fraud
حَدِيث (أَحَادِيْث)	*ḥādīth (aḥādīth)*	Sayings of the Prophet Mohammed
هَدِيَّة (هَدَايَا)	*hadiyyah (hadāya)*	Gift(s), donation(s)
حَاجَة (حَاجَات)	*ḥājah (ḥājāt)*	Need(s)
حَاجِيَات	*hajiyāt*	Basic needs
حَج	*ḥajj*	Pilgrimage
حَلَال	*ḥalāl*	Permissible, lawful, allowed
حَقّ (حُقُوق)	*ḥaqq (ḥuqūq)*	Right(s)
حَرَام	*ḥarām*	Not permissible, unlawful, not allowed
حَوَالَة	*ḥawālah*	Bill of exchange, promissory note, cheque, draft
هِبَة (هِبَات)	*hibah (hibat)*	Donation(s), gift(s)
حِفْظ	*ḥifẓ*	Learning by heart
هِجْرَة	*Hijrah*	Migration
حِكْمَة	*ḥikmah*	Wisdom, rationale
حِيلَة (حِيَل)	*ḥīlah (ḥiyal)*	Trick(s), ploy(s), ruse(s)
حِمَىٰ	*ḥimá*	
حِسْبَة	*ḥisbah*	Ombudsman, regulation
حُكْم (أَحْكَام)	*ḥukm (aḥkām)*	Ruling, decision
عِبَادَة (عِبَادَات)	*'ibādah ('ibādāt)*	Ritual(s), act(s) of worship
عِلَّة (عِلَل)	*'illah ('ilal)*	Defect(s), justification(s), reason(s), rationale(s)
عِلْم (عُلُوم)	*'ilm ('ulūm)*	Knowledge(s)
عِينَة	*'īnah*	Debt buying and selling
عِوَض	*'iwaḍ*	Compensation

Arabic original word	Transliterated as	English meanings
إعَارَة	*i'ārah*	Lending
إعْسَار	*i'sār*	Insolvency
إعْتِدَال	*i'tidāl*	Moderation
إعْتِمَاد	*i'timād*	Approval
إبَاحَة	*ibāḥah*	Permission
إبْدَال	*ibdāl*	Change
إبِل	*ibil*	Camels
ابْن	*ibn*	Son
ابْنُ السَّبِيْل	*ibn al-sabīl*	Traveler
ادِّخَار	*iddikhār*	Saving
إذْن	*idhn*	Permission
إفْلَاس	*iflās*	Bankruptcy
إغَاثَة	*ighāthah*	Relief
إحْسَان	*iḥsān*	Benevolence, compassion, kindness
احْتِكَار	*iḥtikār*	Hoarding
إحْيَاء	*iḥyā'*	Reform, revival, restoration
إيجَاب	*ijāb*	Offer (in contract)
إجَارَة	*ijārah*	Leasing, rent
إجَارَة مُنْتَهِية بِالتَّمْلِيك	*ijārah muntahia-bi-tamlīk*	Hire purchase
إجَارَة واقْتِنَاء	*ijārah wa-iqtina'*	Hire purchase
إجْمَاع	*ijmā'*	Consensus
إجْتِهَاد	*ijtihād*	Effort, exertion, diligence, legal reasoning
إخْلَاص	*ikhlāṣ*	Sincerity
اخْتِيَار	*ikhtiyār*	Choice
إكْرَاه	*ikrāh*	Compulsion
إكْتِسَاب	*iktisāb*	Earning
إلْغَاء	*ilghā'*	Cancellation
إلْحَاق	*ilḥāq*	Annexation
إلْتِزَام	*iltizām*	Commitment
إمَام	*imām*	Leader, guide, ruler
إيمَان	*imān*	Faith, conviction, belief
إنَابَة	*inābah*	Repentance
إنْفَاذ	*infādh*	Enforcement, execution
إنْفَاق	*infāq*	Expenditure, spending
إنْفِصَال	*infiṣāl*	Separation
إنْسَان	*insān*	Human being
إنْتِفَاع	*intifā'*	Utilization
إنْتِقَال	*intiqāl*	Movement, transmission
إقَالَة	*iqālah*	Dismissal, firing, sacking

Arabic original word	Transliterated as	English meanings
إِقَامَة	*iqāmah*	Residence, establishment
إِقْرَار	*iqrār*	Declaration, assertion, testimony
إِقْطَاع	*iqṭā'*	Deduction
إِقْتِنَاء	*iqtinā'*	Acquisition
إِقْتِصَاد	*iqtiṣād*	Economics
إِرْفَاق	*irfāq*	Attachment, concession
إِرْث	*irth*	Inheritance
اشْتِرَاك	*ishtirāk*	Contribution, participation, premium
إِصْلَاح	*iṣlāḥ*	Improvement, reform
إِسْلَام	*islām*	Submission, peace
إِسْرَاف	*isrāf*	Wasteful expenditure, extravagance
إِسْتِعْمَال	*isti'māl*	Use
اسْتِعْمَار	*isti'mār*	Colonization
اسْتِئْجَار	*isti'jar*	Hiring, renting
إِسْتِبْدَال	*istibdāl*	Exchange
اسْتِغْلَال	*istighlal*	Exploitation
إِسْتِهْلَاك	*istihlāk*	Consumption
إِسْتِحْقَاق	*istiḥqāq*	Maturity
إِسْتِحْسَان	*istiḥsān*	Juristic preference, approbation
إِسْتِجْرَار	*istijrār*	Recurring or repeat sale
إِسْتِخْلَاف	*istikhlāf*	Succession
إِسْتِلَام	*istilām*	Receipt
إِسْتِمْرَار	*istimrār*	Continuity
إِسْتِنْبَاط	*istinbāṭ*	Elicitation
اسْتِصْلَاح	*istislāh*	Improvement, refurbishment, renovation
إِسْتِصْنَاع	*istiṣnā'*	Manufacturing contract whereby a manufacturer agrees to produce (build) and deliver a well-described good (or premise) at a given price on a given date in the future
إِسْتِثْمَار	*istithmār*	Investment
إِسْتِثْنَاء	*istithnā'*	Exception
إِثْبَات	*ithbāt*	Proof, evidence
إِثْم	*ithm*	Sin
إِتْلَاف	*itlāf*	Damage, spoliation
إِتِّجَار	*ittijār*	Doing business, trafficking
جَهَالَة	*jahālah*	Lack of knowledge, ignorance
جَهْبَذ (جَهابِذَة)	*jahbad, (jahābidah)*	Financial expert(s)
جَاهِلِيَّة	*jāhilīyah*	In the Days of Ignorance
جَهْل	*jahl*	Ignorance, unfamiliarity
جِهَاد	*jihād*	Striving, doing one's utmost

Arabic original word	Transliterated as	English meanings
جِزْيَة	*jizyah*	Poll tax paid by members of other religious groups in a Muslim state for protection of life and property. Muslims on the other hand pay *zakāt* as part of their religious obligation to help the poor.
جُعَالَة	*ju'ālah*	Commission, fee, wage
كَفَالَة	*kafālah*	Guarantee
كَفِيْل	*kafīl*	Guarantor
خَلِيْفَة (خُلَفَاء)	*khalīfah (khulafa')*	Leader(s), successor(s), ruler(s)
خَمْر (خُمُور)	*khamr (khumur)*	Intoxicant(s)
خَرَاج	*kharāj*	A levy on land use, revenue
خَسَارَة (خَسَائر)	*Khasārah (khasā'ir)*	Loss(es)
خَطَر (مَخَاطِر)	*Khatar (ma khātir)*	Danger, risk
خَيْر	*khayr*	Good, beneficial
خِلَافَة	*khilāfah*	Leadership, succession
خِيَانَة	*khiyānah*	Betrayal
خِيَار	*khiyār*	Choice, option
خِيَار الشَّرْط	*khiyār al-shart*	Optional condition
خِيَار الوَصْف	*khiyār al-wasf*	Optional specifications
خُلْع	*khul'*	Divorce, separation
خُمْس	*khums*	One-fifth
خُسْرَان	*khusrān*	Loss, failure
لَازِم	*lāzim*	Necessary, compulsory
لُقَطَة	*luqaṭah*	Found property
مَعْدُوم	*ma'dūm*	Nonexistent
معْلُوم	*ma'lūm*	Known, defined
مَذْهَب (مَذَاهِب)	*madhhab (madhāhib)*	School(s) of Islamic jurisprudence, regime(s), system(s)
مَفْسَدَة (مَفَاسِد)	*mafsadah (mafāsid)*	Spoiler(s)
مَجْهُوْل	*majhūl*	Not known, anonymous
مَكْرُوْه	*makrūh*	Reprehensible, discouraged
مَال (أَمْوَال)	*māl (amwāl)*	Capital, money, property, wealth
مَنْفَعَة (مَنَافِع)	*manfa'ah (manāfi')*	Benefit(s), utility(ies), usufruct(s)
مَقْصَد (مَقَاصِدُ الشَّرِيعَة)	*maqsad (maqāṣid al-sharī'ah)*	Objectives of Islamic Law
مَصْلَحَة (مَصَالِح) مُرْسَلَة	*maṣlaḥah (maṣāliḥ) mursalah*	General benefits, public interest(s)
مَوْقُوف	*mawqūf*	Suspended
مَيْسِر	*maysir*	Gambling
مِلْكِية	*milkiyyah*	Ownership
مِيرَاث	*mirāth*	Inheritance
مِسْكِين (مَسَاكِين)	*miskīn (masakīn)*	Poor, poor people
مِيثَاق	*mīthāq*	Charter

Arabic original word	Transliterated as	English meanings
مِثْلًا بِمِثْل	*mithlan-bi-mithl*	Like for like
مِثْلِي	*mithlī*	Similar
مُعَلَّق	*mu'allaq*	Suspended
مُعَامَلَة (مُعَامَلَات)	*mu'āmalah (mu'āmalāt)*	Transactions
مُعَاوَضَة (مُعَاوَضَات)	*mu'āwaḍāt*	Exchange, compensation
مُبَاح	*mubāḥ*	Permissible
مُضَارَبَة	*muḍārabah*	A partnership whereby one party (the capital owner) provides capital to an entrepreneur to undertake a business activity. Profits are shared between them as agreed, but any financial loss is borne only by the capital owner, as his loss is his unrewarded efforts put into the business activity.
مُضَارِب	*muḍārib*	The partner in *muḍārabah* contract providing work, entrepreneurship, and management
مُفْلِس	*muflis*	Bankrupt
مُفْتِي	*mufti*	Jurist who provides legal *shari'ah* opinions
مُغَارَسَة	*mughārassah*	Sharecropping between two parties whereby one provides land, equipment, and shoots of trees and the other agrees to plant the trees and take care of them in return for a share in the harvest or the profit
مُحْتَسِب	*muḥtasib*	Ombudsman
مُجْتَهِد	*mujtahid*	Legal expert or a jurist who exerts great effort in deriving a legal opinion
مُجْتَمَع (مُجْتَمَعَات)	*mujtama' (mujtama'āt)*	Community, society
مُخَاطَرَة	*mukhāṭarah*	Taking risk
مُلَامَسَة	*Mulāmasah*	Touching
مُقَارَضَة	*muqāraḍah*	Same meaning as *muḍārabah*
مُقَايَضَة	*muqāyadah*	Barter
مُرَابَحَة	*murābaḥah*	Mark-up sale, sale at a margin
مُسَاقَاة	*musāqāh*	A sharecropping contract whereby the owner of a garden/orchard shares the produce with a worker in return for his services in irrigating the garden/orchard
مُسَاوَمَة	*musāwamah*	Bargaining on price, haggling
مُشَارَكَة	*mushārakah*	Partnership whereby all the partners contribute capital for a business venture. The partners share profits on pre-agreed ratios while losses are shared according to each partner's capital contribution.
مُشَارَكَة مُتَنَاقِصَة	*mushārakah mutanāqiṣah*	Diminishing partnership
مُشْتَرِك	*mushtarik*	Participant
مُسْتَحَب	*mustahab*	Meritorious
مُسْتَحِق	*mustahiq*	Eligible for recipient of *zakāt*
مُتَوَلِّي	*mutawallī*	Manager, director
مُطْلَق	*mutlaq*	Absolute

Arabic original word	Transliterated as	English meanings
مُزَكِّي	*muzakki*	*Zakāt* payer
مُزَارَعَة	*muzāra'ah*	A sharecropping contract whereby one party agrees to provide land, seeds, and equipment and the other agrees to do the work needed in return for a part of the produce of the land
مُزَايَدَة	*muzāyadah*	Auction sale, bidding
نَفَقَة / نَفَقَات	*nafaqah (nafaqāt)*	Expense(s)
نَجَش	*najash*	Prohibited practice of deceiving and inciting a potential buyer of goods during the course of pre-sale negotiations or bidding to secure a greater value for the goods
نَصّ	*naṣṣ*	Text, scripture
نِصَاب	*nisāb*	Threshold, exemption limit for the payment of *zakat*
نِيَّة	*nīyyah*	Intention
قَبْض	*qabḍ*	Receipt
قَبُول/ قُبُول	*qabūl/qubūl*	Acceptance
قَاضِي	*qāḍi*	Judge
قَرْض (قُرُوض)	*qarḍ (qurūḍ)*	Loan(s)
قَرْض حَسَن	*qarḍ ḥasan*	Interest-free loan
قِيمَة (قِيَم)	*qīmah (qiyam)*	Value(s)
قِمَار	*qimār*	Gambling
قِرَاض	*qirāḍ*	Another name for *muḍārabah*
قِصَاص	*qiṣāṣ*	Punishment
قِيَاس	*qiyās*	Analogical reasoning
قُرْآن	*Qur'ān*	The sacred book of Islam
قُرُوض	*qurūḍ*	Loans
رأس المَال رُؤُوس الأَمْوَال	*ra's al-māl* *ru'ūs al-amwāl*	Capital(s)
رَبُّ المَال (أَرْبَابُ المَال)	*rabb al-māl arbāb al-māl*	Capital owner(s)
رَهْن	*rahn*	Collateral, pledge, guarantee
رَمَضَان	*ramadān*	Month of fasting for muslims
ربَا	*ribā*	Usury, interest
رِبَا البُيُوع	*ribā al-buyū'*	Usury of trade; another name for *riba al-fadl*
رِبَا الدُّيُون	*ribā al-duyūn*	Interest/usury of debt; another name for *riba al-nasi'ah*
رِبَا الفَضْل	*ribā al-faḍl*	Difference in exchanging two similar commodities
رِبَا النَّسِيئَة/النَّسَأ	*ribā al-nasī'ah/al-nasa'*	Interest-based lending for the delay in repayment
رِبَا القُرُوض	*ribā al-qurūḍ*	Interest on loans
رِبْح (أَرْبَاح)	*ribḥ (arbāḥ)*	Profit(s)
رِكَاز	*rikāz*	Treasure
رِشْوَة	*rishwah*	Bribe
رِزْق	*rizq*	Sustenance

Arabic original word	Transliterated as	English meanings
رُكْبَان	*rukbān*	Business traveler
رُكْن	*rukn*	Pillar
رُقْعَة	*ruq'ah*	Promissory note
رُشْد	*rushd*	Maturity
صَدَقَة جَارِية	*ṣadaqah jāriyah*	Perpetual charity
صَدَقَة (صَدَقَات)	*ṣadaqāt*	Charity(ies)
سَدُّ الذَرِيعَة	*sadd al-dharī'ah*	Prohibition of a deed that, if permitted, may lead to another prohibited deed
صَحَابِي / صَحَابَة	*ṣaḥābī (ṣaḥābah)*	Companion(s)
صَحِيح	*ṣaḥīḥ*	Valid; opposite of *bāṭil and fāsid*
سَهَم/أسْهُم	*sahm (ashum)*	Share(s)
صَكّ (صُكُوك)	*ṣakk (ṣukūk)*	Asset-based or asset-backed financial certificate(s)
سَلَف	*salaf*	Loan; another name for *salam*
صَلَاة	*ṣalāh*	Prayers offered by muslims
سَلَم	*salam*	Forward sale where the price of a specific good is paid in advance for its delivery at a specified time in the future
سَنَد (سَنَدَات)	*sanad (sanadāt)*	Bond(s)
صَرْف	*ṣarf*	Currency exchange
صَوْم	*ṣawm*	Fasting
شَهَادَة	*shahādah*	Testimony, certification
شَحْن	*shaḥn*	Shipping
شَرَاكَة	*sharākah*	Partnership
شَرِيعَة	*shari'ah*	Islamic law
شَرِكَة (شَرِكَات)	*sharikah (sharikāt)*	Company(ies), enterprise(s), partnership(s)
شَرِكَة عُقُود	*sharikat 'uqūd*	Contractual partnership
شَرِكَة أبْدَان	*sharikat abdān*	A partnership company based on the skills of professionals working together and sharing the proceeds
شَرِكَة أمْوال	*sharikat amwāl*	Financial partnership
شَرِكَة عِنَان	*sharikat 'inān*	Limited liability partnership
شَرِكَة مِلْك	*sharikat milk*	Joint property partnership
شَرِكَة مُفَاوَضَة	*sharikat mufawadah*	Unlimited liability partnership
شَرِكَة صَنَائِع	*sharikat sanāi'*	A partnership company based on the skills of professionals working together and sharing the proceed. Same as *sharikat abdān.*
شَرِكَة وُجُوه	*sharikat wujūh*	A partnership company based on the credibility and creditworthiness of the partners
شَرْط	*sharṭ*	Condition
شُفْعَة	*shuf'ah*	Right of preemption
شُوْرَىٰ	*shūrá*	Consultation

Arabic original word	Transliterated as	English meanings
سِمْسَار	*simsār*	Middleman, broker
سُفْتَجَة	*suftajah*	Bill of exchange
صُكُوك	*sukūk*	Equity-based certificates of investment
سُنَّة	*sunnah*	Tradition of the prophet mohammed
سُوْرَة	*sūrah*	Qur'anic chapter
تَعَامُل	*ta'āmul*	Dealing
تَعَاوُن	*ta'āwun*	Cooperation
تَعَاوُني	*ta'awuni*	A principle of mutual assistance
تَبَرُّع (تَبَرُّعَات)	*tabarru' (tabarru'āt)*	Donation(s), gift(s), charity(ies)
تَبْذِير	*tabdhīr*	Wastage
تَدَاوُل	*tadāwul*	Circulation
تَفْوِيض	*tafwīd*	Authorization
تَحَوُّط	*taḥawwuṭ*	Hedging
تَحْسِينَات	*tahsināt*	Luxuries
تَكَافُل	*takāful*	Solidarity, mutual support
تَكافُل تعاوُني	*takāful ta'awuni*	Cooperative risk sharing and mutual insurance
تَأمِيْن	*ta'mīn*	Insurance
تَمْلِيك	*tamleek*	Transfer of ownership
تَقْلِيد	*taqlīd*	Imitation
تَقْوَى	*taqwá*	God consciousness
تَوَكُّل	*tawakkul*	Trust in God
تَوَرُّق	*tawarruq*	The process of buying a commodity at a deferred price, in order to sell it in cash at a lower price. Usually, the sale is to a third party, with the aim to obtain cash. This is the classical form *tawarruq,* which is permissible. Organised *tawarruq,* where the bank plays both the roles of seller and buyer, is not permissible according to the majority of contemporary *fuqaha'* (jurists, scholars)
تَوْحِيد	*tawhid*	Oneness of Allah
تَعْوِيض (تَعْوِيضَات)	*ta'wīḍ (ta'wiḍat)*	Compensation(s)
ثَمَن	*thaman*	Price
ثَوَاب	*thawāb*	Reward
تِجَارَة	*tijārah*	Business, commerce, trade
أُجْرَة	*ujrah*	Allowance, commission, fee, salary, wage
أُخُوَّة	*ukhuwah*	Brotherhood
أُمَّة	*ummah*	Muslim community
عُمْرَة	*'umrah*	Mini-pilgrimage to Makkah that is not compulsory but highly recommended. It can be performed at any time of the year.
أوقِيَّة	*ūqīyyah*	Ounce

Arabic original word	Transliterated as	English meanings
عُرْف	*'urf*	Custom, common practice
عُشْر (عُشُور)	*'ushr ('ushūr)*	Ten percent of *zakāt* on nonirrigated agricultural produce payable by the Muslim at the time of the harvest
أُصُول	*uṣūl*	Origins
أُصُوْل الفِقْه	*uṣūl al-fiqh*	Islamic legal bases
وَعْد (وُعُود)	*wa'd (wu'ūd)*	Promise(s), undertaking(s)
وَدِيعَة (وَدَائِع)	*wadī'ah (wadā'i')*	Deposit(s)
وَاجِب	*wajib*	Obligatory, compulsory, mandatory
وَكَالَة (وَكَالَات)	*wakālah (wakālat)*	Agency; a contract whereby one party appoints another party to perform a certain task on its behalf, usually for payment of a fee or a commission
وَكِيل (وُكَلَاء)	*wakil (wukalā')*	Representative(s), agent(s)
وَلِي	*wali*	Guardian
وَقْف (أَوْقَاف)	*waqf (awqāf)*	Endowment(s), foundation(s), trust(s)
وَصِيَّة	*waṣīyah*	Will. bequest
زَبُون (زَبَائِن)	*zabūn (zaba'in)*	Customer(s)
زَكَاة	*zakāh, zakāt*	Obligatory contribution or poor due payable by all Muslims having wealth above *nisab* (threshold or exemption limit)
زَكَاة الفِطْر	*zakāt al-fiṭr*	Poll tax payable on every muslim at the end of Ramadan (the month of fasting)
زَكَاة المَال	*zakāt al-māl*	An annual levy on the wealth of a Muslim (above a certain level). The rate paid differs according to the type of property owned.
زَكَاة الرِكَاز	*zakāt al-rikāz*	Levy on treasure trove
زَكَاة التِجَارَة	*zakāt al-tijārah*	Levy on business
ظُلْم	*ẓulm*	Injustice, oppression, exploitation

Abbreviations

10-PoA	Ten-Year Program of Action
10YF	Ten-Year Framework and Strategies document for the development of the Islamic financial sector
10-YS	10-Year Strategy (Islamic Development Bank Group)
AAOIFI	Accounting and Auditing Organization for Islamic Financial Institutions
AUM	Assets under management
BMI	Broader Market Index
BNM	Bank Negara Malaysia (central bank, Malaysia)
CAGR	Compound annual growth rate
CAR	Capital adequacy ratio
CDD	Community-driven development
CIBAFI	General Council for Islamic Banks and Financial Institutions
CSR	Corporate social responsibility
EC	European Commission
ETFs	Exchange traded funds
FTSE	Financial Times Stock Exchange
G-20	Group of Twenty
GCC	Gulf Cooperation Council
GDP	Gross domestic product
GEI	Government Effectiveness Index
GIFR	Global Islamic Finance Report
HQLA	High Quality Liquid Assets
IDB	Islamic Development Bank
IDBG	Islamic Development Bank Group
IEI	Islamic equity index
IFIs	Islamic financial institutions
IFSB	Islamic Financial Services Board
IFSIs	Islamic financial services institutions
IICRA	International Islamic Center for Reconciliation and Arbitration
IIFM	International Islamic Financial Markets
IIRA	International Islamic Rating Agency
IMF	International Monetary Fund
IPOs	Initial public offerings
IRTI	Islamic Research and Training Institute (Islamic Development Bank)
ISRA	International Shari'ah Research Academy
IT	Information technology
KPIs	Key Performance Indicators
MDGs	Millennium Development Goals
MENA	Middle East and North Africa
MFI	Microfinance institution
MSCI	Morgan Stanley Capital International
MSE	Micro and small enterprises

MSMEs	Micro, small, and medium enterprises
MTR	Mid-Term Review of the Ten-Year Framework and Strategies document
NBFIs	Nonbank financial institutions
NGOs	Nongovernmental organizations
NPLs	Nonperforming Loans
OECD	Organisation for Economic Co-operation and Development
OIC	Organisation of Islamic Cooperation
OJK	Otoritas Jasa Keuangan (Financial Services Authority, Indonesia)
PCA	Prompt Corrective Action
PLS	Profit and loss sharing
PPP	Purchasing power parity
PRs	Pakistan rupees
RBC	Risk-based capital approach
REITs	Real estate investment trusts
SAMA	Saudi Arabian Monetary Authority
SDGs	Sustainable Development Goals
SMEs	Small and medium enterprises
SRI	Socially responsible investment
UCTs	Unconditional cash transfers
UN	United Nations

All dollar-denominated currency is in U.S. dollars, unless otherwise noted.

Overview

There is broad consensus that the objective of economic development is not only to boost economic growth but also to share prosperity with all segments of society through equitable distribution of income and wealth. The trickle-down approach asserts that higher productivity and industrial advancement lead to higher gross domestic product (GDP) growth, which will improve the well-being of all segments of the society, including the poorest and most marginalized in a country. However, recent experience has shown that the immediate impact of such a growth-led policy can be an undesirable concentration of wealth in the hands of a few, while the growth benefits trickle down to the extremely poor only over a relatively long period of time. Inequality increased considerably in the aftermath of the financial crisis of 2007–08. The seriousness of the problem is highlighted by a few striking facts:

- Almost half of the world's wealth is now owned by just 1 percent of the population (Working for the Few 2014).
- The richest 10 percent of the world's population holds 86 percent of the world's wealth, and the top 1 percent alone accounts for 46 percent of global assets (Credit Suisse 2013).
- In the United States, the wealthiest 1 percent has captured 95 percent of growth since 2009, while the bottom 90 percent has become poorer (Working for the Few 2014).

There is growing realization that despite good intentions, development policies have led to an undesirable imbalance in income and wealth distribution. Given the significant evidence of growing inequality, its adverse effects on economic growth, and its social costs, among other wide-ranging negative impacts, there is an ongoing debate as to how to minimize extreme inequality and enhance shared prosperity. Much has been said about the damages of high inequality of income and wealth to society. It erodes trust, creates barriers to social mobility for current and future generations, increases social resentment, undermines effective governance, creates a "winner-takes-all" society, and breaks down social solidarity. While income and wealth inequality undermines economic performance, shared prosperity and economic performance support each other; there is no trade-off.

In this regard, several global agencies, including the United Nations, place an emphasis on inclusive and sustainable development rather than mere economic development.

The World Bank Group has revised its mission for the first time in 30 years and has included promotion of shared prosperity, one of the two goals, in addition to reducing the number of people living in extreme poverty.[1] Similarly, the new 10-Year Strategy of the Islamic Development Bank Group (IDBG) (2016–25) also aims at promoting inclusive and sustainable socioeconomic development among member-countries by providing a leadership role in promoting Islamic finance globally.

Although the development community's concern about growing inequality and the imbalance in distribution of wealth has led to a realization that equitable sharing of prosperity is essential, there is a difference of opinion as to the approaches to achieve this goal. Islamic economics and finance provide an alternative perspective and solution to the development challenges mentioned. Given the potential role of Islamic finance in economic development, the World Bank Group and IDBG decided to focus on the topic of "Islamic Finance and Shared Prosperity" as the general theme for the inaugural edition of the *Global Report on Islamic Finance (GRIF)*. This Report has three main objectives:

- To develop understanding of the theoretical foundation of Islamic finance and shared prosperity
- To review recent development and trends in various sectors of Islamic finance, such as banking, capital markets, and social finance
- To identify policy interventions and tools for policy makers to leverage Islamic finance to eradicate extreme poverty and ensure equitable distribution of wealth.

The Report develops a theoretical framework to analyze the progress of Islamic economics and finance based on four fundamental pillars: an institutional framework and public policy oriented to the objectives of sustainable development and shared prosperity in line with the broader objectives of Islam; prudent governance and accountable leadership; promotion of an economy based on risk sharing and entrepreneurship; and financial and social inclusion for all, thereby promoting development, growth, and shared prosperity. The risk-sharing and asset-based financing nature of Islamic finance and its potential contribution to growth and inclusive prosperity have considerable merit, particularly in light of the mounting evidence of the negative effects of debt and leverage on the economy. For example, two recent seminal works by Mian and Sufi (2014) and Turner (2015) document the strong relationship of household leverage to financial crisis and instability, and their adverse effects on economic growth.

Islamic finance, through its core principles, advocates for the just, fair, and equitable distribution of income and wealth during the production cycle and provides mechanisms for redistribution to address any imbalances that may occur. Islamic finance's approach to redistribution is based on a balanced blend of income-based redistribution through redistributive instruments and asset-based redistribution through the notion of risk sharing (dispersion of ownership). The income-based redistribution approach offers only a partial solution because it takes the current income distribution as given and aims at fairer distribution of future GDP. By contrast, asset-based redistribution is basically a risk-sharing approach; it empowers equity participation by the lower-income groups in the society. Rewards are shared, but so is risk. Making the poor direct holders of real assets in the real sector of the economy reduces their aversion to risk. It also creates positive incentives for behavioral factors that enhance productivity (such as trust, truthfulness, and hard work) through the design of contracts that reduce or eliminate the difference between principals and agents and are conducive to the advancement of the interests of all parties to a contract (Mirakhor 2015).

Islamic finance is very relevant to the Sustainable Development Goals (SDGs)—the global development agenda for 2015–30—which require unprecedented mobilization of resources to support their implementation. Because of the transformative and sustainable nature of the new development agenda, all possible resources must be mobilized if the world is to succeed in meeting its targets. Given the principles of Islamic finance that support socially inclusive and development-promoting activities, the Islamic financial sector has the potential to contribute to the achievement of the SDGs. Particularly in member-countries of the Organisation of Islamic Cooperation (OIC)—where policy makers are challenged with high levels of inequality and highly indebted households, firms, and sovereigns—a solution provided by Islamic finance could lead to sustainable development and enhanced shared prosperity. Mobilization of Islamic financial institutions, capital markets, and the social sector in promoting strong growth, enhanced financial inclusion and intermediation; reducing risks and vulnerability of the poor; and more broadly contributing to financial stability and development will be pivotal in achieving the SDGs in countries with a serious commitment to Islamic finance.

Despite encouraging developments and a rich theoretical foundation, there are a number of aspects where policy interventions or improvements in policy effectiveness are needed to develop Islamic finance to boost shared prosperity. These include enhancing the harmonization, implementation, and enforcement of regulations; creating institutions that provide credit and other information, which in turn support the provision of equity-based finance, particularly to small and medium enterprises (SMEs) and microenterprises; development of capital markets and *sukūk* (Islamic bond) products to help finance large infrastructure projects; and regulatory recognition of products from other jurisdictions to expand the markets through cross-border transactions.

To overcome challenges and to realize the full potential of Islamic finance, a serious and concerted effort by stakeholders is required. A summary of findings of the Report follows.

Going Beyond Banking

The Islamic banking sector is the dominant component of the Islamic finance industry. It has grown exponentially in the past two decades, accumulating nearly US$1.9 trillion in assets and spreading across 50 Muslim and non-Muslim countries around the world.

Financial intermediation through risk-sharing contracts, as well as financial inclusion by Islamic banks, could contribute to shared prosperity—provided that Islamic banks pursue risk-sharing intermediation and increase the allocation of credit to the micro, small, and medium enterprise (MSME) sector. Islamic banking is not typical conventional banking; rather, it is a mode of financial intermediation offering banking and asset management services. Current practices are restraining its full potential because of attempts to replicate conventional banking.

To live up to the ideals of Islamic finance, Islamic banks face many challenges, ranging from the gap between the prevalence of debt-based instruments and the aspirations of financing predominantly through equity and risk sharing, to the need for increased social capital, and to the challenges of creating an enabling regulatory framework. To contribute to shared prosperity, the Islamic banking sector should focus on six key areas of improvement and adopt best practices. These include the following:

1. Creating an enabling regulatory environment by supporting consistent regulations, ensuring consistent implementation of the Basel III and Islamic Financial Services Board (IFSB) frameworks, ensuring that systemic risks in dual banking systems (conventional and Islamic) are addressed, and implementing cross-border supervision
2. Introducing innovative risk-sharing products and services, rather than replicating conventional risk-transfer products
3. Harmonizing *shari'ah* governance through efforts to unify cross-country *shari'ah* rulings about Islamic finance, which would help accelerate the growth of the industry
4. Enhancing the scale of and access to Islamic finance to include low-income earners
5. Improving liquidity and ensuring stability
6. Bolstering human capital and literacy in Islamic finance.

Developing Vibrant Capital Markets

Capital markets through equity- and asset-based finance could play a critical role in reducing poverty by providing opportunities for the poor to build assets. Islamic capital markets are relatively young, but they are the second largest segment of the Islamic finance sector after banking. The *sukūk* market has grown considerably over the last decade. *Sukūk* offer great potential for promoting shared prosperity because of their suitability for financing infrastructure, raising funds for new businesses, encouraging entrepreneurship, and supporting economic development. Unlike other asset classes, *sukūk* offer a hybrid profile between pure equity and debt, and are thus attractive to a wide range of investors and finance seekers, again with a positive potential for shared prosperity.

Development of vibrant capital markets is the essential ingredient for Islamic finance. There is the need for incentives to encourage risk sharing, particularly through the development of markets for equity trading. This is hindered by the perverse tax treatment that classifies interest as a tax-deductible expense. In order to create a level playing field for debt and equity, there is a need to eliminate the tax shelter on interest payments. Tax neutrality for *sukūk* issuers and investors could further boost the market. The use of *sukūk* by governments and governmental agencies to mobilize financing is essential to develop a long-term yield curve and to develop a corporate *sukūk* market, as well as to promote transparency and efficiency of asset pricing.

Promoting the Nonbank Financial Institutions Sector

International financial systems are realizing the growing importance of nonbank financial institutions (NBFIs)—such as housing finance, leasing, and asset management—and especially their potential contribution to economic development. The risk-sharing and asset-backed nature of Islamic finance products is more suitable for providing financial services through NBFIs. This sector is currently underdeveloped and underutilized in Islamic finance and therefore should be given priority by policy makers.

A good place to start is with Islamic insurance. In addition to providing protection against risk and uncertainty, *takāful* could play a critical role in enhancing financial inclusion, reducing poverty, achieving inclusive economic growth, and boosting shared prosperity. *Takāful* can provide important benefits to households and firms. Greater access to financial services for both households and firms may help reduce income inequality and accelerate economic growth. Protection against unexpected shocks to income and enhanced productivity through better health for the poor and vulnerable segments of society through micro*takāful* could become effective tools for combating poverty. With the growth of Islamic microfinance, especially in member-countries of the OIC, there is a need to develop the micro*takāful* industry to provide protection against uncertain events and loss of income.

To attain a robust Islamic NBFI sector that will promote inclusive economic development and shared prosperity, certain requirements must be met, including supportive institutions and public policy, responsible governance and leadership, promotion of risk sharing and entrepreneurship, and a sound regulatory and supervisory framework. Serious supply- and demand-side and legal challenges must be overcome. Increasing the number and diversity of Islamic NBFIs, together with increasing the range of products offered to various segments, are two major challenges on the supply side. On the demand side, low levels of financial literacy about the products and services offered by Islamic NBFIs; cultural, social, and physical barriers; insufficient consumer protection practices; and reputation- and credibility-related challenges are the biggest obstacles hindering further improvement of Islamic NBFIs. A balanced and enabling regulatory and taxation framework that also fosters cross-border investments in the Islamic NBFI sector is also needed.

Alleviating Poverty and Sharing Prosperity through Islamic Social Finance

Islamic social finance advocating a sharing economy and promoting redistribution could play a significant role in helping achieve the twin development objectives of ending extreme poverty globally by 2030 and promoting shared prosperity by raising the incomes of the bottom 40 percent of the population. The institutions and instruments of Islamic social finance are rooted in redistribution and philanthropy. Such interventions, involving *qarḍ ḥasan*, *zakāt,* and *ṣadaqāt*,[2] can potentially address the basic needs of the extremely poor and the destitute and create a social safety net. The instrument of *awqāf* (Islamic endowments or trusts) is ideal for the creation and preservation of assets that can ensure a flow of resources to support the provision of education, health care, and other social goods. These Islamic institutions can play a critical role in the realization of the global vision of generating sufficient income-earning opportunities; investing in people's development prospects by improving the coverage and quality of education, health, and sanitation; and protecting the poor and vulnerable against sudden risks of unemployment, hunger, illness, drought, and other calamities. These measures would greatly boost shared prosperity, improving the welfare of the least well-off.

The role of Islamic social finance has great significance in countries with high levels of exclusion and deprivation. This Report estimates that for most countries in South and Southeast Asia and Sub-Saharan Africa, the resource needs to alleviate deprivation could be met adequately if the potential of institutions of *zakāt* and *waqf* were realized, even if only in part.

Public Policy Interventions

In an environment of constrained sources of development financing, timely public policy interventions are the need of the hour. Islamic finance, with its rich theoretical promise to fight poverty and enhance prosperity, could play the role of a catalyst. Despite recent encouraging developments and the growth of Islamic finance, there are a number of areas in which policy interventions or improvements in policy effectiveness are needed to further develop Islamic finance and boost shared prosperity. Lower-income countries are lagging behind higher-income countries in terms of developing Islamic finance to enhance shared prosperity. The significance of timely and effective policy cannot be overemphasized.

This Report identifies areas in different sectors that could guide policy makers in formulating policy interventions to meet the objective of leveraging Islamic finance to alleviate poverty and enhance shared prosperity. These include enhancing implementation and enforcement of regulations; creating institutions that provide credit and information that in turn support the provision of equity-based finance, particularly to SMEs and microenterprises; developing capital markets and *sukūk* products to help finance large infrastructure projects; harmonizing regulations; and using regulation to recognize products from other jurisdictions to expand the markets through cross-border transactions.

The process of identifying policy interventions and areas to focus on has been going on for more than a decade. Notably, the IDBG and IFSB jointly prepared a Ten-Year Framework and Strategies document and Mid-Term Review (MTR). These and other initiatives emphasize incorporating the use of Islamic finance in national development plans, as well as building master plans to develop the Islamic finance sector domestically. Recently, the Group of Twenty (G-20) has made similar recommendations to better integrate Islamic finance with global financial systems. This Report identifies additional areas for policy recommendations.

Table O.1 summarizes recommendations and policy measures for each sector with respect to each pillar of the development framework for Islamic finance discussed in this Report. Without the right enabling environment, Islamic finance may not be able to attain the potential expected from it. However, with

TABLE 0.1 Recommendations and Policy Interventions by Sector

	Institutional framework and public policy	Governance and leadership	Risk sharing and entrepreneurship	Financial and social inclusion
Banking	• Create an enabling regulatory environment by supporting consistent regulations and ensuring consistent implementation of the Basel III and Islamic Financial Services Board (IFSB) framework. • Ensure that systemic risks in dual banking systems (conventional and Islamic) are addressed. • Implement cross-border supervision. • Improve liquidity. • Ensure stability.	• Harmonize *shari'ah* governance through efforts to unify cross-country *shari'ah* rulings about Islamic finance.	• Introduce innovative risk-sharing products and services, rather than replicate conventional risk-transfer products.	• Enhance the scale and access to Islamic finance to include low-income earners. • Bolster human capital. • Increase Islamic finance literacy.
Capital markets	• Create a level playing field for debt and equity instruments by o Eliminating the tax shelter on interest expense, o Allowing tax-free transfer of assets in asset-backed *sukūk*—or at least treating the transfer fee as a tax-deductible expense.	• Incorporate higher ethical standards through transparent governance mechanisms and a robust regulatory framework. • Improve *shari'ah* governance: o Align *shari'ah* screening standards for equities across jurisdictions. o Publish *shari'ah* screening standards, and list compliant equities for the convenience of investors on a periodic basis. • Provide disclosures relevant to *shari'ah* compliance, especially events that may trigger noncompliance in the regular reporting of firms. • Strengthen resolution frameworks and investor protection mechanisms.	• Encourage investment in equities, which is the purest form of risk sharing that not only distributes wealth more equitably but also creates more jobs and enhances shared prosperity. • Improve the scalability and liquidity of *sukūk* by providing an enabling environment for trading *sukūk* in secondary markets. • Provide incentives for issuing long-term *sukūk* based on more equity-like structures such as *muḍārabah* and *mushārakah*.	• Introduce retail *sukūk* for smaller investors • Relax the condition for listing of companies in order to provide a larger universe of equities for investment.

table continues next page

TABLE 0.1 **Recommendations and Policy Interventions by Sector** *(continued)*

	Institutional framework and public policy	Governance and leadership	Risk sharing and entrepreneurship	Financial and social inclusion
Takāful	• Adopt a holistic approach while formulating the policy guidelines for the industry that takes into consideration both the industry and consumers in a *shari'ah*-compliant manner. • Design policies that balance the protections for participants' rights with the need for effective pricing, greater solvency, operators' financial sustainability, good business conduct, and relevant disclosures. • To avoid confusion among Muslims, a board consisting of *shari'ah* scholars at the national level may provide guidance as to how to implement *takāful*. • Expand investment through the Islamic capital market to provide flexibility in the implementation of the risk-based capital regime.	• Establish clear and transparent corporate governance and regulatory framework for formal as well as informal *takāful* operations. • Regulate the *takāful* industry based on its risk characteristics. A risk-based approach may be desirable; however, this should take into consideration the difference between conventional insurance and *takāful*. • Set requirements for solvency purposes on the investment activities of *takāful* in order to address the risks faced by the operators.	• Introduce *takāful* and micro*takāful* as a mode for pooling risk and assets. • The long-term *shari'ah*-compliant investment from the savings and investments in *takāful* funds can be a critical source for economic development. • Encourage investment in capital market instruments.	• Allow participants to use micro*takāful* for savings and investment. • Allow micro*takāful* for family, health, crops, livestock, and property based on the cooperative (*wakālah*-partner) model.

table continues next page

TABLE O.1 **Recommendations and Policy Interventions by Sector** *(continued)*

	Institutional framework and public policy	Governance and leadership	Risk sharing and entrepreneurship	Financial and social inclusion
Nonbank financial institutions (NBFIs)	• Develop policies that require strong investor protection and stringent disclosure requirements as far as the investment is concerned. • Ensure that the products and activities of NBFIs comply with *shari'ah.*	• Develop legal infrastructure to support contract enforcement—a prerequisite for the development of the financial sector, as it not only reduces transaction costs but also enhances investor confidence. • Clearly define regulatory requirements such as licensing, disclosure, and corporate governance.	• Enhance diversification by directing more financing to small and medium enterprises relative to larger firms. • Develop skills and alternative approaches to mitigate risks (moral hazard) through proper monitoring and evaluation.	• Increase the number and diversity of Islamic NBFIs. • Encourage Islamic NBFIs to provide Islamic financial services in countries where establishing Islamic banks is not possible because of legal and regulatory restrictions.
Islamic social finance	• Recognize the diversity in *zakāt* management practices across the globe and create an adequately flexible and enabling regulatory environment. • Introduce/reform the *waqf* regulatory framework in order to establish *waqf* as an institution in the voluntary sector. • Recognize Islamic social finance as sustainable means of absorbing operational costs and providing "affordable" financing to the poor.	• Create a network of supporting infrastructure institutions, including research, training, and advocacy for the sound and orderly function of Islamic social finance institutions. • Develop a sound governance system that recognizes the significance of trust and credibility as key drivers underlying Islamic social finance. • Harmonize the financial reporting of Islamic social finance institutions to enhance transparency.	• Mitigate and absorb high risks with financing to the poor through mechanisms rooted in philanthropy and benevolence. • Make innovative use of *zakāt* and *waqf* to create risk management tools (credit enhancement/guarantees and micro*takāful*).	• Recognize self-exclusion as a key problem resulting from religious, cultural, and ethical beliefs of the poor. • Enhance social and human capital through community empowerment initiatives funded through the sustainable Islamic social funding instrument.

adequate policy interventions and an enabling financial infrastructure, Islamic finance could become a catalyst for alleviating poverty and promoting inclusive prosperity.

Brief Overview of Chapters

Chapter 1 lays the theoretical framework of the role of Islamic economics and finance in promoting development, growth, and shared prosperity. This framework is based on four fundamental pillars: an institutional framework and public policy oriented to the objectives of sustainable development and shared prosperity in line with the broader objectives of Islam; prudent governance and accountable leadership; promotion of an economy based on risk sharing and entrepreneurship; and financial and social inclusion for all.

The first pillar is crucial because having a sound institutional framework and appropriate public policies are the foundation upon which the other pillars must rest and can function optimally. Institutions play a critical role in this framework, as they implement the rules prescribed by the tenets of Islam. The institutions also adhere to the core objectives of Islam (commonly known as *maqāsid al-sharī'ah*, or Objectives of *Shari'ah*) that lay the foundation to formulate the policies promoting economic and social justice, preservation of human rights, dignity, health, and the intergenerational wealth of the society.

The second pillar focuses on developing a governance mechanism and accompanying compliance system based on the objectives and institutions prescribed by the first pillar. The ethically based governance, leadership, and compliance system helps increase the transparency and accountability in the public, private, and social sector institutions of the overall economic system, and hence strengthens trust in the system. Trustworthy and capable leadership can ensure protection of rights of the vulnerable or those who could be vulnerable (as in future generations). Increased trust and better governance in turn strengthen the institutional framework, which enables better implementation of better public policies.

The third pillar is the distribution channel; it works at both the individual and organizational level. One of the central features is the advocacy of risk sharing and promotion of entrepreneurship. This is one of the most important aspects of Islamic finance, which differentiates it from the conventional approach of overreliance on debt-dominated instruments that shift or transfer risk. Sharing the risks of economic and financial transactions also ensures the stability of the financial system. In addition, risk sharing with equitable sharing mechanisms encourages entrepreneurship and innovation because counterparties receive their fair share in the investment. This in turn will increase the allocation of resources to the real sector, rather than channeling excessive financial flows to the financial sector, leading to overfinancialization of economy.

An important component of risk sharing in Islamic economics is risk sharing through Islamic instruments of redistribution. Without this channel, certain segments of the society could easily be left out of the system, which would marginalize them and decrease the full productive potential and social harmony of society. This redistribution of income and wealth is not charity; rather, it is an endowment that would enable them to conduct their lives honorably and have an equal opportunity to contribute productively to society.

The fourth pillar aims to ensure that the fruits of higher growth are distributed to every segment of the society inclusively, either through participation in the economic growth or through Islam's instruments of redistribution. Since member-countries of the OIC have predominantly Muslim populations—for whom certain methods of conventional finance could contradict their faith and thus exclude them from the financial system—using a new framework of economic development and finance could help increase financial and social inclusion, which could facilitate equal opportunity.

Chapter 2 presents a snapshot of the current state of the extreme poverty and income disparity globally and compares it with the

OIC countries. A brief analysis of the historical trend also is provided in several metrics with respect to select benchmarks against the framework of economic development developed in chapter 1. Finding and discussing the root causes of the disparities between OIC and non-OIC countries is beyond the scope of this Report and is left for future research.

Extreme poverty has been reduced considerably around the world in the past two decades—although at a slower pace within the group of OIC countries than globally. OIC countries are very diverse in terms of income group, geography, and culture and are tied only by religion. The rate of poverty alleviation among the extreme lower-middle-income and lower-income countries is higher for OIC member-countries than for the non-OIC group. Among the regional differences, in Sub-Saharan Africa, OIC countries have exhibited higher poverty reduction than the non-OIC countries in the same region. However, OIC countries have lagged non-OIC countries in poverty reduction in East Asia and South Asia. In income disparity, there is no significant difference between OIC and non-OIC countries. In both groups of countries, the top decile receive the major share of the income.

To assess the state of shared prosperity, various indexes are used as a proxy for each pillar of shared prosperity, as discussed in chapter 1. In the institutional framework and public policy, the Rule of Law Index score is negative for all groups of countries except for the high-income group, clearly highlighting the need to strengthen the legal system in order to break out of the poverty cycle. The Government Effectiveness Index indicates a similar trend for governance and leadership; on average, countries from the lower-income and lower-middle-income groups trail behind the high-income group, highlighting the importance of governance and leadership in enhancing shared prosperity.

As an admittedly imperfect proxy for risk sharing, this Report uses the inverse of the correlation between consumption and income. OIC countries on average have a better risk-sharing environment than non-OIC countries. The capital market could be a better proxy for entrepreneurship. However, stock markets are not established in most lower-middle- and lower-income countries. The development of capital markets with wider access to the public under a strong legal and governance framework is desirable to promote shared prosperity in countries where poverty is still prevalent. In social and financial inclusion, OIC countries tend to borrow less from formal financial institutions, which may indicate self-exclusion because of religious reasons. Developing the Islamic finance sector may enhance financial inclusion.

In summary, chapter 2 presents the state of affairs with respect to trends in poverty alleviation and income distribution, which can be used by policy makers to formulate policy interventions and to identify areas to strengthen, keeping in mind the objective of leveraging Islamic finance for alleviating poverty and enhancing shared prosperity.

Chapter 3 focuses on the Islamic banking sector, which is the dominant component of the Islamic finance industry, accounting for more than three-quarters of the industry's assets. Islamic banking is based on key Islamic principles of prohibiting exploitation, emphasizing ethical standards, promoting moral and social values, and rewarding enterprise (linking risk and reward). The aspiration of Islamic banking is the creation, equitable distribution, and circulation of wealth in order to promote economic and social justice and to satisfy customers' needs for *shari'ah*-compliant investments and financing opportunities. This wealth creation and its fair distribution ensure shared prosperity. Islamic banking contributes to shared prosperity through its effect on economic growth, as a provider of capital for economic activities, and through the risk-sharing characteristics of its products.

The key features of risk-sharing contracts, and financial inclusion through increased banking options, contribute to shared prosperity. Islamic banking can have a positive effect on financial intermediation by the poor, which ultimately should boost the mobilization of savings and prosperity. In addition, Islamic banks have a social responsibility that transcends the maximization of profits.

Chapter 4 addresses how capital markets can contribute to enhancing shared prosperity by facilitating long-term financing through tradable instruments that enable easy market entry and exit. In a pure equity-based and risk-sharing framework, Islamic capital markets can serve the real sector of economy more effectively in an equitable and sustainable manner than conventional capital markets. The main requirements to facilitate the development of Islamic capital markets are similar to those for conventional capital markets: notably, protecting property rights, controlling market manipulation and fraudulent practices, maintaining fair pricing, and supporting the rule of law. However, there are additional requirements for the sound development of Islamic capital markets—particularly the promotion of risk sharing and asset-based finance in light of the prohibition of debt-based finance.

At present, there is no organized stock exchange that is operating in full compliance with *shari'ah* principles. Any investor in the Islamic equity market invests in the shares of *shari'ah*-compliant companies or in a publicly offered portfolio consisting of these equities offered through unit trusts, mutual funds, or exchange traded funds (ETFs). There are several prevailing standards for screening equities, including screens offered by major index provider companies such as the Financial Times Stock Exchange (FTSE), Standard and Poor's (S&P), Dow Jones, and Morgan Stanley Capital International (MSCI). The empirical evidence provided in the Report suggests that Islamic equity indexes based on the S&P's *shari'ah* screening standard perform at least as well on average as their conventional counterparts—despite lower diversification due to the exclusion of financial products and stocks backing activities prohibited by *shari'ah.*

The *sukūk* (Islamic bond) market has grown considerably over the last decade. *Sukūk* are now used for financing by corporate and sovereign entities. The *sukūk* market recovered quickly after the global financial crisis and peaked in 2012. Issuance declined somewhat in 2014 and 2015, but it is still considerably higher than its precrisis level. *Sukūk* offer great potential for promoting shared prosperity due to their suitability for financing infrastructure, raising funds for business, and supporting economic development. Unlike other asset classes, they offer a hybrid profile between pure equity and debt, and are thus attractive to a wide range of investors and finance seekers, again with a positive potential for shared prosperity.

An MTR of the Islamic financial services industry jointly prepared by the Islamic Research and Training Institute (IRTI) of the Islamic Development Bank and the IFSB highlights some of the major challenges hindering the development of Islamic capital markets. First is the need for incentives to encourage risk sharing, in particular, through the devel opment of markets for equity trading. This is hampered by the perverse tax treatment that classifies interest as a tax-deductible expense. In order to create a level playing field for debt and equity, there is a need to eliminate the tax shelter on interest payments. Second, because asset-backed *sukūk* could be more costly to structure than conventional securities, there is a case for allowing these expenses to be tax-deductible. In addition, provision should be made for tax exemption on the asset transferred in sale-based structures because such transfers are a precondition for *shari'ah* compliance. The authorities may wish to extend the favorable treatment of *sukūk* further by exempting investors from income and capital gains tax. This could apply where *sukūk* are used to fund specific development projects, rather than for unspecified government or corporate expenditures.

The MTR highlights the lack of a uniform approach to Islamic capital market regulation and governance. It is important for Islamic capital markets to be seen as incorporating higher ethical standards through transparent governance mechanisms and robust regulatory frameworks. It would also be helpful for market confidence and perceptions of financial product integrity if *shari'ah* governance standards were harmonized. This would facilitate cross-border activities in both primary and secondary markets, and the acceptance of contracts across regions and across schools of thought and markets. The MTR urges the adoption of the *shari'ah* standards proposed by the Accounting and Auditing Organization for Islamic Financial Institutions (AAOIFI) and the IFSB, with *shari'ah* boards taking full responsibility for the capital market products they approve.

The chapter also cites liquidity constraints as an impediment: notably the lack of depth in the secondary market in *sukūk,* reflecting limited issuance and the preference of investors to hold *sukūk* to maturity rather than trade. Greater pricing transparency and faster settlement procedures are recommended to encourage *sukūk* trading. Revaluation of the underlying assets may also be justified for the resolution of disputes and investor protection. A high level of financial literacy is needed by those investing and trading in Islamic financial markets, especially with respect to legal and *shari'ah* safeguards and the nature of the risks shared rather than transferred.

Chapter 5 focuses on *takāful,* the Islamic counterpart of conventional insurance. The scheme is similar to a mutual insurance concept, but it complies with Islamic Law and is based on concepts of mutual solidarity and risk sharing. A group of participants agree to support one another jointly for the losses arising from specified risks. The scheme is managed on the participants' behalf by a *takāful* operator. The *takāful* industry has two unique characteristics: mutual risk sharing and *shari'ah* compliance. In order to make it feasible, viable, and accessible to all segments of the society, there should be a globally acceptable *takāful* business model.

Takāful, as an infant industry, faces many challenges. Sound public policy is needed to balance protection for participants' rights with the requisite for effective pricing, greater solvency, operators' financial sustainability, good business conduct, and relevant disclosures. One of the major challenges for *takāful* operators is that *shari'ah*-compliant investment opportunities are lacking in many jurisdictions; thus the operators do not have adequate venues for long-term and stable investments offering desirable risk and return profiles. As a result, *takāful* operators lack access to adequate portfolio and risk management instruments to adequately match and hedge their liabilities. Development of Islamic capital markets, particularly *sukūk*, is essential for further development of the *takāful* industry.

Chapter 6 discusses the growing importance of NBFIs and highlights the important links of the products and services offered by NBFIs to shared prosperity. The chapter covers Islamic asset management, housing finance, and some specialized NBFIs, such as *muḍārabah* (risk-sharing partnerships) and *ijārah* (leasing) financing companies. The chapter argues that NBFIs in an economy add to the development of a diverse financial sector that expands the menu of products to better serve dynamic needs of the society.

A diverse financial sector also increases the stability of the financial system. NBFIs can serve as backup institutions that may help stabilize the financial sector when negative shocks adversely affect the dominant financial institutions, notably banks. Moreover, a well-developed NBFI sector can provide services to those segments of the society that are not adequately served by the formal banking sector. In this way, NBFIs have great potential to promote shared prosperity more effectively.

Despite the low levels of development in most of the countries with a high Muslim population, Islamic NBFIs have gained momentum since the global financial crisis, especially on the asset-management side. Assets under management of Islamic funds exceeded US$60 billion as of 2014, with an average annual growth of 13.5 percent between 2008 and 2014. A case can be made to exploit the synergies between socially responsible investments and *sukūk* as an alternative tool for mobilizing financing that could attract Islamic and socially responsible investors to make a visible contribution to sustainable development. Advocating for the potential of Islamic NBFIs for SMEs, chapter 6 presents a case study of novel *shari'ah*-compliant crowdfunding to demonstrate how Islamic finance can be deployed to enhance SMEs' access to finance. The chapter also includes some highlights and cases on Islamic house financing, *muḍārabah,* and *ijārah* companies that when properly implemented have the potential to improve financial inclusion in most OIC developing markets.

Chapter 7 provides an overview of alternative asset classes in Islamic finance and explores how this sector could enhance shared prosperity. As alternative investments are a diverse asset class, there are no all-embracing regulations or guidelines that can be applied. Usually alternative investments are under the remit of securities or capital market regulators, rather than being the responsibility of central banks. Among OIC countries, the Malaysian Securities Commission and the Capital Markets Authority of Saudi Arabia have played leading roles in identifying the issues that arise with alternative investments. The Kuala Lumpur-based IFSB has not yet issued any standards specifically on alternative investments, as it focuses more on Islamic banking, capital markets, and *takāful*, although it has published Guiding Principles for Islamic Collective Investment Schemes. There is clearly a case for more comprehensive guidance on alternative investments by the IFSB, as its membership includes regulatory authorities from the OIC states.

Regulators should at least try to ensure that their policies do not inhibit risk sharing and asset-based financing. These are core principles of Islamic finance that are particularly applicable to investment in alternative assets. There is a case for encouraging the establishment of nonbank Islamic financial institutions that can serve investors seeking alternative assets. The IFSB and national regulators should take the initiative in providing an enabling environment, specifically by drafting guidelines that could be applied to *shari'ah*-compliant alternative investment. They need to consider the incentive structures for new entrants and the governance framework that can best promote the use of risk-sharing partnerships such as *muḍārabah* and *mushārakah* for alternative investments.

At the same time, it must be recognized that those involved in alternative investments are typically sophisticated investors who do not need protection in the same way as retail investors. Many analysts urge so-called "light touch" regulation for alternative investments, as this reduces transaction costs, which ultimately get passed on to the investors. The European Union and the United Kingdom have relatively liberal directives on alternative investments. Nevertheless, in the case of Islamic investment, the *shari'ah* oversight should not be "light touch": otherwise this might undermine the credibility of the investments for the pious. There would be reputational risks to the financial institutions offering such investments and potential reputational damage to the scholars involved in approving the investments.

Shari'ah scholars working on Islamic finance need to address the issue of the permissibility of alternative asset classes more comprehensively. At the international level, this includes the OIC Islamic *Fiqh* Academy (IFA), which has issued *fatāwá* (religious opinions) on many Islamic financing contracts, but not specifically on alternative investments. The *shari'ah* scholars advising securities regulators also have a role to play, although at present only the Securities Commission in Kuala Lumpur has a formal *shari'ah* board. It has produced a joint report on Islamic capital markets in collaboration with another Kuala Lumpur–based institution, the International *Shari'ah* Research Academy (ISRA). A similar joint initiative in the field of Islamic alternative asset classes would be welcomed by the worldwide Islamic finance community.

Chapter 8 advocates that Islamic social finance could play a significant role in helping achieve the twin development objectives of ending extreme poverty globally by 2030 and promoting shared prosperity by raising the incomes of the bottom 40 percent of the population. The institutions and instruments of Islamic social finance are rooted in redistribution and philanthropy. Such intervention, involving *zakāt* and *ṣadaqāt* (charity), can potentially address the basic needs of the extremely poor and the destitute and create a social safety net. The chapter reports several creative experiments using *zakāt* and *waqf*, including creating an interest-free credit pool funded with *zakāt* and *ṣadaqāt*, supporting community-driven development using *zakāt* and *ṣadaqāt* funds, creating a guarantee fund with *zakāt*; providing affordable health care through corporate *waqf*, and engineering a *waqf* to provide relief and rehabilitation.

Policies are needed to support the efficient mobilization of Islamic social finance, efficient use and management of such resources, and their integration with microfinance to make it more inclusive and affordable. At the macro and meso levels, these include policies to create enabling legal, regulatory, and fiscal frameworks and to provide a supportive infrastructure. At a micro level, these include policies to enhance the accountability and transparency of the institutions, improve their governance structures, and diversify their product offerings, while transforming the poor into financially literate and more responsible clients.

Chapter 9 provides a road map for supportive public policy, a sound enabling environment, and conducive financial infrastructure to support the development of Islamic finance and its effectiveness in delivering the socioeconomic benefits expected from it. As Islamic finance caters to the needs of real economic activities and provides financing by taking on the risk of the business or the economic activities it finances, policies to develop that Islamic financial sector cannot be pursued in isolation from broader public policy concerning economic development, business promotion, and social advancement.

Islamic finance at present is working within a system that is heavily biased in favor of debt-based financing. The financial infrastructure, peripheral support institutions, and legal environment are more conducive to debt than other modes of financing. Thus, creating an enabling environment to support the proper growth and socially beneficial development of the risk-sharing aspect of Islamic finance is important. This entails cross-sectoral, well-coordinated, and timely reforms in financial sector regulations, in legal provisions for new types of institutions, in contract enforcement, and in tax treatment. Such changes lie beyond the capacities of individual financial institutions; hence the role of government and financial sector regulators and stakeholders is particularly important.

Efforts are under way at the national and supranational levels to develop and enhance the impact of Islamic finance. At the international level, various financial infrastructure institutions are developing standards for accounting, auditing, governance, *shari'ah* compliance, regulation, and supervision for the Islamic financial sector. Multilateral cooperation at the international level helped create a Ten-Year Framework and Strategies document for the development of the Islamic financial sector, which underwent a MTR in 2013. The MTR emphasizes enablement, performance, and reach as three pillars of strategic importance, and proposed 20 initiatives within these three pillars that can be pursued by individual countries and their respective regulatory authorities. It is hoped that this undertaking will help coordinate policies and consolidate efforts to develop Islamic finance across countries. Some countries have used these recommendations as guides to come up with their own national plans to foster the development of Islamic finance.

The issue of development of the Islamic financial sector to increase shared prosperity was also a part of the agenda of the G-20 in 2015. The World Bank and the International Monetary Fund (IMF) offered suggestions at the national and international level to better integrate Islamic finance with the global financial system. At the national level, recommendations included adapting regulatory and supervisory frameworks to take into account the industry's specific features such as risk sharing where deemed appropriate; exploring means for enhancing the liquidity management of Islamic banks; adapting tax systems to avoid placing Islamic finance instruments at a disadvantage; and providing the right incentives to ease access to asset-based and equity-like financing, particularly for SMEs. At the global level, the G-20 calls for systematically incorporating the industry's features in global standards and guidance and developing accounting and statistics standards, especially for *sukūk;* granting membership to Islamic finance standard-setters in the consultative groups of global standard-setters, with the view to strengthen the emerging cooperation between these institutions; and stepping up the engagement of international financial institutions and multilateral development banks in Islamic finance through analytical work, policy advice, and capacity development.

Chapter 9 also provides an overview of recent policy initiatives undertaken as case studies by Indonesia, Malaysia, and Pakistan to highlight recent developments in, and the enactment and implementation of, policies to promote shared prosperity. Islamic financial sector development and financial inclusion are integrated within the national development or financial development plans of these three countries. Strengthening *shari'ah* governance, improving the alignment of the national-level banking regulations with the principles issued by international Islamic financial infrastructure institutions, and establishing diversified financial institutions have become explicit parts of their agenda. Similarly, financial inclusion, its promotion by integrating *zakāt* and *awqāf*, and fostering the financing of a wider set of economic sectors are gaining policy importance.

In an effort to align Islamic financial sector development with its long-term economic development plan, Indonesia has issued a road map for Islamic banking development, a road map for Islamic capital market development, and a road map for sustainable finance. These are targets for improving the resilience and competitiveness of the Islamic financial sector, promoting economic growth and well-being, and supporting the national commitment to environmental protection. Indonesia is also working toward integrating the collection and distribution of *zakāt* into its financial system.

Islamic finance has been a priority area in Malaysia for three decades. In 2013, it enacted a comprehensive Financial Services Act to consolidate Islamic financial sector regulations, improve *shari'ah* governance, properly differentiate Islamic deposit taking from investment activities, and provide relevant regulations for both. These efforts foster proper risk sharing between the financial institutions and their clients.

Pakistan has a strategic plan in place to develop Islamic finance. It also developed a National Financial Inclusion Strategy that encompasses many of the areas needed to develop Islamic finance. It is one of the few countries that has a well-developed regulatory framework for microfinance and a microfinance credit information bureau. Pakistan has a system of *zakāt* collection and distribution at both the private and public levels.

Notes

1. Specifically, the goals are to end extreme poverty globally by 2030 and to promote shared prosperity by raising the incomes of the bottom 40 percent of the population. See "Ending Poverty and Sharing Prosperity," http://www.worldbank.org/content/dam/Worldbank/gmr/gmr2014/GMR_2014_Full_Report.pdf.
2. *Qarḍ ḥasan* is a voluntary loan, without any expectation by the creditor of any return on the principal. *Zakāt* are obligatory contributions to the poor and marginalized, payable by all Muslims having wealth above a certain threshold. *Ṣadaqāt* are recommended contributions to the less privileged or less able.

References

Credit Suisse. 2013. *Global Wealth Report 2013.* Zurich: Credit Suisse.

Mian, Atif, and Amir Sufi. 2014. *House of Debt, How They (and You) Caused the Great Recession, and How We Can Prevent It from Happening Again.* Chicago, IL: University of Chicago Press.

Mirakhor, Abbas. 2015. "Risk Sharing and Shared Prosperity." Paper presented at the inaugural World Bank–Islamic Development

Bank Guidance Financial Symposium on Islamic Finance and Shared Prosperity, Istanbul, September 8–9.

Turner, Adair. 2015. *Between Debt and the Devil: Money, Credit, and Fixing Global Finance.* Princeton, NJ: Princeton University Press.

Working for the Few. 2014. "Political Capture and Economic Inequality." Oxfam Briefing Paper 178, Oxfam GB for Oxfam International, Oxford, U.K. https://www.oxfam.org/sites/www.oxfam.org/files/bp-working-for-few-political-capture-economic-inequality-200114-summ-en.pdf.

1

Islamic Finance and Shared Prosperity

There is broad consensus that the objective of economic development is not only to boost economic growth but also to share prosperity with all segments of society through the equitable distribution of income and wealth. In recent decades, policy makers—including multilateral development organizations such as the World Bank Group—have often applied a "trickle-down" approach to reduce levels of absolute poverty. This approach asserts that higher productivity and industrial advancement lead to higher gross domestic product (GDP) growth in a country. However, the immediate impact of such a growth-led policy could be an undesirable concentration of wealth in the hands of a few, while the growth benefits trickle down to the extremely poor only over a relatively long period of time. This approach has resulted in only partial success at the cost of social disequilibrium.

Rising inequality and ways to cope with this growing problem top the agenda of multilateral development institutions and the policy makers in both developed and developing countries. International organizations such as Organisation for Economic Co-operation and Development (OECD) and the International Monetary Fund (IMF) and multilateral development institutions including the World Bank Group have repeatedly warned about the dire consequences of the increasing gap between the incomes of the very rich and the very poor. Professor Thomas Piketty's influential 2013 book, *Capital in the Twenty-First Century,* highlighted the inequality in 20 countries during the past three centuries. The drastic deterioration in the distribution of wealth and income between the very rich and the very poor in the world is highlighted by a few striking facts:

- Almost half the world's wealth is now owned by just 1 percent of the population (Working for the Few 2014).

- The richest 10 percent of the population hold 86 percent of the world's wealth, and the top 1 percent alone account for 46 percent of global assets (Credit Suisse 2013).
- In the United States, the wealthiest 1 percent has captured 95 percent of growth since 2009, following the financial crisis, while the bottom 90 percent became poorer (Working for the Few 2014).

Income distribution is worsening around the world, leading to widening inequality.[1] Recent research on inequality and growth has provided strong evidence that inequality has damaging effects not only on economic development and growth but also on social mobility and the social contract,[2] as follows:

- An extensive literature review in a 2012 report by the European Commission (EC) finds that high inequality has adverse effects on household well-being, criminality, health, social capital, education, political participation, and female labor market participation.
- The same report (EC 2012) notes that according to human capital accumulation theory, in imperfect financial markets, an agent's ability to invest is determined by his or her own wealth. Hence a highly unequal income distribution would block agents with insufficient funds from contributing to economic growth.
- Considering all the negative externalities of income distribution, a 2014 report for the OECD (Cingano 2014) concludes that unequal distribution of income slows economic growth. Enhancing the income of the lowest 10 percent of the population is especially needed to increase economic growth.[3]
- A 2010 study for the IMF (Kumhof and Rancière 2010) shows that the precrisis periods of 1920–29 and 1983–2008 were both characterized by a large increase in the income share of the rich and a large increase in leverage.[4]
- The influential book *Fault Lines* (Rajan 2012) argues that rising income inequality in the United States was one of the main reasons behind the 2007–08 global financial crisis. Rajan's thesis is that the declining share of low-income households was compensated by ever-expanding credit facilities, which in turn increased fragilities in the economic system through high leverage ratios, creating systemic risk.
- A 2013 study of Asia (Egawa 2013) finds that the middle-income trap problem can be alleviated by creating a more equal distribution of income.

The economists' perception that there is always a trade-off between growth and inequality and their notion that redistributive policies are necessarily not conducive to growth are both gradually changing (Ostry, Berg, and Tsangarides 2014). In the context of finance, the recent literature also emphasizes how inequality intensifies leverage, produces financial cycles, and precipitates a crisis (Rajan 2012). A host of political-economic factors also comes into play through the power of the richer few (Stiglitz 2012). Against the backdrop of growing inequality and more refined understanding of its harmful effects, this chapter focuses on an alternative perspective that could assist countries in reaching the goals of reducing poverty and promoting shared prosperity. We should emphasize that the perspective presented in this chapter is not intended to substitute for but to augment the World Bank Group perspective.

Reducing Extreme Poverty

In 2000, United Nations member-countries unanimously agreed on achieving eight development goals, commonly known as Millennium Development Goals (MDGs), by 2015.[5] Several international and multilateral development organizations, including the World Bank, IMF, and Islamic Development Bank (IDB), have pledged to help achieve these eight development goals. Progress has been made in several MDG goals, such as reducing extreme poverty, narrowing disparities of primary school participation between girls and boys, and decreasing tuberculosis and malaria (UN 2014).

Under a new initiative that followed the MDGs, the Sustainable Development Goals (SDGs), a new goal to reduce the number of people living on less than $1.25 a day to 3 percent globally by 2030 follows the success of the MDG. Set in 2000 to be achieved by 2015, the goal of reducing the percentage of people living on less than $1.25 a day by half was reached ahead of its target in 2010. By 2011, the share of the worldwide population living on less than $1.25 a day had decreased from 43 percent in 1990 to 17 percent (table 1.1). The share has declined in every region.

Reaching the target of reducing the extreme poverty level to 3 percent by 2030 is not impossible, but it is certainly very ambitious. It requires developing countries to maintain the growth rates they have achieved since the late 1990s (figure 1.1).

The recent decrease in global poverty was mainly the result of rapid growth in China. As China's growth rate starts to slow down, reducing poverty will be more complex (Narayan and others 2013). Even if developing countries achieve the high growth rates of the past decade, the benefits of high growth may not be evenly distributed to different income groups in the society. In addition to maintaining high growth rates, low-income countries urgently need to implement institutional and governance reforms that enhance the accountability of the State, raise the quality of service delivery, and improve the overall economic and social environment.

TABLE 1.1 Percentage of Population Living below $1.25 a Day, 1981–2011

Region	1981	1984	1987	1990	1993	1996	1999	2002	2005	2008	2011
East Asia and Pacific	77.95	65.63	54.27	57.01	51.66	38.27	35.89	27.34	16.56	13.72	7.93
Europe and Central Asia	2.92	2.31	1.88	1.54	2.87	4.28	3.83	2.13	1.26	0.49	0.49
Latin America and the Caribbean	11.66	13.38	12.47	12.63	11.14	10.57	10.95	10.22	7.35	5.37	4.63
Middle East and North Africa	8.85	6.62	7.24	5.77	5.33	4.78	4.79	3.83	2.99	2.05	1.69
South Asia	61.35	57.73	56.85	54.09	52.07	48.55	44.96	44.10	39.28	34.05	24.50
Sub-Saharan Africa	52.81	56.29	55.81	56.78	60.84	59.75	59.40	57.18	52.86	49.65	46.85
World total	52.71	47.53	42.98	43.44	41.56	35.87	34.24	30.62	24.77	21.85	16.99

Source: http://iresearch.worldbank.org/PovcalNet/index.htm?4.
Note: Data are in 2005 U.S. dollars in purchasing power parity terms.

FIGURE 1.1 GDP Growth Reduces Poverty

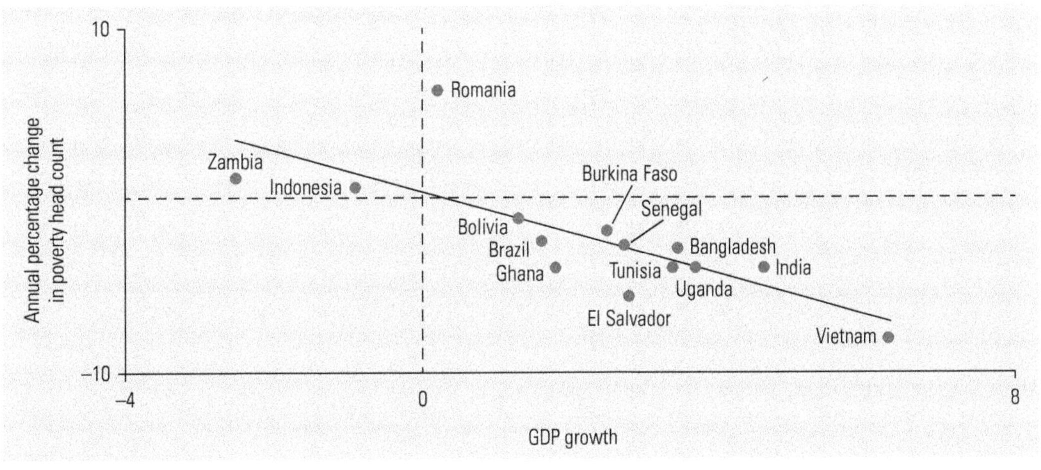

Source: AFD and others 2005.
Note: The downward sloping line (the decrease in poverty relative to the increase in growth) represents the best fit of the data of countries in the sample.

Complementing Poverty Reduction with Shared Prosperity

There are various approaches designed to deal with inequality. Those approaches fall into two main categories: those dealing with income-based distribution and those dealing with asset-based distribution.

Income-based distribution approaches take the current income distribution as given and aim at fairer distribution of future GDP. Within this approach, there are "soft" and "hard" redistribution proposals. The World Bank Group's proposal is considered a soft solution, as it requires no immediate redistribution. It does recommend that member-countries consider a new social contract, labor and gender empowerment, and institutional reforms, and that they redirect public expenditures.

Almost all income-based redistribution proposals require a new social contract. Nobel Prize winner and former World Bank Chief Economist Joseph Stiglitz (2014) argues that without a new social contract, the problem of inequality will remain intractable. He proposes rewriting the rules of the game (40 different rules) in economic and financial areas. This approach presents a serious challenge in terms of political acceptability and viability because existing rules, Stiglitz argues, are put in place for the benefit of the "haves" who control the legislative and enforcement power of the State. His proposals, like those of Thomas Piketty—high-income taxes, property taxes, and inheritance taxes—are considered "hard" redistribution precisely because they entail such difficult political, economic, and social challenges.

The second approach is asset-based redistribution. The approach is explained best in Samuel Bowles's 2012 book, *The New Economics of Inequality and Redistribution*. This approach does not require an explicit new social contract, does not propose explicit changes in the rules of the game, and does not pose a political challenge. It relies principally on the methods of contracting, financing, and ownership through the market. Its major objective is changing financial and labor contracts to create an incentive structure that improves productivity by better aligning the interests of principles and agents in such a way that avoids moral hazard and other informational problems.[6] The intention is not only to include the excluded in the financial system, but also to empower them to become asset and wealth builders, thus effectively addressing the dual problems of poverty and inequality simultaneously.

Given the strong evidence of the negative impact of inequality on economic growth, the social and economic costs associated with inequality, and the risks high inequality poses to any economic system, it is difficult to argue that inequality in a society can be ignored. Inequality in a society not only damages the growth prospects of a country but also creates social unrest and has negative effects on mobility between different income groups. No country has managed to escape from the middle-income trap while maintaining high levels of inequality. Hence, shared prosperity could be instrumental both in decreasing extreme poverty and in increasing average growth rates of countries (Ostry, Berg, and Tsangarides 2014).

The shared prosperity indicator (figure 1.2) focuses directly on the income of the less well-off, rather than focusing only on growth rates of GDP per capita. Shared prosperity is not a simple redistributive policy where wealth is taken from the rich and given to the poor. Instead, shared prosperity aims not only to increase the economic resources of the countries, but also to maximize the share of those continuously increasing resources going to the bottom 40 percent of the income distribution. Hence shared prosperity mainly relies on enforcing a social contract where all agents in society have a fair opportunity to realize their full potential, contribute to economic growth, and receive their fair share of income and wealth.

The adoption of the SDGs by the development community, including the IDB, signifies the shared belief that achieving the SDGs will lead to sustainable development and shared prosperity. However, one of the key constraints in achieving the SDGs will be funding the huge investments necessary to

FIGURE 1.2 **Percentage of Income Held by the Top and Bottom 10 Percent in Select Countries**

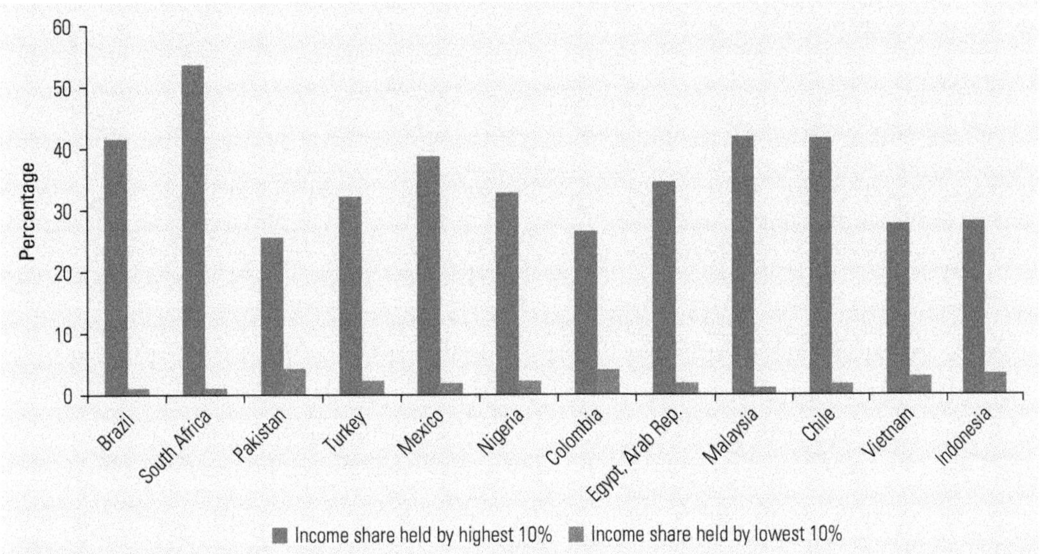

Source: World Bank, World Development Indicators, 2014.

achieve the goals. At current levels of investment, the developing countries will face an annual gap of $2.5 trillion to achieve the SDGs, the United Nations Conference on Trade and Development (UNCTAD 2014) estimates. Given the scale of funding requirements, promotion of sustainable development will need "significant mobilization of resources from a variety of sources and the effective use of financing," the United Nations concludes.[7] It will also require the engagement of different stakeholders, including government, businesses, civil society, and the financial sector.

Boxes 1.1 and 1.2 briefly present the development strategies from two multilaterals—the World Bank and the IDB. Both strategies have common goals but different approaches. The key difference in the two approaches is the use of Islamic finance by IDB, but the end goals are the same—reducing poverty and enhancing shared prosperity.

The Islamic Perspective on Development and Shared Prosperity

The Islamic perspective on income distribution shares many similarities with the asset-based approach to redistribution.[8] The asset-based approach is basically a risk-sharing approach. It converges with Islamic finance's contractual framework in terms of empowering equity participation by the lower-income groups in a society. Making the poor direct holders of real assets in the real sector of the economy reduces their high risk aversion. It also creates positive incentives for behavior to enhance productivity (such as trust, truthfulness, and hard work) through the design of contracts that reduce or eliminate the difference between principals and agents and are conducive to achievement of interests of all parties to a contract.

The foundations of human and economic development in Islam are well defined. The Islamic system of economics can be regarded as a rule-based system with well-defined principles, rules, and institutions. Compliance with this rule-based system leads to material and nonmaterial progress of society as a whole. The conventional perspective on economic development during the 1950s equated economic development with economic progress without taking into consideration the well-being of individuals. This paradigm evolved and has shifted considerably

BOX 1.1 The World Bank Group Approach to Enhancing Shared Prosperity

For the first time in 30 years, the development community, led by the World Bank Group, has revised its objectives to give priority to inequality. The new mission of the World Bank Group, introduced in 2013, has two pillars: reducing the number of people living in extreme poverty and promoting shared prosperity. The World Bank Group defines promoting shared prosperity as boosting the incomes of the bottom 40 percent of the population in every country. By focusing on the advancement of the poor and vulnerable segment of the society, the World Bank Group aims to achieve a more equitable distribution of growth revenues.

The World Bank Group's approach in promoting shared prosperity relies on five sets of policies.

Raising growth potential

Increasing economic growth is the most efficient method of reducing poverty levels and promoting shared prosperity of the poorest 40 percent of the population. Dani Rodrik (2008) has stated that "historically nothing has worked better than economic growth in enabling societies to improve the life chances of their members, including those at the very bottom." These groups are mostly excluded from the economic developments benefiting the other segments of their society. Without access to proper health care, education, credit, and land use, they are trapped in a spiral of extreme poverty. To tackle these problems, policy makers should carefully analyze the needs of those people and consider specific microeconomic policies reflecting the realities of each different geographic location.

Financial and social inclusion

To improve the prospects and well-being of the marginalized extreme poor, the World Bank Group is also focusing on enhancing social and financial inclusion of the society, in addition to increasing growth rates. These two priorities are connected. Increasing financial and social inclusion would also help boost overall economic growth by promoting countercyclical economic policy and by helping poor people maintain their human capital for the future and assist in the recovery of the economy. In addition to increasing financial access, increasing the financial literacy of low-income groups is important.

Fiscal sustainability

Fiscal sustainability became an important focus after public debt-to-GDP ratios rose rapidly in the aftermath of the global financial crisis. The high level of public indebtedness not only limits the functionality of welfare states but also makes using Keynesian types of growth policies less plausible. Throughout history, the prevailing financial system has created a growth path that many experts describe as a boom-bust cycle. During the boom period, high growth rates have been accompanied by high levels of leverage. When the level of leverage reaches a certain inflection point, the system collapses and a rebound follows. Smoothing out this cycle through fiscal sustainability is an important task for the economy and society, as recognized by the World Bank Group strategy.

Environmental sustainability

In addition to fiscal responsibility, creating environmentally friendly economic growth strengthens the sustainability of economic growth. The World Bank Group has committed to develop new metrics to measure the true positive effects of economic growth that takes into account not only the economic growth but also the negative effects of pollution and depletion of natural resources.

Institutional and governance reforms

In order to create a well-functioning social contract where all income groups—not just the very few privileged ones—are included in the prospects of economic growth, trust in government and institutions should be established and strengthened. Measures to increase accountability of institutions will reduce corruption and make institutions more efficient in fulfilling their responsibilities.

BOX 1.2 The Islamic Development Bank Group Strategy for Development

In 2015, the Islamic Development Bank Group (IDBG) adopted its 10-Year Strategy (10-YS) to be implemented during the period 2016–2025. The new 10-YS is based on the IDBG Vision, and is in line with the 10-Year Program of Action (10-PoA) of the Organisation of Islamic Cooperation (OIC) and the Sustainable Development Goals (SDGs) adopted by the United Nations General Assembly in September 2015. The new 10-YS aims to promote inclusive and sustainable socioeconomic development and enhance cooperation between IDB member-countries. It enables the IDB Group to serve the varying development needs of its 56 member-countries. It also aspires for the IDB Group to take a leadership role in promoting Islamic finance globally.

The 10-YS is founded on a framework that revolves around three strategic objectives, five priority areas, and seven guiding principles for effective and efficient implementation. These strategic objectives translate the vision in the member-countries into IDBG goals for the next 10 years. The five strategic pillars have been chosen to reflect three main considerations: the uniqueness, by mandate, of IDBG; the strengths and capabilities accumulated over decades of experience; and the relative position and potential of IDBG in the context of the evolving development landscape.

Infrastructure development and private sector support are critical areas because of their role in fostering growth and because they offer the potential to build on capabilities already in place. Social development (including agriculture and rural development, education, and health) as a priority area would provide solutions to problems of the neediest and underserved populations, build on widespread experience, and fulfill the IDBG's inclusive mandate. Islamic finance and cooperation are unique areas of activities and core mandates for IDBG. In each of the pillars, capacity development will play a very important role.

In order to translate the strategic pillars into action, given the existing constraints, the strategy includes a set of guiding principles to improve operational effectiveness and organizational efficiency. These guiding principles will help IDBG continue growing, with greater emphasis on mobilization of external resources and implementation through gradual decentralization; be more selective, to maximize the impact in development given the available resources; build capabilities in strategic areas in a cost-efficient manner; and better integrate and coordinate activities across the Group to maximize synergies.

during the past 50 years. Today, development economists acknowledge the importance of individuals as well as the state of institutions. The Islamic perspective on economic development encompasses this revised view. It has three dimensions: the development of the material world, self-development, and development of the society as a whole (Iqbal and Mirakhor 2013).

The central economic tenet of Islam is to develop a prosperous and egalitarian economic and social system wherein all members of society can maximize their intellectual capacity; preserve and promote their faith, health, and wealth among generations; and actively contribute to the economic and social development of society. From this perspective, Islamic economics and finance offer an alternative and viable framework that can play an important role in achieving sustainable development and boosting shared prosperity. This framework is based on four fundamental pillars, depicted in figure 1.3:

1. An institutional framework and public policy in line with the objectives of Islam
2. Prudent governance and accountable leadership
3. Promotion of the economy based on risk sharing and entrepreneurship (distribution)
4. Financial and social inclusion for all (redistribution).

FIGURE 1.3 Islamic Framework to Achieve Sustainable Development and Shared Prosperity

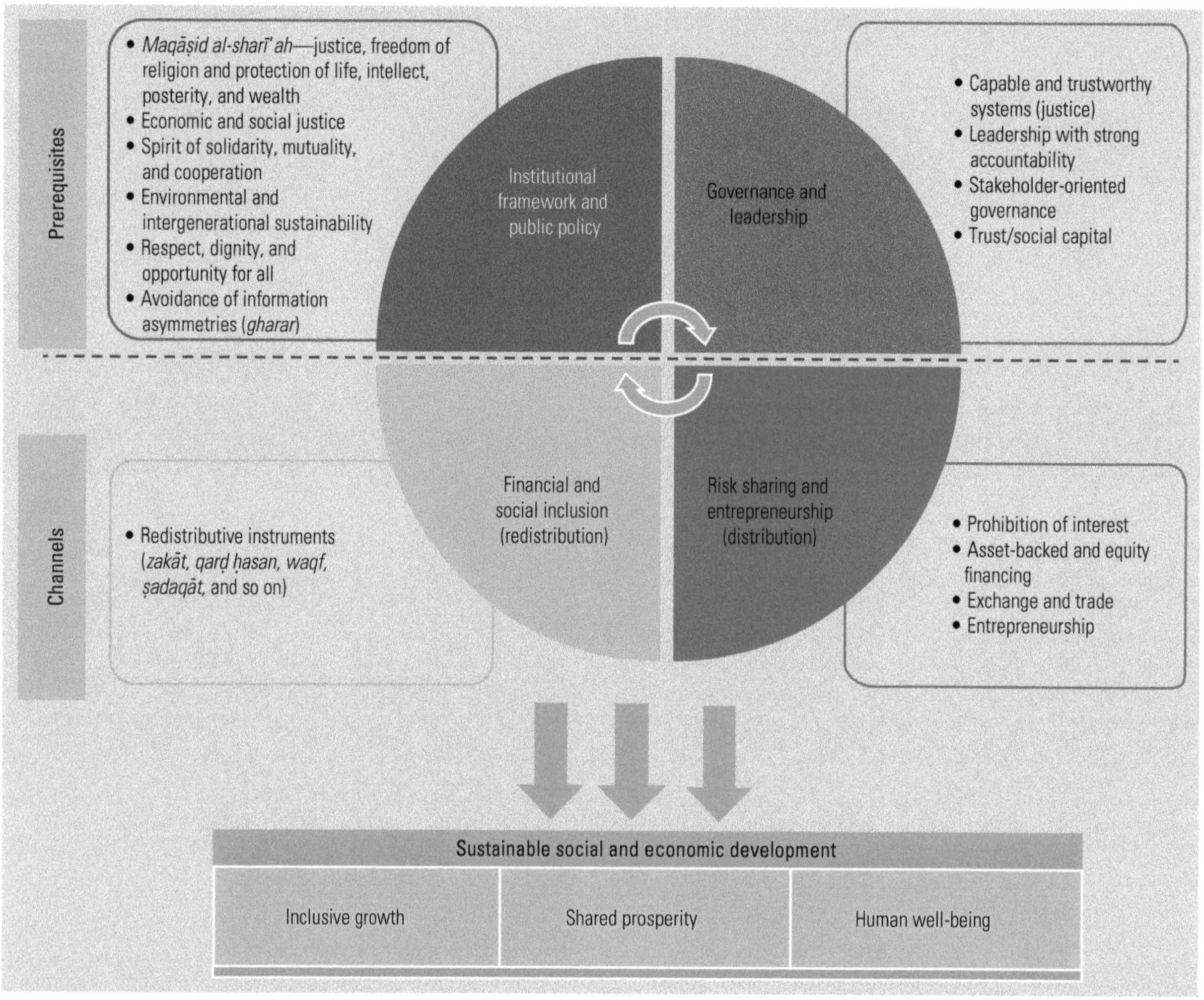

Note: For definitions of the terms of Islamic finance, see the glossary.

The first two pillars are prerequisites, while the last two are the channels to achieve sustainable development with equitable distribution of both opportunities and wealth, which are the main objectives of the concept of economic development in Islam. The proposed framework, which is constructed by interpreting central tenets of Islamic principles, could be used in creating a universal strategy and policy that align with the principles of Islamic finance to achieve the goal of sustainable development and to increase the welfare of all members of the society.

The first pillar is crucial because having a sound institutional framework and appropriate public policies are the foundation upon which the other pillars must rest and can function optimally. Institutions play a critical role in this framework, as they implement the rules prescribed by the tenets of Islam. The institutions also must adhere to the core objectives of Islam (commonly known as *maqāṣid al-sharī'ah,* or Objectives of Islamic Law)[9] that lay the foundation to formulate the policies promoting economic and social justice, preservation of human rights, dignity, health, and the intergenerational wealth of the society.

The second pillar focuses on developing a governance mechanism and accompanying compliance system based on the objectives and institutions briefly outlined in the first step. The ethically based governance, leadership, and compliance system helps increase the transparency and accountability in the public, private, and social sector institutions of the overall economic system and hence strengthens trust in the system. Trustworthy and capable leadership can ensure protection of rights of the vulnerable or those who could be vulnerable (as in future generations). Increased trust and better governance in turn strengthen the institutional framework that enables better implementation of better public policies. The desired institutional and governance structure must be able to do the following:

1. Design policies to foster inclusive growth and development by promoting entrepreneurship, risk-sharing financial transactions, and equity participation, and by discouraging financial leverage and speculation.
2. Encourage all members of society to contribute to the creation of economic, social, human, and moral capital.
3. Enhance the equitable distribution of wealth by promoting sharing of both risk and rewards.
4. Alleviate poverty by redistributing wealth, with special focus on the poorest.
5. Achieve economic and social justice by the correct use of material growth and development that enhances the overall well-being of the society.

The third pillar is the distribution channel; it works at both the individual and organizational level. One of the main features is the advocacy of risk sharing and promotion of entrepreneurship. This is one of the most important aspects of Islamic finance, which differentiates it from the conventional approach of overreliance on debt-dominated risk-shifting or risk-transfer mechanisms.[10] Sharing the risks of economic and financial transactions also ensures the stability of the financial system (Askari and others 2010). In addition, risk sharing with equitable sharing mechanisms encourages entrepreneurship and innovation, since counterparties receive their fair share in the investment. This in turn will increase the allocation of resources to the real sector, rather than channeling excessive financial flows to the financial sector (overfinancialization).[11]

The fourth pillar aims to ensure that the fruits of the higher growth are distributed to every segment of the society inclusively, either through participation in the economic growth or through Islam's instruments of redistribution.

Pillar I. Institutional Framework

Establishing efficient institutions and an institutional framework in line with the principles of Islam—that emphasize universal values such as protecting life, preserving property rights and sanctity of contracts, building a more just society, protecting the rights of future generations, fostering mutuality and solidarity, and being sensitive to environmental issues—is essential in creating an enabling environment for the Islamic economic and financial systems to flourish.

The institutional framework of the ideal economy consists of a collection of institutions: rules of conduct and their associated means of enforcement to deal with the allocation of resources, production, and exchange of goods and services and the distribution and redistribution of the resulting income and wealth. The objective of these institutions is to achieve social justice. Each economic system has an "institutional matrix" that "defines the opportunity set ... that makes the highest payoffs in an economy's income distribution or ... that provides the highest payoffs to productive activity" (North 2005, 61). Douglass North, in his 2005 book *Understanding the Process of Economic Change*, contends that in all economic systems, institutions (rules of behavior) are designed by humans to impose constraints on human interaction. These institutions "structure human interaction by providing an incentive structure to guide human behavior. But an incentive structure requires a theory of the way the mind perceives the world and its functioning so that institutions can provide those incentives" (North 2005, 66). At this point, paradigms become relevant because paradigms in economics include conceptions of humankind and society and their interrelationships.

An important function of the institutional framework is reducing uncertainty caused by lack of information, which can hinder decision making. Rules specify what kind of conduct is most appropriate in achieving just results, especially when individuals face alternative choices and must take action. Rules impose restrictions on what society's members can do, without upsetting the social order upon which all members depend in choosing their own actions and forming their expectations of how others will respond and act. Compliance with the rules makes people more certain in forming those expectations, prevents conflict, reconciles differences, coordinates actions, facilitates cooperation, promotes social integration and social solidarity, and strengthens the social order. In an ideal society, the degree of effectiveness in enforcing rules is determined by the degree to which the objective of achieving social justice becomes integral to members of the society.

Key Institutions of Islamic Finance

The Islamic economic paradigm is a Creator-centered conceptualization of reality (box 1.3). Its view of the institutional framework is based on the following:

- Clear and secure property rights
- Contract enforcement
- Trust among people and between government and people, and among people and other institutions. Such abiding trust can reduce risk, uncertainty, and ambiguity; strengthen social solidarity; bring private and public interests into closer harmony; and ensure coordination so risk can be shared better.

One of the main advantages of having a well-established institutional framework is that it improves the flow of information and can reduce information asymmetries. The Islamic institutional framework has well-defined rules and guidance on everyday life and economic transactions. Rules governing transactions—such as trustworthiness, truthfulness, faithfulness to the terms and conditions of contracts, transparency, and noninterference with the workings of the markets and the price mechanism so long as market participants are complying with the rules—provide a reasonably strong economy where information flows without hindrance. Participants can engage in transactions confidently, with minimal concern for uncertainty regarding the actions and reactions of other participants. Because of the high level of trust, transaction costs can be minimal. Due to the level of depth and clarity in these rules, if agents in an economy comply with them, the problem of information asymmetry would be minimized, which in turn would encourage Islamic financial instruments to function.

The Role of Public Policy

In all economic systems, the State plays a role in the economy. Only the extent of the State's involvement differs, depending on the common values and belief system shared by the individuals that make up the particular society and the political structure that is in power during a particular period. The Islamic economy is to ensure that everyone has equal access to resources and means of livelihood, that markets are supervised so that justice is attained, that transfers take place from the more able to the less able, and that distributive justice is ensured for the next generation (Al-Hasani and Mirakhor 2003).

The role of the government is only that of a trustee to society, and it is to act according to the rules prescribed in the *Qur'ān* and *sunnah*.[12] The role of the government is broadly divided into two functions: a policy function that ensures that private interest does not diverge too far from public interest, and a function to design and implement an incentive structure to encourage rule compliance, coordination, and cooperation.

BOX 1.3 Key Institutions in an Ideal Islamic Economy

The institutional structure of the ideal Islamic economy rests on rules governing property, production, exchange, trust, markets, and distribution and redistribution, among others.

Property rights

All property ultimately belongs to the Creator, who has made all created resources available for humans, to empower them to perform what their Creator expects of them. Individuals are free to acquire and accumulate property as long as it does not violate the rights and the interests of the society and individuals. Islam prohibits the concentration of wealth and imposes limits on consumption through its rules prohibiting overspending (*isrāf*), waste (*itlāf*), and ostentatious and opulent spending (*itrāf*).

Contracts

Islam places great significance on the sanctity of and commitment to contracts. Islam's strong emphasis on the strictly binding nature of contracts covers private and public contracts, as well as international treaties. Moreover, every public office in Islam is regarded as a contract, that is, an agreement that defines the rights and obligations of the parties. Every contract entered into by the believer must include a forthright intention to remain loyal to performing the obligations specified by the terms of the contract.

Trust

Trust is considered the most important element of social capital in Islam, which considers being trustworthy an obligatory personality trait. In the *shari'ah*, the concepts of justice, faithfulness, reward, and punishment are linked with the fulfillment of obligations incurred under the stipulations of the contract. Being trustworthy and remaining faithful to promises and contracts are absolute requirements, regardless of the costs involved or whether the other party is a friend or a foe.

Markets

The market's institutional structure is built around five pillars: property rights, the free flow of information, trust, contracts, and the right not to be harmed by others and the obligation not to harm anyone. Together, they serve to reduce uncertainty and transaction costs and enable cooperation and collective action to proceed unhindered.

Distribution and redistribution

The most important economic institution of the Islamic economic paradigm to achieve social justice is its set of rules regarding distribution and redistribution. Distribution takes place after production and sale, when all factors of production are given what is due to them commensurate with their contribution to production, exchange, and sale of goods and services. Redistribution occurs after the distribution phase, when the charges due to the less able are levied. These expenditures are essentially repatriation and redemption of the rights of others in one's income and wealth.

Source: Iqbal and Mirakhor 2011.

Islam uses the market as a mechanism to solve part of the coordination problem within the economy. The State enters the market as the supervisor/regulator of economic activity. It is the combination of State supervision/regulation and free enterprise that will be used to maximize social welfare. The State must actively complement market forces to ensure that individual initiative does not degenerate into a private greed for gains, especially when the gains are nonproductive.

The symbiotic relationship of humankind, the Creator, and the environment can offer an alternative in achieving sustained and civilized development that could augment the proposed framework proposed by the World Bank Group. Macroeconomic policies are taking cognizance of social and environmental elements as integral parts of the decision process (Mirakhor and Askari 2010). Hence there is a clear link between public policy based on Islamic principles and the emphasis on inclusive and environmentally friendly and fiscally sustainable development policies.

Islamic finance clearly states that the sole owner of all the property, including natural resources, is the Creator. Hence any abuse of natural resources, their wasteful or inefficient use, or disregard or negligence in creating externalities such as pollution is forbidden (Majah 1952). The Islamic perspective places a strong emphasis on intergenerational sustainability in both environmental and fiscal issues.

In addition, Islamic public policies are required to pay a great deal of attention to inclusiveness and efficiency. *Maqāṣid al-sharīʻah* principles direct the State to implement socially optimal and effective public policies that encourage cooperation rather than competition and support basic freedoms under which a market-oriented and socially inclusive economic system can flourish. Public policy to support financial integration with the real economy and to mobilize savings in developing countries could help promote risk mitigation and risk sharing, thus building resilience in the face of shocks.

Pillar II. Responsible Governance and Leadership

Governance can be regarded as the set of rules and norms that deals with the process and structures with which entities are managed, and that define the distribution of responsibilities between the management and related parties that are to gain or lose from the actions of the entity. The main objective of governance is to maximize the gains of the related parties and stakeholders within the social, legal, and market environment. The governance model in the Islamic economic system is a stakeholder-oriented model where the governance structure and process at the system and firm level protect the rights of stakeholders that are exposed to any risk as a result of a firm's activities. Whereas the conventional financial system is struggling to find convincing arguments to justify stakeholders' participation in governance, a stakeholder model is built into Islam's principles of property rights, commitment to explicit and implicit contractual agreements, and implementation of an effective incentive system.

The design of the governance system in Islam can be best understood in light of principles governing the rights of the individual, society, and the State; the laws governing property ownership; and the framework of contracts. Islam's recognition and protection of rights is not limited to human beings but encompasses all forms of life as well as the environment. Each element of Allah (swt)'s creation has been endowed with certain rights, and each is obligated to respect and honor the rights of others (Iqbal and Mirakhor 2004).

The principles of property rights and contracts in Islam offer theoretical foundations to acknowledge the rights of all stakeholders, Iqbal and Mirakhor (2004) argue. Islam's principles of property rights, contracts, and a just social order define the business environment where economic agents are morally conscious of protecting property rights and contractual obligations to one another, whether acting as public servants, managers, employees, suppliers, or customers, or in any other capacity. All participants in economic activities—whether individuals, firms, corporations, nonprofit organizations, or public institutions—are subject to the same degree of commitment. The notion of the sanctity of contractual obligations is not limited to explicit contracts, which are well defined, stipulated, and documented, but is equally applicable to implicit contracts, which are incomplete by nature. Property rights of all contractual parties—whether individuals, local communities, intangible legal entities, or the society—are preserved and protected.

A financial sector with weak governance and lack of transparency is bound to lead to debt financing, market frictions, inefficiencies, and financial exclusion. Strong corporate governance values would increase the accountability and transparency of the financial system.

In Islam, the expected behavior of a firm is not any different from the expected behavior of any other member of the society. Although the entity itself does not have a conscience, the behavior of its managers becomes the behavior of the firm, and their actions are subject to the same high standards of moral and ethical commitment as expected from any member of society. A firm's economic and moral behavior is shaped by its managers acting on behalf of the owners, and it is their fiduciary duty to manage the firm for the benefit of all the stakeholders and not for the owners alone. Consequently, it will be incumbent upon managers and owners to ensure that the behavior of the firm conforms to the principles and the rules of Islamic law.

Notions of responsibility and accountability play an important role in shaping the behavior of the leaders in the public and private sector. Business leaders are expected to act prudently as opposed to recklessly and to act with the best ethical behavior. For example, taking excessive risks is a form of acting without prudence and probably in one's own self-interest rather than the larger interest of the shareholders and stakeholders. Similarly, attempts to circumvent regulatory constraints,[13] find loopholes in the law, and misrepresent matters, and acts of willful negligence that were common practice among top business leaders during the global financial crisis would not be the traits of a leader compliant with the rules of Islam.

Pillar III. Risk-Sharing Finance

The core principle of Islamic finance (Askari and others 2010) is risk sharing among the investors and the users of funds that stipulates that both share the outcome of the business or asset being financed —whether positive or negative.[14] Unconditional prohibition of interest in any form by Islamic Law eliminates unsecured debt from the financial system. Instead, preference is given to asset-backed and equity or participatory finance, as well as financing of trading and exchange activities.

Encouraging financial instruments that promote risk sharing and asset-backed financing could help deleverage financial systems (box 1.4) and make them more stable and resilient to economic shocks. The development of equity-based capital markets could play an important role in mobilizing resources without creating leverage in the economy. A financial system based on asset-backed financing would encourage real transactions and growth in the real sector. A financial system based on risk-sharing principles would smooth out the boom-bust cycles in the economy, thus creating a more just and equitable society, because in such a system the distribution of profit and loss would be determined according to the risks each agent bears.

Because counterparties would receive their fair share of proceeds in investments according to the risk they bear, the entrepreneurial spirit in a society would be invigorated. Agents would be willing to take judicious risk in developing innovative ideas and actually bringing these ideas to life if they were rewarded according to the risk they would bear. A growing body of evidence demonstrates the significance of developing entrepreneurship in the economy through micro, small, or medium enterprises, which could serve as the engine for growth. Entrepreneurship encourages socially optimum risk sharing and promotes innovation.

An economic system based fully on the principle of risk sharing mitigates the negative effects of recessions on certain investors while enabling the returns during high-growth episodes to be distributed in a more equitable manner. Hence the risk-sharing principle not only can help create smoother business cycles but also can enhance a more sound and equitable pattern of income distribution in a society.

Islamic finance, through its core principles, advocates for just and fair distribution of income and wealth during the production

BOX 1.4 Why Is Debt Finance So Prevalent?

In 2013, outstanding global debt reached $199 trillion (Dobbs and others 2015)—almost triple the capitalization of the equity market, at $64 trillion (Deutsche Bank Research 2014) (figures B1.4.1 and B1.4.2).

One of the major reasons why debt finance is so prevalent is because the interest payments are tax deductible. Tax breaks for debt occur in two principal forms. Interest payments on mortgages are tax deductible for personal income tax purposes in many countries. Meanwhile, firms can deduct interest payments to debtholders from their taxable earnings. By contrast, the dividend payments and retained profits that flow to shareholders are taxable (*Economist* 2015). It could be argued that debt finance is being subsidized by sovereigns, and this subsidy makes it more favorable than equity finance.

Another reason is information asymmetry. Investors have insufficient information regarding the state of investment projects. Townsend (1979) argues that debt contracts are optimal when only the entrepreneur can observe the state of the world and his or her project; investors must pay a fixed

FIGURE B1.4.1 Global Outstanding Debt

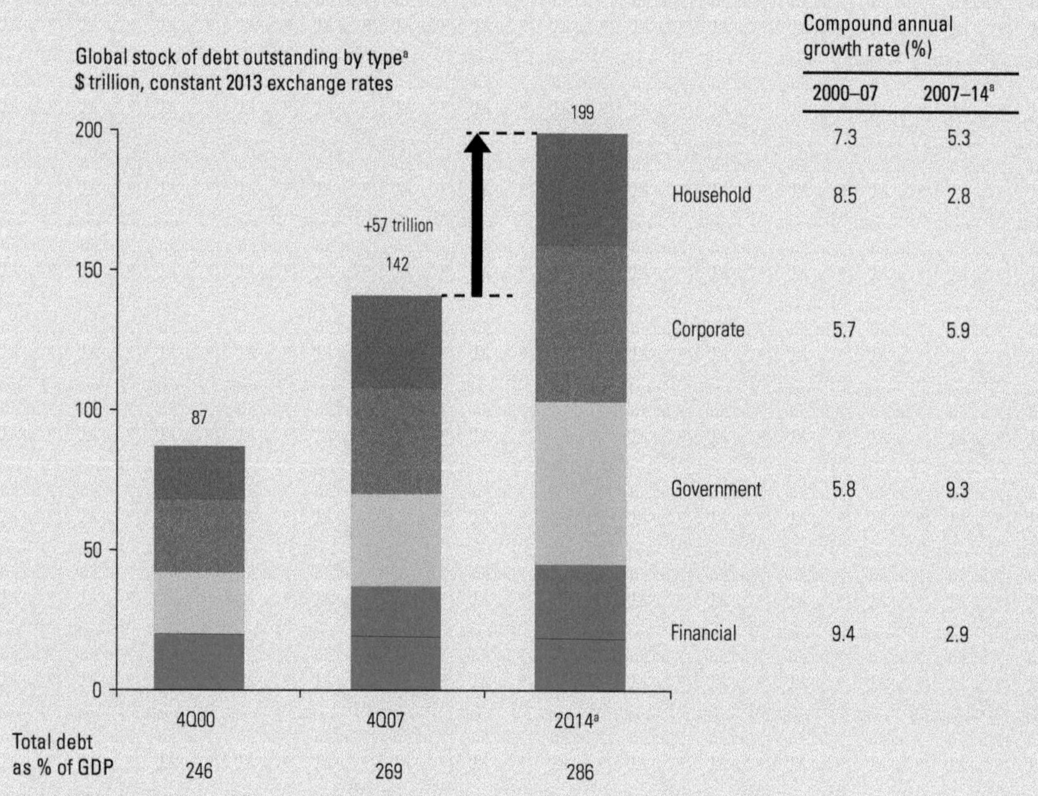

Source: Dobbs and others 2015.
Note: Numbers may not sum due to rounding.
a. 2Q14 data for advanced economies and China; 4Q13 data for other developing economies.

box continues next page

BOX 1.4 Why Is Debt Finance So Prevalent? *(continued)*

cost (in terms of time, money, and/or effort) to verify the prospects of the project. However, if the probability of monitoring the environment in which the future stream of investment are to be realized is somehow endogenized through some sort of screening process, then a debt contract is no longer efficient even after the debt contract has matured. Furthermore, considering the systemic risks posed by the debt-fueled growth that this strategy poses, the optimality of contracts would change drastically, favoring instruments based on risk sharing.

Another reason why debt financing is much more prevalent is because investors might prefer the relative safety of bonds to equities. Moreover, the entrepreneur retains the entire marginal return through a debt contract; the entrepreneur does not have to share the future stream of profits with other investors. This creates incentives for debt financing rather than equity financing (Jensen and Meckling 1976).

FIGURE B1.4.2 Stock Markets versus Debt Securities

$ trillion

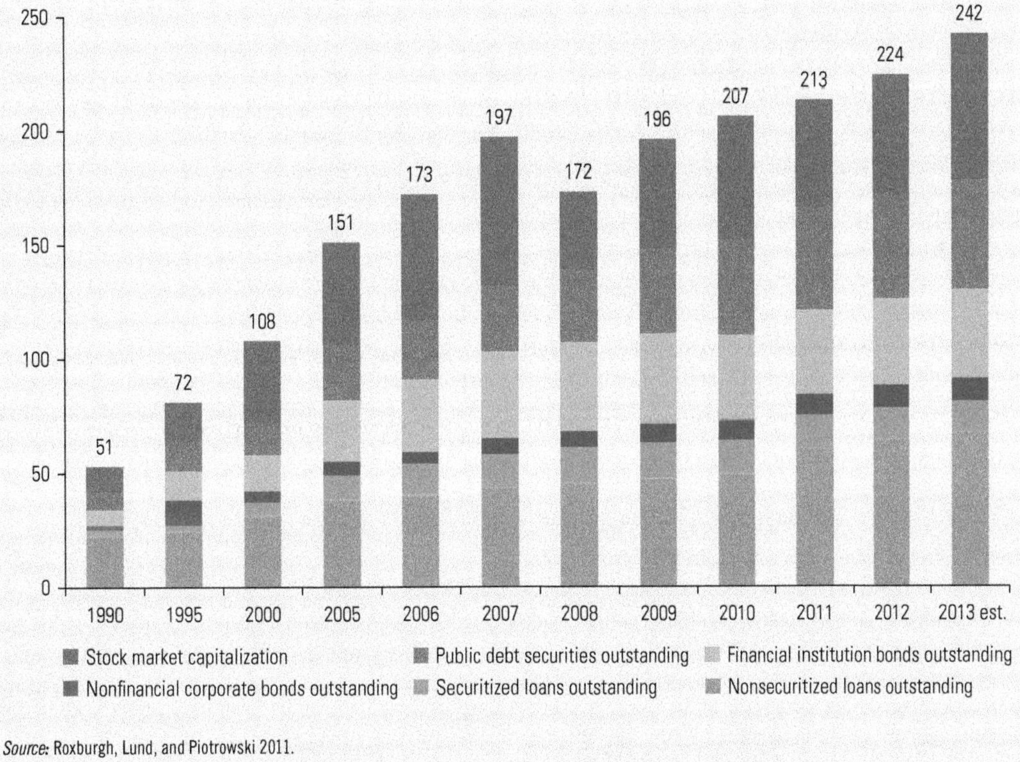

Source: Roxburgh, Lund, and Piotrowski 2011.

cycle and provides mechanisms for redistribution to address any imbalances that may occur. Islamic finance's approach to redistribution is based on a balanced blend of income-based redistribution through redistributive instruments and asset-based redistribution through the notion of risk sharing. Whereas the income-based redistribution approach offers only a partial solution—as it takes the current income distribution as given and aims at fairer distribution of future GDP—the asset-based redistribution is basically a risk-sharing approach and converges to Islamic finance's contractual framework in terms of empowering equity participation by the lower-income groups in the society. Analytically, by making the poor direct holders of real assets in the real sector of the economy, the approach reduces their empirically observed high aversion to risk. It also creates positive incentives for promoting behavioral factors that enhance productivity (such as trust, truthfulness, and hard work) through the design of contracts that reduce or eliminate the difference between principles and agents and are conducive to achievement of the interests of all parties to a contract.

Researchers suggest that good public policy and strengthened institutional frameworks in developing countries can go a long way toward reducing aggregate risk in an economy. Policy improvements include strengthening governance to reduce damage to households due to excessive risk taking; achieving and sustaining economic and political stability; and promoting financial sector development. In terms of the institutional framework, clear and secure property rights, contract enforcement, and trust among people and between government and people and other institutions can reduce risk, uncertainty, and ambiguity; strengthen social solidarity; bring private and public interests into closer harmony; and ensure coordination to encourage risk sharing (North 2005; Mirakhor 2009; Mirakhor and Askari 2010).

A system based on risk sharing has the potential of not only creating a smoother business cycle and a more equitable distribution of wealth but also speeding up the deleveraging of the financial system while encouraging the entrepreneurial spirit. Figure 1.4 illustrates how equity finance is more conducive to economic growth than other forms of financing.

Pillar IV. Financial and Social Inclusion

The main problems in enhancing financial inclusion are linked to risks arising from information asymmetries and the high transaction costs of processing, monitoring, and enforcing small loans. Information asymmetries can result from adverse selection (the inability of the lender to distinguish between high- and

FIGURE 1.4 The Contrasting Effects on Growth of Different Forms of Financial Expansion

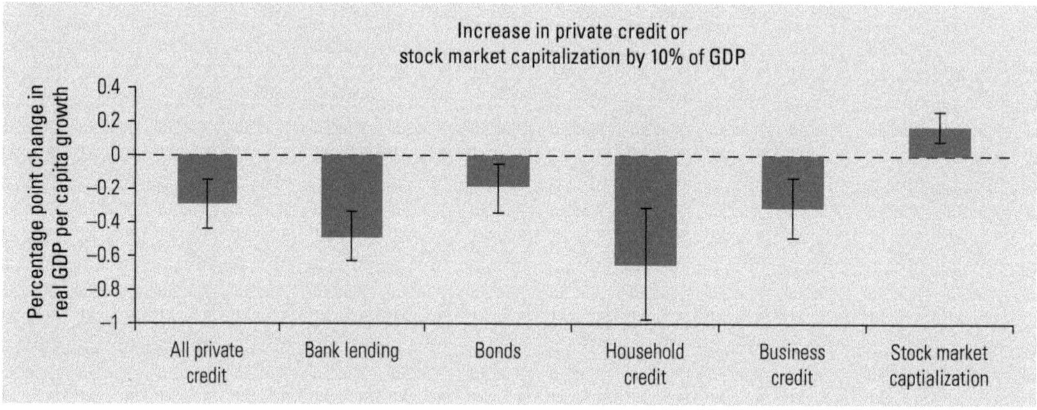

Source: OECD 2015, http://www.oecd.org/eco/How-to-restore-a-healthy-financial-sector-that-supports-long-lasting-inclusive-growth.pdf.

low-risk borrowers) or from moral hazard (the tendency for some borrowers to divert resources to projects that reduce their likelihood of being able to repay the loan, and the inability of the lender to detect and prevent such behavior).

From an Islamic perspective, property is not a means of exclusion but of inclusion, in which to redeem the rights of those less able through the income and wealth of the more able. Islam emphasizes financial inclusion more explicitly than conventional finance; inclusion is embedded in core economic and social institutions of Islam. Two distinct features of Islamic finance—the notions of risk sharing and redistribution of wealth—differentiate its path of development significantly from the conventional financial model.

The following are the main drivers of financial inclusion:

- Contracts of exchange and risk-sharing instruments in the financial sector
- Redistributive risk-sharing instruments that the economically more able segment of society uses to share the risks faced by the less able segment of the population (Askari, Iqbal, and Mirakhor 2015; Iqbal and Mirakhor 2011)
- Inheritance rules specified in the *Qur'ān*, through which the wealth of a person at the time of death is distributed among current and future generations of inheritors (Mirakhor and Iqbal 2012).

Instruments of redistribution are used to redeem the rights of the less able through the income and wealth of the more able. Rules of redistribution ensure that those unable to benefit by participating directly in production and consumption in the market, through a combination of their labor and their right of access to resources provided by the Supreme Creator for all humans, can redeem their rights through various redistributive mechanisms (see box 1.5). Once these rights have been redeemed out of the income and wealth of the more economically able, the latter's property rights on the remaining income and wealth are held inviolable. Contrary to common belief, these are not instruments of charity, altruism, or beneficence, but instruments of redemption of rights and repayment of obligations (Iqbal and Mirakhor 2013).

The *Qur'ān* considers the more able as trustee-agents in using these resources on behalf of the less able. In this view, property

BOX 1.5 Key Instruments of Redistribution in Islamic Finance

Ṣadaqah (recommended contributions)

Ṣadaqah is intended to redeem the rights of the less privileged in society. *Ṣadaqāt* is the plural of the term *ṣadaqah*, a derivative of the root meaning truthfulness and sincerity.

Zakāt (mandatory levy)

Zakāt is one of the key pillars of Islam and is ordained to mobilize funds for the welfare of the poor. Its collection was enforced by governments in early Islamic history.

Qarḍ ḥasan (benevolent loan free of any charge)

Qarḍ ḥasan, a loan mentioned in the *Qur'ān* as "beautiful" (*ḥasan*), is a voluntary loan, without any expectation by the creditor of any return on the principal.

Waqf (endowment)

A *waqf* is a trust established when the contributor endows the stream of income accruing to a property for a charitable purpose in perpetuity.

Source: Iqbal and Mirakhor 2013.

is not a means of exclusion but inclusion, in which the rights of those less able are redeemed through the income and wealth of the more able. The result would be a balanced economy without extremes of wealth and poverty. The operational mechanism for redeeming the right of the less able in the income and wealth of the more able are the network of mandatory and voluntary payments such as *zakāt* (a 2.5 percent levy on asset-based wealth), *khums* (a 20 percent levy on income), and payments referred to as *ṣadaqāt* (recommended contributions). Finally, individuals who for some reason were left marginalized in the system without having the necessary resources to meet their basic needs are provided with the necessary social safety net through redistributive instruments.

For centuries, Islamic redistributive instruments such as *zakāt, qarḍ ḥasan, waqf,* and *ṣadaqāt* have played a vital role of ensuring social protection and alleviating poverty in a dignified manner that has led to wider social and financial inclusion. These instruments need to be revived and institutionalized to gain optimal benefits.[15] Through these redistributive instruments, the rich share the risk by helping the poor, which creates a more equitable society where everyone would have equal opportunity and contribute to economic development of the society.

Although periodic income redistribution can reduce inequality in the dimension of income, the change may not persist over the longer run. For example, incomes through redistribution could be subject to misuse by the recipient or allocated to consumption, which could bring the system back to the same state of inequality. Compared with income redistribution, asset redistribution is potentially more durable because it affects the potential future stream of earnings, not one-time income. For these reasons, Islam not only puts in place a method of redistribution of wealth—for example, at the time of distributing an inheritance—but also a method of periodically redistributing income and wealth in the form of *zakāt*, *waqf*, and more frequent *ṣadaqāt* and other contributions. This not only directly helps the poorer segment of the population but also brings idle wealth into circulation and productive use. Islam also puts in place an overall system of fairness, unambiguity in transactions, risk sharing, and equitable dealings. This is important to avoid nullifying any redistributive effect and to ensure proper incentives for members of society to work, take risks, and share in the outcomes. Together these elements of distribution and redistribution of income and wealth ensure circulation of wealth and avoid its concentration among the rich.

The Role of the Financial Sector in Achieving Shared Prosperity

The financical sector can promote shared prosperity by facilitating economic growth, decreasing income inequality, and reducing vulnerability. On a macroeconomic level, academic research has shown that not all types of growth contribute to the reduction in poverty rates in the same manner. Even though overfinancialization poses dangers to economic stability, in order to achieve sustainable growth, it is essential to have a well-functioning financial system that can channel the funds to the most productive resources. Growth fueled by the financial sector generates less employment for the lower-income segment of the society than growth driven by labor-intensive sectors. For example, growth favoring the agricultural sector helps improve the conditions of the very poor. Hence, channeling the resources of the financial sector into the development of the real sector is crucial to realizing the World Bank Group goals. Several studies have shown that financial sector development can make positive contributions to economic development (Levine 1997).

Development of the financial sector can make a significant contribution to achieving shared prosperity in several areas. Table 1.2 presents the relationships of the functions that the financial sector typically performs and the factors that can contribute to enhancing shared prosperity.

Box 1.6 describes how the development of the financial sector could contribute to shared prosperity under each pillar of Islamic finance's framework of development.

TABLE 1.2 Functions of the Financial Sector and Factors Affecting Shared Prosperity

	Mobilizing savings/ managing assets	Allocating capital/financing	Managing risks
Facilitating growth	Mobilize financial resources for investments.	Allocate capital for production.	Avoid economic crisis and promote innovation.
Decreasing income inequality	Manage assets for poorest 40 percent of the population.	Provide financing to the poor and micro and small enterprises.	Protect the poor against downturns and negative shocks.
Reducing vulnerability	Allow savings for emergencies.	Reduce risk by monitoring and provide financing for short-term needs and emergencies.	Provide insurance and protection against risks and uncertain events.

Source: Ahmed 2015.

BOX 1.6 How Development of the Financial Sector Could Promote Shared Prosperity

Institutions and Public Policy

Institutional framework: Establish efficient, well-run institutions in line with the principles of *maqāṣid al-sharī'ah* that emphasize universal values such as protecting life, preserving property rights and the sanctity of contracts, building a more just society, protecting the rights of future generations, fostering mutuality and solidarity, and being sensitive to environmental issues.

Fiscal prudence and environmentally sustainable development: Develop risk-sharing instruments to finance fiscal deficits. Ensure that prudent fiscal policies are in place to protect the rights and wealth of future generations. Pay special attention to the negative externalities higher economic growth might create, such as pollution and depletion of resources. Not taking these effects into account would shift the burden from the current generation to future generations.

Socially optimal and inclusive public policy: Use *maqāṣid al-sharī'ah* principles to implement socially optimal and effective public policies that encourage cooperation rather than competition, and basic freedoms under which a market-oriented and socially inclusive economic system could flourish.

Responsible Governance and Leadership

Enhanced governance: A financial sector with weak governance and lack of transparency is bound to lead to debt financing, market frictions, inefficiencies, and financial exclusion.

Enhanced accountability: Greater accountability would induce policy makers and agents within an economy to act according to the predefined set of rules that would enhance property rights, contracts, and trust in the entire economic system. This, in turn, would lead to more efficient resource allocation and a more vibrant economy. An increase in trust would reduce the cost of screening and monitoring and encourage investments in the real economy.

Strong leadership to implement policies: Strong political will and leadership is of utmost importance to implement the theoretical goals of responsible governance.

Promotion of Risk Sharing and Entrepreneurship

Deleveraging the financial system and promoting risk sharing: Financial instruments promoting risk sharing and asset-based financing can help deleverage financial systems to make them more stable and robust, thus promoting sustainable growth. Similarly, the development of equity-based capital markets can play an important role in mobilizing resources without creating leverage in the economy. A financial system based on asset-based financing would encourage transactions and growth in the real sector. A financial system

box continues next page

BOX 1.6 How Development of the Financial Sector Could Promote Shared Prosperity *(continued)*

based on risk-sharing principles would smooth out the boom-bust cycles in the economy. This would create a more just and equitable society, because in such a system, the distribution of profit and loss would be determined according to the risks agents bear.

Reducing information asymmetries (*gharar*): Because agents are rewarded according to the risk they bear, counterparties have incentives to act in a responsible manner without taking unnecessary risk. This mutuality increases the trust in counterparties, which decreases *gharar* and results in a more efficient allocation of resources. Because Islamic principles strictly prohibit the existence of vagueness in contracts, this also reduces information asymmetries.

Promoting entrepreneurship: Promoting entrepreneurship through micro, small, and medium enterprises can serve as an engine for growth. Entrepreneurship encourages socially optimal risk sharing and promotes innovation. However, every owner of a micro, small, or medium enterprise is not an entrepreneur. A key consideration is how to develop such skills and encourage calculated risk taking to promote development, and how to make opportunities available to share in the prosperity.

Financial and Social Inclusion

Revitalizing and institutionalizing redistributive instruments: For centuries, redistributive instruments such as *zakāt, qarḍ ḥasan, waqf,* and *ṣadaqāt* have played a vital role of social protection and alleviation of poverty in a dignified manner that have led to wider social and financial inclusion. These instruments need to be revived and institutionalized to yield optimal benefits.

Creating innovative social finance: Both social inclusion and financial inclusion are critical tools in boosting shared prosperity. However, the conventional means of financial inclusion through microfinance and SME financing face serious challenges, including the high cost of borrowing and lack of affordable funding. This problem is even more serious for countries with massive poverty, including the majority of OIC countries. There is a need to develop financial mechanisms that make affordable financing available to the poor. Market-based solutions, public-private partnerships, and social finance instruments can help.

Creating unconventional means of social protection: Conventional finance's answer to increasing social inclusion mainly relies on the activities of the welfare state. However, the spike in government indebtedness after the financial crisis, especially in developed countries, has limited the availability of sovereign financial resources and thus the role welfare states might play in terms of reducing income inequality. Countries that have high levels of poverty also often have very weak institutions, which makes it difficult to support a welfare state. Hence a different framework is needed to reach the poor and marginalized.

Conclusion

This chapter presents a perspective based on Islamic economics and finance that offers an alternative approach to achieving two key development objectives: reducing extreme poverty to 3 percent globally by 2030, and promoting shared prosperity. Given the severity of these problems in member-countries of the OIC, where policy makers are challenged with high levels of inequality and highly indebted households, firms, and sovereigns, a solution provided by Islamic finance could lead to sustainable development and enhanced shared prosperity.

The main core principles of Islamic finance are its asset-based and risk-sharing principles. The asset-backed nature of Islamic finance prevents an economy from becoming overfinancialized and leveraged. Risk sharing not only offers the foundation for a more stable financial system but also more equitable growth because the proceeds of returns to growth are shared by agents in line with the risk they bear.

For those core principles to be realized, certain preconditions must be met. The starting point is establishing a sound institutional framework that has well-defined rules and reduces information asymmetries in economic transactions. The institutional framework should be strengthened by governance structures that take into account all the stakeholders, as well as the broader society. Finally, adherence to redistributive principles could enhance financial inclusion and would enable the proceeds of growth to be redistributed to the marginalized groups who for some reason did not have the necessary resources to participate in the growth strategies.

Notes

1. Various theories have been proposed to explain the deterioration in income and wealth distribution. One strand of academic literature considers the globalization of finance and trade to be the main culprit of rising inequality around the world (Krugman and Venables 1995). Another strand focuses on recent technological advances, and identifies a "skill bias" that tends to benefit skilled workers more in comparison to unskilled workers (Acemoglu 2002).
2. Earlier views on inequality thought that it might help spur growth. For example, Lazear and Rosen (1981) argue that high inequality might strengthen the incentives for workers to work harder and take on risk and pursue innovative ideas. Okun (1975) argues that there is a negative relationship between policies addressed to reducing inequality and productivity and coined the term "equity-efficiency trade-off." Kaldor (1955) argues that since rich people have a higher saving rate than poor people, higher inequality results in higher savings and capital accumulation, which spur economic growth.
3. From a different perspective, and drawing on extensive empirical data and theory, Kuznets (1955) argues that at the early stages of economic development, equality declines, but as the development process proceeds, there will be a turning point as equality begins to improve. He postulates that the relationship between economic development and inequality is in the form of an equality U-curve or an inequality inverse U-curve.
4. Kumhof and Rancière (2010) present a dynamic general equilibrium model that produces these stylized facts.
5. The eight main MDGs seek to (1) eradicate extreme poverty and hunger; (2) achieve universal primary education; (3) promote gender equality; (4) reduce child mortality; (5) improve maternal health; (6) combat HIV/AIDS, malaria, and other diseases; (7) ensure environmental sustainability; and (8) develop a global partnership for development.
6. Moral hazard is a situation in which one party gets involved in a risky event knowing that it is protected against the risk, and the other party will incur the cost.
7. United Nations Economic and Social Council. "Millennium Development Goals and Post-2015 Development Agenda," page 3. http://www.un.org/en/ecosoc/about/mdg.shtml.
8. For an in-depth discussion of development issues in Islam, see Chapra (2007); Mirakhor and Askari (2010); and Askari, Iqbal, and Krichene (2010).
9. For purposes of this book, and as an oversimplification, the *shari'ah* is Islamic Law derived from two divinely revealed sources: the *Qur'ān* and the Tradition of the Prophet Mohammed. There are other means of ascertaining the *shari'ah* from nonrevealed sources, such as *ijma* (the contemporary consensus of scholars of the *shari'ah*) and *qiyās* (reasoning); however, there are many others.
10. Islamic finance comprises four areas of activity that are conducted in accordance with *shari'ah* principles: banking, financing, investing, and *takāful* (*shari'ah*-compliant cooperative insurance).
11. Financialization is a term sometimes used to describe the form of financial capitalism that developed between 1980 and 2010, in which financial leverage tended to override capital (equity), and financial markets tended to dominate over the traditional real sector economy.
12. The *Qur'ān* is the holy book of Islam. The *sunnah* are established practices that Muslims are required to follow, embodied in *ḥādīth*, or verified reports of the utterances, actions, and tacit approvals of the Prophet Mohammed.
13. The financial sector and its lobbyists are often accused of resisting any substantial regulation that attempts to restrict the sector's risky behavior. If one believes the accusation of Nobel laureate Joseph Stiglitz that the financial sector in the United States prefers to return to the golden (unregulated) days before

the crisis (Stiglitz 2014), the world is in for another financial and humanitarian catastrophe (Graafland and van de Ven 2011).

14. Arrow (1971, 121–33, 143, 239–66) demonstrated that in a competitive market economy, in which markets are complete and Arrow securities whose payoffs are State-contingent are available, it would be Pareto optimal for the economy if its members were to share risk according to each participant's ability to bear risk (Askari and Mirakhor 2014).
15. For example, a World Bank study estimates the resource shortfall to close the poverty gap in countries using *zakāt* collection and finds that 20 out of 39 OIC countries could lift the poorest, living on less than $1.25 per day, above the poverty line simply with adequate *zakāt* collection (Mohieldin and others 2011). See also chapter 8.

References

Acemoglu, Daron. 2002. "Technical Change, Inequality, and the Labor Market." *Journal of Economic Literature* 40 (1): 7–72.

AFD (Agence Française de Développement), Bundesministerium für Wirtschaftliche Zusammenarbeit und Entwicklung, U.K. Department for International Development (DFID), and the World Bank. 2005. *Pro-Poor Growth in the 1990s: Lessons and Insights from 14 Countries.* Washington, DC: World Bank, on behalf of the Operationalizing Pro-Poor Growth Research Program.

Ahmed, Habib. 2015. "The Role of Islamic Finance in Achieving Sustainable Development Goals and Shared Prosperity." Paper presented at the inaugural World Bank-Islamic Development Bank-Guidance Financial Symposium on Islamic Finance and Shared Prosperity, Istanbul, September 8–9.

Al-Hasani, Baqir, and Abbas Mirakhor. 2003. *Iqtisad: The Islamic Approach to Economic Problems.* New York: Global Scholarly Publications.

Arrow, K. J. 1971. *Essays in the Theory of Risk-Bearing.* Chicago, IL: Markham Publishing Company.

Askari, Hossein, Zamir Iqbal, and Noureddine Krichene. 2010. "The Inherent Stability of Islamic Finance." In *The Stability of Islamic Finance: Creating a Resilient Financial Environment for a Secure Future*, edited by Hossein Askari, Zamir Iqbal, Noureddine Krichene, and Abbas Mirakhor, 75–81. Singapore: John Wiley & Sons (Asia).

Askari, Hossein, Zamir Iqbal, Noureddine Krichene, and Abbas Mirakhor, eds. 2010. *The Stability of Islamic Finance: Creating a Resilient Financial Environment for a Secure Future.* Singapore: John Wiley & Sons (Asia).

Askari, Hossein, and Abbas Mirakhor. 2014. "Risk Sharing, Public Policy and the Contribution of Islamic Finance." *PSL Quarterly Review* 67 (271): 345–79.

Askari, Hossein, Zamir Iqbal, and Abbas Mirakhor. 2015. *Introduction to Islamic Economics: Theory and Application.* Singapore: John Wiley & Sons (Asia).

Bowles, Samuel. 2012. *The New Economics of Inequality and Redistribution.* Cambridge, U.K.: Cambridge University Press.

Chapra, Muhammad Umer. 2007. *Islam and Economic Development: A Strategy for Development with Justice and Stability.* New Delhi: Adam Publishers.

Cingano, F. 2014. "Trends in Income Inequality and Its Impact on Economic Growth." OECD Social, Employment and Migration Working Paper 163, Organisation for Economic Cooperation and Development, Paris.

Credit Suisse. 2013. *Global Wealth Report 2013.* Zurich: Credit Suisse.

Deutsche Bank Research. 2014. *Mapping the World's Financial Markets.* https://etf.deutscheawm.com/ITA/ITA/Download/Research-Global/47e36b78-d254-4b16-a82f-d5c5f1b1e09a/Mapping-the-World-s-Financial-Markets.pdf.

Dobbs, Richard, Susan Lund, Jonathan Woetzel, and Mina Mutafchieva. 2015. *Debt and (Not Much) Deleveraging.* London; Washington, DC; Shanghai, China; Brussels: McKinsey Global Institute.

EC (European Commission). 2012. *Literature Review on Income Inequality and the Effects on Social Outcomes.* Brussels: European Commission Publications Office.

Economist. 2015. "A Senseless Subsidy; Ending the Debt Addiction." May 16.

Egawa, Akio. 2013. "Will Income Inequality Cause a Middle-income Trap in Asia?" Bruegel Working Paper 2013/06, Brussels European and Global Economic Laboratory, Brussels.

Graafland, Johan J., and Bert W. van de Ven. 2011. "The Credit Crisis and the Moral Responsibility of Professionals in Finance." *Journal of Business Ethics* 103 (4): 605–19.

Iqbal, Zamir, and Abbas Mirakhor. 2004. "Stakeholders Model of Governance in the Islamic Economic System." *Journal of Islamic Economic Studies* 11: 44–63.

———. 2011. *An Introduction to Islamic Finance: Theory and Practice*. New Delhi: John Wiley & Sons.

Iqbal, Zamir, and Abbas Mirakhor, eds. 2013. *Economic Development and Islamic Finance*. Washington, DC: World Bank.

Jensen, Michael C., and William H. Meckling. 1976. "Theory of the Firm: Managerial Behavior, Agency Costs and Ownership Structure." *Journal of Financial Economics* 3: 305–60.

Kaldor, N. 1955. "Alternative Theories of Distribution." *Review of Economic Studies* 23: 83–100.

Krugman, Paul, and Anthony J. Venables. 1995. "Globalization and the Inequality of Nations." Working Paper 5098, National Bureau of Economic Research, Cambridge, MA.

Kumhof, M., and R. Rancière. 2010. "Inequality, Leverage, and Crises." IMF Working Paper WP/10/268, International Monetary Fund, Washington, DC.

Kuznets, Stanley. 1955. "Economic Growth and Income Inequality." *American Economic Review* 45 (1): 1–28.

Lazear, Edward P., and Sherwin Rosen. 1981. "Rank-Order Tournaments as Optimum Labor Contracts." *Journal of Political Economy* 89 (October): 841–86.

Levine, Ross. 1997. "Financial Development and Economic Growth: Views and Agenda." *Journal of Economic Literature* 35 (June): 688–726.

Majah, Ibn. 1952. "*Sunan Ibn Majah*." Beirut: Darul Kutub Al Ilmiyyah.

Mirakhor, Abbas. 2009. "Islamic Economics and Finance: An Institutional Perspective." MPRA Paper 56017, Munich Personal RePEc Archive, University Library of Munich, Germany.

Mirakhor, Abbas, and Hossein Askari. 2010. *Islam and the Path to Human Economic Development*. New York: Palgrave Macmillan.

Mirakhor, Abbas, and Zamir Iqbal. 2012. "Financial Inclusion: Islamic Finance Perspective." MPRA Paper 55977, Munich Personal RePEc Archive, University Library of Munich, Germany.

Mohieldin, Mahmoud, Zamir Iqbal, Ahmed Rostom, and Xiachen Fu. 2011. "The Role of Islamic Finance in Enhancing Financial Inclusion in Organisation of Islamic Cooperation (OIC) Countries." *Islamic Economic Studies* 20 (2): 55–120.

Narayan, Ambar, Sailesh Tiwari, Pedro Olinto, Maximillian Ashwill, Francisco Ferreira, Jaime Saavedra, Luis-Felipe Lopez-Calva, John Newman, Gabriel Demombynes, Anna Reva, and Mary Anne Mulligan. 2013. "Analyzing the World Bank's Goal of Achieving 'Shared Prosperity.'" *Inequality in Focus* 2 (3), World Bank, Washington, DC. http://www.worldbank.org/content/dam/Worldbank/document/Poverty%20documents/inequality-in-focus-october2013-v12.pdf.

North, Douglass. 2005. *Understanding the Process of Economic Change*. Princeton, NJ: Princeton University Press.

OECD (Organisation for Economic Co-operation and Development). 2015. "How to Restore a Healthy Financial Sector That Supports Long-Lasting, Inclusive Growth?" Economics Department Policy Note 27, OECD, Paris.

Okun, Arthur M. 1975. *Equality and Efficiency: The Big Tradeoff*. Washington, DC: Brookings Institution Press.

Ostry, Jonathan David, Andrew Berg, and Charalambos G. Tsangarides. 2014. "Redistribution, Inequality, and Growth." IMF Working Paper 14/02, International Monetary Fund, Washington, DC.

Piketty, Thomas. 2013. (English translation, 2014). *Capital in the Twenty-First Century*. Cambridge, MA: Harvard University Press.

Rajan, R. 2012. *Fault Lines: How Hidden Fractures Still Threaten the World Economy*. Noida, India: HarperCollins Publishers.

Rodrik, Dani. 2008. *One Economics, Many Recipes: Globalization, Institutions, and Economic Growth*. Princeton, NJ: Princeton University Press.

Roxburgh, Charles, Susan Lund, and John Piotrowski. 2011. "Mapping Global Capital Markets 2011." Research update, McKinsey Global Institute, Washington, DC.

Stiglitz, Joseph. 2012. *The Price of Inequality: How Today's Divided Society Endangers Our Future*. New York: W. W. Norton & Company.

———. 2014. "Reforming Taxation to Promote Growth and Equity." Roosevelt Institute White Paper, Roosevelt Institute, New York.

Townsend, R. 1979. "Optimal Contracts and Competitive Markets with Costly State Verification." *Journal of Economic Theory* 22: 265–93.

UN (United Nations). 2014. *The Millennium Development Goals Report 2014*. http://www.un.org/millenniumgoals/2014%20MDG%20Report/MDG%202014%20English%20web.pdf.

UNCTAD (United Nations Conference on Trade and Development). 2014. *The Trade and Development Report 2014: Global Governance and Policy Space for Development*. New York: United Nations.

Working for the Few. 2014. "Political Capture and Economic Inequality." Briefing Paper 178, Oxfam GB for Oxfam International, Oxford, U.K. https://www.oxfam.org/sites/www.oxfam.org/files/file_attachments/bp-working-for-few-political-capture-economic-inequality-200114-en_3.pdf.

2

The State of Development and Shared Prosperity in OIC Countries

This chapter provides a brief overview of economic development in the 57 countries belonging to the Organisation of Islamic Cooperation (OIC) in relation to the goals of the World Bank Group, Islamic Development Bank, and other multilateral development institutions.[1] The aim is to provide an overview of the state of development and shared prosperity in those countries and to identify the gaps in meeting the goals set by the global development community. Such an analysis is vital for formulating effective policy responses in OIC countries, some of which are facing serious development and income distribution issues.

The Millennium Development Goals

At the turn of the new millennium, all member-states of the United Nations and more than 20 international organizations identified eight development goals, known as the Millennium Development Goals (MDGs), and pledged to achieve them by 2015. The eight goals aimed to achieve the following:

1. Eradicate extreme poverty and hunger
2. Achieve universal primary education
3. Promote gender equality
4. Reduce child mortality
5. Improve maternal health

6. Combat HIV/AIDS, malaria, and other diseases
7. Ensure environmental sustainability
8. Develop a global partnership for development.

Good progress has been made, and some of the development goals have been met ahead of the target deadline. Figure 2.1 presents progress in the first five MDGs as of 2014. The red dotted line represents the MDG target for every metric. For the sake of brevity, the comparison is reported at the level of the world compared with the OIC countries as a group.[2] Except for goal 1, of reducing the extreme poverty by 50 percent, no other MDGs were attained by either the world or the OIC countries. In terms of comparative performance, the OIC countries as a group, on average, did not deviate significantly from the world as a group.

The world has witnessed a reduction by half in the share of people living under extreme poverty; however, this success has not been distributed evenly across different income groups or regions. Figure 2.2 shows the state of poverty according to two different benchmarks: the poverty headcount ratios at $1.25 a day and at $2 a day, grouped by different income levels.[3] Overall, the headcount ratio of people living in extreme poverty (on less than $1.25 a day) has declined considerably among OIC countries and worldwide. However, there is a great variation between the distributions of the ratio of people living on less than $1.25 a day. The trend lines clearly indicate that the reduction of the poverty among the OIC member-countries was much faster than their non-OIC counterparts in almost all income groups, as highlighted with solid lines in figure 2.2.

Figure 2.3 presents the regional distribution of poverty ratios by both measures. As expected, the region that is worst off in terms of people living in extreme poverty is Sub-Saharan Africa. In contrast, East Asian nations succeeded in reducing the extreme poverty ratios significantly between 1990 and 2014, thanks to their high growth rates.

The State of Shared Prosperity

Despite progress made toward reducing extreme poverty ahead of the target deadline, the gap between the rich and poor has widened, especially after the global financial crisis. The proceeds of the economic growth seemed to be concentrated in the very top layer of economies, creating social unrest.

FIGURE 2.1 Progress in Meeting Millennium Development Goals 1–5

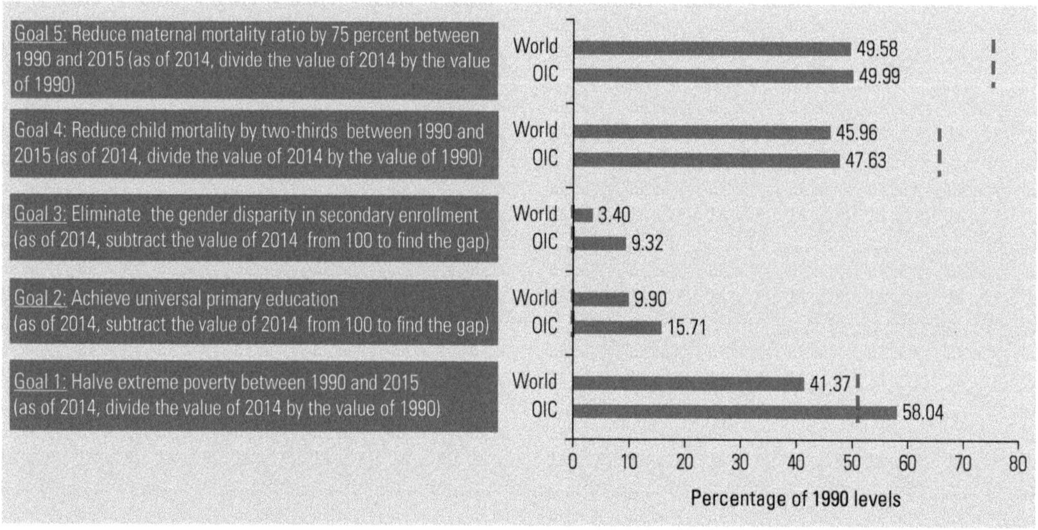

Source: http://mdgs.un.org/unsd/mdg/Data.aspx.
Note: The red dotted line indicates the MDG targets for each subcategory. OIC = Organisation of Islamic Cooperation.

FIGURE 2.2 Poverty Headcount Ratios, Income-Level Classification

Percentage of population

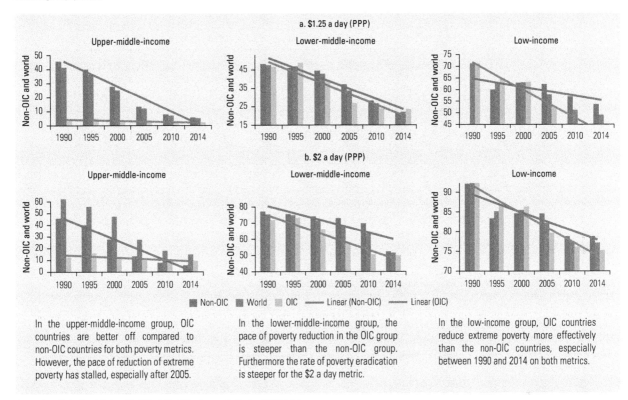

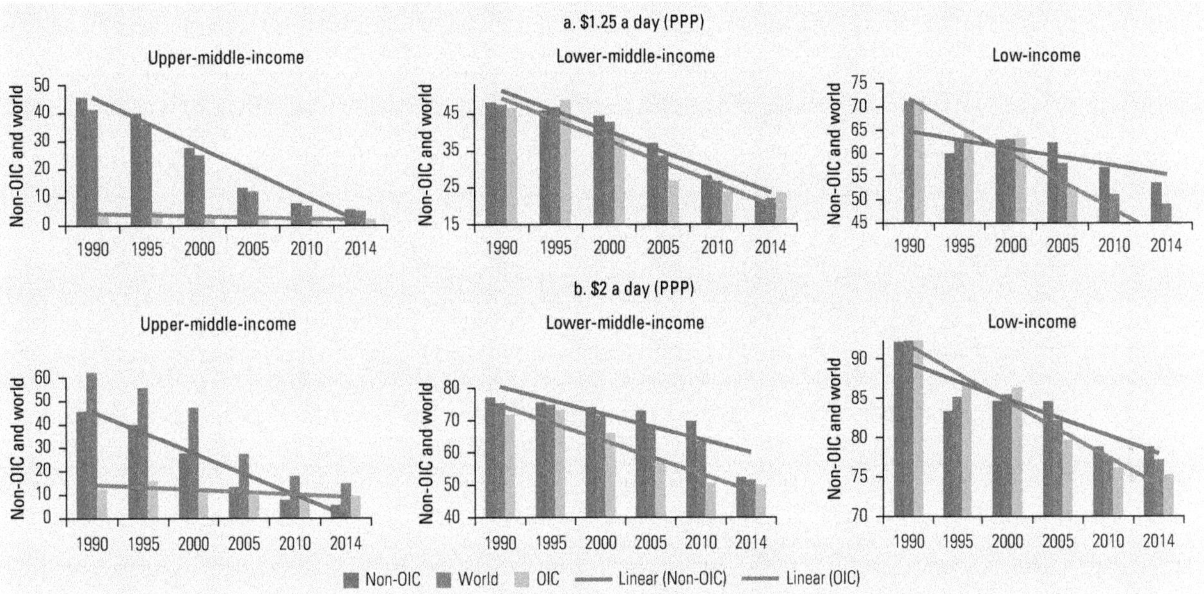

In the upper-middle-income group, OIC countries are better off compared to non-OIC countries for both poverty metrics. However, the pace of reduction of extreme poverty has stalled, especially after 2005.

In the lower-middle-income group, the pace of poverty reduction in the OIC group is steeper than the non-OIC group. Furthermore the rate of poverty eradication is steeper for the $2 a day metric.

In the low-income group, OIC countries reduce extreme poverty more effectively than the non-OIC countries, especially between 1990 and 2014 on both metrics.

Source: Compiled using data from World Bank World Development Indicators (WDI) database.
Note: OIC = Organisation of Islamic Cooperation; PPP = purchasing power parity.

Figure 2.4 makes it clear that the share of the income going to the top 10 percent is significantly higher than the income of the rest of the deciles throughout the world. This is the case for both OIC countries and non-OIC countries.

Figure 2.5 presents survey data on consumption or income (depending on the type of survey) of the bottom 40 percent and the total population. Unfortunately, the lack of continuous survey data hampers analysis. However, based on the available data, the figure depicts the state of OIC and non-OIC countries with respect to regional and income classifications.

Panel a of figure 2.5 compares the non-OIC and OIC member-countries. The OIC countries in the lower-middle-income group increased the income for the bottom 40 percent of their populations by 10 percent, while the income of the total population increased by only 6 percent. For the lower-income group, the gap is narrowing in OIC countries; however, in non-OIC, the per capita income for the bottom 40 percent increased at almost the same rate as the total population from 2007 to 2014. The growth rate in per capita income for the non-OIC group is much higher than that of the OIC group. While in the upper-middle-income group, the growth rate of per capita income for the total population and the bottom 40 percent within the group for OIC countries and non-OIC countries is not very different, the growth rate for non-OIC countries is higher than that of the OIC group. The slower growth rates for the OIC group clearly indicate the need for a policy response to boost the distribution of economic growth overall, as well as for the bottom 40 percent.

Figure 2.6 analyzes whether the gap between per capita consumption (income)

FIGURE 2.3 **Poverty Headcount Ratios, Regional Classification**

Percentage of population

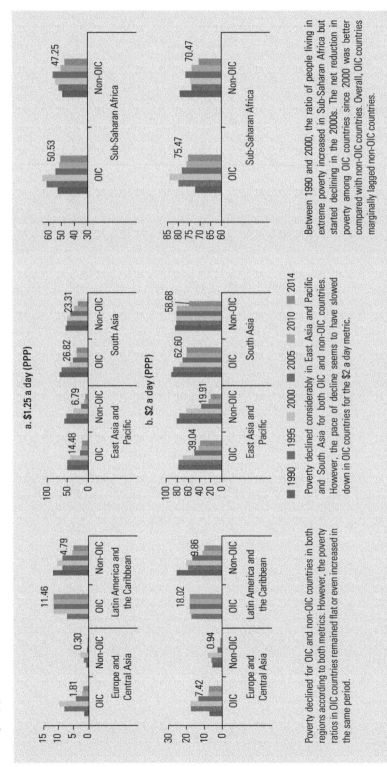

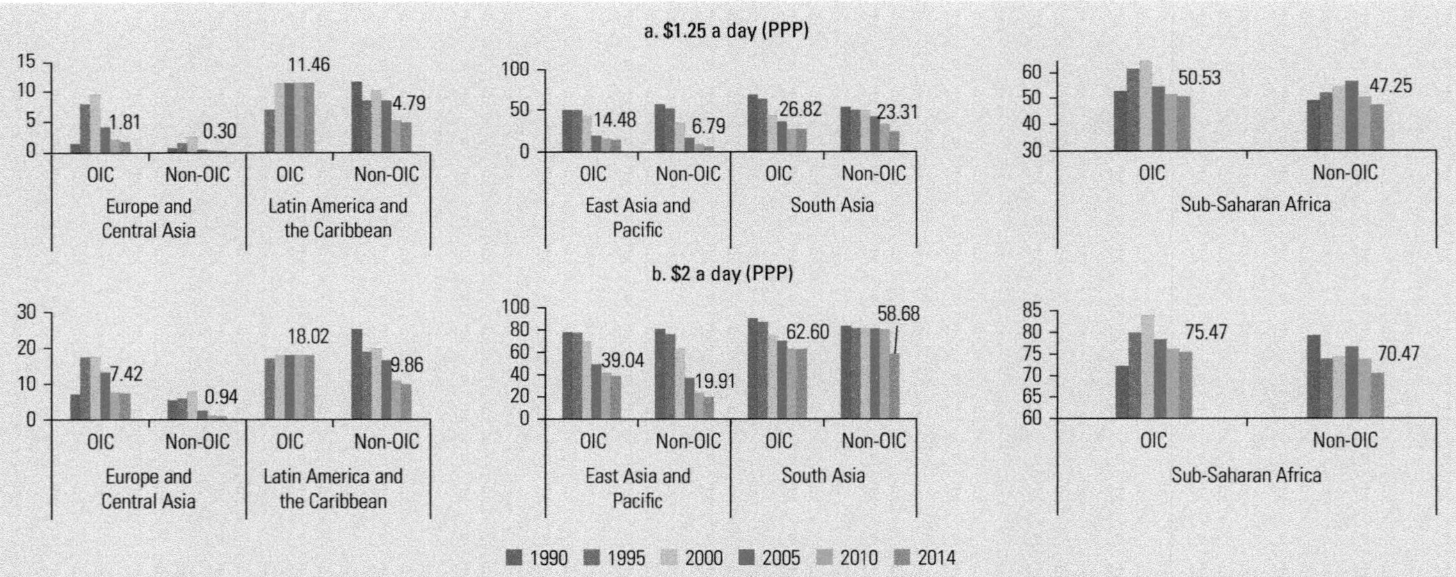

Poverty declined for OIC and non-OIC countries in both regions according to both metrics. However, the poverty ratios in OIC countries remained flat or even increased in the same period.

Poverty declined considerably in East Asia and Pacific and South Asia for both OIC and non-OIC countries. However, the pace of decline seems to have slowed down in OIC countries for the $2 a day metric.

Between 1990 and 2000, the ratio of people living in extreme poverty increased in Sub-Saharan Africa but started declining in the 2000s. The net reduction in poverty among OIC countries since 2000 was better compared with non-OIC countries. Overall, OIC countries marginally lagged non-OIC countries.

Source: Compiled using data from World Bank World Development Indicators (WDI) database.
Note: OIC = Organisation of Islamic Cooperation; PPP = purchasing power parity.

FIGURE 2.4 **Income Distribution by Decile**

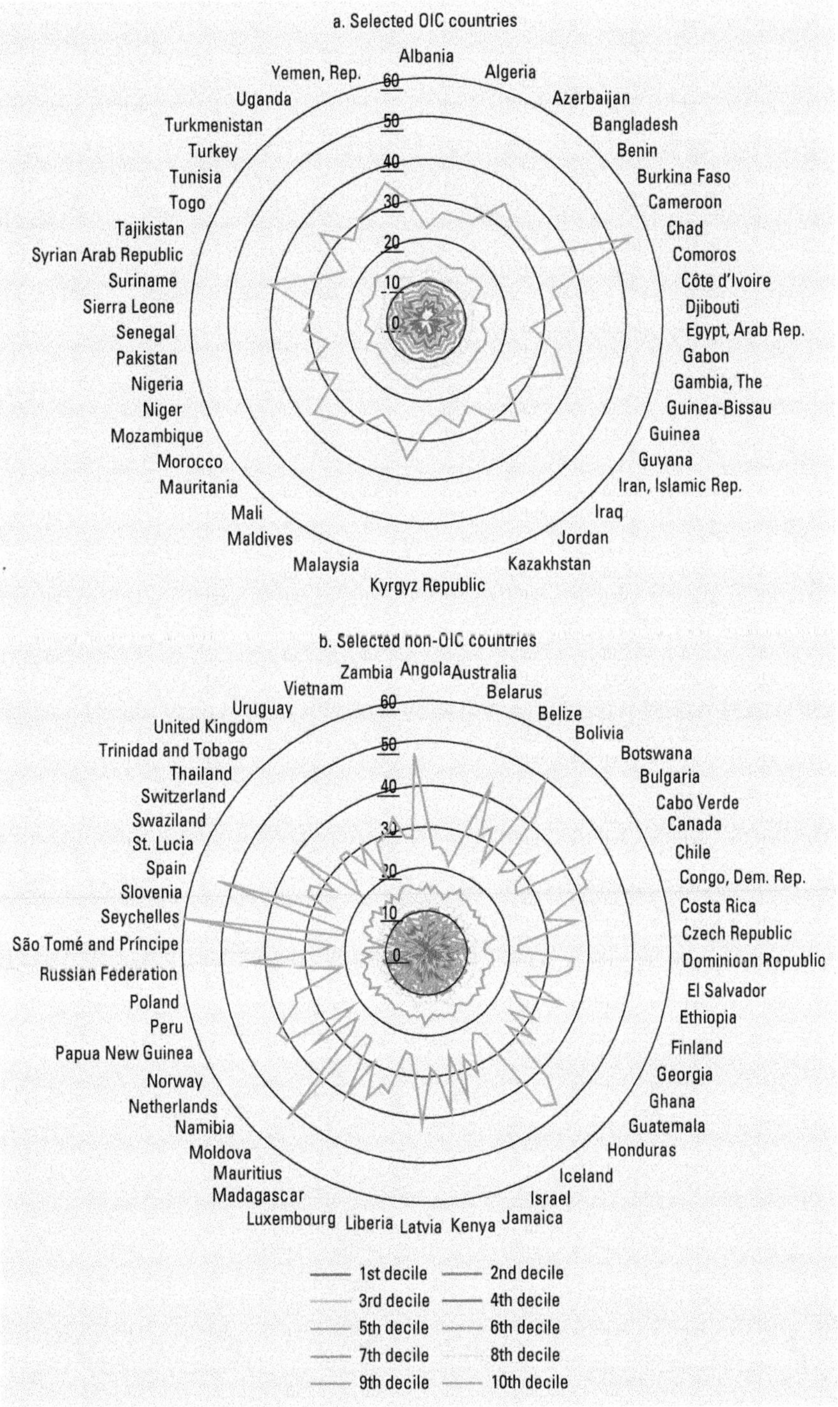

Source: Compiled using data from World Bank World Development Indicators (WDI) database.

FIGURE 2.5 Per Capita Income (Consumption) of the Bottom 40 Percent and the Total Population

2005 PPP $ per day

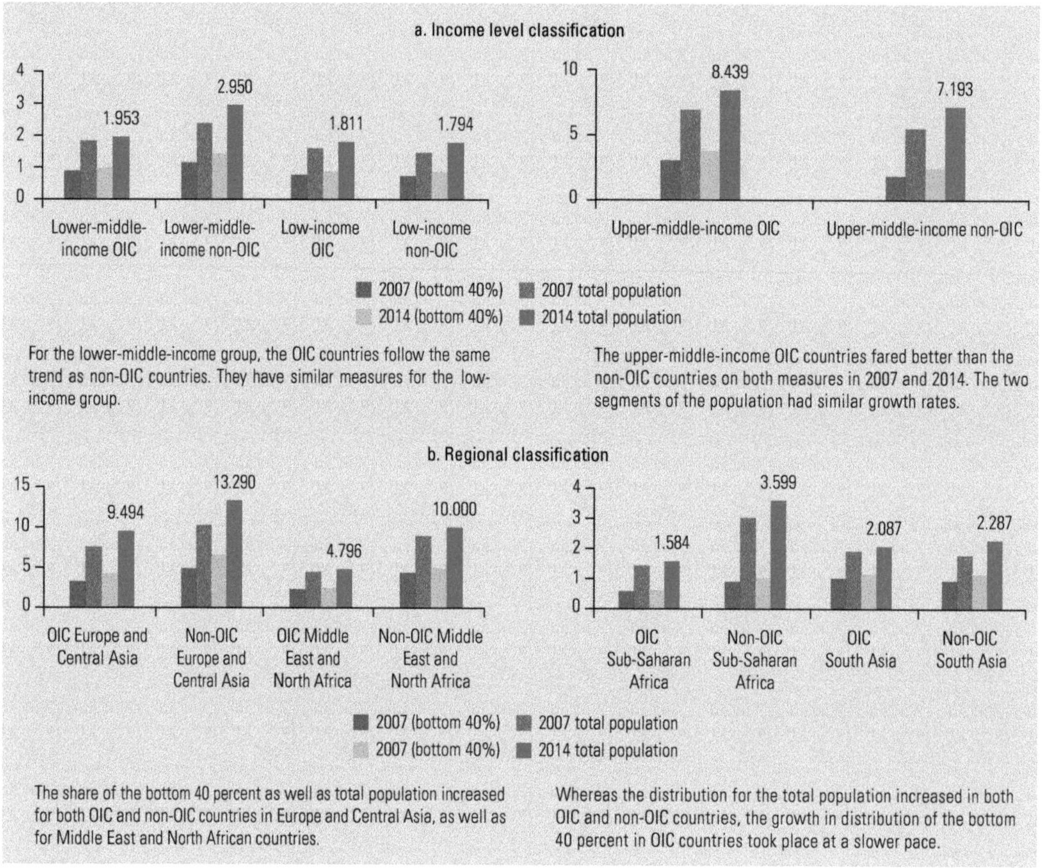

Source: Calculations using data from World Bank World Development Indicators (WDI) database.
Note: OIC = Organisation of Islamic Cooperation; PPP = purchasing power parity.

FIGURE 2.6 Change in the Gap between Per Capita Consumption (Income) of the Bottom 40 Percent and the Overall Population between 2007 and 2014

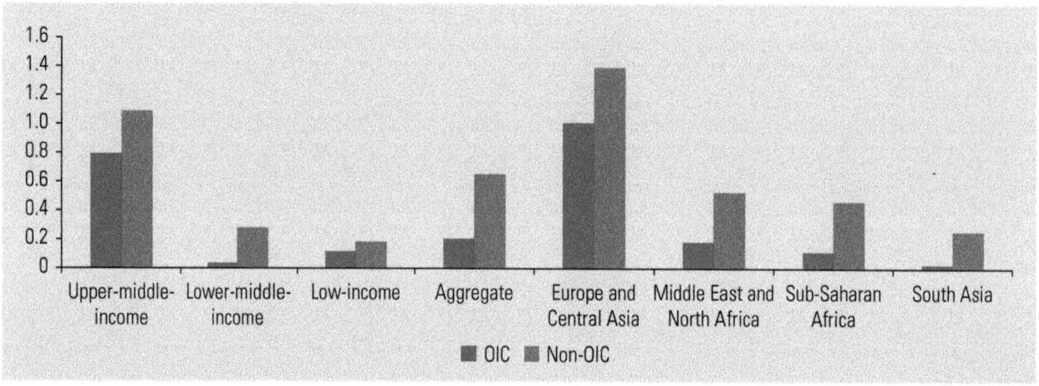

Source: Calculations using data from World Bank World Development Indicators (WDI) database.
Note: OIC = Organisation of Islamic Cooperation.

of the bottom 40 percent and overall population increased or decreased between 2007 and 2014. To be more specific, the gap between the bottom 40 percent and the overall population (Δ) was calculated as the difference between the gaps in 2007 and 2014 to observe whether that gap between the bottom 40 percent and overall population in terms of income per capita has been increasing or decreasing. A positive value for Δ implies that the relative position of the bottom 40 percent has worsened. Overall, the gap was positive in all countries, but more so in non-OIC countries. This indicates that the bottom 40 percent were worse off in all regions, but the disparity in OIC countries was lower compared to other countries in the region. In other words, the relative gap between the bottom 40 percent and overall population diverged less in OIC countries than that in non-OIC countries. It is difficult to attribute this trend to any specific factor; it could be a result of various factors that require further research.

The State of the Pillars of the Economic Development Framework of Islamic Finance

Chapter 1 presented a theoretical framework of how inclusive growth and shared prosperity could be achieved through principles of Islamic economics and finance. The Islamic perspective on economic development was presented as based on four pillars:

1. An institutional framework and public policy in line with the objectives of Islam
2. Prudent governance and accountable leadership
3. Promotion of the economy and entrepreneurship based on risk sharing
4. Financial and social inclusion for all.

This section takes this general framework as the starting point and examines the state of each pillar to enhance our understanding to suggest an adequate policy response. Since each component is a composite of various variables, some of which are not directly observable, proxies are used to analyze the state of each component. Given the complexities of the framework and the broad nature of the components, developing a comprehensive analytical tool would require extensive effort and resources. This section includes a very broad analysis to get a sense of the state of affairs without delving too deeply into subcomponents. Several studies have been undertaken to determine the observation and implementation of Islamic principles in Islamic countries.[4]

Table 2.1 presents these proxies, which are used to quantify the relative status of OIC countries with respect to other countries according to several classifications.

TABLE 2.1 Factors to Measure Core Development Components

Dimension	Proxy
Institutional framework and public policy	Rule of Law Index
Governance and leadership	Government Effectiveness Index
Risk sharing and entrepreneurship	Correlation between real GDP and consumption
	Relative value of market capitalization of listed companies
Financial and social inclusion	Alternative sources of funding (percentage of population, age 15^+)
	CPIA (Country Policy and Institutional Assessment) policies for social inclusion/equity cluster average
Financial sector depth and interaction with shared prosperity and poverty reduction	Domestic-credit-to-private-sector ratio (percentage of GDP)
	Gross-portfolio-debt-assets-to-GDP ratio (percent)
	Gross-portfolio-equity-assets-to-GDP ratio (percent)

Additional measures are included to understand the dynamics of the financial sector with respect to poverty and shared prosperity.

Institutional Framework and Public Policy

A well-established institutional framework is one of the major requirements for Islamic finance to flourish and to achieve fairness in a society. In a panel of around 100 countries from 1960 to 1990, Barro (1996) finds that among other factors, better maintenance of the rule of law enables countries to grow faster. He argues that a country where rule of law principles are strongly adhered to would grow faster because the environment for investment would be sound.

The core foundation of a sound institutional framework is the strength of the legal structure. To assess the quality of the institutional framework in OIC countries, the World Bank's Rule of Law Index is used as a proxy. The Rule of Law Index, shown in figure 2.7, captures the essential elements that should be present in a well-functioning judicial system. The values of this index range between -2.5 (weak) and 2.5 (strong). On aggregate, the value of the index was below zero in both the world and the OIC group, with the low-income group at the bottom. Since, as mentioned, economic growth is the main force that reduces poverty, strengthening the legal system should be a priority in supporting development in OIC countries. In particular, the largest discrepancy between OIC and non-OIC countries is in the lower-middle-income group, which constitutes roughly 54 percent of the overall OIC population. Hence, policy makers from these countries should especially focus on strengthening the legal system.

Governance and Leadership

Sound public policy is essential to providing services in an efficient manner and addressing the needs of the public. Strong leadership is needed to implement the necessary reforms. Conversely, the lack of a well-functioning and effective government could result in an environment that is chaotic and unfriendly toward market practices and economic growth. For example, Middle East and North African countries with better measures of political stability, government effectiveness, and corruption control metrics grow by as much as 2.5 percentage points a year faster in terms of GDP than those that score lower in

FIGURE 2.7 Rule of Law Index, Income-Level Classification

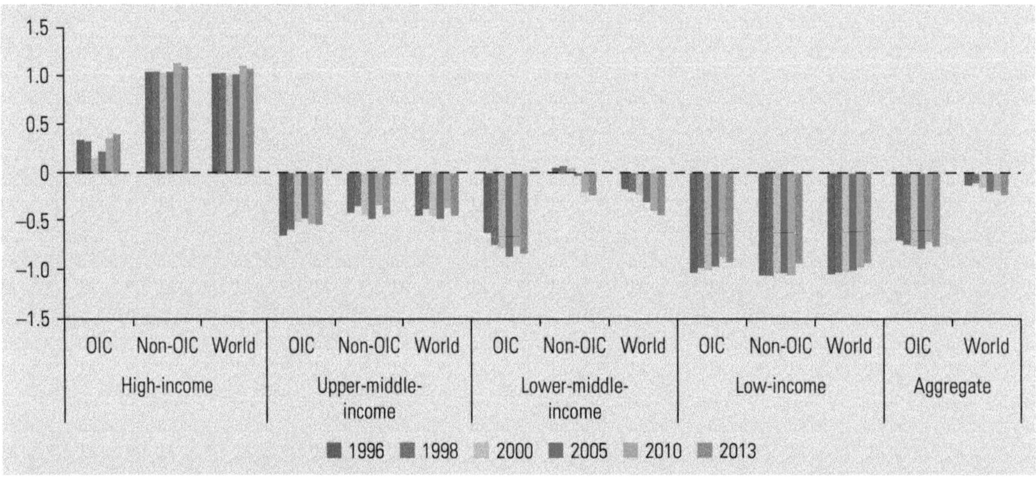

Source: http://info.worldbank.org/governance/wgi/index.aspx#home.
Note: The Rule of Law Index captures perceptions of the extent to which agents have confidence in and abide by the rules of society, particularly the quality of contract enforcement, property rights, the police, and the courts, as well as the likelihood of crime and violence. The estimate gives the country's score on the aggregate indicator, in units of a standard normal distribution, ranging from approximately –2.5 to 2.5. OIC = Organisation of Islamic Cooperation.

these indicators, according to Han, Khan, and Zhuang (2014).

Good governance also ensures that the rights of shareholders and all stakeholders will be protected. This will promote investment because investors will feel secure in making investments. Good governance will also strengthen the soundness and effectiveness of institutions. Rodrik, Subramanian, and Trebbi (2004) analyze the relative contributions of institutions, geography, and trade in determining income levels around the world and conclude that the quality of institutions "trumps" everything else.[5]

To capture the state of the quality of governance, the World Bank's Government Effectiveness Indicators (GEI) are used as a proxy. Figure 2.8 shows that on average, the countries from the lower- and lower-middle-income group have low GEI scores, trailing non-OIC countries from the same group in terms of the effectiveness of government.

Risk Sharing and Entrepreneurship

A core concept of Islamic finance, which clearly distinguishes it from conventional financing, is risk sharing. Quantifying the extent of risk sharing in an economy is very difficult because risk sharing is an abstract term that encompasses many channels, including the welfare state, financial globalization, and revenues from the export of natural resources. Despite these difficulties, a proxy for risk sharing—the inverse of the correlation between domestic aggregate consumption and GDP—can be used. If there is perfect risk sharing in a given economy, then the evolution of consumption should not be determined solely by movements of income; other factors would smooth the negative and positive effects on the consumption (Kalemli-Ozcan, Sørensen, and Yosha 2003).

As figure 2.9 shows, the correlation between consumption and income is very high, but on an aggregate level, OIC countries seem to be faring better in terms of risk sharing than the world as a whole (that is, the correlation of OIC countries is lower). However, it is important to keep this result in regional context. The slightly lower correlation between income and consumption in OIC countries might not necessarily indicate better risk sharing, but might reflect the high

FIGURE 2.8 **Government Effectiveness Index, Income-Level Classification**

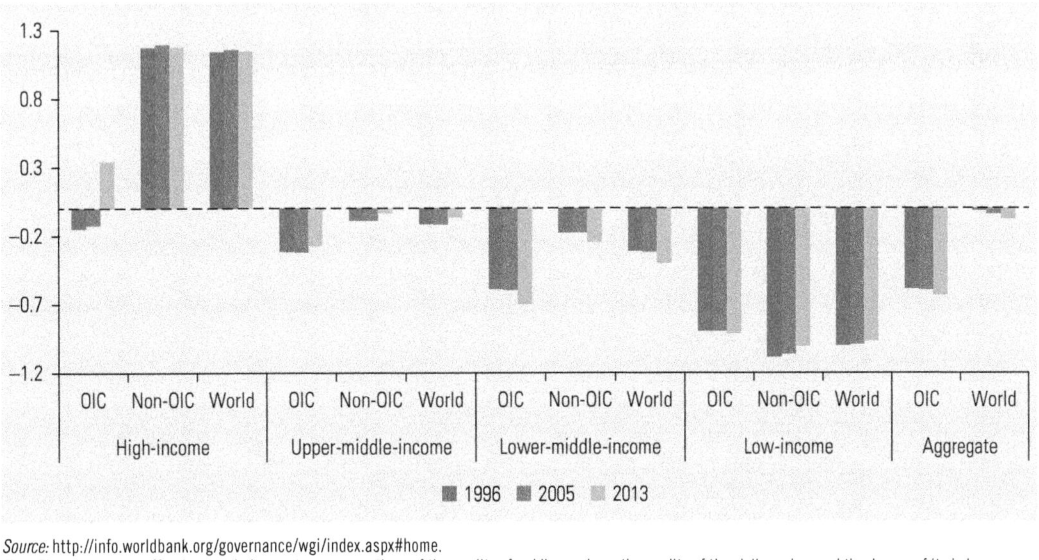

Source: http://info.worldbank.org/governance/wgi/index.aspx#home.

Note: The government effectiveness index captures perceptions of the quality of public services, the quality of the civil service, and the degree of its independence from political pressures; the quality of policy formulation and implementation; and the credibility of the government's commitment to such policies. Estimate gives the country's score on the aggregate indicator, in units of a standard normal distribution, ranging from approximately −2.5 to 2.5.

OIC = Organisation of Islamic Cooperation.

FIGURE 2.9 **Correlation between Consumption and Real GDP, Income-Level Classification**

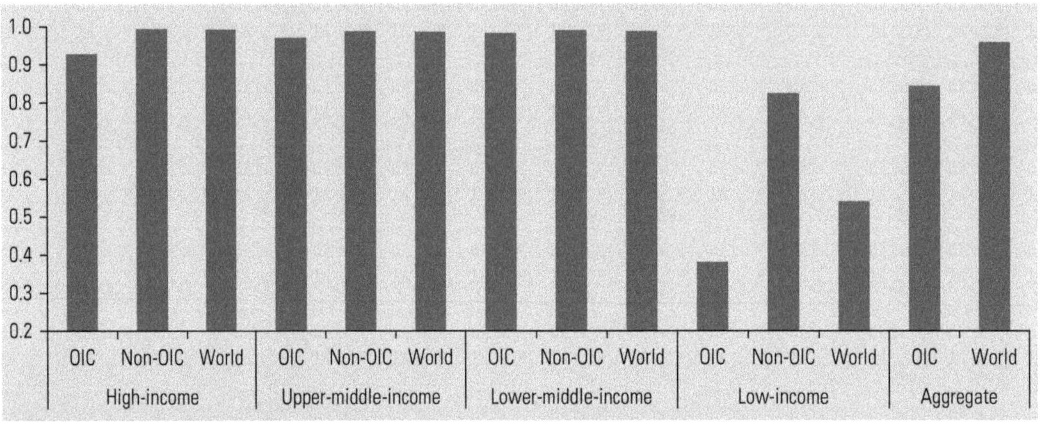

Source: http://www.rug.nl/research/ggdc/data/pwt/pwt-8.1.

Note: Consumption includes both private and government consumption. The Penn World Table (PWT), upon which this figure is based, is a set of national accounts data developed and maintained by scholars at the University of California, Davis, and the Groningen Growth Development Centre of the University of Groningen, the Netherlands, to measure real GDP across countries and over time. Successive updates have added countries (currently 167), years (1950–2011), and data on capital, productivity, employment, and population. OIC = Organisation of Islamic Cooperation.

level of oil revenues that have accumulated in sovereign wealth funds, which could offset the negative effect of recessions on consumption, hence weakening the correlation between income and consumption.

In all income levels, OIC countries perform better than non-OIC countries. A value of 1 indicates that OIC and non-OIC countries are on a par. In all income groups and regions, the relative ratio is less than 1. The relative spikes in 1995 could partially be explained by the booms and busts in commodity markets, which might be important for OIC countries.

Stock market development is positively and robustly associated with long-term economic growth, Levine and Zervos (1996) find, using cross-country growth regressions. Figure 2.10 presents the relative value of market capitalization to GDP between OIC and non-OIC countries. Since Islamic finance is based on risk sharing and has an asset-backed nature, one would expect to see a higher ratio of this metric among OIC countries compared to the others. However, due to the less developed capital markets for equities and asset-based securities, the OIC countries' relative performance is not impressive. Without developed capital markets, the full potential of a risk-sharing financial system such as Islamic finance cannot be envisioned. Hence in order for OIC countries to grow faster in a development model based on risk sharing, stock markets must play an essential role; to materialize, OIC countries need to reform legal and governance structures and strengthen their institutions.

Financial and Social Inclusion

While Islamic principles stress the importance of hard work and free market enterprise where everyone is expected to contribute according to his or her ability, they also emphasize that individuals who are left behind should be protected and provided with the basic needs that would enable them to live their life in a humane way.

To analyze the extent of financial inclusion in the world and in OIC countries, two metrics were used. Figure 2.11 depicts the various sources people use in obtaining funds. A value of 1 indicates that OIC and non-OIC countries are on a par. A value greater than 1 indicates that OIC countries use a particular type of funding more extensively than non-OIC countries. In almost all income groups and regions, the relative ratio is less than 1. The use of formal financial institutions is limited in OIC countries

FIGURE 2.10 Relative Value of Market Capitalization of Listed Companies, Ratio of OIC to Non-OIC Countries

Percentage of GDP

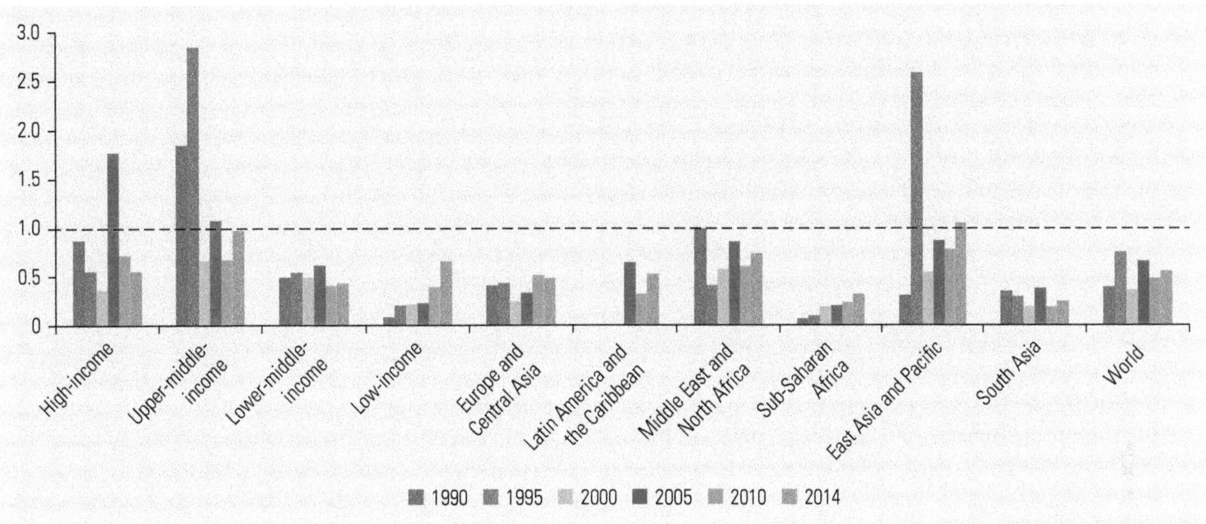

Source: Calculated using data from http://data.worldbank.org/indicator/CM.MKT.LCAP.GD.ZS.
Note: A value of 1 indicates that OIC and non-OIC countries are on a par. Market capitalization (also known as market value) is the share price times the number of shares outstanding. Listed domestic companies are the domestically incorporated companies listed on the country's stock exchanges at the end of the year. Listed companies do not include investment companies, mutual funds, or other collective investment vehicles. OIC = Organisation of Islamic Cooperation.

FIGURE 2.11 Sources People Use to Obtain Funds, Ratio of OIC to Non-OIC Countries, Regional and Income-Level Classification

Percentage of population age 15+

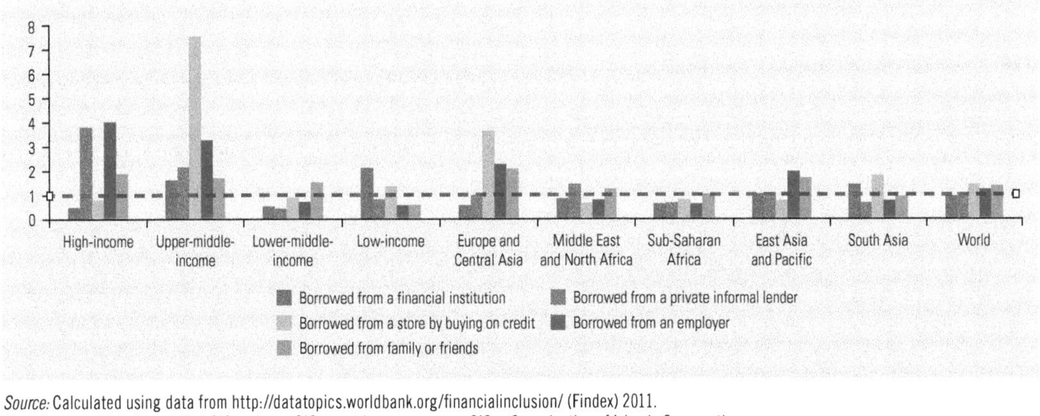

Source: Calculated using data from http://datatopics.worldbank.org/financialinclusion/ (Findex) 2011.
Note: A value of 1 indicates that OIC and non-OIC countries are on a par. OIC = Organisation of Islamic Cooperation.

compared to non-OIC countries. Other sources—such as private informal lenders, buying on credit, or borrowing from family or friends—are more common.

Several factors could affect the level of access of citizens in a country to financial services. For example, countries where the population is condensed rather than dispersed, where citizens have higher income per capita, and/or where the banking system is more competitive may find it easier to provide financial services to their citizens. In addition, some individuals may stay away from financial services due to religious principles.

Demirgüç-Kunt, Klapper, and Randall (2014) find that Muslims are less likely to have an account at official financial institutions. This could be one factor that explains the patterns for OIC countries depicted in figure 2.11.

Figure 2.12 is intended to capture the degree of social inclusion in the world and in OIC countries. In terms of social inclusion, OIC countries lag behind the world on an aggregate basis.

The figure depicts the World Bank's social inclusion metric as a ratio of OIC to non-OIC countries. OIC countries in the upper-middle-income and Europe and Central Asia regions have greater social inclusion than their counterparts in the same classification.

Variations in the social inclusion metric across countries could have various sociological, economic, political, and other dimensions. Minorities and different ethnic and religious groups could be marginalized, depending on the historical and cultural situation of a country. Income level could be another factor that could make it difficult for certain individuals to participate in the society productively, utilize education and health care, and earn a living. Hence, when trying to pinpoint the root causes of the social exclusion in their countries, policy makers in OIC countries should take a broad perspective and design policies to effectively deal with these causes.

Financial Sector Depth and Interaction with Shared Prosperity and Poverty Reduction

The positive relationship between financial sector development and economic development has been well established; various studies have shown the contribution of a developed financial sector to overall economic growth.[6] In this respect, it is important to understand the degree of financial sector development in any country. It is particularly important for a risk-sharing financial system such as Islamic finance, which requires a well-developed financial sector with reduced information asymmetry.

The next three figures examine the financial depth of countries with respect to certain metrics. Figure 2.13 examines domestic credit to the private sector as a ratio of GDP and compares the OIC and non-OIC countries belonging to the same income-level groups. The OIC group in all income-level groups lags the non-OIC group, implying that the financial sector in select OIC countries is in the early stages of development and, with further development, could contribute to economic growth. In addition, businesses do not usually borrow from financial institutions; this could be due to lack of access to financial services or to voluntary religious constraints

FIGURE 2.12 Social Inclusion, Ratio of OIC to Non-OIC Countries

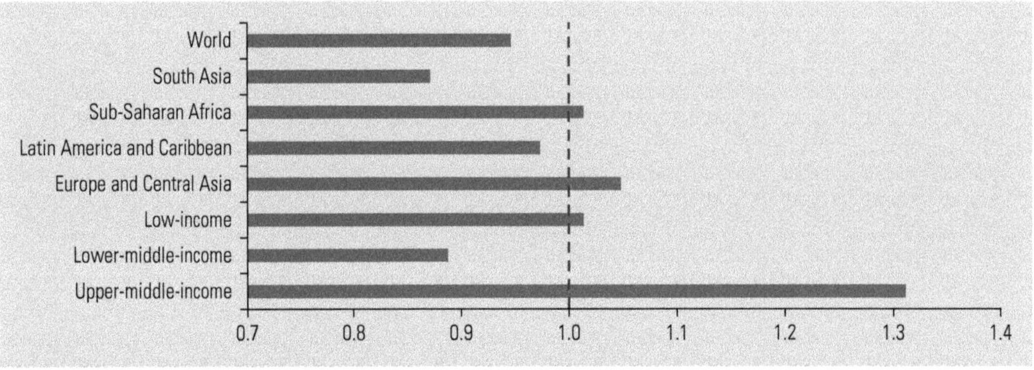

Source: Calculated using data from http://data.worldbank.org/indicator/IQ.CPA.SOCI.XQ/countries.
Note: A value of 1 indicates that OIC and non-OIC countries are on a par. The figure presents the Country Policy and Institutional Assessment policies for social inclusion/equity cluster average. The policies for social inclusion and equity cluster include gender equality, equity of public resource use, building human resources, social protection and labor, and policies and institutions for environmental sustainability. Scores range from a low of 1 to a high of 6.
OIC = Organisation of Islamic Cooperation.

FIGURE 2.13 Domestic Credit to the Private Sector

Percentage of GDP

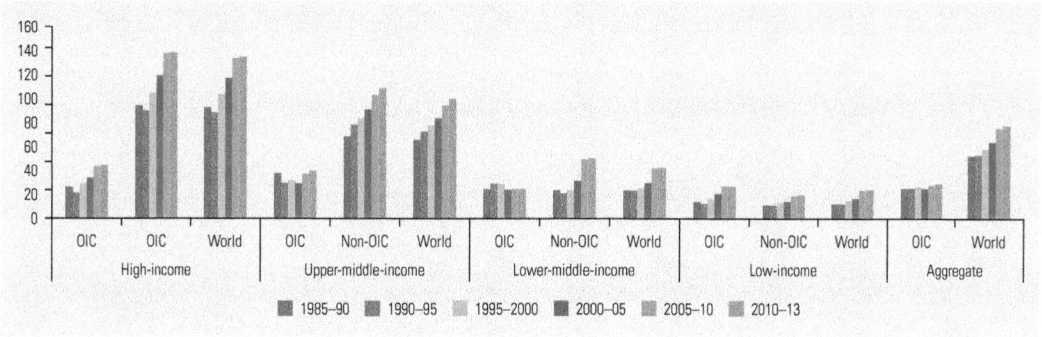

Source: Calculated using data from http://data.worldbank.org/indicator/FS.AST.PRVT.GD.ZS.

Note: Domestic credit to the private sector refers to financial resources provided to the private sector by financial corporations, such as through loans, purchases of nonequity securities, and trade credits and other accounts receivable that establish a claim for repayment. OIC = Organisation of Islamic Cooperation.

on borrowing from conventional modes of financing. This practice underscores the importance and potential of the provision of Islamic finance in the OIC member-countries.

Using the World Bank's Business Enterprise surveys, Bhattacharya and Wolde (2012) quantify the impact of the various constraints faced by local businesses in the Middle East and North Africa (MENA) Region and conclude that the main difficulties are access to finance, labor skill mismatches and shortages, and constraints on electric power. Hence easing the financial access to firms and individuals in the MENA Region would promote growth and speed up their convergence to better-off nations.

Figures 2.14 and 2.15 analyze the forms of financing (equity versus debt financing) relative to GDP, and contrast OIC countries to non-OIC countries belonging to the same income level groups. The objective is to determine how conducive a country is to developing risk-sharing finance as advocated by Islamic finance. Given the prohibition of interest-based debt by Islamic finance, the equities market and asset-based securities market become the preferred capital markets. Figure 2.14 shows the gross-portfolio-debt-assets-to-GDP ratio, while figure 2.15 depicts the gross-portfolio-equity-assets-to-GDP ratio and contrasts OIC countries to non-OIC countries belonging to the same income level groups.

In the aggregate, OIC countries have reduced the amount of debt assets in their portfolios, while that ratio has been increasing in the world. Similarly, in the aggregate, OIC countries have reduced the amount of equity assets in their portfolios in recent years, while the same ratio has been increasing in the world. This could indicate a shift toward alternative asset classes, but further analysis and research is required to understand these trends.

Policy Response

While there is strong theoretical support for Islamic economics and finance to lead to sustainable growth and enhance shared prosperity, the enabling environment is lacking to reap the benefits. Public policy measures are needed to develop and strengthen institutions in key areas of governance, the legal system, and government effectiveness. In addition, strengthening the financial sector in ways that are conducive to risk-sharing finance based on the core principles of Islam should be the main objective of policy makers wishing to exploit the full potential of Islamic finance. Until these reforms are undertaken, it would be unrealistic to expect Islamic finance to fulfill the promise of developing a more stable, sustainable, and inclusive economic system.

FIGURE 2.14 Gross Portfolio Debt Assets to GDP

Percentage of GDP

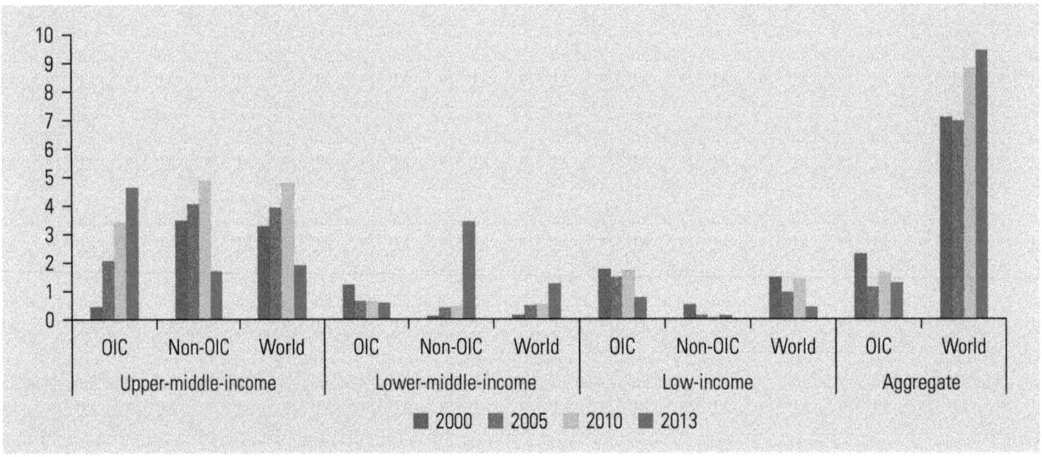

Source: Compiled using data from the World Bank Global Financial Development Database.
Note: Ratio of gross portfolio debt assets to GDP. OIC = Organisation of Islamic Cooperation.

FIGURE 2.15 Gross Portfolio Equity Assets to GDP

Percentage of GDP

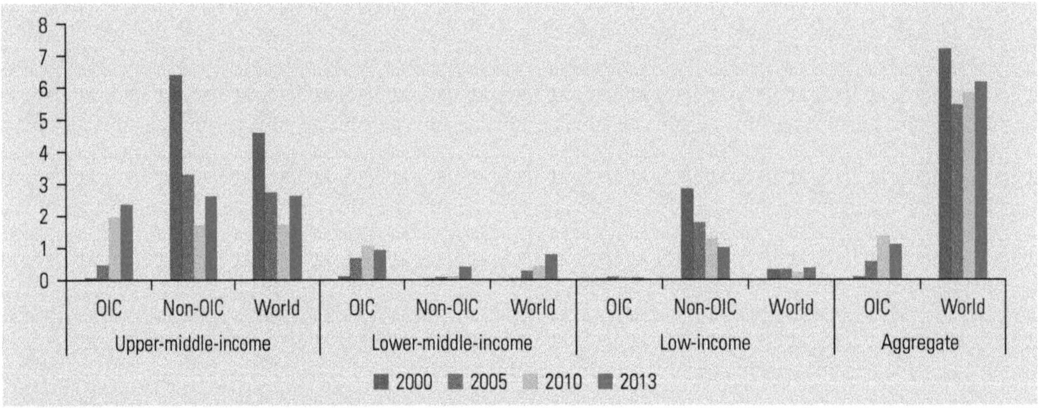

Source: Compiled using data from the World Bank Global Financial Development Database.
Note: Ratio of gross portfolio equity assets to GDP. Equity assets include shares, stocks, participation, and similar documents (such as American depository receipts) that usually denote ownership of equity. OIC = Organisation of Islamic Cooperation.

The analysis in this chapter assesses the state of affairs with respect to trends in poverty alleviation and income distribution, which can be used by the policy makers to formulate policy interventions and to identify areas to strengthen, keeping in mind the objective of leveraging Islamic finance for alleviating poverty and enhancing shared prosperity. Chapter 9, the final chapter, provides a road map for such policy measures.

Notes

1. The Organisation of Islamic Cooperation (OIC) (formerly the Organisation of the Islamic Conference) has a membership of 57 countries spread over four continents, covering around 1.7 billion people. It is the collective voice of the Muslim world, dedicated to ensuring and safeguarding the interests of the Muslim world in the spirit of promoting international peace and harmony among various people of the world. http://www.oicun.org/.

2. We are thankful to Ishrat Husain for urging caution in making interpretations based on aggregate data for a group as heterogeneous as the OIC. Furthermore, data on various variables used in this chapter are not consistent, as highlighted by Bello and Suleman (2011). Hence, the interpretation should be used cautiously.
3. For each five-year period, the latest available data for every country were used. High-income OIC countries were excluded from the analysis because no data were available. The income and regional classifications are adopted from World Bank Group classifications. Aggregate values were computed with a weighted average, using the overall population of a given country. Data are in purchasing power parity (PPP) terms.
4. For example, see Askari and Rehman (2010), who construct an Islamicity index of various countries. See also Askari and Rehman (2013).
5. Adam Smith, in *The Wealth of Nations* (1776), long ago recognized the significance of the first two pillars as the prerequisites for the development model described in chapter 1: "Commerce and manufactures can seldom flourish long in any state which does not enjoy a regular administration of justice, in which the people do not feel themselves secure in the possession of their property, in which the faith of contracts is not supported by law, and in which the authority of the state is not supposed to be regularly employed in enforcing the payment of debts from all those who are able to pay. Commerce and manufactures, in short, can seldom flourish in any state in which there is not a certain degree of confidence in the justice of government" (cited in Rodrik, Subramanian, and Trebbi 2004).
6. In a seminal paper, Levine (1997) finds evidence suggesting a positive, first-order relationship between financial development and economic growth. Enhancing financial services could make it easier for firms to obtain funds to make additional investments and for individuals to smooth their consumption and weather the negative income shocks to their income stream. Furthermore, a well-functioning financial system not only channels funds to the most efficient sectors, but also enables risk and assets to be priced; such prices are essential for reducing uncertainty about future investments. All these factors contribute to economic growth.

References

Askari, H., and S. Rehman. 2010. "An Economic Islamicity Index." *Global Economy Journal* 10 (September): 1–37.

———. 2013. "A Survey of the Economic Development of OIC Countries." In *Economic Development and Islamic Finance*, edited by Zamir Iqbal and Abbas Mirakhor. Washington, DC: World Bank.

Barro, Robert J. 1996. "Determinants of Economic Growth: A Cross-country Empirical Study." NBER Working Paper 5698, National Bureau of Economic Research, Cambridge, MA.

Bello, Abdullateef, and Areef Suleman. 2011. "The Challenge of Achieving the Millennium Development Goals in IDB Member Countries in the Post-Crisis World." IDB Occasional Paper 16, Islamic Development Bank, Jeddah, Saudi Arabia.

Bhattacharya, Rina, and Hirut Wolde. 2012. "Business Environment Constraints on Growth in the MENA Region." *Middle East Development Journal* 4 (1): 1250004-1–125994-18.

Demirgüç-Kunt, Asli, Leora Klapper, and Douglas Randall. 2014. "Islamic Finance and Financial Inclusion: Measuring Use of and Demand for Formal Financial Services among Muslim Adults." *Review of Middle East Economics and Finance* 10 (2): 177–218.

Feenstra, Robert C., Robert Inklaar, and Marcel P. Timmer. 2015. "The Next Generation of the Penn World Table." *American Economic Review* 105 (10): 3150–82. http://www.ggdc.net/pwt.

Han, Xuehui, Haider Ali Khan, and Juzhong Zhuang. 2014. "Do Governance Indicators Explain Development Performance? A Cross-Country Analysis." Economics Working Paper 417, Asian Development Bank, Manila.

Kalemli-Ozcan, Sebnem, Bent E. Sørensen, and Oved Yosha. 2003. "Risk Sharing and Industrial Specialization: Regional and International Evidence." *American Economic Review* 93 (3): 903–18.

Levine, Ross. 1997. "Financial Development and Economic Growth: Views and Agenda." *Journal of Economic Literature* 35 (June): 688–726.

Levine, Ross, and Sara Zervos. 1996. "Stock Market Development and Long-Run Growth." *The World Bank Economic Review* 10 (26): 323–39.

Rodrik, Dani, Arvind Subramanian, and Francesco Trebbi. 2004. "Institutions Rule: The Primacy of Institutions over Geography and Integration in Economic Development." *Journal of Economic Growth* 9 (2): 131–65.

3

The Islamic Banking Sector

The Islamic banking sector, which is the dominant component of the Islamic finance industry, has grown dramatically since the first known experiment started in the Egyptian village of Mit Ghamr in 1963. Today, more than 300 Islamic finance institutions, with assets close to $1.9 trillion (IFSB 2016), are spread across 50 economies around the world in both Muslim and non-Muslim countries.

This chapter discusses the theoretical channels through which Islamic banking contributes to shared prosperity, presents an overview of Islamic banking, examines the key challenges facing Islamic banks, and offers policy recommendations.

Islamic Banking and Shared Prosperity

The aspiration of Islamic banks is the creation, equitable distribution, and circulation of wealth in order to promote social justice and to satisfy customers' needs for *shari'ah*-compliant investment opportunities. This wealth creation and its fair distribution ensure shared prosperity. Islamic banking contributes to shared prosperity through its impact on economic growth, as a provider of capital for economic activities, and through the characteristics of its products. Islamic economics is normative in nature, with the objective of complying with *shari'ah* (*maqāṣid al-sharī'ah*). The Islamic economy is built upon a set of objectives, or *maqāṣid,* that are the underlying principles that promote the well-being of all humanity.[1] The existence of Islamic finance and banking is supported by these key Islamic principles, which can be summarized as showing a preference for risk sharing over risk transfer through debt, prohibiting social and economic exploitation, emphasizing ethical standards, promoting moral and social values, and rewarding enterprise (linking risk and reward) that would boost shared prosperity, as discussed in chapter 1.

The Abu Halima projects in Sudan are a good illustration of the potential for Islamic banking to take advantage of business opportunities and enhance living conditions in low-income settings (see box 3.1). Justice demands that resources be employed in a manner that benefits the whole of society and is accompanied by an underlying productive economic activity that generates real wealth.

How Risk Sharing through Islamic Banking Promotes Shared Prosperity

Islamic banking is built on the principle of risk sharing in the financial system. Islamic financing instruments ensure that the sharing of the rewards from economic activity is not skewed by individuals' initial endowment of financial resources. Furthermore, the prohibition of interest and usury is intended to create more favorable conditions for shared prosperity by removing guaranteed returns and safeguarding the fair transfer of property and value among all economic actors. Islam banking adheres to certain conditions for financing real economic activities that help prevent the excessive expansion of debt (Chapra 2011) and for moving the economy from a debt-based, risk-shifting economy to a risk-sharing economy (Askari and others 2012).

Islamic banking, in its essence, should help mobilize resources from a large spectrum of the population, substantially increase the share of equity financing in business, and advance risk sharing in entrepreneurial activities. A close examination of Islamic modes of finance reveals that they keep finance tied to real economic activity. Islamic modes of profit and loss–sharing share this characteristic, whether through partnership (*mushārakah*), agency (*muḍārabah*), trade-based contracts such as deferred payment mark-up sales (*murābaḥah*), the sale of goods to be manufactured (*istiṣnā'*), or forward sales (*salam*).

BOX 3.1 Abu Halima *Muḍārabah* Greenhouse Project in Sudan

This small project, located in Abu-Halima, a rural community in north Khartoum, is an example of how Islamic banking products have the potential to contribute to shared prosperity. This initiative by the Islamic Development Bank, the Bank of Khartoum (Sudan), and the Central Bank of Sudan aims to empower low-income households by financing 125 graduates of colleges of agriculture who work with their families to set up and operate greenhouses through the profit-sharing contract of *muḍārabah* (see details to follow). The project supports shared prosperity through two modalities.

First, by targeting low-income households, it ensures an efficient way of reducing poverty and income inequality. One of the qualifying criteria is that the young graduate's income must not exceed twice the Sudanese minimum wage.

Second, by adopting profit sharing, the project helps low-income households build equity, acquire productive capacities, and develop human capital. The adopted mode of financing is restricted *muḍārabah*, a joint venture in which the financier attaches some conditions to the use of funds.

The project has the following characteristics:

- Beneficiaries: 125 families headed by college of agriculture graduates, forming one cooperative.
- Business type: Greenhouses for production of 1,400 tons of vegetables annually.
- Mode of financing: *Muḍārabah* (capital management). Profits are shared on a ratio of 40 percent for the project managers and 60 percent for the bank. Losses are absorbed by the bank. However, each family receives a living allowance throughout the production process, whether there is a loss or not.
- Finance amount: $4 million for the cooperative, which works out to $30,000 for each family.
- Partners: One technical consultant and two private supermarkets for commercialization.

Today, these units are among the most important providers of vegetables near Khartoum.

Source: Bank of Khartoum, Sudan.

This concept of financing helps promote growth of the financial sector in tandem with that of the real sector.

Risk sharing ensures that banks thoroughly evaluate business proposals because it creates an incentive for financial institutions to internalize costs related to bankruptcy. In addition, risk sharing is implemented through equity-based financing. This type of financing helps foster cooperation, interdependence, and above all universal brotherhood by involving everyone in both production and investment. Advocates of shifting the reliance from debt-based to equity-based financing are growing in mainstream economics. Greater reliance on equity also opens the door to greater demands by investors for shareholder values. The International Monetary Fund, in a *World Economic Outlook* on the causes and indicators of financial crises, acknowledges the advantage of equity financing in sustaining financial stability, noting that foreign direct investment, in contrast to inflows that create debt, is often regarded as providing a safer and more stable way to finance development (IMF 1998).

Although Islamic banking may not be the ultimate answer to improving socioeconomic justice and shared prosperity, the ethical aspects ingrained in the principles of Islamic banking can lead to increased transparency and social accountability, which in turn can help societies achieve economic growth and prosperity.[2]

How Islamic Banking Promotes Shared Prosperity through Financial Stability

The pass-through nature of Islamic banking eliminates the asset-liability mismatch inherent in classical conventional banking, thereby promoting a stable financial system. In case of a financial crisis, portfolios are balanced automatically, and there is less need for any bailouts by the governments (Askari and others 2010). The built-in stabilizing feature of Islamic banking could protect poor segments of the society from the financing of bailouts through additional taxes and higher costs. In this respect, shared prosperity can be protected because the bottom 40 percent of the population will be less burdened.

How Islamic Banking Promotes Shared Prosperity through Financial Inclusion

The concepts of financial and social inclusiveness and income equality are central to Islamic economic teaching. Islamic finance can be effectively used to address the issue of financial inclusion (see box 3.2) because it can provide a viable alternative to conventional debt-based financing by promoting risk-sharing contracts. It can also utilize specific wealth redistribution instruments to aid access to finance for the poorest in society. These instruments distribute income from the wealthy and privileged to those defined as poor and needy, through voluntary or involuntary levies (Mirakhor and Iqbal 2012).

BOX 3.2 Channels of Financial Inclusion from an Islamic Finance Perspective

Islamic financial services can address the issue of financial inclusion with two approaches: by promoting risk-sharing contracts, which provide a viable alternative to conventional debt-based financing; and by using specific wealth redistribution instruments (Mirakhor and Iqbal 2012).

The users of formal Islamic financial services can be categorized into user and nonuser groups. Nonusers may not be able to access the financial system (involuntary exclusion) or may opt out of the financial system (voluntary exclusion) (figure B3.2.1). The financially excluded do not have access to the

box continues next page

BOX 3.2 Channels of Financial Inclusion from an Islamic Finance Perspective *(continued)*

financial system because they do not have enough income or present too high a lending risk; certain segments of the population are subject to social, religious, ethnic, gender, or other discrimination; and/or the informational and contractual framework might prevent financial institutions from reaching out to certain segments because outreach is too costly to be commercially viable.

FIGURE B3.2.1 Channels of Financial Inclusion

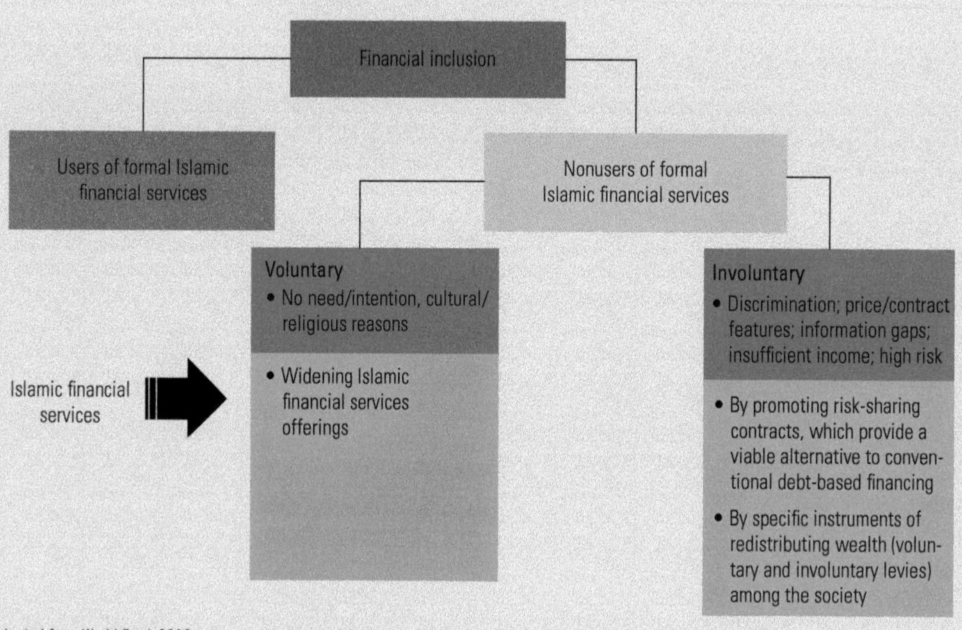

Source: Adapted from World Bank 2008.

This redistribution not only ensures social justice, but also mobilizes resources, making finance available to the poor and improving the productive capacity of the community.

Table 3.1 shows the state of Islamic banking and financial inclusion in selected Muslim-majority countries. The degree of religiosity[3] is on average about 85 percent in these countries, highlighting the important role of religion in daily life and society. About 9 percent of the population of these countries is financially excluded due to religious reasons (World Bank 2014). Hence Islamic finance can play a role in bringing more than 40 million financially excluded individuals into the formal financial system.

At present, however, the number of banks that offer *shari'ah*-compliant financial services per 10 million adults is low except in a few countries such as Bahrain, Kuwait, Malaysia, and Qatar (Zulkhibri 2016). Geographical reach is also limited for banks offering *shari'ah*-compliant financial services (as measured by such banks per 10,000 square kilometers). Efforts to increase financial inclusion in countries with Muslim populations thus require sustainable mechanisms to be able to offer

TABLE 3.1 Islamic Financial Institutions and Financial Inclusion by Country

Economy	Religiosity and financial inclusion				Islamic financial institutions (IFIs)			
	Religiosity[a] (%)	Account at a formal financial institution (%, age 15+)	Adults with no account due to religious reasons[b] (%, age 15+)	Adults with no account due to religious reasons[b] (thousands, age 15+)	Number of IFIs	Islamic assets per adult[c] ($)	Number of IFIs per 10 million adults	Number of IFIs per 10,000 km^2
Afghanistan	97	9.0	33.6	5,830	2	—	1.1	0.03
Albania	39	28.3	8.3	150	1	—	4.0	0.36
Algeria	95	33.3	7.6	1,330	2	—	0.8	0.01
Azerbaijan	50	14.9	5.8	355	1	—	1.4	0.12
Bahrain	94	64.5	0	0	32	29,194	301.6	421.05
Bangladesh	99	39.6	4.5	2,840	12	14	1.2	0.92
Benin	—	10.5	1.7	77	0	0	0	0
Burkina Faso	—	13.4	1.2	98	1	—	1.1	0.04
Cameroon	96	14.8	1.1	114	2	—	1.7	0.04
Chad	95	9.0	10.0	573	0	0	0	0
Comoros	97	21.7	5.8	20	0	0	0	0
Djibouti	98	12.3	22.8	117	0	0	0	0
Egypt, Arab Rep.	97	9.7	2.9	1,480	11	146	1.9	0.11
Gabon	—	18.9	1.5	12	0	0	0	0
Guinea	—	3.7	5.0	279	0	0	0	0
Indonesia	99	19.6	1.5	2,110	23	30	1.3	0.13
Iraq	84	10.6	25.6	4,310	14	98	7.4	0.32
Jordan	—	25.5	11.3	329	6	1,583	15.4	0.68
Kazakhstan	43	42.1	1.7	126	0	0	0	0
Kuwait	91	86.8	2.6	7	18	28,102	87.2	10.10
Kyrgyz Republic	72	3.8	7.3	272	0	0	0	0
Lebanon	87	37.0	7.6	155	4	—	12.4	3.91
Malaysia	96	66.2	0.1	8	34	4,949	16.8	1.03
Mali	95	8.2	2.8	218	0	0	0	0
Mauritania	98	17.5	17.7	312	1	76	4.7	0.01
Morocco	97	39.1	26.8	3,810	0	0	0	0
Mozambique	—	39.9	2.3	189	0	0	0	0
Niger	99	1.5	23.6	1,910	0	0	0	0
Nigeria	96	29.7	3.9	2,520	0	0	0	0
Oman	—	73.6	14.2	78	3	—	14.4	0.10
Pakistan	92	10.3	7.2	7,400	29	40	2.5	0.38

table continues next page

TABLE 3.1 Islamic Financial Institutions and Financial Inclusion by Country *(continued)*

Economy	Religiosity and financial inclusion				Islamic financial institutions (IFIs)			
	Religiosity[a] (%)	Account at a formal financial institution (%, age 15+)	Adults with no account due to religious reasons[b] (%, age 15+)	Adults with no account due to religious reasons[b] (thousands, age 15+)	Number of IFIs	Islamic assets per adult[c] ($)	Number of IFIs per 10 million adults	Number of IFIs per 10,000 km^2
Qatar	95	65.9	11.6	64	14	13,851	86.5	12.08
Saudi Arabia	93	46.4	24.1	2,540	18	1,685	9.2	0.08
Senegal	96	5.8	6.0	411	0	0	0	0
Sierra Leone	—	15.3	9.9	287	0	0	0	0

Sources: Bankscope; Global Findex; World Bank, World Development Indicators (database); World Bank 2014.
Note: — = not available.
a. Percentage of adults in a given country who responded affirmatively to the question, "Is religion an important part of your daily life?" in a 2010 Gallup poll.
b. Number of adults and percentage of adults that point to a religious reason for not having an account at a formal financial institution.
c. Islamic assets per adult ($)/Size of Islamic assets in the banking sector of an economy per its adult population.

shari'ah-compliant financial services to all residents, especially the Muslim poor and near poor, estimated at around 700 million people who are living on less than $2 a day.

A substantial number of Muslims have voluntarily shunned formal banking activities because of their religious beliefs (Zulkhibri 2016). At the same time, as the Islamic financial sector has deepened, many previously excluded individuals have started to undertake Islamic banking transactions. This suggests that Islamic banking can have a positive impact on financial intermediation by the poor, which ultimately should boost the mobilization of savings and prosperity. The opportunities for Islamic banking to offer financial products and services to the poor, especially in Muslim-dominated populations, are expected to grow. Islamic banking may also be more likely to finance projects that can be beneficial for low-income people, given the religious nature of its business and the ethical objectives enshrined in Islamic financing principles.

Despite the apparent difficulties in applying principles in practice, Islamic banking may increasingly play an important and positive role in improving financial inclusion. Structured approaches can be applied to enhance financial inclusion for individuals and households experiencing extreme poverty (via *zakāt, ṣadaqāt, waqf*, and collective risk sharing); poverty (via *qarḍ ḥasan, zakāt, waqf*, microfinance, and micro*takāful*); and low income (via market-based solutions and support to micro, small, and medium enterprises) (see chapter 8, on social finance). The uniqueness of the risk-sharing principle should be promoted more in rural areas in Muslim-majority countries. The availability of profit and loss–sharing instruments helps individuals mitigate their market risks because it contributes to portfolio diversification.

A World Bank (2014) study shows that the greater the number of Islamic banks per 100,000 adults, the lower the proportion of firms identifying access to finance as a major constraint. This finding suggests that increasing the number of *shari'ah*-compliant financial institutions can make a positive difference in the operations of small firms (0–20 employees) in countries with Muslim populations by reducing barriers to accessing formal financial services.

Recent Developments in Islamic Banking and Current Status

Recently, the Islamic Financial Services Board (IFSB 2015) estimated the size of the industry in terms of assets at $1.87 trillion and the size of the banking sector at $1.4762 trillion as of mid-2014.[4]

Size and Structure

Islamic banking has been growing not only in Muslim countries, but also in the non-Muslim world. The global spread of Islamic banks has transformed the financial systems of a growing number of Muslim countries. According to Bureau van Dijk Bankscope data, there were 161 deposit-taking Islamic banks globally as of the end of 2014, a 28 percent increase from 2010. Net income, total assets, and total equity have also grown (figure 3.1). Globally, the Islamic Republic of Iran accounts for one-third of the assets of Islamic banks (table 3.2). Together with Sudan, these are the only two countries with a financial system based solely on Islamic finance. The rapid increase in Islamic banking and the importance of the sector for the economies of various other countries, particularly the member-countries of the Gulf Cooperation Council (GCC), Indonesia, Malaysia, and Pakistan, make it important to increase the understanding of recent developments, current trends, and industry drivers.

Recent increases in Islamic banking activity have been driven by a number of factors. First, increased oil prices prior to 2015, particularly in GCC states, have bolstered liquidity in these economies, increasing demand for financial services. However, the substantially lower oil prices in 2014 and 2015 and projected for 2016 has raised issues related to sustainability. Second and more positively, Islamic banks were not as adversely affected by the 2008–09 global financial crisis as were conventional banks. Finally, Islamic banking has gained momentum as a credible competitor to conventional banking. Its products and services continue to evolve, as has the legal and regulatory frameworks under which it operates.

Together, the GCC countries and the Islamic Republic of Iran constitute the dominant players with the majority of the assets in the banking industry. As a consequence, the Middle East dominates the growth of Islamic banking globally. The South and Southeast Asia Region ranks as second globally for Islamic banking, with 15 percent of the market share. The region includes Malaysia, the second largest economy in terms of total *shari'ah*-compliant financial assets, and Indonesia, the country with the world's largest Muslim population. Pakistan and Bangladesh are two other emerging countries in the region, with combined assets of almost 2 percent of the global market. Overall, there is a large potential for Islamic

FIGURE 3.1 **Average Percentage Increase in Various Elements of Islamic Banking, 2010–13**

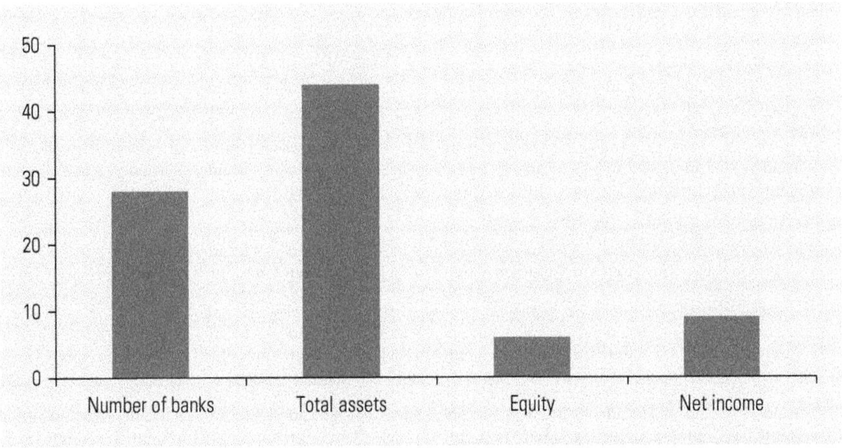

Source: Figures calculated from data extracted from Bankscope 2015.

TABLE 3.2 Islamic Banking Assets by Region, 2013

Region/country	Total assets ($billion)
Middle East, including the Islamic Republic of Iran	
Iran, Islamic Rep.	482.40
Saudi Arabia	121.70
United Arab Emirates	100.30
Kuwait	78.70
Qatar	59.00
Bahrain	46.20
South and Southeast Asia	
Malaysia	156.70
Bangladesh	17.00
Indonesia	13.00
Pakistan	6.20
Africa	
Sudan	6.50
Egypt, Arab Rep.	5.00
Tunisia	0.76
Gambia, The	0.02
Other	
Turkey	44.80
United Kingdom	3.30

Source: Figures calculated from data extracted from Bankscope 2015.

banking to continue growing, taking into account income growth rates in these countries, in addition to the large and growing population of Muslims. Turkey and the United Kingdom complete the current picture, accounting for 4 percent and a symbolic fraction of 1 percent of bank assets, respectively.

In addition, there are a larger number of countries that have less developed Islamic banking sectors but that host substantial Muslim populations. Thus there are two clear potential areas for expansion: the entry of new Islamic banks, as well as the expansion of existing banks, in countries where Islamic banking already exists; and the introduction of new Islamic banks, and expansion of existing institutions, where Islamic banking is underdeveloped despite a substantial Muslim population. Countries such as Nigeria and Senegal in West Africa are good candidates for an expansion of Islamic banking in the near future. Other candidates include Afghanistan, Algeria, Azerbaijan, Cameroon, Libya, Mali, Kazakhstan, Morocco, Mozambique, and Uzbekistan.

Although data availability is an issue in most of the 57 member-countries of the Organisation of Islamic Cooperation (OIC), there is some evidence that Islamic banks are contributing to shared prosperity through the modes of financing they are offering, as well as the sectors they are supporting (see chapter 2 of this Report).

Figure 3.2 shows the distribution by sector of financing provided by Islamic banks, reported as a percentage of the total, and

FIGURE 3.2 **Financing by Sector, Islamic Banks, 2012**

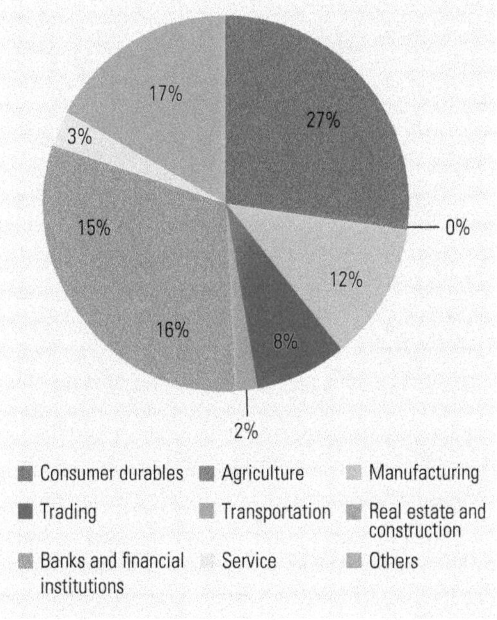

Source: Ibisonline.net /IRTI.

aggregated by country. More than one-quarter of financing facilitates the acquisition of consumer durables, while financing for real estate and construction, manufacturing, and trading accounts for 16 percent, 12 percent, and 8 percent, respectively. All these sectors are drivers of economic development, a necessary condition for shared prosperity.

Performance of Islamic Banks: Indicators of Financial Soundness

The Islamic banking system as a whole is well capitalized and liquid, although the degree of liquidity varies by region and according to the market share of Islamic banks. The capital adequacy ratio (CAR) for Islamic banks is generally well above the regulatory requirement (see table 3.3). Major portion of the risk weighted capital ratio consists of Tier 1 capital.

In 2014, Islamic banks in the United Kingdom, Turkey, Africa, the GCC, and the Islamic Republic of Iran had the strongest capital positions, followed by countries where Islamic banks were relatively important in terms of market share. For instance, in 2014 the CARs for Islamic banks in the United Kingdom, Turkey, the GCC, and the Islamic Republic of Iran were all satisfactory, averaging 33, 32, 26, and 19 percent, respectively, well above the minimum 8 percent requirement for total capital under Basel III.

In terms of profitability, return on assets of Islamic banks is positive, with banks operating in Africa, the GCC, the Islamic Republic of Iran, the Middle East, and Asia scoring better than their counterparts elsewhere, with a return on assets above 0.5 percent. One possible reason is that some of the banks in these regions are state-owned banks and for the most part finance state-owned enterprises and government projects at concessionary rates.

In terms of credit risk, nonperforming loans (NPLs) have declined across the regions, although they have remained relatively high in the GCC, the Islamic Republic of Iran, and Africa, averaging double digits from 2010 to 2013. The GCC and the Islamic Republic of Iran made significant progress in reducing the ratio of NPLs to total loans from double digits in 2010–13 to single digit in 2014. Islamic banks in Indonesia, Malaysia, Pakistan, and Sudan have relatively lower levels of credit risk, averaging 6 percent in the period under review. In 2014, the level of NPLs for the United Kingdom, Turkey, the GCC, and the Islamic Republic of Iran averaged 9 percent, 8 percent, 7 percent, and 6 percent, respectively.

The high level of NPLs in the Middle East and Asia highlights the relatively high level of credit risk in the region and calls for greater regulatory oversight. Regulatory frameworks for banking supervision need to be scaled up. Banks with double-digit NPLs need more intensive credit risk supervision from their central banks to mitigate such risks. In particular, central banks in these countries need to pay greater attention to Islamic banks and also monitor the banks' largest clients more closely. In addition, both central credit registries and credit reference bureaus could be established to check borrowers' credit histories. There is also the need in these jurisdictions to establish Asset Management

TABLE 3.3 Financial Soundness Indicators, All Islamic Banks

	2010	2011	2012	2013	2014
GCC, including the Islamic Republic of Iran					
Capital adequacy ratio (CAR)	27.7	36.7	29.5	30.8	26.3
Tier 1 ratio	27.0	33.0	29.6	30.0	25.4
Nonperforming loans to total loans	10.1	12.3	10.1	9.2	6.0
Return on assets	–2.5	0.5	0.3	1.5	0.5
Return on equity	–2.0	4.9	5.2	6.4	5.8
Liquid assets/Deposits and short-term funding	50.7	85.6	60.1	63.6	45.1
Liquid assets/Total deposits and borrowing	47.6	50.2	47.5	46.6	51.4
Middle East and Asia (excluding GCC/Iran, Islamic Rep.)					
Capital adequacy ratio	45.6	27.4	24.9	19.0	19.1
Tier 1 ratio	25.0	24.1	20.4	15.3	14.4
Nonperforming loans to total loans	6.6	7.9	7.0	9.2	9.2
Return on assets	0.3	1.1	0.9	1.3	0.7
Return on equity	6.5	7.5	4.3	–2.4	7.4
Liquid assets/Deposits and short-term funding	110.5	85.4	52.2	44.2	35.1
Liquid assets/Total deposits and borrowing	23.6	26.2	19.5	17.9	18.9
Africa					
Capital adequacy ratio (CAR)	35.2	102.8	26.7	30.2	32.2
Tier 1 ratio	22.9	163.1	22.2	25.3	27.9
Nonperforming loans to total loans	6.5	11.5	10.8	10.8	7.8
Return on assets	3.7	2.4	2.7	1.6	2.7
Return on equity	17.1	9.6	10.3	12.3	18.4
Liquid assets/Deposits and short-term funding	83.8	97.6	74.9	81.7	48.8
Liquid assets/Total deposits and borrowing	93.3	112.0	77.1	115.7	29.7
United Kingdom and Turkey					
Capital adequacy ratio	36.2	30.4	30.1	28.4	32.8
Tier 1 ratio	14.3	13.0	12.9	11.6	12.5
Nonperforming loans to total loans	3.5	3.0	2.9	3.1	7.2
Return on asset	8.1	6.3	4.9	1.1	–0.1
Return on equity	21.1	18.5	16.3	11.2	–0.9
Liquid assets/Deposits and short-term funding	161.1	216.2	86.0	176.9	22.5
Liquid assets/Total deposits and borrowing	158.2	265.7	101.6	176.2	21.1

Source: Figures calculated using data extracted from Bankscope 2014/2015.
Note: GCC = Gulf Cooperation Council.

Recovery Corporations in order to recover some of the bad loans.

Islamic banks in the GCC and the Islamic Republic of Iran are more liquid than their counterparts elsewhere, followed by banks in Africa. The reason for this pattern is that the lion's share of Islamic banks in Africa are located in Sudan—one of the two countries, with the Islamic Republic of Iran, where the whole banking system is *shari'ah* compliant, and Islamic banks are not in competition with conventional banks. Compliant Islamic banks in the Middle East, Asia, the United Kingdom, and Turkey appear to have only moderate liquidity positions.

Regional Perspectives

Assets and deposits in the global Islamic banking industry are highly concentrated, yet the majority of Islamic banks are small. Eleven percent of the 161 banks identified as Islamic banks with Bankscope data have assets above $20 billion; 11 percent have assets between $10 billion and $20 billion; 12 percent have assets between $5 billion and $10 billion; 27 percent have assets between $1 billion and $5 billion; and 40 percent have less than $1 billion in assets.

The bulk of the world's assets (77 percent) in Islamic banking are in the Middle East and North Africa (MENA) Region, followed by Asia (18 percent), Europe (3.73 percent), and Sub-Saharan Africa (less than 1 percent) (see figure 3.3). The pattern for the number of Islamic banks is similar, with 50 percent of Islamic banks located in the MENA Region, 30 percent in Asia, and 15 percent in Sub-Saharan Africa, despite having less than 1 percent of total assets. In the MENA Region, which has the bulk of Islamic bank assets, more than half the assets belong to Iranian banks ($451 billion), and the largest seven banks account for 80 percent of the Iranian market. These banks individually have assets valued at more than $20 billion.

Challenges Facing the Islamic Banking Sector

Over half a century since the establishment of modern Islamic banking, the evidence from Muslim-majority countries remains mixed concerning the sector's contribution to socio-economic development. A few studies have found that Islamic banking has yet to make a significant contribution to financial inclusion and economic development (Abedifar and others 2015), while others find a positive link (Imam and Kpodar 2015). Some studies have found that gains from Islamic banking have been limited to only a small segment of the general population.

The main reason is that the benefits of Islamic banking can be achieved only if it is practiced in its true spirit and form. Its misuse,

FIGURE 3.3 Regional Shares of Number of Banks, Deposits, and Assets
Percentage share

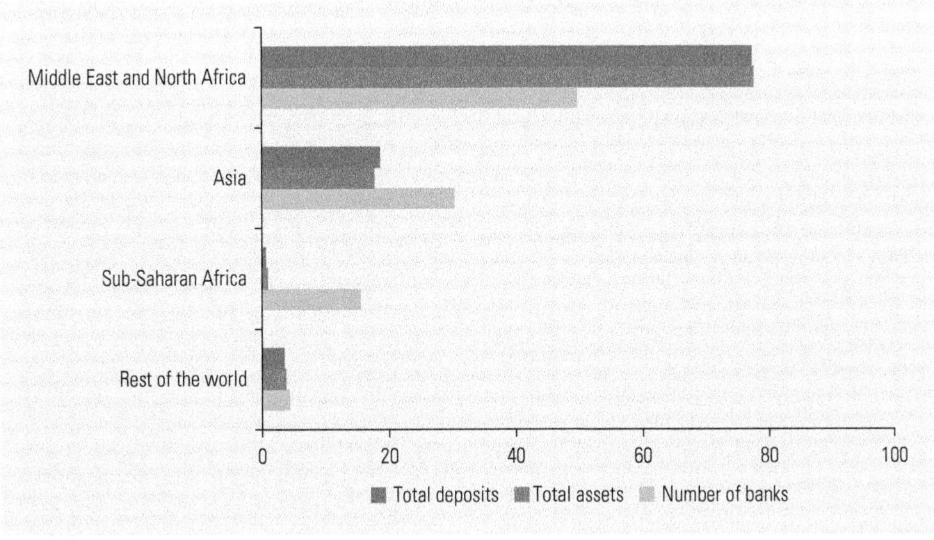

Source: Figures calculated using data extracted from Bankscope 2014.

like the misuse of any system, can preclude the attainment of its benefits. Another reason has to do with how the business and industry of Islamic banking evolved and how it has been preoccupied with high–net worth individuals, making it difficult to develop a healthy socio-economic environment that would be close to the ideal of Islam. *Shari'ah*-compliant practices may have created additional burdens, inefficiencies, and operational constraints, undermining the original *shari'ah* objectives of fairness, inclusiveness, equity, and economic justice (Sufian, Noor, and Zulkhibri 2008). There is empirical evidence that Islamic finance contributes positively to growth, and the literature argues that there is a large potential for *shari'ah* financial products to play a role in this growth (see box 3.3). This suggests that the litmus test of the usefulness of Islamic banking would be its ability to induce growth and reduce poverty through its chief characteristic, risk sharing (Askari and others 2012). Islamic banks have social responsibilities that transcend the goal of profit maximization. In reaching these goals, many challenges exist that need to be addressed by all stakeholders.

Divergence between Theory and Practice of Islamic Banking

Closing the gap between theory and practice is the most important issue facing Islamic banks. To date, Islamic banks have tended to position themselves close to conventional banks through product innovations, such as *tawarruq*, commodity *murābaḥah*, Islamic repos, and asset-based securities, which some argue are detached from the real economy

BOX 3.3 Islamic Banking: Is It Good for Growth?

Islamic banking, with unique attributes that differentiate it from its conventional counterpart, seems better adapted to characteristics prevailing in poorer countries of the Middle East and North Africa, Sub-Saharan Africa, and parts of South Asia and Southeast Asia. The distinct attributes of Islamic banking that encourage sharing risk, prohibiting interest, enhancing financial stability, and promoting investment in morally acceptable projects are advantages that could make it better adapted to the local environment, not only in Islamic countries, but also in low- and middle-income non-Muslim countries. Under certain circumstances it could be better at stimulating growth than conventional banking.

A study by Imam and Kpodar (2015) investigates whether the development of Islamic banking has had a positive impact on growth, using a sample of low- and middle-income countries with data from 1990 to 2010. The study uses the following regression:

$$G_{it} = \alpha + \beta IslBank_{it} + \delta FD_{it} + \varphi X_{it} + u_{it} + \varepsilon_{it} + v_t, \qquad (3.3.1)$$

where G is the growth rate of real GDP per capita; *IslBank* is the indicator of Islamic banking development (ratio of loans, assets, or deposits in Islamic banks to GDP); *FD* is the measure of overall financial development (ratio of private sector credit by commercial banks to GDP); *X* is the set of control variables described above; u is the country-specific effect; ε is the error term; and v is the time-specific effect.

The results show that, holding constant the level of financial development and other growth determinants, countries where Islamic banking is developing—and hence its impact on growth is measurable—experience faster economic growth than others. This suggests that despite its relatively small size compared to the economy or the overall size of the financial system, Islamic banking is positively associated with economic growth. The results are robust across different measures of Islamic banking development, econometric estimators (pooling, fixed effects, and system generalized method of moments), and the sample composition and time periods.

Thus, the empirical evidence examined in Imam and Kpodar (2015) suggests that as the industry matures and the obstacles it faces are addressed over time, Islamic banking represents a growth opportunity for countries.

and move too far away from the theoretical underpinnings of Islamic economics. There is a need to develop policies that could narrow the gap between the aspirations of Islamic banking to be based essentially on risk-sharing instruments such as *muḍārabah* and *mushārakah*, and the reality of Islamic banks relying heavily on debt-based instruments such as *murābaḥah*.[5]

Nowhere is such a gap between aspiration and reality more apparent than on the asset side of the balance sheets of Islamic banks. Islamic banking is still largely based on mark-up or profit margin techniques—a pattern identified over a decade ago (Iqbal and Molyneux 2005). This shift from equity-based financing or profit and loss–sharing contracts to debt-based financing poses the risk of negating their advantages in terms of financial stability, and the systemic benefits in terms of promoting sustainable development. Figure 3.4 clearly illustrates this challenge: more than 75 percent of the financing offered by Islamic banks globally is in the form of *murābaḥah* and deferred sales contracts. Leasing and hire purchase contracts come second, with about 11 percent. The shares of profit-sharing instruments (*mushārakah* and *muḍārabah*) remain at a lowly 4.17 percent and 1.67 percent, respectively. To put it another way, it appears that less than 6 percent of global Islamic financing is on a profit-sharing basis. The benevolent *qarḍ ḥasan* contract stands at 1.53 percent. Overall, the "star" Islamic banking products represent less than 8 percent of the total of Islamic financing globally.

Governments and the relevant authorities should look to remove barriers in order to boost the attractiveness of risk-sharing contracts in Islamic banking. The issues of clearly defining property rights and improving tax rate treatment will be a starting point to provide a level playing field. Internalizing the social dimension and social justice aspects into Islamic banks' own operational functions also may help close the gap between theory and practice. Extending financial inclusion via profit and loss–sharing Islamic modes of finance will extend this economic dynamic to a larger section of society.

FIGURE 3.4 Islamic Modes of Finance by Islamic Banks, 2012

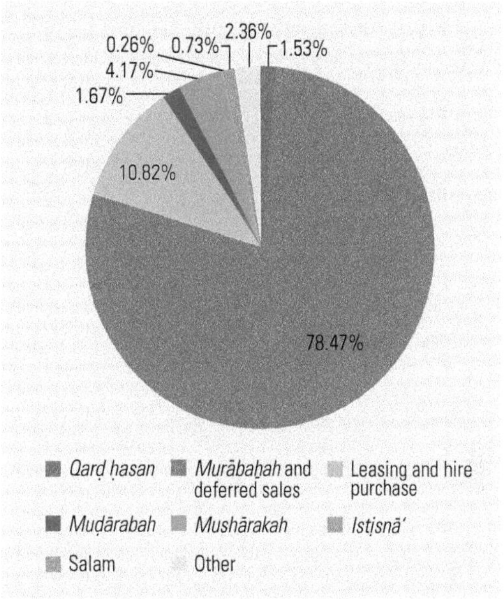

Source: Islamic Banks and Financial Institutions Information, Ibisonline.net/IRTI.

Scale, Access, and Outreach of Islamic Banking

Underdevelopment of risk-sharing instruments discourages investors from investing in sectors that are perceived as high risk, such as micro, small, and medium enterprises (MSMEs). The MSME market is largely untapped in emerging markets and has huge potential (World Bank-IDB-IRTI 2015). With the proper enabling environment, investors with a matching risk appetite are likely to be attracted to providing capital for these sectors. Increasing the access of poor and low-income groups to wider Islamic financial services and products could be a way forward to achieving the goal of ending poverty, particularly in Muslim countries.

To create real impact, Islamic finance needs to reach a critical mass by exploring untapped markets or by consolidating existing platforms to build an entity with the required expertise and capital that can influence multiple areas of the market. A large-scale Islamic financial institution, with a large amount of capital, is needed to generate change. The fragmentation in domestic markets has led to the erosion of banks' profit margins and difficulties for banks that want to scale up their business operations. However, a large-scale Islamic financial institution would be able to scale up through its presence in key financial markets. This, in turn, would make vital funding sources available to a wider range of consumers, generating new product profiles to penetrate new markets, influencing global markets, and increasing investor awareness.

Soundness, Stability, and Efficiency of Islamic Banking

Islamic banks pose several regulatory, market behavioral, and legal challenges. One challenge is designing and implementing an effective financial regulation and supervisory framework for Islamic banking that takes into account the unique features of the Islamic banking business, without increasing the regulatory burden and restricting its growth potential. The soundness of Islamic banking is important for the overall stability of the domestic and global financial system. One way to ensure stability is to reduce asset-liability risks and to adopt policies that minimize moral hazard and adverse selection, excessive debt creation, and leverage.

An appropriate and robust legal, regulatory, and tax framework is a basic requirement for establishing sound Islamic financial institutions and markets. It is also important to ensure a more integrated Islamic financial services industry globally so it can withstand shocks and adverse market developments. Putting in place these building blocks and applying mutually acceptable rules and standards will strengthen the resilience of the Islamic financial system. Innovation and knowledge sharing between various market players at the global level can facilitate the standardization and globalization of Islamic financial products. Accelerating the development of these critical building blocks of the Islamic financial system is vitally needed to respond to the changing economic and financial landscape.

Leveling the playing field with respect to the tax treatment of financial instruments is urgently needed. Conventional debt often receives advantageous tax treatment, while some Islamic finance products face double taxation. Treatment of such products requires uniform regulation, as well as a supportive legal framework. Similarly, existing legal and supervisory frameworks that are based on the conventional banking model may also create difficulties in the longer term for the efficient running of Islamic banks. An accounting procedure based solely on conventional banking practice is inadequate because of the different nature and treatment of financial instruments.

Liquidity and Basel III Compliance

Issues of liquidity and compliance with the Basel III capital requirements also present challenges. Banks in general, and Islamic banks in particular, are inherently subject to liquidity risk, relying mostly on relatively short-term demand deposits to finance illiquid investments. For example, in 2012, 77 percent of Islamic bank liabilities consisted of demand deposits, while 76 percent of their assets were in the form of investments (see table 3.4). Issues of maturity mismatch are therefore unavoidable. It is critical for Islamic financial institutions to innovate and revolutionize *shari'ah*-compliant products to enhance and manage liquidity.

By relying on equity-based finance, Islamic banks incur a higher charge of regulatory capital, since by definition Islamic banks are

TABLE 3.4 Demand Deposits and Investments of Islamic Banks, 2012

Region	Total deposits over total liabilities, percent	Total investments over total assets, percent
Europe	30.47	69.85
Middle East	83.15	76.23
Asia	73.67	75.41
Africa	87.04	73.38
Global	76.95	75.60

Source: Ibisonline.net/IRTI.

required to hold more equity than conventional banks. This places Islamic financial institutions at a disadvantage under Basel III's new capital requirements. A further complication concerns the calculation of risk-weighted assets, given variation across jurisdictions in the treatment of profit-sharing investment accounts (PSIAs). It is important to ensure proper regulatory treatment of the PSIAs of Islamic banks. It is also essential to identify instruments eligible for treatment as additional Tier 1 and Tier 2 capital, bearing in mind revised IFSB standards on capital adequacy (IFSB 15).[6]

Shari'ah Governance Credibility in Islamic Banking

Improvement in the *shari'ah* governance framework is needed to enhance *shari'ah* compliance, credibility, and integrity. A strong *shari'ah* governance framework helps increase consumer confidence and provides greater flexibility for Islamic financial institutions to be innovative within the boundaries of *shari'ah*. The *shari'ah* board contributes to public awareness about the philosophical basis and concepts of Islamic banking and finance. *Shari'ah* governance adds value to the existing corporate governance framework in Islamic financial institutions. Furthermore, *shari'ah* compliance is not just restrictive with respect to investment in companies with unacceptable business; it also promotes investment in businesses that contribute to the ethical values of Islam and purification of dubious profits by distributing them to charity for the welfare of the community as a whole.

On the other hand, standardized *fatāwá* (religious opinions) and centralized *shari'ah* boards help unify operations between Islamic banks and also increase public awareness and confidence. Differences in *shari'ah* interpretations can lead to a lack of harmonization both within and across borders, which can affect trust in the industry. The IFSB and Accounting and Auditing Organization for Islamic Financial Institutions (AAOIFI) recommend establishing, at the bank level, an independent *shari'ah* supervisory board (SSB), a well-resourced internal *shari'ah* review process, and periodic external *shari'ah* reviews (Kammer and others 2015). However, a centralized *shari'ah* board, in addition to bank-level *shari'ah* boards, can be advantageous in ensuring consistent *shari'ah* compliance approaches. Malaysia is a leader in terms of *shari'ah* regulatory and governance framework for its Islamic financial services industry. An increasing number of countries (including Bahrain, Indonesia, Morocco, Nigeria, Oman, Pakistan, and Sudan) are moving in the same direction in putting in place their own *shari'ah* regulatory and governance framework. For Islamic finance to move to the mainstream and extend into a broader range of jurisdictions, it must resolve inefficiencies associated with the *shari'ah* compliance process.

Adequately Trained and Skilled Human Capital

The institutional, technical, and human resource requirements of Islamic banks are unique. The Islamic banking industry requires human capital with a combination of competencies in accounting, finance, and *shari'ah*. Without appropriate training and skilled human resources, even if demand for Islamic banking services increases, the supply of such services cannot be met unless the industry has suitably qualified staff at all levels of management. Even so, if skilled human capital is not of the highest standard, the credibility, competitiveness, and stability of the Islamic banking industry will be at stake. Hence a critical and unique challenge of Islamic banking institutions is to address the shortfall of trained and skilled human capital for the industry to adequately meet its operational requirements and *shari'ah* governance standards.

Many banks still have limited capabilities and expertise to consistently originate and structure large Islamic finance deals, which often include pioneering arrangements and features. The need for highly skilled staff will increase with the development of innovative Islamic financial products and services.

Shari'ah experts need to have an adequate knowledge of banking and finance, while Islamic bankers, finance specialists, and regulators need an adequate knowledge of the applicable *shari'ah* rules and principles. Specialized training and educational institutions to provide Islamic financial knowledge to the populace are also needed, along with collaboration and exchange of knowledge across jurisdictions, and supplementary research into and development of key specialized and human resource areas. To meet this human capital requirement, large financial institutions can act as knowledge centers to attract foreign talent from the existing international financial hubs, as well as retain local talent.

Policy Recommendations

The rapid development of Islamic banking is adding considerable variety and choice for both Muslims and non-Muslims who wish to engage in financial activities. However, the absence of a truly global Islamic financial system based on *shari'ah* principles, as well as the varying ways in which Islamic banking business is conducted in different jurisdictions, has led to somewhat haphazard growth and development of Islamic banking and finance. In terms of policy response, the Islamic banking sector should focus on six key priorities to improve and adopt best practices for the sector to contribute to shared prosperity. The joint IMF-World Bank Group of Twenty note on integrating Islamic finance with global financial systems could serve as a good road map as discussed in chapter 9.

1. Shift toward *shari'ah*-based banking and practices. Currently, Islamic banking based on *shari'ah* compliance is primarily serving established corporate entities and relatively high–net worth individuals. The operating model of Islamic financial institutions needs to be revisited to promote *shari'ah*-based banking models. This will ensure that a greater portion of finance is available for micro, small, and medium enterprises through the use of risk-sharing instruments.
2. Harmonize *shari'ah* standards. Efforts must be made to develop global *shari'ah* reference bodies that can assist in harmonizing cross-country *fatāwá* relating to Islamic finance and help in accelerating the growth of the industry. Facilitating regional harmonization may be the first step toward greater harmonization of the Islamic banking system. It would be desirable to have clear and consistent rulings by scholars on *shari'ah* issues so that no ambiguity remains.
3. Create an enabling regulatory environment. Given the evolving global financial landscape, critical regulatory challenges include ensuring a level playing field for both conventional and Islamic banks through consistent regulations, ensuring consistent implementation of the Basel III framework, ensuring that systematic risks in dual banking systems are addressed, and implementing cross-border supervision.
4. Enhance the scale of and access to Islamic finance. For Islamic banking to live up to the promise of delivering equitable growth, it is vital that the scale, access, and outreach of Islamic banking be increased to include low-income earners. There is a need to enhance risk management practices; reduce costs; make best use of available technology; and use a range of channels, such as branchless banks, e-money, and mobile banking, to deliver financial services.
5. Improve liquidity and ensure stability. The problem of liquidity management needs to be addressed by developing new instruments through research and innovation. Developing a credible liquidity management framework will help accelerate the growth of the industry. Sustainable growth and stability in Islamic banks require the development of a comprehensive risk management framework geared to their specific situation and requirements.
6. Bolster human capital and Islamic finance literacy. The human capital of the industry could be strengthened by creating credible Islamic finance knowledge platforms through regular training, seminars, and workshops, as well as by developing

frontier knowledge in Islamic finance for the industry, with the support of the industry and academia. Trust and confidence in using Islamic financial services needs to be increased. Public awareness can be increased by promoting Islamic financial literacy, including knowledge of which financial products are best suited for particular purposes.

Notes

1. For more on this, see the *maqāṣid al-sharīʿah* as developed by al-Ghazel and al-Shatibi, in Zarqa (1980).
2. Askari and Krichene (2014) provide a review of the arguments in support of risk sharing being the essence of Islamic banking and the major reason for its stability. Hassan and Dridi (2010) also argue that risk-sharing characteristics of Islamic banking should increase stability, thereby stimulating growth.
3. Religiosity was measured as the percentage of adults in a given country who responded affirmatively to the question, "Is religion an important part of your daily life?" in a 2010 Gallup poll.
4. There are many reports on the state of Islamic banking, but they adopt different approaches, leading to a wide range of estimates of the size of the industry. Data on Islamic banks often cover commercial as well as investment banks, and sometimes they even include multilateral institutions such as the Islamic Development Bank. Such differences in the choice of institutions to include explain the wide range of estimates of the size of the Islamic banking industry.
5. Dar and Presley (2000) suggest several explanations for the tendency of Islamic banks to prefer to use modes of financing other than profit and loss–sharing (overwhelmingly *murābaḥah*).
6. IFSB-15 provides guidelines for the components of regulatory capital (Tier 1 and Tier 2). IFSB-15 also defines common equity as the Tier 1 core capital and preferred stock as the additional Tier 1 capital. Currently, the IFSB standard is the only international guideline to integrate Islamic contracting principles into the global financial system. A unified adoption of this standard would ensure that institutions offering Islamic financial products and services assign sufficient capital to cover the risk of the institution's Islamic operations.

References

Abedifar, P., S. Ebrahim, P. Molyneux, and A. Tarazi. 2015. "Islamic Banking and Finance: Recent Empirical Literature and Directions for Future Research." *Journal of Economic Surveys* 29 (4): 637–70.

Askari, H., Z. Iqbal, N. Krichene, and A. Mirakhor. 2010. *The Stability of Islamic Finance: Creating a Resilient Financial Environment for a Secure Future.* Singapore: John Wiley and Sons (Asia).

———. 2012. *Risk Sharing in Finance: The Islamic Finance Alternative.* Singapore: John Wiley and Sons (Asia).

Askari, H., and N. Krichene. 2014. "Islamic Finance: An Alternative Financial System for Stability, Equity, and Growth." *PSL Quarterly Review* 67 (268): 9–54.

Bankscope. 2014/2015. Database. https://bankscope.bvdinfo.com/version-2016114/home.serv?product=scope2006.

Chapra, M. U. 2011. "The Global Financial Crisis: Can Islamic Finance Help?" In *Islamic Economics and Finance: A European Perspective,* edited by J. Langton, C. Trullols, and A. Turkistani. London: Palgrave Macmillan.

Dar, H., and J. Presley. 2000. "Lack of Profit Loss Sharing in Islamic Banking: Management and Control Imbalances." *International Journal of Islamic Financial Services* 2 (2): 3–18.

Hassan, M., and J. Dridi. 2010. "The Effects of Global Crises on Islamic and Conventional Banks: A Comparative Study." IMF Working Paper WP/10/201, International Monetary Fund, Washington, DC.

IFSB (Islamic Financial Services Board). 2015. *Islamic Financial Services Industry Stability Report 2015.* Kuala Lumpur: IFSB.

———. 2016. *Islamic Financial Services Industry Stability Report 2016.* Kuala Lumpur: Islamic Financial Services Board.

Imam, P., and K. Kpodar. 2015. "Is Islamic Banking Good for Growth?" Working Paper WP/15/81, International Monetary Fund, Washington, DC; also presented at the inaugural World Bank-IDB-Guidance Financial Symposium on Islamic Finance, Istanbul, September 8–9.

IMF (International Monetary Fund). 1998. *World Economic Outlook: Financial Crises: Causes and Indicators.* Washington, DC: International Monetary Fund.

Iqbal, M., and P. Molyneux. 2005. *Thirty Years of Islamic Banking: History, Performance and Prospects*. New York: Palgrave Macmillan.

Kammer, A., M. Norat, M. Pinon, A. Prasad, C. M. Towe, and others. 2015. "Islamic Finance: Opportunities, Challenges, and Policy Options." IMF Staff Discussion Note SDN/15/05, International Monetary Fund, Washington, DC.

Mirakhor, Abbas, and Zamir Iqbal. 2012. "Financial Inclusion: Islamic Finance Perspective." *Journal of Islamic Business and Management* 2 (1): 35–64.

Sufian, F., M. A. Noor, and M. Zulkhibri. 2008. "The Efficiency of Islamic Banks: Empirical Evidence from the MENA and Asian Countries Islamic Banking Sectors." *Middle East Business and Economic Review* 20 (1): 1–19.

World Bank. 2008. *Finance for All? Policies and Pitfalls in Expanding Access*. World Bank Policy Research Report. Washington, DC: World Bank.

———. 2014. *Global Financial Development Report 2014: Financial Inclusion*. Washington, DC: World Bank.

World Bank-IDB-IRTI (World Bank, Islamic Development Bank, Islamic Research and Training Institute). 2015. *Leveraging Islamic Finance for Small and Medium Enterprises (SMEs)*. Washington, DC: World Bank.

Zarqa, A. 1980. "Islamic Economics: An Approach to Human Welfare." In *Studies in Islamic Economics*, edited by K. Ahmad. Leicester, U.K.: The Islamic Foundation.

Zulkhibri, M. 2016. "Financial Inclusion, Financial Inclusion Policy and Islamic Finance." IRTI Working Paper 1437-01, Islamic Research and Training Institute, Jeddah, Saudi Arabia.

4

Islamic Capital Markets

The purpose of capital markets is to facilitate long-term investment. The principles of Islamic finance promote risk sharing in lieu of risk transfer in conventional markets. The risk-sharing and equity participation principles of Islamic finance promote the long-term value of investments in real assets rather than the maximization of short-term profits. The ethical dimension of Islamic finance ensures the long-term sustainability of society. The main components of Islamic capital markets are equity markets and *sukūk* (asset-backed securitized Islamic products). This chapter evaluates the current state of the equity and *sukūk* markets and analyzes their role in fostering economic development with shared prosperity.

The Role of Capital Markets in Enhancing Shared Prosperity

A well-functioning capital market not only improves the capital allocation in the economy but also enhances productive growth. Islamic capital markets can make a significant contribution to achieving economic development and enhancing shared prosperity using the principles of risk sharing and equity participation. There is ample research supporting the contribution of the financial sector to economic development and its impact on income distribution. Levine (1997, 2005) clearly demonstrates that financial development produces faster average growth. Pagano (1993); King and Levine (1993); Bekaert and Harvey (1997); and Beck, Demirgüç-Kunt, and Levine (2007) emphasize the importance of capital markets development on the path of economic growth. Similarly, Agarwal and Mohtadi (2004) find that stock market development is positively associated with economic growth. Pradhan and others (2014) investigate the linkages between stock market development, bank development, and economic growth and find that stock market development is an important ingredient of growth.

It is well documented that when risk is spread among a large number of participants through an efficient capital market, closer coordination between the financial and real sector is promoted, as well as better sharing of the benefits of economic growth and greater stability for the financial system. By contrast, risk transfers through debt instruments, along with higher leverage, weaken the link between the financial and real sector, thus posing a threat to financial stability. The growth of pure financial assets can outpace the growth of the real sector, a phenomenon known as decoupling (Menkoff and Tolksdorf 2001) or financialization (Epstein 2006; Palley 2007), whereby economic growth is no longer anchored with growth of the real sector. Excessive financialization of assets may result in bubbles (Parenteau 2005). All too often, financial sector crises have required large government interventions and massive bailouts. Thus while private financiers enjoy the gains of robust pure financial innovations, which ultimately lead to decoupling, the society at large suffers the pain of saving the real sector from the vagaries of financial sector crises.

Efficient risk sharing requires that economic risks are allocated among participants in accordance with their respective degree of risk tolerance (Mirakhor 2010).[1] Efficient capital markets allow risky investments to be matched with those investors who have the appetite for risk taking in the expectation of better returns. The alignment of risk taking with the expected returns of investment enhances risk-sharing opportunities, improves the dissemination of information, lowers the cost of mobilizing funds, facilitates investments in the most productive technologies, and enhances the efficient allocation of capital (Levine and Zervos 1998; Agarwal and Mohtadi 2004). Furthermore, liquidity in capital markets encourages firms to invest in long-term and more productive projects. This higher productivity raises the return on the investment and encourages more saving and investment in physical capital, which lead to faster economic growth.

What makes the Islamic capital market different from the conventional capital market is the ethical dimension, which focuses on the long-term sustainability of society, and its principles of risk sharing (dispersion of ownership) and avoidance of excessive leverage and speculation. Figure 4.1 depicts the mechanism of an Islamic stock market based on respect for core values. Economic and social justice, the spirit of solidarity, and intergenerational respect supersede the market structure. Organizations that are socially and ethically responsible can raise funds in this market on the basis of sharing both risk and reward. In the absence of

FIGURE 4.1 The Values-Driven Structure of the Islamic Capital Market

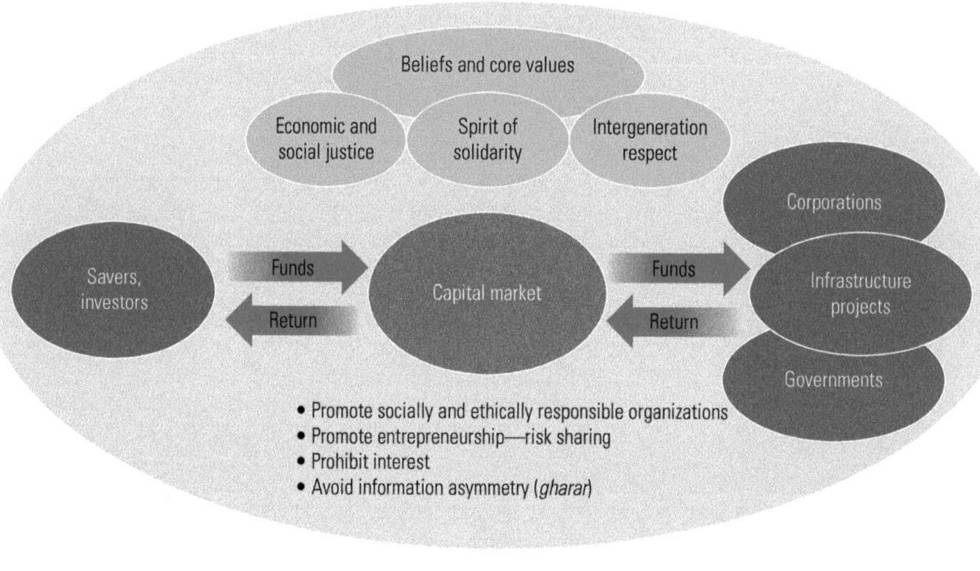

interest and speculation, the possible return is based purely on the underlying economic activity. The Islamic principles of finance thus help in the allocation of more resources to the real sector of the economy, create more job opportunities, and ultimately distribute wealth more equitably.

Equity-based investment is well established in the world of Islamic finance. Investment in instruments such as common stocks and *sukūk* is permissible in those companies that are not engaged in businesses such as gambling or production or trade in prohibited items like alcohol or pork (*harām*), and those that are engaged in socially irresponsible activities (usually referred to as sin stocks). Although investment in stocks is permitted, many of the practices associated with stock trading are not. Speculation through derivative positions and short selling are some of the practices not allowed under *shari'ah* principles (Naughton and Naughton 2000). The main distinction between the conventional and Islamic capital market is the lower leverage and the absence of speculative behavior promoted by short selling and derivative trading.

Sukūk are one of the two pillars of Islamic capital markets. Instead of conventional bonds that are based on a debt contract, *sukūk* are based on risk-sharing contracts backed by real underlying assets, such as asset-backed securitization. The aim for *sukūk* is to develop innovative assets and distribute income from entrepreneurial activities funded by the *sukūk* (Jobst 2007).

In summary, equity-based financing and asset-backed securitization have a positive impact on economic growth. The absence of leverage in a risk-sharing framework will lower riskiness and risk premiums on financial assets such as stocks and *sukūk*. This will support shared prosperity. The risk-sharing framework links the financial sector to the real sector. Thus the risk premium on financial assets directly reflects the riskiness of the real sector. The stock market will have low correlation with the rest of the world, which makes it a good alternative for foreign investors looking to diversify their portfolio. It facilitates capital inflows, which lower the cost of capital and support economic growth. It does all this in a way that does not increase risk—unlike debt-based speculative capital.

Current Status of Islamic Capital Markets

Despite the extraordinary growth of the Islamic banking industry, there is a great need for vibrant and efficient capital markets in the area of Islamic finance. The Islamic capital market is underdeveloped—which is not surprising, because Islamic finance is a relatively new industry.

There is no organized stock exchange dedicated to trading in equities that are compliant with the Islamic investment principles. Organized markets for conventional stocks exist in a number of member-countries of the Organisation of Islamic Cooperation (OIC), and some are quite mature, as in Indonesia, Malaysia, Pakistan, and Saudi Arabia. However, growth in market capitalization does not necessarily contribute to economic development or the more equitable distribution of wealth (Ali 2005, 2013). Figure 4.2 shows the relationship between capital formation (gross domestic investment) and market capitalization.

As the figure shows, market capitalization does not translate into capital formation in any income group, including the high-income countries. However, there is a stark difference between the low-income and higher-income groups of countries. For low-income countries, no relationship between market capitalization and capital formation seems to exist, which suggests either the nonexistence or lower depth of the stock market. Other factors may also be at play. Investors may voluntarily exclude themselves because of their conservative nature (their risk aversion to the speculative nature of markets). Or they may stay out of the market because of their faith, especially in countries where a majority of the population is Muslim. This factor is evident in the figures depicting the OIC member-countries. The only exception is the OIC high-income group—and even here, capital formation remains well below the market capitalization ratio. Interestingly, peaks in

FIGURE 4.2 Market Capitalization versus Capital Formation in OIC and Non-OIC Member Countries by Income Group

Ratios

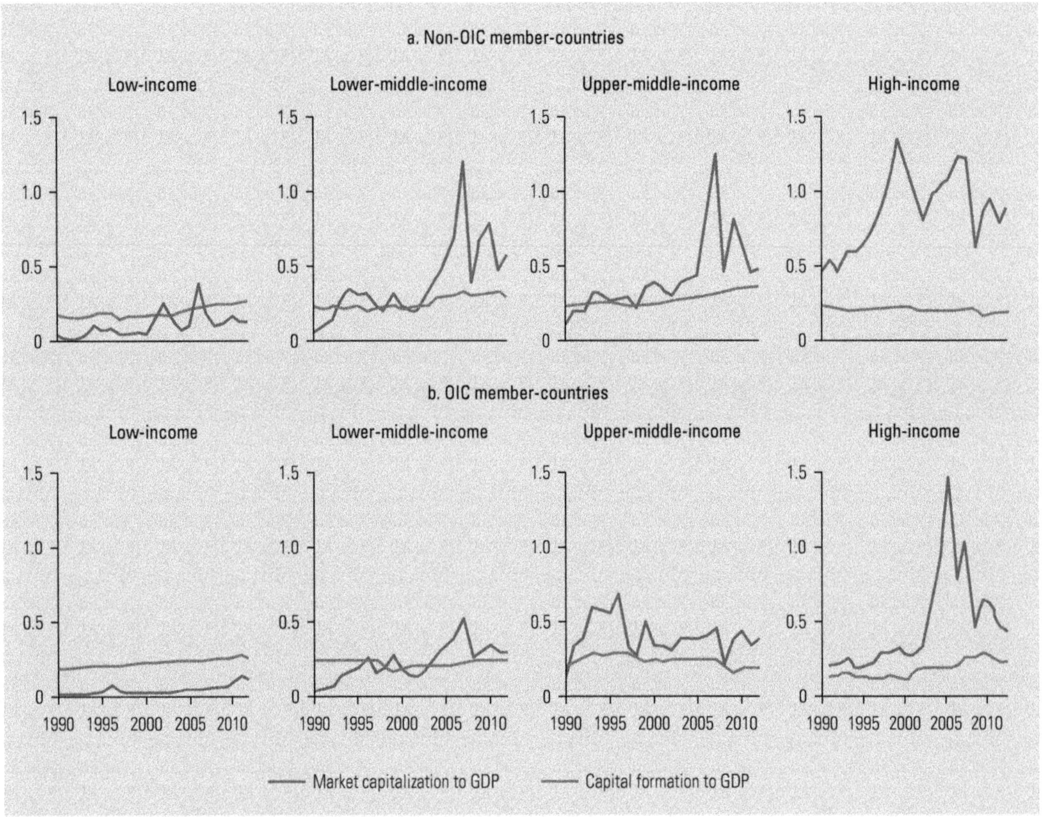

Source: World Bank, World Development Indicators (database).
Note: OIC = Organisation of Islamic Cooperation.

the market capitalization ratio for the non-OIC member-country groups coincide with the formation of bubbles in those markets, especially before the onset of the global financial crisis in 2008.

In summary, stock markets in their current form contribute relatively less to economic development than their potential and expectations because of the speculative nature of these markets. The rise in speculation in recent years has been the result of easy access to leverage in a very low interest-rate environment, and has led to the formation of asset bubbles. If the capital markets are to play any role in economic development, there is a need for a comprehensive policy initiative covering both regulatory and governance mechanisms to curb the speculative behavior in those markets. Al-Masri (2007) highlights the difference between speculation and investment in stock markets and suggests that although speculators in the market provide liquidity and depth to the market, by trading stocks or futures without actually possessing those assets at any point in time, they ultimately increase speculation in those markets.

Risk-Return Analysis of Main *Shari'ah* Indexes

Whether to invest in equity stocks through stock markets is a matter of heated debate among Muslim scholars. On the one hand, some believe that investment in the stock market encourages speculation among market participants, which is not a permissible activity, since the outcome of speculation is similar to that of gambling (Taj El-Din 2009). On the other hand, most scholars consider investment through stock markets to be permissible, based on the view that shareholders are similar to the partners in a partnership firm (Naughton and Naughton 2000). However, these scholars endorse only long-term investment, in which an investor seeks dividend income or long-term gains by investing in shares of those companies with sound management, a good business model, positive future growth potentials, and *shari'ah*-compliant business activities.

Any investor in the Islamic equity market invests in the shares of *shari'ah*-compliant companies[2] or in a publicly offered portfolio consisting of these equities offered through unit trusts, mutual funds, or exchange traded funds (ETFs). Measuring the performance of fund managers is one of the major challenges for investors in Islamic capital markets. To meet this need, all the major index providers—the Financial Times Stock Exchange (FTSE), Standard & Poor's (S&P), Dow Jones, and Morgan Stanley Capital International (MSCI)—now build and provide Islamic equity index (IEI) data based on independent *shari'ah* screening criteria at the global, regional, and country level. Each of these index providers follows slightly different screening criteria for including equities in IEIs, based on the interpretation of the *shari'ah* board.[3]

To avoid unnecessary confusion, this Report uses *shari'ah* screening standards for performance comparison only as proposed by S&P.[4] Since the scope of this Report is global, this chapter provides a detailed analysis of the global and regional index performance. Figure 4.3 compares the performance of S&P *shari'ah*-compliant indexes with that of the conventional indexes. Panel a compares the performance of the S&P Global 1200 with that of the *shari'ah*-compliant version of the same index, titled S&P Global 1200 Shariah. The performance of the *shari'ah*-compliant index was superior over the entire period. However, a similar comparison of the S&P/OIC COMCEC 50 Shariah index,[5] as shown in panel b, reveals that the performance of the *shari'ah*-compliant index was quite similar to the index for the 50 biggest listed companies in OIC member-states, as measured by the S&P Frontier Broader Market Index (BMI).

Figure 4.4 provides a similar analysis on the regional level for the S&P indexes. The *shari'ah*-compliant indexes usually outperform the conventional indexes for developed markets in the United States, Europe, and Asia. However, for the Pan Arab Region with a majority Muslim population, the *shari'ah*-compliant index lags behind the conventional index. This can be attributed to the fact that in developed markets, *shari'ah* screening filters out financial sector companies, resulting in a lean portfolio with lower financial risk. Since most of the listed Islamic banks are in the Pan Arab Region, the performance of the *shari'ah*-compliant index is not very different from that of the conventional index.

Figure 4.5 provides the sectoral breakdown of conventional indexes versus *shari'ah*-compliant S&P indexes. One of the important differences between the indexes is the absence of the financial sector from the IEIs. The information technology (IT) sector dominates the IEIs globally and in the developed markets of the United States and Japan. The proportion of financial sector firms is similar in the Islamic index and the conventional index for the Pan Arab Region, suggesting the presence of a strong Islamic banking sector. The sectoral breakdown further confirms the assertion that the diversification of the IEIs and the conventional indexes are similar, even though a major portion of equities have been screened from the Islamic index.

Table 4.1 reports the return on risk of S&P conventional and *shari'ah* indexes. In terms of excess return, it is evident that *shari'ah*-compliant indexes outperform their benchmark, with the exception of the indexes for the OIC countries and the United States. For other indicators, higher correlation, lower tracking error, and positive information ratios clearly indicate that investors in Islamic equities do not have to sacrifice return to reap the benefits of adhering to their faith. Although not reported here, a comparison of performance based on the MSCI standard was made following a book value of equity approach. No significant difference was found between

FIGURE 4.3 Relative Performance of Conventional versus *Shari'ah*-Compliant Stocks, Global Indexes

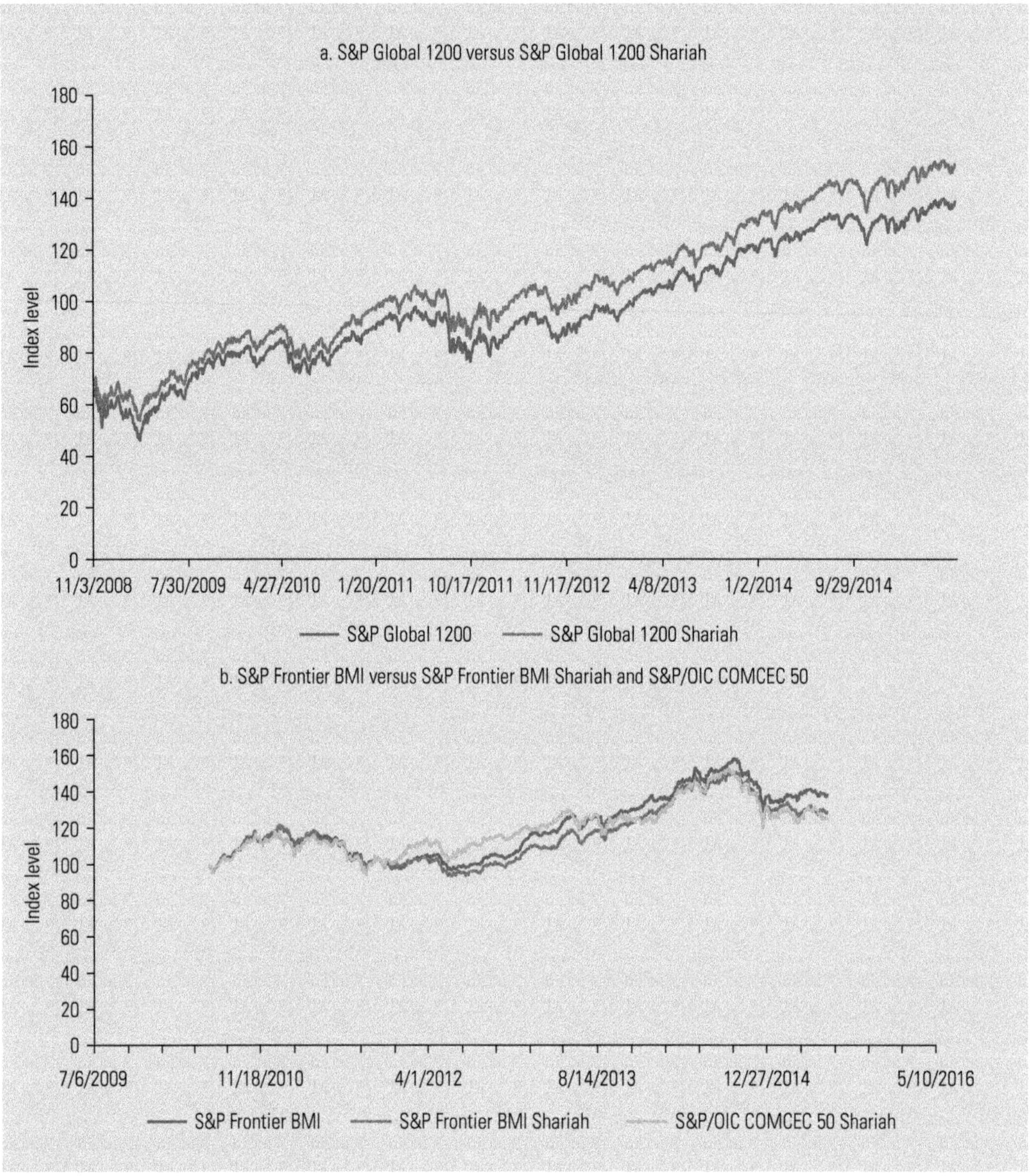

Source: S&P Dow Jones Indexes, http://eu.spindices.com/.
Note: BMI = Broader Market Index; COMCEC = Committee for Economic and Commerical Cooperation of the OIC; OIC = Organisation of Islamic Cooperation; S&P = Standard & Poor's.

shari'ah-compliant S&P indexes and the conventional S&P indexes on the global scale or in the developed markets of the United States and Europe. The similar performance pattern suggests that different *shari'ah* screening standards only add confusion for investors. This further suggests that policy makers and *shari'ah* scholars need to closely work and align these standards to provide a single benchmark to measure performance, to avoid confusing the investing public. A good example is the revision of *shari'ah* screening standards released by the Malaysia Securities Commission in November 2013.

FIGURE 4.4 **Relative Performance of Conventional versus *Shari'ah*-Compliant Stocks, Regional Indexes**

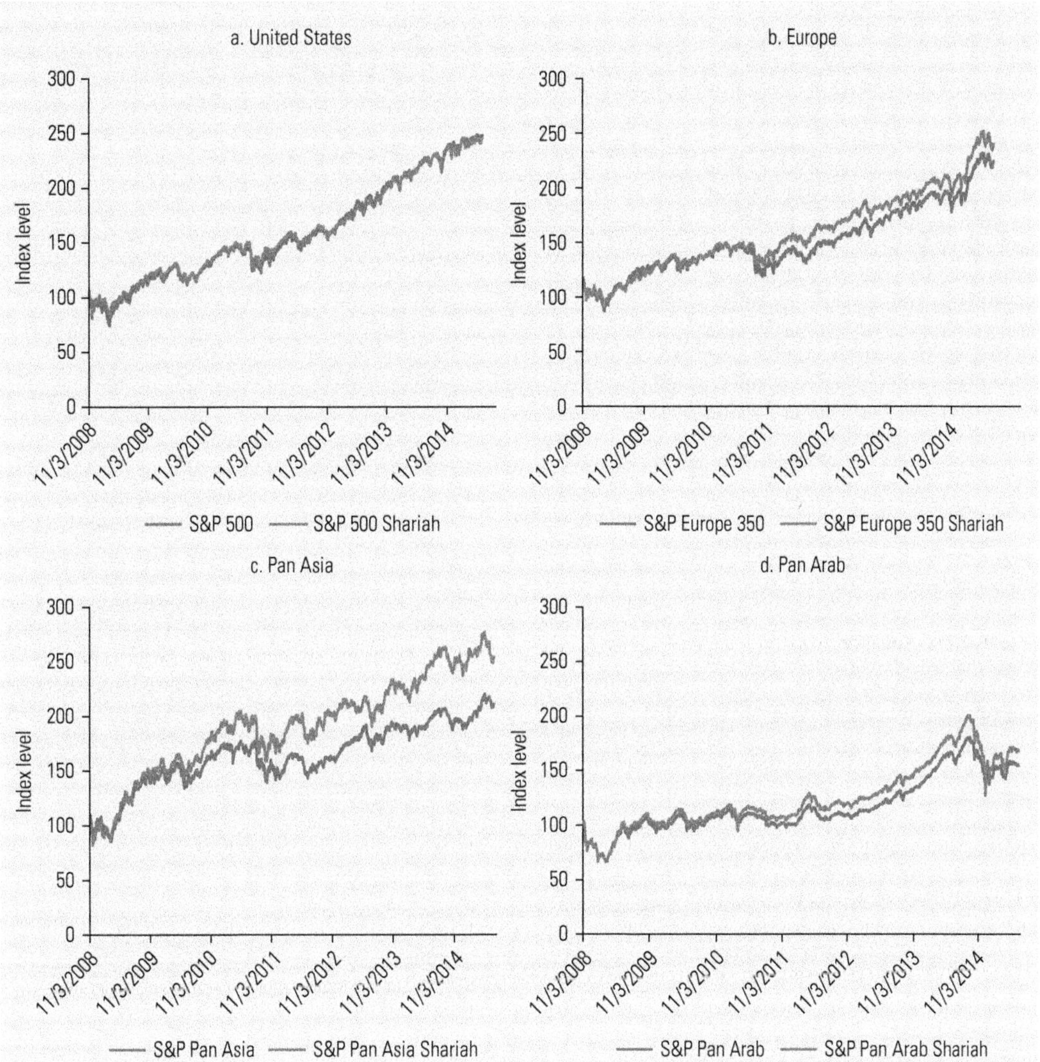

Source: S&P Dow Jones Indexes (http://eu.spindices.com/).
Note: S&P = Standard & Poor's.

In summary, the investors in a passive *shari'ah*-compliant portfolio do not lose in terms of diversification or returns, whether on a nominal or risk-adjusted basis. The performance of *shari'ah*-compliant portfolios is at least as good as the performance of more diversified portfolios with higher financial and lower operating leverage. Since the Islamic portfolio represents shares of those companies in the real sector, it thus helps create more jobs and distribute wealth more equitably.

The Status and Contribution of the Asset-Based Securities (*Sukūk*) Market to Economic Development with Shared Prosperity

Global Trends in *Sukūk*

Sukūk products have been used to raise funds for businesses, support economic development, provide government financing, and manage liquidity in financial institutions. Because they are different from stocks and

FIGURE 4.5 Breakdown by Sector of Major Conventional and *Shari'ah*-Compliant Indexes

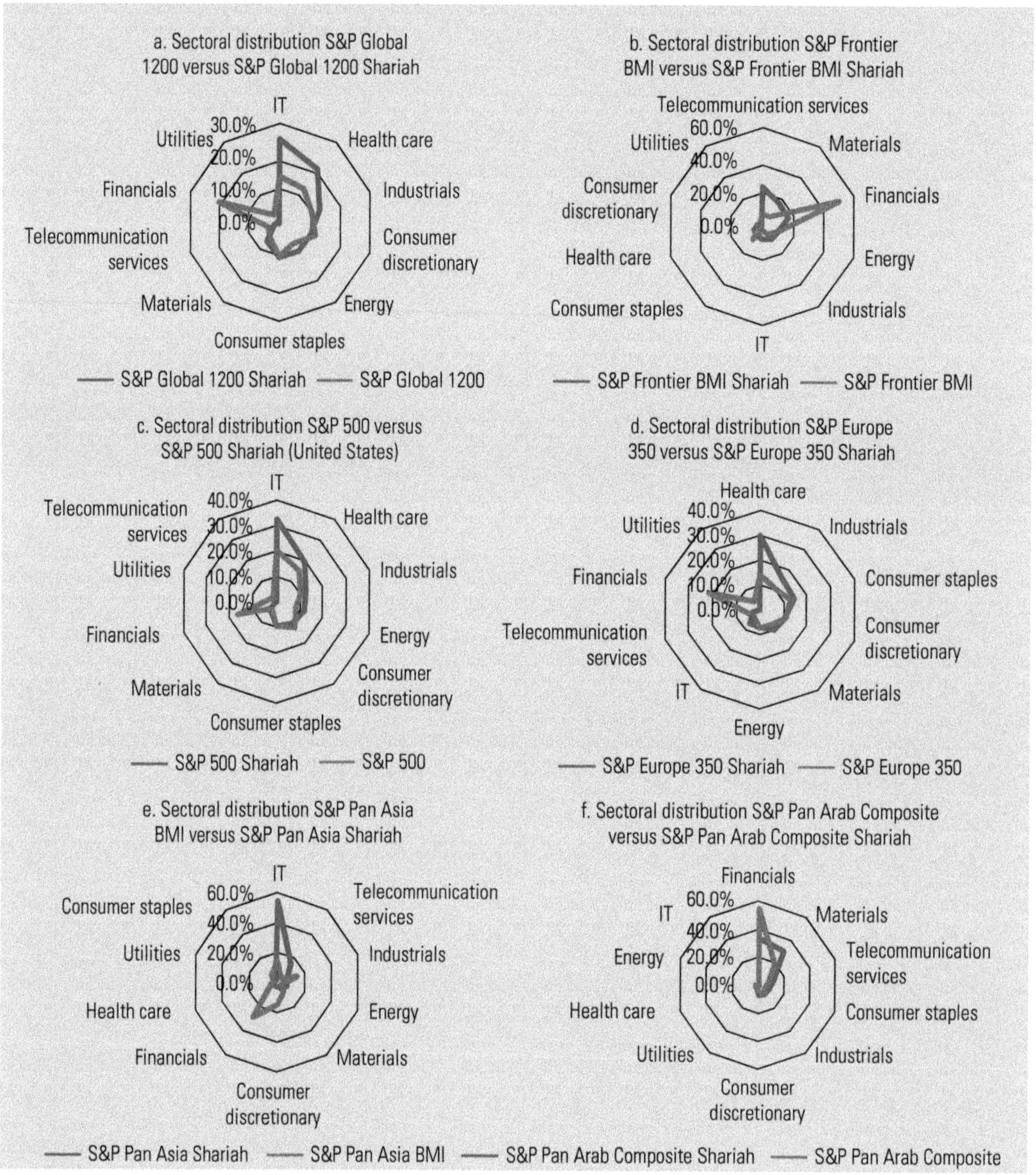

Source: S&P Dow Jones Index Website, various fact sheets as of May 31, 2015.
Note: BMI = Broader Market Index; IT = information technology; S&P = Standard & Poor's.

can be adjusted to various contractual forms and structures, they suit the needs of both the investors and seekers of funds. *Sukūk* have been growing globally since the debut of the first global *sukūk* in 2001. In 2014 alone, *sukūk* issues totaled $133.26 billion from 22 domicile countries. Of the 826 issues, 54 were international and 772 were domestic. The total *sukūk* outstanding was $310.95 billion as of year-end 2014. Table 4.2 presents summary statistics; figure 4.6 provides a breakdown of *sukūk* issuance by currency from 2001 to 2014. The U.S. dollar-denominated *sukūk* have been growing, but *sukūk* denominated in Malaysian ringgit (RM) are growing even faster and dominate the market.

TABLE 4.1 Measures of Selected *Shari'ah*-Compliant Indexes and Benchmark Indexes for Various Holding Periods

Indexes	Variables	5 years	4 years	3 years	2 years	1 year
S&P Global 1200	Excess return (%)	0.44	0.58	−0.30	0.52	0.61
	Tracking error (%)	2.23	2.18	1.87	1.83	1.64
	Information ratio	0.20	0.27	−0.16	0.28	0.37
	Correlation	0.99	0.99	0.99	0.99	0.99
S&P 500	Excess return (%)	−0.65	−0.36	−0.94	0.37	−0.47
	Tracking error (%)	2.07	1.91	1.68	1.64	1.63
	Information ratio	−0.31	−0.19	−0.56	0.23	−0.29
	Correlation	0.99	0.99	0.99	0.99	0.99
S&P Europe 350	Excess return (%)	1.15	1.99	−0.28	−1.00	2.33
	Tracking error (%)	4.99	4.74	3.91	3.60	3.23
	Information ratio	0.23	0.42	−0.07	−0.28	0.72
	Correlation	0.96	0.96	0.96	0.97	0.98
S&P/OIC COMCEC 50 Shariah	Excess return (%)	−1.63	−0.99	−4.49	−4.51	−2.97
	Tracking error (%)	8.22	8.43	8.63	9.68	9.14
	Information ratio	−0.20	−0.12	−0.52	−0.47	−0.32
	Correlation	0.70	0.69	0.63	0.61	0.70
S&P Pan Asia	Excess return (%)	4.17	3.91	2.14	2.39	2.24
	Tracking error (%)	8.15	8.76	8.68	9.14	7.06
	Information ratio	0.51	0.45	0.25	0.26	0.32
	Correlation	0.88	0.85	0.77	0.73	0.83
S&P Pan Arab	Excess return (%)	0.62	0.97	−0.01	−1.05	−0.76
	Tracking error (%)	2.90	3.00	3.13	3.37	4.02
	Information ratio	0.21	0.32	0.00	−0.31	−0.19
	Correlation	0.98	0.98	0.98	0.99	0.99

Source: S&P Dow Jones Indexes, http://eu.spindices.com/.
Notes: Excess return reflects the excess return of the *shari'ah* index over the conventional index. *Tracking error* is the standard deviation of the excess return. *Information ratio* is the ratio of excess return to the tracking error. *Correlation* measures the correlation between the *shari'ah*-compliant index and its conventional benchmark index.

TABLE 4.2 Status of *Sukūk* as of December 31, 2014

Status	Amount ($ billion)
Announced	71.16
Defaulted	1.71
Redeemed early	13.83
Outstanding	310.95
Redeemed	451.57
Restructured	103.97
Total	953.11

Source: Islamic Research and Training Institute (IRTI) calculations based on IFIS (Islamic Finance Information Service) data.

In the first half of 2015, 302 *sukūk* were issued, amounting to $36.845 billion.[6]

After dipping slightly in 2008 in the aftermath of the global financial crisis, *sukūk* issuance has risen and has surpassed the precrisis amounts. *Sukūk* issuance peaked in 2012 at $218.3 billion. In 2013 and 2014, issuance declined (see figure 4.6). However, the market is gaining strength and getting established; during the same period, some very large-size *sukūk* were issued. The total issuance per year for the last four years has been well above $100 billion—a level

FIGURE 4.6 ***Sukūk* Issuance, 2001–14**

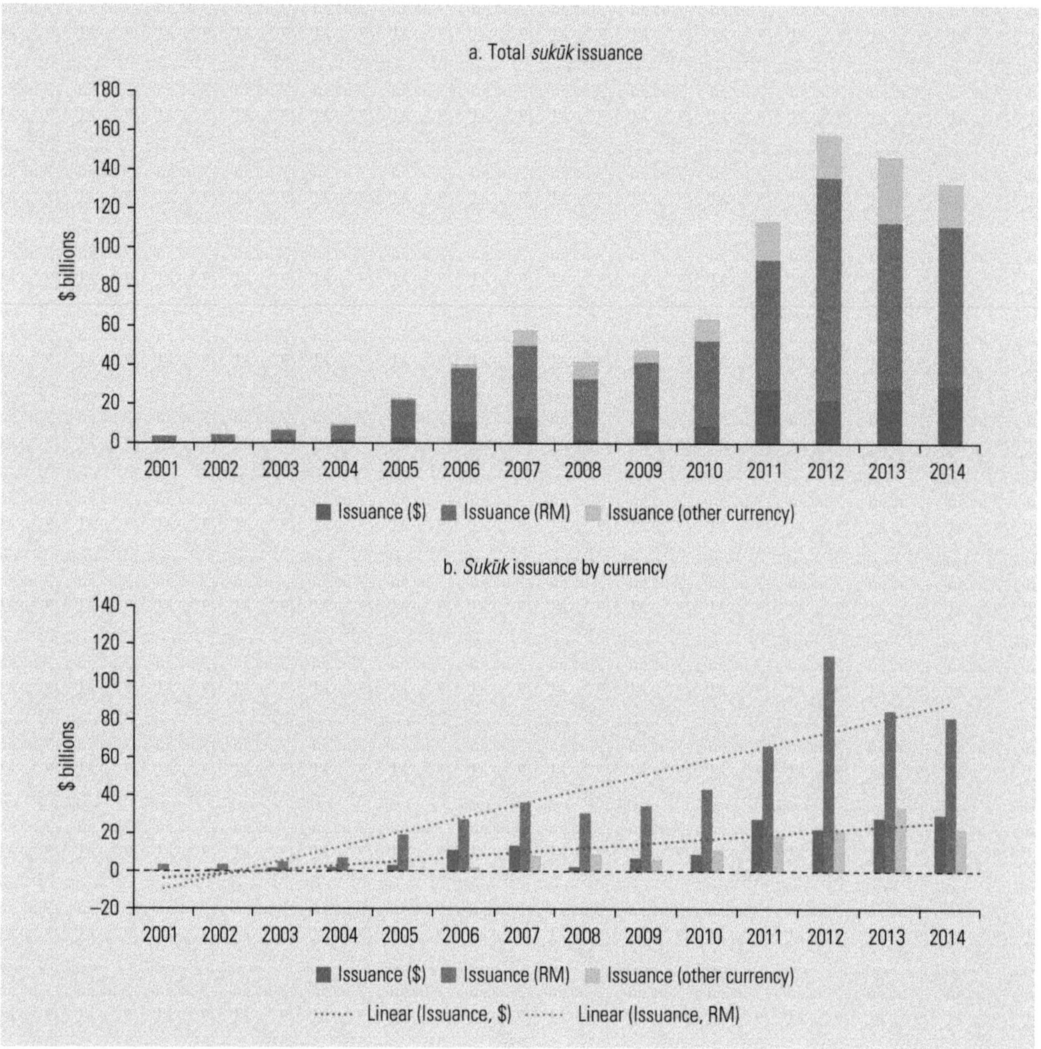

Source: IRTI calculations based on IFIS data.
Note: RM = Malaysian ringgit.

that was not anticipated after the global financial crisis.

Regional Analysis

A regional analysis using four major regions—Asia, the Middle East and North Africa (MENA), Africa,[7] and Europe and North America (Europe/NA)—shows that the bulk of the market is dominated by Asia, followed by the MENA Region (table 4.3). Within Asia, Malaysia has been dominating the *sukūk* issuance market. The cumulative amount and percentage of *sukūk* issued from 2001 to 2014 was $639.9 billion (75 percent) in Asia, compared to $108 billion (13 percent) in MENA, $91 billion (11 percent) in the Europe/NA Region, and about $10.75 billion (1 percent) in Africa (see figure 4.7, panels a and b). The pattern of *sukūk* amounts outstanding is similar across the regions (see panel c).

In 2014 and 2015, several new jurisdictions progressed toward issuing *sukūk*, particularly

TABLE 4.3 **Status of *Sukūk* by Region, 2001–14**

a. Amount ($ billion)

Status	Asia	MENA	Europe/NA	Africa	Others
Announced	34.56	22.68	7.37	6.05	0.50
Defaulted	0.70	0.65	0.37	—	—
Redeemed early	6.08	4.29	3.46	—	—
Outstanding	207.89	42.60	57.31	3.14	—
Redeemed	390.65	37.76	21.57	1.59	—
Restructured	0.02	0.10	0.92	—	—
Total (regional)	639.90	108.09	91.00	10.78	0.50

b. Number of issuances

Status	Asia	MENA	Europe/NA	Africa	Others	Total
Announced	39	25	16	7	1	88
Defaulted	46	1	2	0	0	49
Redeemed early	135	4	5	0	0	144
Outstanding	2,030	70	108	62	0	2,270
Redeemed	5,396	264	54	378	0	6,092
Restructured	1	1	1	0	0	3
Total	7,647	365	186	447	1	8,646

Source: IRTI calculations based on IFIS data.
Note: Europe/NA = Europe and North America; MENA = Middle East and North Africa; — = not available.

in Africa. Some huge *sukūk* at the sovereign and quasi-sovereign levels were launched in MENA and Asia. These include the following:

- Saudi Aviation *sukūk* of $7.7 billion to purchase 50 Airbus aircraft.
- Saudi Aramco SADARA Basic Service Company *sukūk* to fund construction of a chemicals and plastics complex (Saudi Arabian riyal-denominated, totaling $2 billion).
- Malaysia Trust Certificates (*sukūk*) of $1 billion with a 10-year maturity and $500 million with a 30-year maturity. These were long-term *sukūk,* and all of them were oversubscribed.
- The Islamic Development Bank (IDB) has announced expansion of its Medium-Term *Sukūk* Program from $10 billion to $25 billion, and plans to issue at least one *sukūk* publicly each year with a minimum size of $1 billion.

Several Islamic financial institutions (IFIs) have issued perpetual *sukūk* to create a risk-absorbing capital buffer and to use as high-quality liquid assets to meet the capital requirement of the Basel III accord. While this does not promote shared prosperity directly, it does so indirectly by strengthening IFIs, helping them manage their risks, and supporting a continuity of their own business operations that ultimately support the operations of the businesses they invest in.

Despite these developments, more innovation on the *fiqh* and *shari'ah* regulatory side is needed to expand the horizon of *sukūk* and provide refinements to the structuring and operational practices. Nonetheless, every new *sukūk* structure and issuance must undergo evaluation and be endorsed for *shari'ah* compliance. Thus some degree of innovation and changes in practices are taking place.

FIGURE 4.7 Cumulative Issuance of *Sukūk*, 2001–14

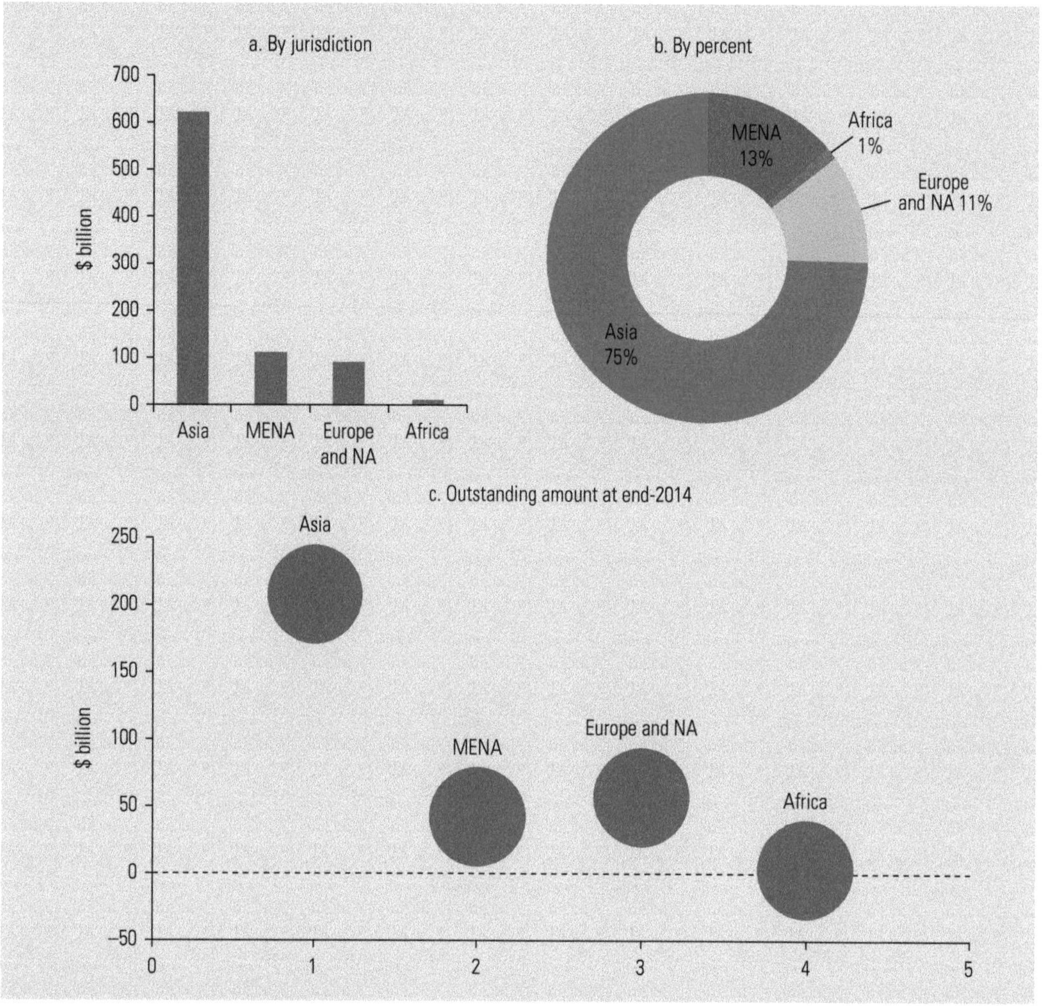

Source: IRTI calculations based on IFIS data.
Note: MENA = Middle East and North Africa; NA = North America.

A Framework for and Analysis of the Contribution of *Sukūk* to Shared Prosperity

Knowing whether *sukūk* are actually contributing to the socioeconomic development and shared prosperity, and if so, by how much, are difficult tasks. However, some informed assessment of *sukūk*'s contribution can be made at the macro level by analyzing various dimensions and compositions of *sukūk*. That is the focus of this section.

The proportion of sovereign *sukūk* in the total issuance compared to the proportion of corporate *sukūk* issuance can reflect the extent of public versus private benefits generated in the economy. However, assuming that the private sector is more efficient than the public sector, the breakdown of sovereign versus corporate issuances can represent different levels of effectiveness in their economic impact. In this regard, both the size and the number of issuances can be analyzed. The average size of the *sukūk* and the long-term versus short-term maturity can also shed light on the possible economic impact over time. The intended use of the funds and the nature of projects and economic subsectors they will support also matter for their impact on the economic development of a country or a region. Since various economic sectors differ in terms of factor intensity, the choice of sector can also have varying implications for job creation and employment generation. *Sukūk* that support the development of infrastructure projects can have long-term and economy-wide impact, compared to general-purpose *sukūk*. Similarly, the accessibility of diversified kinds of investors, including the general public, to *sukūk* purchases has implications for generating savings and channeling them for productive use. The retail-denominated *sukūk* units can diffuse the benefits of *sukūk* more quickly, compared to the large unit value *sukūk* targeting only institutional investors. Moreover, diversifying the investor base by also attracting the retail investors can help in creating an active secondary market in *sukūk*. The more diverse the investor base, the more likely their investment holding horizon will be asynchronous and hence the more likely the *sukūk* will change hands during the maturity period, creating a liquid market. All these comparisons and judgments mentioned are only heuristic because many other factors at the implementation stage, as well as the finer details of the *sukūk* structure, matter for the attainment of economic impact and the sharing of prosperity. Nonetheless, the various ratios and proportions-based criteria can help gauge the direction of the development of the *sukūk* market.

Sovereign versus Corporate Issuance

Sovereign issuers dominate the market in terms of the amounts, number, and average size of *sukūk*. In 2013, 2014, and the first half of 2015, the total amount of sovereign issuance was much higher than the total corporate issuance (see figure 4.8, panel a). The number of sovereign issues was lower than corporate issues in 2013, but the situation reversed with a higher proportion of sovereign issues in 2014. The trend continued in the first half of 2015 (panel b). Despite this, the average size per issue of sovereign *sukūk* had been higher than the average size of corporate *sukūk* (panel c). Overall, corporate *sukūk* issuance remained higher from 2001 to 2014; however, sovereign issues dominated the market in terms of size during the same time period (panel d).

Since the motivations of the government as an economic agent are more social as compared to the motivations and decision-making criteria of other economic agents such as private sector businesses, sovereign *sukūk* are expected to generate wider socioeconomic impacts through the provision of public goods and services, as well as infrastructure development. Sovereign issuance also has positive implications for the development of the *sukūk* market by providing confidence and assurances of the continuity of the market development policies. However, if the *sukūk* mechanism is used by governments simply to finance their current expenditures, then sovereign issuance can contribute to financial repression and crowding out of private investment.

Maturity Structure

The maturity structure of the *sukūk* instruments is presented in figure 4.9. Short-term *sukūk* with tenure of one year or less are the dominant kind, both in the number and in the total amount per year (panel a). These are mostly based on commodity *murābaḥah* or *ʿīnah* sale or *tawarruq* transactions,[8] and commonly are used either for liquidity management by financial institutions or for provision of short-term finance. The trend to issue very short-term *sukūk* of three months or less is increasing. Long-term *sukūk* with a maturity of 10 or more years have been declining and are relatively rare. Medium-term *sukūk* with maturities between 3 to 5 years and 5 to 7 years occupy a middle ground but are increasing (panel b).

Sukūk by Type of Contractual Structure

Murābaḥah-based *sukūk* account for 38 percent of the cumulative amount of *sukūk* issued from 2001 to 2014, followed by *ijārah* at 15 percent and *Bai Bi-Thaman Ajil* at 12 percent (figure 4.10). A disadvantage of

FIGURE 4.8 Characteristics of the *Sukūk* Market

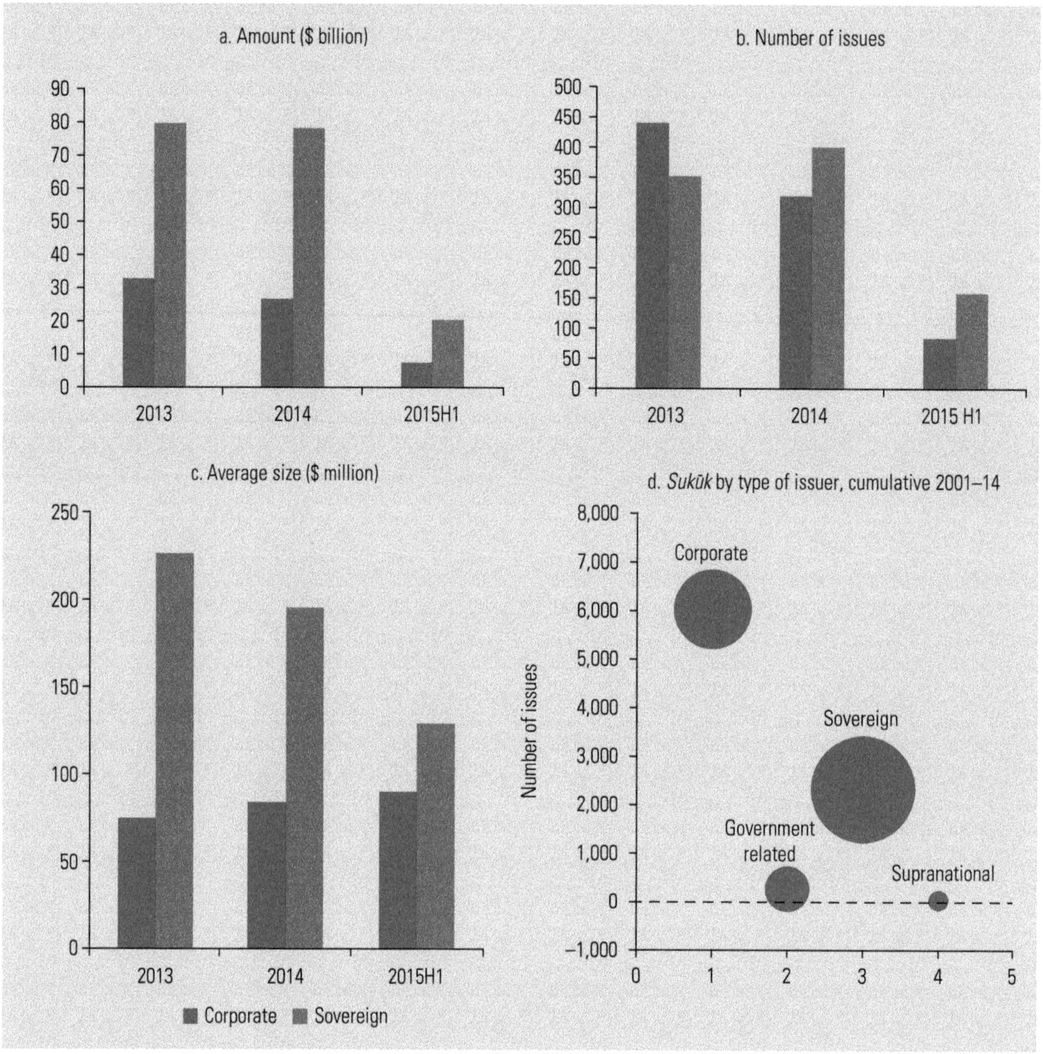

Source: IRTI based on data from Zawya data and IFIS.
Note: 2015H1 = first half of 2015.

murābaḥah sukūk is that they are not tradable in the secondary market;[9] this reduces their potential to change and diversify ownership through secondary trades and lowers the potential for shared prosperity. Moreover, a large proportion of these *murābaḥah sukūk* are issued only to manage liquidity. Hence, they do not directly contribute to economic development; they contribute only indirectly, by strengthening IFIs.

The composition of the types of contractual structure used in *sukūk* has kept changing since 2001. In recent years, the most commonly used structure has been *ijṣrah* (43 percent). This has been followed by *wakālah* (34 percent), which are becoming more prominent (see table 4.4). *Murābaḥah* constituted a smaller proportion (13 percent) in 2013–14. Factors for these changes include *shari'ah* rulings and revisions in the standards issued by the Accounting and Auditing Organization for Islamic Financial Institutions (AAOIFI). However, the main drivers of change have

FIGURE 4.9 **Maturity Structure of *Sukūk* Instruments**

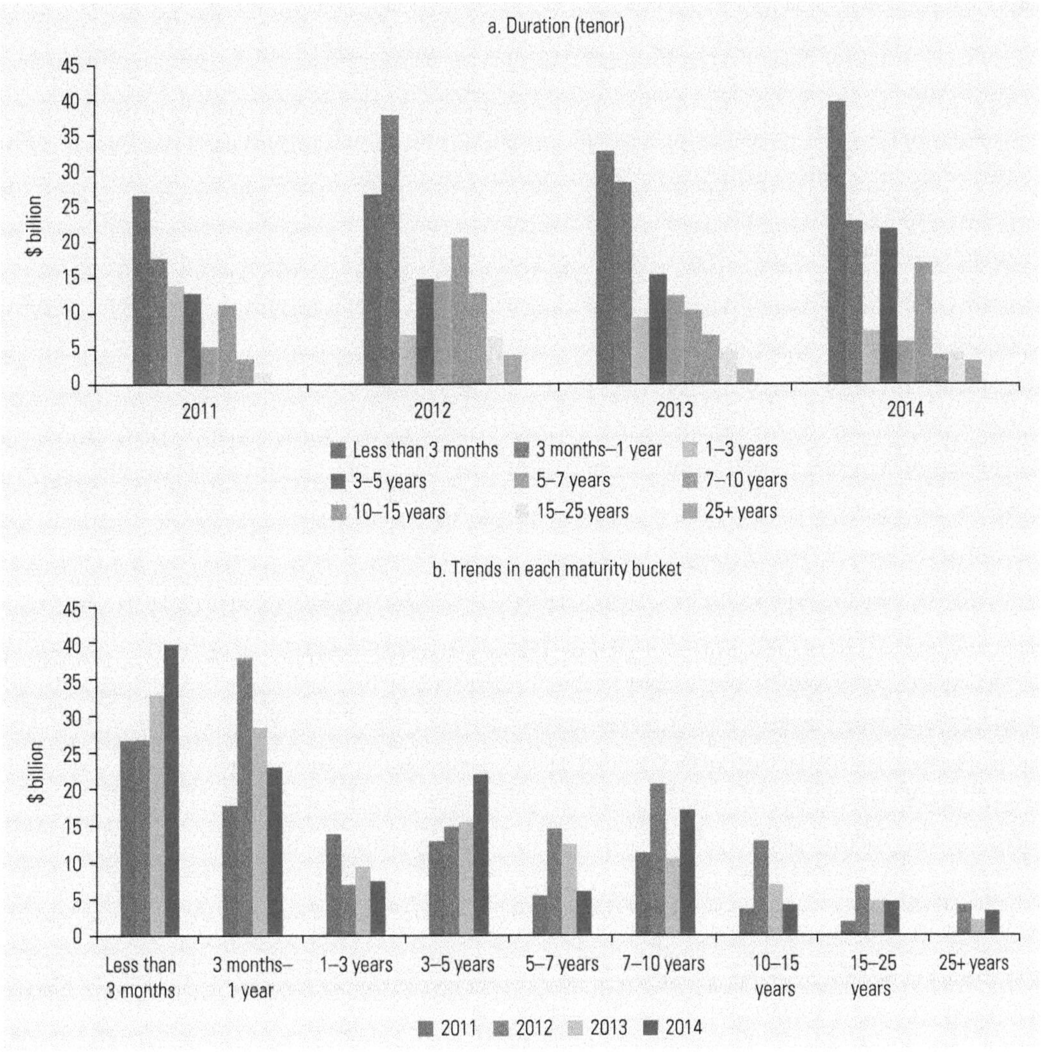

Source: IRTI based on IFIS data.

been issuers' quest to issue *sukūk* without the requirement of qualifying assets, and investors' demand for secured returns.

Sukūk Issuance by Sector

Sovereign *sukūk* had a larger share of the market (58 percent) than private *sukūk* (42 percent) from 2001 to 2014 (figure 4.11, panel a). For private *sukūk*, the largest share of the total cumulative *sukūk* issuance has been for the financial sector (12 percent), followed by real estate (7 percent), energy (5 percent), transport (5 percent), industrial manufacturing (4 percent), utilities (3 percent), telecommunication (2 percent), water and power (2 percent), and services (2 percent) (panel b). Issues for agriculture, food, health care, education, and other sectors have been very small. This was the case from 2001 to 2014. In recent years, the share of sovereign issuance and the share of issuance for the financial sector have increased, while issuance for other private nonfinancial

FIGURE 4.10 *Sukūk* by Structure, 2001–14

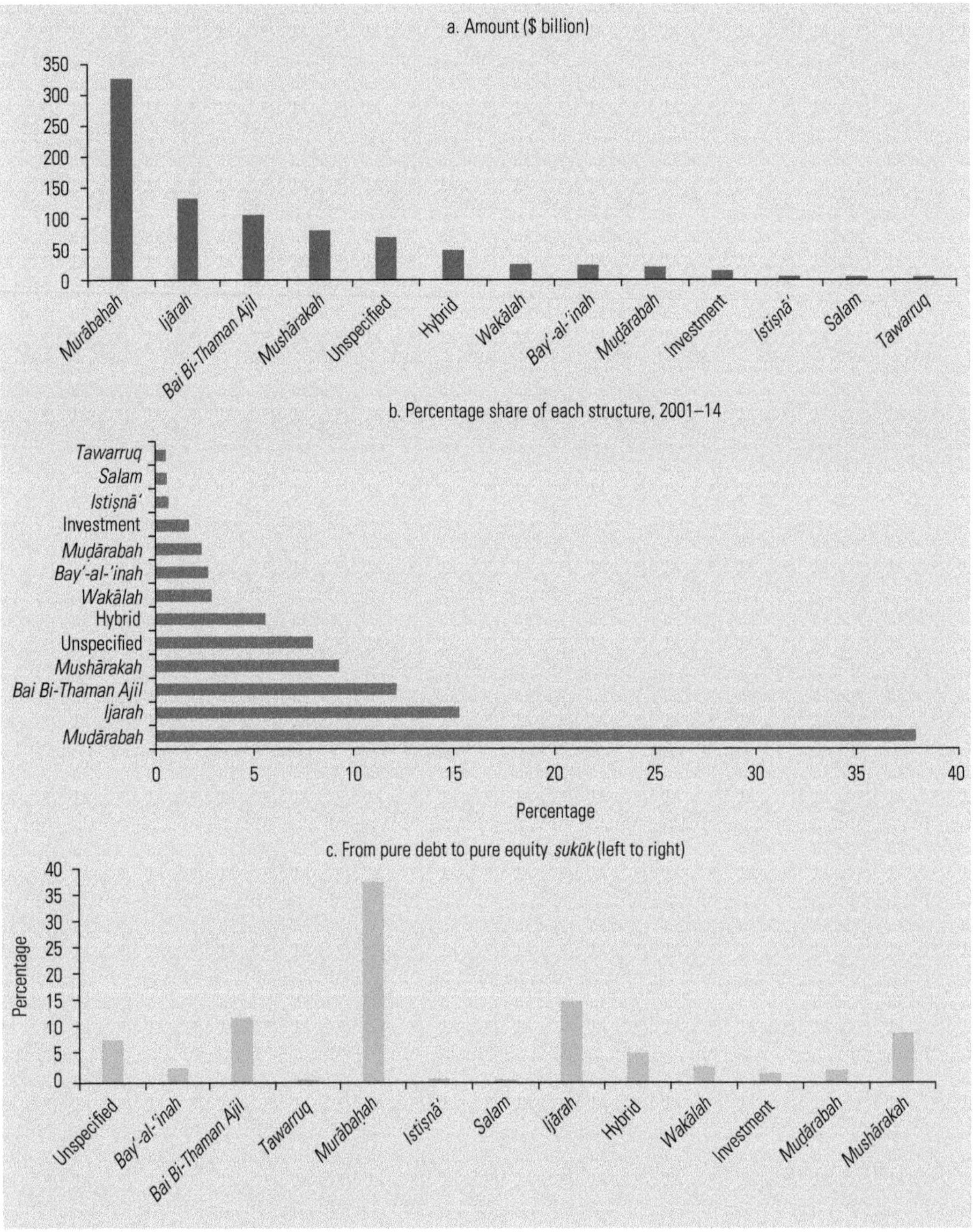

sectors has declined. In 2013–14, the share of sovereign issuance and financial sector issuance reached 61.4 percent and 21.5 percent, respectively, while the issuance for the private nonfinancial sector declined to 17 percent.[10]

Economic Development and Shared Prosperity through *Sukūk* Markets

Potential for Infrastructure Financing

Physical infrastructure plays an important role in the socioeconomic development of

FIGURE 4.11 ***Sukūk* Issuance by Sector, 2001–14**

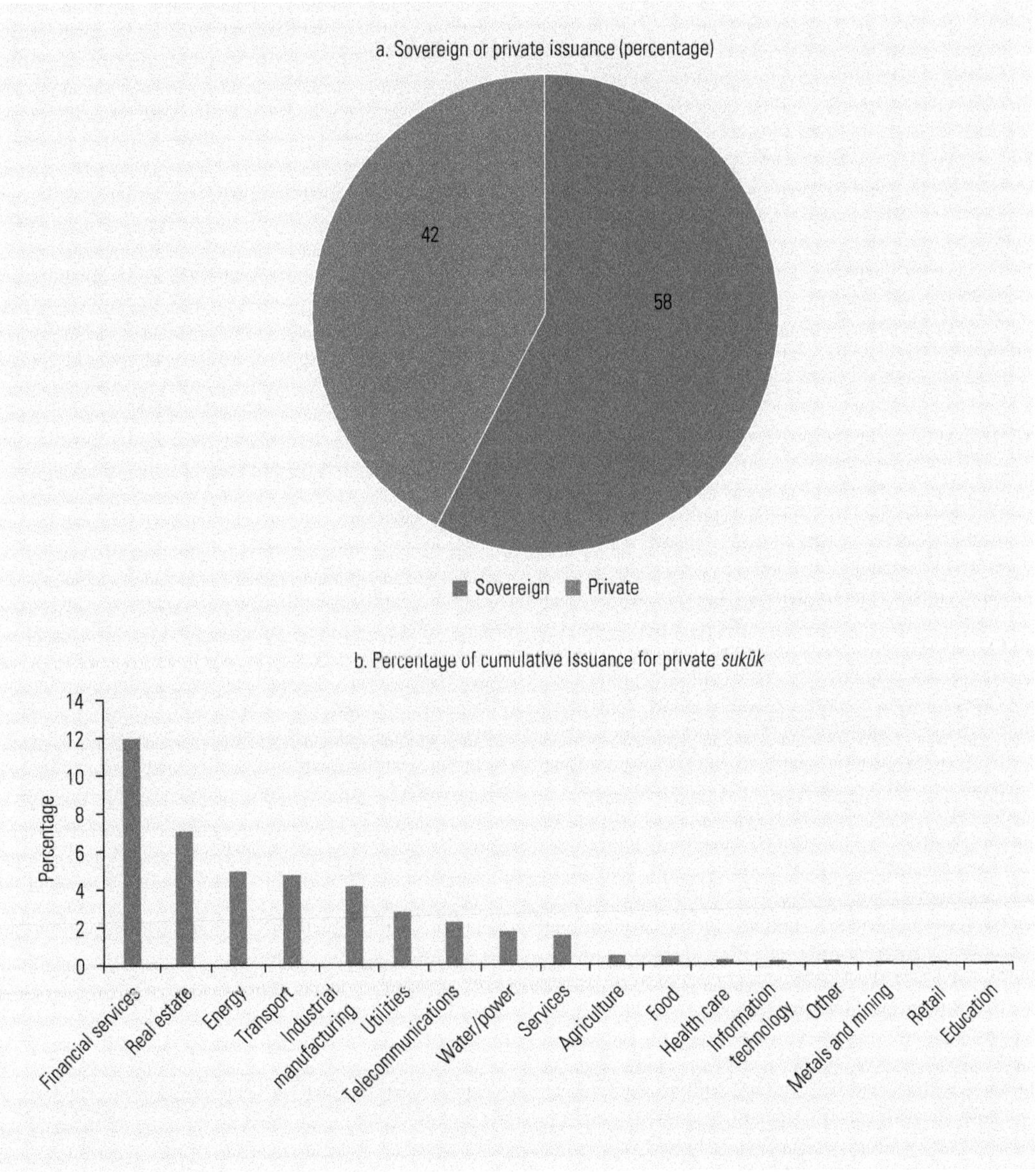

Source: IRTI, based on IFIS data.

countries and regions in many ways, both during its construction phase and for a long period after its construction. It helps long-term development by lowering the costs of economic activity and by facilitating connections and networks. Its benefits reach a wide range of the population, thus contributing to shared prosperity. Often the investments required for such infrastructure projects are quite large and long term. A common problem encountered is the mismatch in maturities between the underlying assets and funding.

Some projects can generate revenues, while others may be in the nature of a public good. In such cases, some kind of public-private partnership may be needed. Yet another issue is scalability: Some projects may offer sufficient incentives for the private sector to

TABLE 4.4 *Sukūk* by Their Underlying Contracts

Underlying contract structure	2013–14		2009–12	
	($ million)	Percent	($ million)	Percent
Ijārah	17,295	43	19,085	48.000
Wakālah	13,628	34	10,670	27.000
Murābaḥah	5,047	13	1,942	5.000
Hybrid	1,964	5	5,408	14.000
Muḍārabah	1,599	4	1	0.002
Mushārakah	391	1	2,605	6.000

Source: IIFM 2014.

step in, but the size of the individual projects may be small and thus have little or no economy-wide impact. Scaling up and coordination would be required to have a wider development impact. An example could be renewable energy projects, such as those promoting wind power. Each windmill is a small investment, but thousands of windmill generators are required to create an economy-wide impact.

Harmonization and connectedness of one infrastructure project with another are also important. For example, the usefulness and impact of some infrastructure projects in one country can depend on the development of coordinated infrastructure projects in neighboring countries. The impact of a cross-country highway built in country A will be enhanced if a highway is also constructed in country B and linked to it. The impact of the infrastructure will be amplified both nationally and regionally. This implies the need for regional initiatives for large infrastructure projects and coordinated issuance of *sukūk*.

In short, infrastructure investment requires more than a financial instrument. On the financial instruments side, it requires scalability and liquidity so that all types of investors are able to participate. On the institutional side, it requires supportive laws, adequate enforcement, and good governance to create an environment where just and fair treatment of all parties is ensured. On the political side, it requires coordination and public will. On the financial sector side, it requires domestic banking and nonbanking financial institutions, along with capital markets.

Given these complexities, less developed countries tend to rely more on external debt and foreign aid for infrastructure projects. This adds to their debt burden, particularly when projects get delayed or remain incomplete or are even abandoned because of the institutional development difficulties mentioned. Even for better performing developing countries, only 2.5 to 3 percent of infrastructure investment comes from international donors (World Bank 2013). Private sector financing from big private international banks is also drying up, as these banks are also facing deleveraging and will not be funding large infrastructure projects.

In this environment, *sukūk* have the opportunity to play a role in increasing shared prosperity (see Ali 2014). Given that the size of the Islamic capital market is small, a strategic use of sovereign and quasi-sovereign *sukūk* can be to finance crucial enabling infrastructure projects that can facilitate further inflows of private funding for infrastructure. Project-specific *sukūk*, instead of general-purpose *sukūk*, would be ideal to overcome some of the problems encountered in infrastructure financing. *Sukūk* can facilitate risk sharing between the investors, the project company, the government, and the operators. These risk-sharing arrangements can vary in different parts of a large project. Financing infrastructure would also require longer-term *sukūk*.

Potential for Social Inclusion and Poverty Alleviation through *Awqāf*

The nonprofit, voluntary sector is a privately initiated sector that provides social goods and works in parallel to the government public sector. *Awqāf* (singular, *waqf*), a kind of trust institution (see glossary), can be used to support the voluntary sector. *Awqāf* can be used not only to provide immediate necessities to the poor, but also to create or strengthen business support institutions that can lower the cost of doing business for the poor. *Awqāf* can also be used to support and build infrastructure institutions that can improve corporate governance and reduce the cost of doing business. For example, information bureaus, market regulatory bodies, the provision of accountancy services, and other such shared services for a group or for the entire society can be funded through *waqf*.

Many of the properties of *awqāf* are amenable to securitization through the issuance of *sukūk* on the usufruct of those properties. The proceeds can be used to expand operations and build new social projects. These *sukūk*, like government *sukūk*, have multiple benefits. They help expand the provision of social goods and services. The issuance and performance of these *sukūk* require appropriate monitoring, reporting, and payment mechanisms. Thus, as a by-product these *sukūk* foster institutionalization of reporting and monitoring practices that can also become useful for the entities in the for-profit sector. By fostering shared institutions, *awqāf* can help reduce the cost of doing business. Equally important, the public provision of social goods through the voluntary sector, such as *awqāf*, builds mutual trust in society, which is a requirement for exponential growth and economic development.

Sukūk for Socioeconomic Development: Experiences and Lessons

Case 1. The Islamic Development Bank's Use of *Sukūk* for Development Financing[11]

The IDB promotes economic development in its 56 member-countries, as well as in Muslim communities in non-member-countries. It has traditionally relied on capital contributions from its members to fund its operations. As the demands for development assistance have been rising faster than the Bank's equity capital, the IDB has been resorting to the capital market. Its debut issue in 2003 of a stand-alone, five-year, $400 million *sukūk* was done as an experiment with the market and to convey the IDB's intentions of using market resources in the coming years.

In 2005, IDB established its $1 billion Medium-Term Note (MTN) Program, which allowed issuance of *sukūk* in multiple currencies as and when needed (box 4.1). The program was initially listed on the Luxembourg Stock Exchange, but was later shifted to the London Stock Exchange and Bursa Malaysia. The MTN program was updated and expanded several times in tandem with the bank's growing operational funding needs. It was increased to $10 billion in 2013. By 2014, it was listed in multiple markets, including Nasdaq Dubai, to further enhance IDB's *sukūk* profile and improve its liquidity for investors. In June 2015, IDB increased the ceiling of its *sukūk* program from $10 billion to $25 billion, in keeping with its aim to expand its financing across member-countries. The expanded program will take advantage of IDB's AAA rating. It seeks to issue one *sukūk* publicly every year, with a minimum size of $1 billion, while keeping pace with growing investor requests for private placements.

The proceeds from the *sukūk* are mainly used to complement IDB's equity resources for its development funding. The funding needs are expected to grow 10 percent a year in the years to come. So far, using proceeds from the *sukūk*, the bank has been able to expand its development assistance in energy, infrastructure, agriculture, health, and other sectors to its member-countries. This has been achieved at a much lower cost than what the beneficiary countries would have paid if they had raised the funds themselves from the international markets.

IDB *sukūk* can be considered hybrid balance sheet asset *sukūk* because these *sukūk* are issued against a specified pool composed of *ijārah* (leasing) and non-*ijārah* (non-leasing)

BOX 4.1 Issuances in IDB's Medium-Term Note Program

Under the Medium-Term Note (MTN) Program, IDB had issued 17 series of *sukūk* as of April 2014. In 2015, IDB announced that it intends to issue up to $25 billion in *sukūk* cumulatively over the next several years under the MTN program, with at least $1 billion issued each year. In addition, IDB also issued three tranches of Malaysian ringgit (RM) *sukūk* in 2008, 2009, and 2013, with a cumulative total of RM 700 million, under a different MTN program of 1.000 RM billion, with maturity dates of August 2013, March 2014, and August 2018, respectively.

Series	Currency	Amount (million)	Type of issuance	Issue date	Maturity date
1	USD	500	Public issuance	2005	June 2010
2	SRls	200	Private placement	2009	September 2012
3	USD	850	Public issuance	2009	September 2014
4	SRls	1,875	Private placement	2010	September 2020
5	SRls	1,875	Private placement	2010	September 2020
6	USD	500	Public issuance	2011	October 2015
7	£	60	Private placement	2011	February 2016
8	USD	750	Public issuance	2011	May 2016
9	£	100	Private placement	2012	January 2017
10	USD	800	Public issuance	2012	June 2017
11	£	100	Private placement	2012	August 2015
12	USD	300	Private placement	2012	October 2015
13	USD	500	Private placement	2012	October 2017
14	USD	700	Private placement	2013	March 2018
15	USD	1,000	Public issuance	2013	June 2018
16	USD	1,500	Public issuance	2014	March 2019
17	USD	100	Private placement	2014	April 2017

Source: Omar and others 2014.
Note: SRls = Saudi riyals.

assets segregated from the balance sheet of IDB. The asset pool contains a significant proportion of *ijārah* compared to receivables (or nontangible assets) so that the composite pool itself can be considered as a tangible asset class for all practical purposes and in the legal classification. Hence the laws pertaining to tangible asset class are applicable to it, and the *sukūk* issued against this pool become eligible to receive a return and also eligible for sale in the secondary market, making them liquid. Each issuance of *sukūk* represents a different pool. *Sukūk* cannot be issued against the same assets until those assets come back into the ownership of IDB.

Using this type of *sukūk* structure for development funding poses challenges. In order to be continually able to issue *sukūk* backed by assets, the IDB must be able to increase the creation of tangible assets or tradable contracts in the IDB balance sheet more quickly before it can issue further *sukūk*. Moreover, most of the assets held by IDB on its balance sheet are development projects or development financing contracts that are not rated; because they are development oriented, they do not generate commercial rates of return. How to induce investors to accept low-return *sukūk* in the market is a challenge.

Therefore, IDB *sukūk* are asset based rather than asset backed. This essentially means that the ultimate recourse in case of default on the *sukūk* would be to IDB as the obligor and originator of the *sukūk* through a special purpose vehicle (SPV), rather than the *sukūk* assets themselves. This does not meet AAOIFI *sukūk* standards or conform to the views of the majority of *shari'ah* scholars, who hold that *sukūk* should represent undivided ownership in the specified assets (or pool of assets) that are sold to the SPV and held in trust with it. This would justify the periodic payments (rents) to the *sukūk* holders as the de facto owners of the underlying assets. In case of default, they would have recourse to those assets in some form. However, this defect exists, and the reasons for this anomaly in IDB *sukūk* are economic and legalistic in nature. Thus, to give comfort or rather to enhance the credit profile of its *sukūk*, IDB has to link the performance of the *sukūk* to the bank's credit strength, which is AAA rated, based on the strength of its capital and the commitment by its member-countries to provide support. In this way, IDB has been able to mobilize resources at a cost much lower than that of the beneficiary countries if they had raised the funds themselves from the international markets.

In addition to its high credit rating, the Basel Committee on Banking Supervision has designated IDB as a "zero-risk weighted" multilateral development bank since 2004. The European Commission has accorded the same treatment to IDB since 2007. All these factors have made it possible for the Islamic financial services industry to use IDB *sukūk* in various ways, including as an acceptable asset class to satisfy Basel III requirements of high-quality liquid assets. It is yet another way in which IDB *sukūk* are contributing to economic progress through the development of the Islamic financial sector globally.

Case 2. Vaccination and Immunization *Ṣukūk*[12]

The *sukūk* issued by the International Financial Facility for Immunization (IFFIm) provide another example of *sukūk* used for social and developmental purposes. The proceeds will be used to fund vaccination development and immunization programs by the Global Alliance for Vaccination and Immunization (Gavi).[13] The $700 million *sukūk* were issued in 2014 and mature in December 2017. They are based on commodity *murābaḥah* structure.[14] Because the *sukūk* are *murābaḥah* based, they are not tradable in the secondary market. Although there is nothing innovative in the structure of the *sukūk*, the fact that they are dedicated to an important social and health purpose is laudable and demonstrates the usefulness of a *shari'ah*-compliant structure in attracting the funding. It is noteworthy that 85 percent of the bids for the *sukūk* came from new investors, mainly from the Middle East (68 percent) and Asia (21 percent). Seventy-four percent of the *sukūk* were taken by Islamic banks, while central banks and other official institutions took 26 percent.[15]

Before it issued the immunization *sukūk*, IFFIm pioneered the issuance of (conventional) vaccination bonds to overcome the problem of slow delivery of money (donations) pledged by sovereigns. Such pledges pass through various channels of approvals until they are delivered, or sometimes they are promised to be delivered several years in the future. IFFIm was created in 2006 to securitize the donation pledges made by certain developed countries for the development of vaccines and immunization programs. IFFIm essentially securitizes and sells these pledged cash receivables at a discount to the investors to get cash-in-hand to finance its immunization projects. Selling of future cash for the present at a discount would not be permissible in Islam. However, by purchasing a commodity on the basis of a deferred payment and selling it on a spot price, the cash-in-hand is generated without explicitly resorting to a sale of pledges.[16] In this process, the AA credit rating of the IFFIm, along with the *shari'ah*-compliant structure of the *sukūk,* also helped. However, greater compliance with *shari'ah* structuring would have been possible without the use of the commodity *murābaḥah* structure, as follows.

The donations from sovereigns are essentially a purchase order for vaccines from the donor countries for distribution to less-developed countries. The IFFIm needs to purchase the available vaccines from Gavi (the vaccine alliance) on spot payment to sell to the purchase orderer at a higher deferred price. IFFIm could have issued *muḍārabah* certificates to investors for this particular deal and shared with them the *murābaḥah* mark-up profit. In this way, the risk of vaccine purchase and sale would have been shared by the investors along with the IFFIm. The deal would have directly linked financing with the actual business and the actual intended commodity (the vaccine), rather than creating a secondary layer of transaction on a second commodity that was not intended for final use by any of the transacting parties. The *muḍārabah* certificates so issued would have been tradable in the secondary market, which would have been good for their liquidity and an added attraction for the investors.

There is another important lesson to be learned in the structuring of this *sukūk*. Although the second *mudārabah*-based structure was possible, the issuers chose the first structure because it was easier to administer. Thus the transaction shifted from the market for the vaccine to the market for the other commodity (such as metals), which was not intended by any party but used for the commodity *murābaḥah* only. A policy recommendation for the development of the Islamic financial sector, and specifically for the development of Islamic capital market products, is that the government and the regulators should take steps to make it easy to do the transaction on the intended commodity and make the use of *ribā* (interest) and its alternate stratagems more difficult and costly.

Recommended Policies to Enhance Shared Prosperity through Islamic Capital Markets

The main requirements of the Islamic capital market framework are not any different from the requirements of the conventional capital market. These include protecting property rights, minimizing corruption and fraudulent practices, and supporting the rule of law. However, there are some differences in the requirements for the sound development of Islamic capital markets. These differences stem from the needs to attain *shari'ah* compliance and the overarching objectives of Islamic teachings. These include the prohibition of interest, and the execution of transactions in ways that neither circumvent nor covertly help in circumventing any *shari'ah* prohibition. The needs arising from meeting the moral and overarching Islamic objectives include facilitating the circulation of wealth instead of its concentration, sharing of risks and rewards more widely instead of shifting risk, and serving the real economy instead of commandeering it.

The growth of the Islamic capital market has been hindered by several challenges. A mid-term review (MTR) of the Islamic financial services industry, jointly prepared by the Islamic Research and Training Institute (IRTI) and the Islamic Financial Services Board (IFSB), highlights some of the major challenges and the policy response needed by the Islamic finance industry. Some policy recommendations emerging from the above discussion follow, including those from the review, specifically addressing the Islamic capital markets in enhancing shared prosperity, along with some context.[17]

Create More Incentives for Risk Sharing

One of the biggest challenges that may hinder the promotion of equity markets in general and Islamic capital markets in particular is the preferential tax treatment of interest expenses paid by corporations. This provides an incentive to corporations to issue more debt than equity. In order to level the playing field for debt and equity, the tax shelter on interest payments needs to be eliminated. Abolishing the tax shelter on interest payments would help reduce reliance on debt markets and increase investment in the equity markets.

Another challenge that Islamic capital markets face is discrimination in the use of financial innovations such as asset-backed securitization. Securitization facilitates risk sharing and thus enhances shared prosperity. In the case of conventional finance, there is no requirement for the assets (title) to be transferred. Moreover, the lack of transfer of the asset does not create a tax liability for the investor. However, in the case of Islamic securitization (*sukūk*), transfer of assets is a *shari'ah* requirement. It incurs additional expenses at the origination and termination of the transaction. There is a need to develop regulations that allow the transfer of ownership without any additional cost for the issuance of *sukūk*.

Sukūk are also failing to meet their goal of sharing prosperity when they are structured to refinance an existing loan as opposed to creating a new economic activity, are general purpose rather than project specific, or are used to finance government budget deficits rather than development financing. The refinancing *sukūk* do not directly contribute to the projects, but only provide continuity to the existing *sukūk*. If the original *sukūk* were not funding economic development projects, extending such *sukūk* would be detrimental to sharing prosperity. Use of such *sukūk* can simply increase public expenditures and adversely affect sustainability.

Short-termism dominates the *sukūk* markets globally as well as regionally, as can be seen from the higher proportion of short-term *sukūk* issuance to total issuance and a trend toward very short maturities. An entire spectrum of maturities would be needed to benefit from the development and orientation of *sukūk* markets. Many of the short-term *sukūk* are based on *murābaḥah* or other such arrangements that are not suitable for developing a secondary market for *sukūk*. Hence the risk sharing that is possible through trade is curtailed by reliance on nontradable *sukūk*. Developing short- and longer-term sovereign and corporate *sukūk* is critical for developing *sukūk* markets. So is addressing legal and fiscal impediments to *sukūk* issuance by corporates.

Standardize and Harmonize the Approach to Islamic Capital Market Regulation

The need for better corporate governance mechanisms and regulatory frameworks cannot be overemphasized for Islamic capital markets. Since Islamic capital market products are based on higher ethical standards than the conventional market because of the requirement to be *shari'ah* compliant, a well-designed regulatory framework is the basic requirement. However, there is a lack of consensus among regulators in terms of devising uniform rules across jurisdictions.

Improve *Shari'ah* Governance

Islamic finance is not a local phenomenon anymore. The Islamic financial services industry exists in some form in at least 50 countries. The need to harmonize *shari'ah* rulings and standardize practices or products in the Islamic finance industry is obvious. To stimulate cross-border activities in both primary and secondary markets, the acceptance of contracts across regions and across schools of thought and markets will also be helpful. Conformity or similarity among the *shari'ah* supervisory boards of IFIs is urgently required to extend the possibilities of the concept and application in the industry. A global approach is required for dealing with governance issues, especially issues related to *shari'ah* governance. Developing and adopting universal standards such as those proposed by AAOIFI and IFSB, among others, is highly recommended.

In the absence of a stock market for the Islamic equities, it may be difficult for investors to identify the investible universe of *shari'ah*-compliant capital market products, especially equities. Policy makers may consider a two-step approach: disclosure by the firm and attestation by the regulator.

- *Disclosures:* Firms are required to report their *shari'ah* compliance status based on a minimum compliance criterion, with the encouragement to provide better disclosures, especially all those events that may result in possible noncompliance in the future.

- *Attestation:* A *shari'ah* board at the apex level validates/attests that the disclosures by the reporting firm are to their satisfaction in terms of meeting the *shari'ah* requirements, and publishes the list of such firms and products on a regular basis.

There is no limit to the financial innovation in Islamic finance, provided that it complies with *shari'ah*. However, several recent financial innovations have attempted to replicate a conventional product, especially leveraged or derivative products. This has led to criticism of Islamic finance practices in general. A clearance requirement from an apex *shari'ah* committee to attest to the *shari'ah* compliance of all financial products offered in any jurisdiction is recommended.

Improve Market Liquidity by Addressing the Constraints

There is evidence that the secondary market in *sukūk* is very thin, due to the limited supply of *sukūk,* as well as the strategy of the *sukūk* buyers to hold their *sukūk* to maturity. *Sukūk* certificates are traded only about 40 percent of the time (Safari 2013), which works out to trading once every 12 trading days. A market infrastructure that facilitates trading, price transparency, and efficient clearing and settlement of transactions is required. According to an IMF report (2014), limited secondary market activity results in lack of adequate pricing and severely hinders effective marking to market. Main factors that hinder the secondary market trading of *sukūk* instruments are lack of supply, incorrect valuations, and the *shari'ah* limitation on tradability. Investors tend to hold their *sukūk* to maturity. Some *sukūk* types are eligible for secondary market trading, such as equity-based *sukūk* (as in *mushārakah* and *muḍārabah*) or those based on the value of an underlying asset (as in *sukūk ijāra*). Others are not, such as debt-based *sukūk* (*murābaḥah sukūk*). The pricing of *sukūk* instruments in the secondary market would require a valuation of the underlying assets pool or business venture. Policies are required to promote correct valuation of the underlying asset pool, enhance standardization of products and the design of structures that can be traded with wide acceptance as compliant with *shari'ah*, and ensure transparency and discourage ambiguities. In addition, targeting a diverse set of investors to buy *sukūk* can also improve liquidity of the secondary markets. A diversity of investor types would mean that different investors would have different investment horizons and their liquidity needs would not be correlated. Thus sale and purchase in the secondary market would remain active.

Strengthen Resolution Frameworks and Investor Protection

Weak or nonexistent default resolution and insolvency regimes to handle *sukūk* defaults pose a challenge. Legal uncertainty about the resolution framework is mitigated in sovereign *sukūk*, which are often issued under international law (IMF 2014). However, there is a need for further clarification of the resolution framework regarding corporate and quasi-sovereign *sukūk*. Most corporate *sukūk* are issued under domestic law in jurisdictions with underdeveloped legal and regulatory infrastructures. Default cases have illustrated that legal uncertainty is high when the performance of the underlying asset falls below expectations and the *sukūk* effectively defaults. Given the lack of a clear legal framework for restructuring, *sukūk* holders must seek resolution in case-by-case negotiations.

In addition, the necessary infrastructure to quickly identify current *sukūk* holders—which would help speed negotiation—is not in place in many jurisdictions. The problem is compounded when the SPV that is normally created to issue the *sukūk* and hold the assets in trust does not have any executive power to negotiate with any party or do any transaction except with the permission of the originator (IIFM 2014). To alleviate these problems, building robust bankruptcy and insolvency frameworks and scenarios of how *sukūk* instruments might unwind in the event of default could be helpful. In the same vein, it would be helpful to have a mechanism for defined executive powers of the SPV in case of default by the obligor.

Notes

1. This process is explored in the Arrow and Debreu (1954) model of competitive equilibrium.
2. *Sharīʿah*-compliant companies include companies whose major source of revenue comes from permissible (*halāl*) activities. Companies that are excluded are predominantly engaged in any of the following nonpermissible (*harām*) activities: trading of alcohol or pork, pornography, gambling, or from profit associated with the charging of interest on loans.
3. The general criteria for including any security in an Islamic index depends on two levels of screening: business and financial. Business screening excludes shares of all companies engaged in activities strictly prohibited (*harām*) in Islam. Financial screening further screens those companies that passes the business screen but have a portion of revenue from *harām* activities, such as borrowing or lending money with interest (*ribā*) and/or have a major proportion of assets in liquid form. These screens are based on arbitrary financial ratios and are quite controversial within the Muslim community (Ashraf 2014; Obaidullah 2005). For a detailed discussion of the different screening criteria and their impact on portfolio performance, see Ashraf (2014).
4. There is no specific reason for the choice of S&P *shari'ah* screening.
5. COMCEC is the Standing Committee for Economic and Commercial Cooperation of the Organisation of Islamic Cooperation.
6. IRTI calculations based on data from Zawya.
7. For the purpose of this chapter, Africa refers to Sub-Saharan Africa, excluding North Africa.
8. See glossary for definitions of *murābaḥah*, *ʿīnah* sale, *tawarruq*, and other Arabic terms.
9. The *murābaḥah* sales contract creates a cash receivable as the asset of the seller. This type of asset cannot be traded at a premium or discount. However, this *sharīʿah* restriction is not operational in Malaysia, which differentiates between a loan (pure debt) and debt resulting from the sale of a commodity at a deferred price (trade-generated debt). The trade-generated debt is tradable in the secondary markets in Malaysia.
10. Percentages for 2013–14 are based on the IFSB (2015) *Islamic Financial Services Industry Stability Report.*
11. This case is based on Ali (2014).
12. This case is based on Ali (2014).
13. Gavi is an international organization created in 2000 to improve access to new and underused vaccines for children living in the world's poorest countries. See http://www.gavi.org/.
14. In a commodity *murābaḥah* structure, the party seeking finance buys a commodity today from the party providing finance for a marked-up price to be paid on a future date. It then sells that commodity in the spot market (or to the same seller) at a discount to get upfront cash. The price payable in the future with a markup becomes a debt obligation for the buyer.
15. http://www.iffim.org/Library/News/Press-releases/2014/International-Finance-Facility-for-Immunisation-issues-first-Sukuk,-raising-US$-500-million/ and http://www.reuters.com/article/2014/12/07/iffim-sukuk-idUSL6N0TI04J20141207.
16. "Under the sukuk Al-Murabaha structure, IFFImSC issued $500 million in sukuk certificates to investors in November 2014. The proceeds of these sukuk certificates were used by IFFImSC to purchase eligible commodities, which were then sold to IFFIm at a pre-specified deferred price. This deferred price included the $500 million principal cost component and a profit component. Simultaneous to its purchase of the commodities, IFFIm on-sold the commodities to a third party commodity purchaser, through a commodity agent, generating $500 million in proceeds for use in funding vaccine programmes and refinancing IFFIm's existing debt" (Gavi 2014, 17).
17. The list of general recommendations is well documented in IRTI and IFSB (2014).

References

Agarwal, Sumit, and Hamid Mohtadi. 2004. "Financial Markets and the Financing Choice of Firms: Evidence from Developing Countries." *Global Finance Journal* 15 (1): 57–70.

Ali, Salman Syed. 2005. *Islamic Capital Market Products: Development and Challenges.* Jeddah, Saudi Arabia: Islamic Research and Training Institute, Islamic Development Bank.

———. 2013. "Islamic Capital Markets: Objectives and the Way Forward." In *Islamic Capital Markets—Competitiveness and Resilience,* edited by Salman Syed Ali. Jeddah, Saudi Arabia: Islamic Research and Training Institute, Islamic Development Bank.

Ali, Salman Syed, ed. 2014. *Islamic Finance and Economic Development: Lessons from the Past and Prospects for the Future.* Jeddah, Saudi Arabia: Islamic Research and Training Institute, Islamic Development Bank.

Al-Masri, Rafic Yunus. 2007. "Speculation between Proponents and Opponents." *Journal of King Abdul-Aziz University: Islamic Economics* 20 (1): 43–52.

Arrow, K. J., and G. Debreu. 1954. "Existence of an Equilibrium for a Competitive Economy." *Econometrica* 22: 265–90.

Ashraf, D., 2014. "Does *Shari'ah* Screening Cause Abnormal Returns? Empirical Evidence from Islamic Equity Indices." *Journal of Business Ethics.* doi:10.1007/s10551-014-2422-2.

Beck, T., A. Demirgüç-Kunt, and R. Levine. 2007. "Finance, Inequality and the Poor." *Journal of Economic Growth* 12 (1): 27–49.

Bekaert, G., and C. R. Harvey. 1997. "Capital Markets: An Engine for Economic Growth." Unpublished paper, National Bureau of Economic Research, Cambridge, MA.

Epstein, Gerald A. 2006. *Financialization and the World Economy.* New York: Edward Elgar.

Gavi Alliance (Global Alliance for Vaccination and Immunization). 2014. *The Vaccine Alliance 2014 Annual Financial Report.* Washington, DC: Gavi Alliance.

IFSB (Islamic Financial Services Board). 2015. *Islamic Financial Services Industry Stability Report 2015.* Kuala Lumpur: IFSB.

IIFM (International Islamic Financial Markets). 2014. *IIFM Sukuk Report: A Comprehensive Study of the Global Sukuk Market.* 4th ed. Manama, Bahrain: International Islamic Financial Markets.

IMF (International Monetary Fund). 2014. *Sukūk Market Surveillance—Market Trends and Financial Stability Implications.* Washington, DC: International Monetary Fund.

IRTI and IFSB (Islamic Research and Training Institute and Islamic Financial Services Board). 2014. *Islamic Financial Services Industry Development: Ten-Year Framework and Strategies—A Mid-Term Review.* Jeddah, Saudi Arabia: Islamic Research and Training Institute.

Jobst, A. A. 2007. "The Economics of Islamic Finance and Securitization." IMF Working Paper, International Monetary Fund, Washington, DC.

King, R., and R. Levine. 1993. "Finance and Growth: Schumpeter Might Be Right." *Quarterly Journal of Economics* 108: 717–38.

Levine, R. 1997. "Financial Development and Economic Growth: Views and Agenda." *Journal of Economic Literature* 35: 688–726.

———. 2005. "Finance and Growth: Theory and Evidence." In *Handbook of Economic Growth,* edited by P. Aghion and S. Durlauf, Vol. 1A, 867–934. New York, Amsterdam: Elsevier B.V.

Levine, R., and S. Zervos. 1998. "Stock Market, Banks and Economic Growth." *American Economic Review* 88: 537–58.

Menkoff, Lucas, and Norbert Tolksdorf. 2001. *Financial Market Drift: Decoupling of the Financial Sector from the Real Economy?* Heidelberg-Berlin: Springer-Verlag.

Mirakhor, Abbas. 2010. "Whither Islamic Finance?" Paper presented at the Inaugural Malaysia Securities Commission and Oxford Center for Islamic Studies Conference, Oxfordshire, U.K. March 15.

Naughton, Shahnaz, and Tony Naughton. 2000. "Religion, Ethics and Stock Trading: The Case of an Islamic Equities Market." *Journal of Business Ethics* 23 (2): 145–59.

Obaidullah, M. 2005. *Islamic Financial Services.* Jeddah, Saudi Arabia: Scientific Publishing Center, King AbdulAziz University.

Omar, Mustafa, Salman Syed Ali, Mohamed Obaidullah, and Turkhan Abdulmanp. 2014. "Funding for Development Finance." In *Islamic Finance and Economic Development: Lessons from the Past and Prospects for the Future,* edited by Salman Syed Ali. Jeddah, Saudi Arabia: Islamic Research and Training Institute, Islamic Development Bank.

Pagano, M. 1993. "Financial Markets and Growth: An Overview." *European Economic Review* 37: 613–22.

Palley, T. J. 2007. "Financialization: What It Is and Why It Matters." Working Paper 252, The Levy Economics Institute, Annandale-on-Hudson, NY.

Parenteau, R. W. 2005. "The Late 1990s U.S. Bubble: Financialization in the Extreme." In *Financialization and the World Economy*, edited by G. Epstein. Cheltenham, UK: Edward Elgar.

Pradhan, R. P., M. B. Arvin, J. H. Hall, and S. Bahmani. 2014. "Causal Nexus between Economic Growth, Banking Sector Development, Stock Market Development, and Other Macroeconomic Variables: The Case of ASEAN Countries." *Review of Financial Economics* 23: 155–73.

Safari, Meysam. 2013. "Contractual Structures and Payoff Patterns of *Sukūk* Securities." *International Journal of Banking and Finance* 10 (2): 1–24.

Taj El-Din, Seif El-Din. 2009. "The Stock-Exchange from an Islamic Perspective." In *Issues in the International Financial Crisis from an Islamic Perspective*, 99–122. Jeddah, Saudi Arabia: Islamic Economic Research Center King Abdulaziz University.

World Bank. 2013. "Long-Term Financing of Infrastructure: A Look at Nonfinancial Constraints." Issues Note No. 6 for Consideration by G-20, coordinated by the Infrastructure Policy Unit, Sustainable Development Network, World Bank, Washington, DC.

5

Takāful (Islamic Insurance), Re*takāful*, and Micro*takāful*

Takāful, or mutual assistance, is the Islamic counterpart of conventional insurance. The word *takāful* is derived from an Arabic word *kafālah,* which means to guarantee. A group of participants agree to support one another jointly for the losses arising from specified risks. They contribute to a fund, and are compensated or reimbursed from that fund in the event of certain risks. The scheme is managed on the participants' behalf by a *takāful* operator. It is similar to a mutual insurance concept, but it complies with *shari'ah* and is based on concepts of mutual solidarity and risk sharing.

Although *takāful* and conventional insurance share the same function of handling pure risks, they differ in a number of ways (box 5.1). From the perspective of insurance policyholders, risk management entails transferring a risk held solely by the policyholder wholly to the insurance company. The underlying contract between the insurance companies and the policyholders is an exchange contract, where the insurance company promises to indemnify any losses in consideration of premiums, and the insurance company's only hope of making a profit would be for the risk covered not to occur, and for the premiums collected to exceed the payouts for claims. However, in *takāful*, the risk is usually borne by the individual participant but is shared and transferred to the group of participants.

The Potential Role of *Takāful* in Promoting Shared Prosperity

Besides being *shari'ah* compliant, *takāful* promotes shared prosperity by helping individuals and businesses reduce their exposure

BOX 5.1 Similarities and Differences between Conventional Mutuals/Cooperatives and *Takāful*

The majority of modern insurance companies in the developed countries (classified as stock insurance companies) are owned by investors who have purchased the company's shares. Any profits generated by this form of insurance company are distributed to the investors in the form of dividend payments. Profits are typically generated if claim experiences are lower than those expected in the pricing assumption. Policyholders are customers who have purchased a policy from the company for protection in the event of unforeseen events. Policyholders usually do not benefit directly when claims are low because the insurance company takes the underwriting surpluses as profits.

By contrast, a mutual insurance company is owned entirely by its policyholders. Any profits may be distributed back to policyholders. They have a stronger influence on the company management practices; they may elect or terminate the company's management at annual meetings. The major disadvantage of mutual insurance companies is the difficulty in raising capital needed to remain solvent or fund expansion. The independence of management can also be limited, as policyholders are the owners.

In both kinds of companies, the contract of insurance is still a bilateral contract of exchange (*mu'āwaḍāt*) involving a seller and buyer. This differs from the *takāful* contract, which is a unilateral contract (*tabarru'āt*). By contributing a sum of money to a common *takāful* risk fund in the form of a donation (*tabarru'*), an individual will become one of the participants and agree to mutually help other participants, should they suffer from a mishap. *Takāful* participants are not owners of any company, though they have a collective interest in the *takāful* risk fund.

The relationship of the *takāful* operator to the participants is that of a manager (*muḍārib*) or agent (*wakil*). The operator administers the schemes and manages the risks and investment aspects of the *takāful* funds for a fee or share of the investment profits. The operator does not cover the risk the participants face because the participants have already agreed to mutually help one another. *Takāful* operators are required by regulation to lend funds to support any deficiency in the *takāful* risk funds to protect the interests of the participants, but are restricted to using only a temporary interest-free loan (*qarḍ ḥasan*). The operators have the right of recovery once the fund is solvent.

Takāful based on a cooperative model may resemble a mutual insurance setup; however, mutual insurance does not have any restriction as to the type of activities and investments that it can enter into. By contrast, *takāful* contributions from participants must be invested in a *halāl* (permissible) or *shari'ah*-compliant type of investments, which are free from *ribā*. If the investments generate a surplus, all the participants will share the benefits. *Takāful* operators are also required to have a *shari'ah* advisory board to monitor the processes and activities of the operations, including their product offerings and investments, so that they are *shari'ah* compliant. In certain jurisdictions, such as in Malaysia, *takāful* companies must undertake a *shari'ah* audit in addition to the customary accounting audit, in each accounting period.

Although the results for both insurance and *takāful* are the same—to provide compensation against possible losses—the central difference lies in the way that each achieves this objective. The notion "the ends will justify the means" does not hold when it comes to *shari'ah*, where both the ends and the means must be compliant.

to risks, increase their savings, and promote long-term capital investment.

Because *takāful* is based on the concept of mutualization (resource pooling and risk sharing), the understanding and acceptance of the *takāful* mechanism is enhanced when traditions of mutual aid exist within the target population. This spirit of mutual aid may arise from a number of situations, such as being members of a community or a cooperative, residents of the same neighborhood, or members of a social or Islamic movement. Such common ties can increase social trust, which underpins micro*takāful*—supporting the growth in Islamic microfinance.

Generally, saving in *takāful,* as opposed to in a commercial bank, is regarded as a better means to accumulate an estate and distribute such wealth to heirs. There may also be other advantages, as risk management practices are a natural discipline of a *takāful* operator, which reduces the possibility of failure. Furthermore, *takāful* operators' businesses focus on investments, while the bank focuses on financing. As a low-yield environment is likely to continue, *takāful* investors will tend to earn higher yields than account holders in a typical conventional or Islamic bank. There is evidence that micro*takāful* has encouraged savings, and thus alleviated poverty, in the Arab Republic of Egypt, as microfinance institutions and microleasing companies are not allowed to accept deposits. Thus while being socially responsible, micro*takāful* helps support poor microfinance consumers by boosting their savings.

Funds from pensions and insurance companies have deepened and widened financial systems in the developed world. In the United States, institutional investors have contributed not only to the deepening of equity markets but also to the development of the corporate bond market, which in 2012 ranked largest in the world, at 140 percent of GDP. The greater involvement of insurance companies and pension funds has also helped reduce the volatility of the equity and bond market. Institutional investors bring stable pools of capital with an interest in long-term positions instead of speculative trades. *Takāful* operators can similarly contribute to the growth of the *sukūk* market (see chapter 4).

Likewise, savings or investments made in *takāful* funds can provide a critical source of funding for a variety of economic activities for the community and even for the country. There is an immense need for infrastructure investments worldwide, especially in developing countries. As traditional sources of public and private financing face greater constraints, institutional investors are increasingly being considered as sources of financing for infrastructure project development and maintenance in developing countries. Together, these institutional investors would benefit from the better return on investment and diversification. Furthermore, infrastructure investments can provide a predictable cash flow that can often keep pace with inflation. While *takāful* and micro*takāful* funds are still small in size, the rapid growth of the industry in such countries is encouraging.

Micro*takāful* has a great role to play to promote financial inclusion. Besides being *shari'ah* compliant, *takāful* promotes social and economic values by helping individuals and businesses reduce their exposure to risks. Though micro*takāful* is still limited in comparison to microinsurance, it has great potential in the light of the growing demand for *shari'ah*-compliant microfinance. Financial institutions are now promoting the use of insurance or *takāful* as a guarantee for credit. This is very important in developing countries, where the poor have low liquidity in general and low capacity to pledge other types of guarantees that might be acceptable to formal banking standards.

Micro*takāful* is a socially responsible tool that aims to reduce poverty, help the vulnerable, and assist the underserved population through financial inclusion and practices such as pooling risks and assets within villages or communities. Micro*takāful* covering family and health benefits and crop, livestock, and property damages can be implemented through a community-based model, a cooperative-based model, a *wakālah* partner model, or even a provider-driven model. People who participate in a micro-level health insurance scheme will be able to reduce their out-of-pocket expenditures and increase their use of health care services (Panda and others 2015).

Micro*takāful* also has several comparative advantages as a means to extend traditional social security schemes. Micro*takāful* has the capacity to reach groups excluded from statutory social insurance, especially where the workers are in the rural and informal economy. The transaction costs necessary to reach these populations can be reduced, since micro*takāful* schemes can be operated by local governmental or social organizations or nongovernment organizations that are usually in the vicinity of their target population; their staffs include social workers who are used to working with and are closer to targeted groups. Micro*takāful* benefits packages can be designed in close partnership with the target population to ensure a higher participation rate.

An area of concern for micro*takāful* is that the poor are more likely to prefer informal *takāful* schemes rather than formal ones, as they are easier to join and more affordable. In addition, while enrollment can be increased through options like subsidies and coupons, complete inclusion will not be possible for all, given the cost.

Awareness programs linked with microinsurance schemes have also increased financial literacy, which in turn can increase participation in the financial system and adoption of financial products and services. This pattern is supported by studies in Burkina Faso (Cofie and others 2013), Cameroon (Noubiap and others 2013), and India (Panda, Chakraborty, and Dror 2015). A study of a farmers' literacy training program in Gujarat, India (Gaurav, Cole, and Tobacman 2011), showed that training through a financial module increased the take-up rate of microinsurance from 8 percent to 16 percent.

The Current State of the *Takāful* Industry

The market for *takāful* is potentially huge. The world's 1.5 billion Muslims represent a potential customer base that no insurer can afford to ignore. Moreover, the majority of the world's Muslim population is young (under 25 years of age). The underinsured status of most Muslims is also a significant enticement to potential *takāful* operators.

The *takāful* market has been growing strongly. It is currently concentrated in Malaysia and the Middle East (primarily Saudi Arabia). The growth rate of the *takāful* market in those areas is well ahead of the conventional insurance market.

Global gross *takāful* contributions amounted to an estimated $14 billion in 2014, up from $12.3 billion in 2013 (figure 5.1). Year-on-year growth has moderated from a high compound annual growth rate of 22 percent in 2007–11 to a still healthy growth rate of 14 percent in 2012–14 (Ernst & Young 2014). The *takāful* market in ASEAN countries (Brunei Darussalam, Indonesia, Malaysia, Singapore, and Thailand), driven by strong economic dynamics and young demographics, continues to grow at 22 percent. The countries of the Gulf Cooperation Council (GCC), including Saudi Arabia, have registered a growth rate of about 12 percent.

Saudi Arabia accounts for nearly half (48 percent) of the share of global gross *takāful* contributions (excluding the Islamic Republic of Iran, which has a unique domestic industry).[1] Malaysia and Indonesia account for nearly one-third (30 percent), followed by other GCC countries (15 percent), and Africa, South Asia, and the Levant (the remaining 7 percent).

Takāful Practices in Selected Countries

The two *takāful* models most widely adopted are *wakālah* (agency) and *muḍārabah* (profit sharing) (see table 5.1). In each case, the operator is responsible for developing the products, underwriting the risk, collecting the contributions, investing the contributions, and dealing with claims. There has also been a significant growth in the use of a mixed or hybrid model, which combines aspects of *wakālah* and *muḍārabah*. Another model, known as the *waqf* model, has also evolved as an enhancement to the governance structure of *takāful*, though it is not widely practiced.

The *Wakālah* Model

In the *wakālah* model, mutual risk sharing occurs among participants who contribute to a *takāful* fund. These contributions include the payment of fees and charges due to the operator, together with a donation to the *takāful* fund. The operator acts as the agent (or *wakil*) of the participants, and is therefore entitled to a fee for the services provided. The fee is deducted up front when participants make contributions, and the balance is channeled into the *takāful* fund. In the strictest sense, the *takāful* operator should not share

FIGURE 5.1 **Total Amounts of Global Gross *Takāful* Contributions by Region, 2009–2014f**

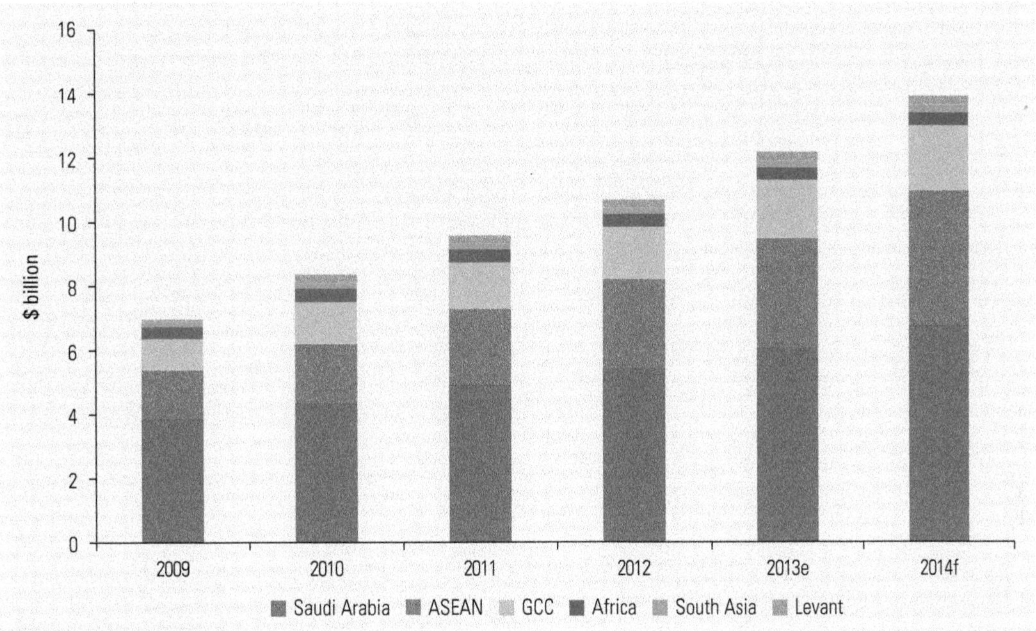

Source: Ernst & Young 2014.
Note: ASEAN = Association of Southeast Asian Nations; GCC = Gulf Cooperation Council; GCC countries include Bahrain, Kuwait, Qatar, and the United Arab Emirates, excluding Saudi Arabia; 2013e = estimate; 2014f = forecast.

TABLE 5.1 ***Takāful* Models**

Properties	*Muḍārabah*	Pure *Wakālah*	Mixed	*Wakālah-Waqf*
Creation of fund	Participants' contributions	Participants' contributions	Participants' contributions	Donations to create initial *waqf*
Fees	None	Up-front fees as agreed	Up-front fees as agreed	Up-front fees as agreed
Underwriting surplus	As per agreed ratio	None[a]	None[a]	None[a]
Underwriting losses	*Qarḍ ḥasan* from *takāful* operator	*Qarḍ ḥasan* from *takāful* operator	*Qarḍ ḥasan* from *takāful* operator	*Waqf* to solicit funds
Investment profits	None	None	Profit-sharing ratio as agreed	Profit-sharing ratio as agreed
Investment losses	Borne by participants	Borne by participants	Borne by participants	Borne by participants
Operational expenses	Borne by *takāful* operator (with some exceptions)	Borne by *takāful* operator	Borne by *takāful* operator	Borne by *takāful* operator
Liquidation	Proceeds accrue only to participants	Proceeds accrue only to participants	Proceeds accrue only to participants	Proceeds accrue only to participants
Jurisdiction	Some GCC members, Malaysia, Saudi Arabia	United Kingdom	Bahrain, Malaysia, Sudan	Pakistan, South Africa

Note: AAOIFI = Accounting and Auditing Organization for Islamic Financial Institutions; GCC = Gulf Cooperation Council.
a. Following the strict AAOIFI interpretation.

directly in either the investment or underwriting risks borne by the *takāful* fund or in any surplus/deficit of the fund. Under the generic *wakālah* model, the operator faces the challenge of ensuring that the operational and management expenses are less than the fees collected; only then can the operator make a profit. Depending on the terms of the contract, the operator's remuneration may include a performance fee, charged against any surplus, as an incentive to effectively manage the *takāful* fund.

This model is gaining popularity across the world due to its transparency and the fixed nature of charges, irrespective of the amount of *takāful* contribution received, as it provides an incentive for the company to act in the best interests of participants and enhance their returns. Moreover, there are fewer issues associated with this model that might create disagreements among *shari'ah* scholars of different schools of thoughts (Akhter 2010).

The *Muḍārabah* Model

In the *muḍārabah* model, the operator is usually entitled to a fixed pre-agreed percentage of any underwriting surplus and/or investment profits of the *takāful* fund. *Takāful* participants are similar to investors who provide capital and contributions in a business venture. Under this arrangement, the operator is allowed to share in the underwriting results from operations, as well as the favorable performance returns on invested premiums. However, the operator's earning is not guaranteed, as there may be no investment return or underwriting surplus at year's end.

The Mixed Model

The mixed model is widely practiced by *takāful* companies around the globe and is currently the dominant model in the Middle East. The Central Bank of Bahrain has also taken the initiative to make it compulsory for *takāful* and re*takāful* companies to adopt this mixed model in their business.

The mixed model combines elements of the *wakālah* and *muḍārabah* models. It is structured so that the *takāful* operator retains two funds: one for the shareholders and the other for participants. The underwriting activities are conducted according to the *wakālah* model; the shareholders manage the funds as an agent on behalf of the participants. In exchange, each participant is charged a *wakālah* fee, which is normally a percentage of their contribution. As an incentive for effective management, the operator is also entitled to earn a fee if there is a surplus in the participants' fund. With regard to investment activities, the operator invests the surplus contributions in different *shari'ah*-compliant instruments based on the *muḍārabah* contract. The operator acts as the investment manager or *muḍārib* on behalf of the participants. The ratio of profit is fixed and agreed between the parties at the time the contract begins. The Accounting and Auditing Organization for Islamic Financial Institutions (AAOIFI) recommends that the mixed model be adopted (Yusof 2001).

The *Waqf* Model

After several objections were raised regarding the *shari'ah* issue that a "profit-sharing" contract should not be applied (as donations cannot simultaneously be capital), the issue of sharing any surplus in the *muḍārabah* model, and the legal status of the *takāful* fund, the *waqf* (Islamic trust) model emerged. The model is a modified form of the *wakālah* model, where a *waqf* fund is created by the initial donations of shareholders. Participants' contributions then go directly to the *waqf* fund. A *waqf* has no owner; however, the operator has the right to devise and administer the fund's rules and regulations. The general idea is that the *takāful* fund should be perpetual communal property devoted to public and community use. *Waqf*-like trusts are legal institutions in their own right and can be governed by the trustees under a civil legal structure. *Waqf* can be expanded beyond the scope of religious activities to cover education, public utilities, social work, and other areas of social services. The *takāful* operator is usually paid its fees from the *waqf* fund as the administrator.

The contributions or donations in the *waqf* fund are invested in *shari'ah*-compliant instruments. The *takāful* operator and participants share the profits from investments according to pre-agreed ratios. The *waqf* fund will pay claims, re*takāful* expenses, and underwriting costs as usual; the net surplus will be vested to the participants. Participants who have no prior claims can be paid the surplus according to their proportion of contribution. The *waqf* model has been adopted by *takāful* operators in South Africa.

Re*takāful*

Re*takāful*[2] allows operators to share risks that they cannot or do not wish to absorb themselves. The main purpose of re*takāful* is similar to that of reinsurance: to spread risk and add capacity, so that larger or more risks can be included. By spreading risk within the industry, *takāful* operators can function more efficiently. Re*takāful* plays a vital role in the general *takāful* sector, especially for large and specialized risks, as compared to family *takāful*.

This arrangement seems very much like reinsurance, but the fundamental difference is that conventional underwriting is about transferring risk, but re*takāful* is about sharing the risk. The operator also becomes a risk manager instead of a risk taker. This is a mirror of the relationship between a *takāful* operator as agent and the *takāful* participants as owners of the *takāful* fund (hence the name, re*takāful*). The risk remains with the participants. By extension to re*takāful*, this implies that the risk remains with the ceding *takāful* operator (Frenz and Soualhi 2010).

Currently, there are a limited number of re*takāful* operators in the industry. Commercial market *takāful* operations have not yet grown to scale in many jurisdictions, except for the GCC countries and Malaysia. On the other hand, *takāful* operators have claimed that their expansion has been limited: particularly their inability to take on large commercial risks, partly due to a lack of scale and re*takāful*. Whatever the situation may be, the wealth from oil-driven growth is encouraging society and businesses to seek protection using *shari'ah*-compliant products and hence will raise the demand for *takāful*, and thus for re*takāful*.

The existing re*takāful* operators are located mainly in GCC states and Malaysia, where the *takāful* businesses are concentrated. Bahrain and Dubai each have two registered re*takāful* operators, Malaysia has four, and Singapore has one. Several renowned companies are also operating from a low tax haven in Malaysia, Labuan Business International Financial Center, mainly as branches of their worldwide entities serving the regional markets in Asia.

One of the main problems worldwide is the lack of re*takāful* companies that are capitalized to the levels required by insurers, and more particularly the lack of A-rated re*takāful* companies. This has resulted in *takāful* companies having to reinsure on a conventional basis, contrary to the preferred option of seeking cover consistent with Islamic principles. About 80 percent of ceded premiums are placed with traditional reinsurers.[3] This practice is allowed under the concept of *ḍarūrah*, or extreme necessity. *Shari'ah* scholars have granted dispensation to *takāful* companies to reinsure on a conventional basis so long as there are no re*takāful* alternatives available, but they may do so for a limited period only. At the same time, industry traditionalists are increasingly challenging whether the necessity (*ḍarūrah*) concept is still applicable in today's market and are encouraging alternatives.

One alternative that some *takāful* operators may embark on is the practice of co*takāful*. In this arrangement, a common *takāful* certificate is issued, and the risk will be shared based on certain agreed percentages between several *takāful* operators. Often, one operator will take the lead. The leading *takāful* operator will be responsible for administering various aspects of the coverage, such as collecting contributions, making claims, and preparing the documents. In this situation, the lead operator may levy a charge (leader fee).

In another practice, a number of large conventional reinsurance companies from Muslim countries take on the risks and retrocede a large proportion of risk with international reinsurance companies that operate on a conventional basis. The cession from *takāful* companies ranges from some 10 percent in Southeast Asia, where *takāful* companies have relatively smaller commercial risks (so far), to the Middle East, where up to 80 percent of risk is reinsured on a conventional basis.

Even though a typical reinsurance transaction is generally based on the principles of contract (*'aqd*), the nature of this transaction is quite different from other forms of commercial contracts in conventional reinsurance. It must also comply with *shari'ah* principles. Reinsurance contracts must essentially be financial transactions that bind both the reinsurance company and the insurance company on the general principles of contract.

All the same, there have been several moves for Islamic reinsurance to displace use of conventional reinsurance. One of the world's largest reinsurer/re*takāful* operators is in talks with Malaysian market players and the Malaysian *Takāful* Association to set up a market re*takāful* pool. This initiative is supported by Bank Negara Malaysia. Given that stricter regulation is likely, especially in GCC countries, *takāful* operators' demand for re*takāful* arrangements should increase. Lloyd's of London is also building its capacity in the *takāful* sector. It has opened an office in Dubai and is in talks with regulators to access the Malaysian market.

Takāful/Re*takāful* Windows

Where the market and its regulation are still in their infancy, as in Indonesia and many countries in Africa, window operations within an insurance company are prevalent. A window is attractive from the standpoint of shareholders, since setting up a separate *takāful* entity requires additional capital. While shareholders see the potential of *takāful,* they also perceive many uncertainties. Usually, companies have segregated the *takāful* funds from other insurance funds, but these companies tend to market *takāful* merely as just another insurance product. Generally, the public lacks awareness of *takāful* and what is *shari'ah* compliant and what is not.

Conflict among brands is also an issue when a company is providing both conventional insurance and *takāful*. Another cause of concern for a window operation is the high likelihood of its Muslim *takāful* intermediaries marketing *takāful* and selling insurance at the same time.

When *shari'ah* compliance is left totally to the producer (in this case, the insurance company), there is a danger as to whether the operator will eventually achieve its status as an Islamic organization. The concept of "permissible in times of necessity" (*ḍarūrah*) may be invoked only sparingly, such as fulfilling the reinsurance needs of the *takāful* operator in the absence of sophisticated re*takāful* arrangements for large and specialized risks. Achieving consistency and standardization in *shari'ah* review may take several years; however, it is a strategy that should be undertaken with full enthusiasm. Similarly, *shari'ah* compliance risk should be minimized by installing a mandatory *shari'ah* board. A definite timeline should be formulated and followed to separate the *takāful* business so that it can be a stand-alone entity. In Indonesia, all windows were given three years to dismantle before the OJK (Otoritas Jasa Keuangan, Indonesia's equivalent of the Financial Services Authority) was inaugurated.

Micro*takāful*

Micro*takāful* can be defined as *takāful* accessed by the low-income market. As such, micro*takāful* is not just a scaled-down version of regular *takāful*; the product and processes need to be completely reengineered to meet the characteristics and preferences of the low-income market, such as farmers, blue collar workers, and small traders. This means that micro*takāful* must have unique product features in line with the income and other realities of the target market. It also requires innovative and cost-effective approaches to reach masses of people who may not be formally employed or have a bank account.

The first micro*takāful* scheme was established in 1997 in Lebanon by the Lebanon Agricultural Mutual Fund. It provides health insurance coverage and meets costs not covered by the Government Social Security Fund, which usually covers 85 percent of hospital fees. The fund covers more than 5,000 families (23,000 beneficiaries). Each family pays a premium of $10 per month. Those who cannot afford the premiums are sponsored by local villagers or other policyholders (Brugnoni 2013).

As with conventional microinsurance, micro*takāful* is delivered with the help of agents and financial institutions. However, to reach the poor, additional innovative distribution channels are organized, including the following:

- *Full-service model:* Regulated *takāful* operators downsize their insurance services and charge a premium the poor can afford. Islamic microfinance institutions can assume the role of insurers by offering basic credit life insurance to protect their loan portfolios.
- *Partnership model: Takāful* operators with products pair with Islamic microfinance institutions and others to provide microinsurance in low-income markets.
- *Community-based model:* Local communities form groups that capitalize and manage a risk pool for their members.
- *Provider model:* Providers, such as hospitals, clinics, or dairy cooperatives, create prepaid or risk pooling coverage for people who use their facilities or services.
- *Social protection models:* National governments underwrite cover for certain risks through social insurance programs, such as for health care, crops, and livestock, as well as covariant risks.[4]

General characteristics of micro*takāful* are presented in table 5.2.

Challenges for the *Takāful* Industry

With regard to regulations, the same regulatory regime cannot be applied to both micro*takāful* and conventional insurance, even for operator-provided schemes. For example, any risk-based requirements will drive up capital costs. The capital requirements for micro*takāful* operators should also be much reduced, and regulations must encourage schemes through cooperatives with additional tax incentives.

Corporate Governance and Regulatory Framework

Although the application of *takāful* products has grown considerably in recent years, only

TABLE 5.2 General Characteristics of Micro*takāful*

Consideration	Micro*takāful*
Extension of social insurance	Yes
Benefits and coverage	Basic assistance, funeral benefits, income during hospital stays, small term life cover benefits
Risks	General, catastrophic
Customer segmentation	Informal economy, affinity groups, cooperatives
Affordability	Salary deductions, benevolent sponsorships, affordable contributions by low-income participants
Underwriting	Group basis, link with microfinance
Distribution	Home service agents, micro Islamic financial institutions , cooperatives, affinity groups, *Masjid* (place of worship)

a few countries have distinct *takāful* regulations, and some countries favor the use of one *takāful* model over another. Regulators need to understand the implications of regulations and accounting standards for how assets are valued and how surplus and profits are computed and distributed. In *takāful*, just like insurance, premiums are due up front before service is rendered. This means that premiums must be invested in suitable *shari'ah*-compliant assets. For contingent benefits where claims can happen at any time, investing solely in volatile assets like equities is not advisable.

Malaysia has one of the most advanced sets of *takāful* regulations. The growth of *takāful* is only one part of the general growth of Islamic finance in the country. Malaysia has a vibrant Islamic banking and capital market, with by far the largest *sukūk* market anywhere in the world (see chapter 4). It also has a large (but not large enough) base of human capital trained in Islamic finance, including *takāful*. Thus, using Malaysia as a standard as to how *takāful* should be regulated may not be appropriate for a country only now venturing into *takāful*.

In contrast to Malaysia, Bahrain's conventional and *takāful* industry remains rules based. Regulations are set out in rulebooks that provide guidance as to how insurance and *takāful* liabilities should be valued (Central Bank of Bahrain 2011). There is built-in flexibility, though, as other methodologies can be acceptable, if justified. As in Malaysia, *takāful* windows are not allowed. However, the regulation says that only the *wakālah* (agency) contract can be used in *takāful*, with a subsidiary *mudārabah* contract for assets being invested.

There is no explicit guidance as to how *takāful* products should be priced. Thus operators are free to set their fee under the *wakālah* contract. This arrangement has been exploited by some *takāful* companies, with little consideration for whether the premium net of *wakālah* fees is sufficient to pay claims.

Regulating *takāful* is different from regulating insurance. This stems from the hybrid nature of its setup. A risk-based approach to regulating *takāful* is desirable, but well-thought-out, rules-based regulation may suffice initially. An important early decision for the regulators is whether to allow *takāful* windows. *Shari'ah* is flexible on this matter only if regulations preclude the setup of stand-alone *takāful* companies.

Having a holistic approach that keeps in mind the viewpoint of both the industry and consumers is a critical factor to nurture industry best practices and market development. Policies need to balance protections for participants' rights with the need for effective pricing, greater solvency, operators' financial sustainability, good business conduct, and relevant disclosures. On the consumer side, there is demand for greater transparency of *takāful* operators and better financial education to unlock various opportunities for industry's growth. To avoid confusion among Muslims, there should be a consensus among *shari'ah* scholars in the country as to how *takāful* is implemented. Although in Malaysia the majority of Muslims are happy for the government to decide what *shari'ah* compliance means, this may not be possible in other jurisdictions. An early consensus among local scholars on how *takāful* is structured is important.

Looking at substance over form is important, as ultimately, if risks are similar, the capital solvency requirements should be the same, no matter how the risk fund is branded. Regulators should look for arbitrage opportunities between *takāful* and the insurance industry. For example, a similar product could require lower solvency capital if it were sold as a *takāful* product than if it were sold as a conventional product. Such arbitrage may harm the *takāful* industry over the long term if such lower solvency capital is not justified.

Lack of Investment Opportunities

The investment environment remains challenging for *takāful* operators. Not only are *shari'ah*-compliant investments lacking in many jurisdictions, but *takāful* operators do not have many options for long-term and stable investments. In addition, as many of the players in the industry are relatively young, the *takāful* industry has generated higher expense ratios in comparison to insurers operating in the same market, reducing operators' profitability. Stricter solvency and capital requirements also make it harder for smaller players to achieve profitability. Young *takāful* players will need to either quickly build scale or consider mergers to meet the regulatory demands. Hence governments wanting higher growth in *takāful* should also look into development of an Islamic capital market and provide flexibility in the implementation of the risk-based capital regime.

Policy Response

Takāful, like Islamic finance, has two sides: financial efficiency and *shari'ah* compliance. There is a need to develop a globally accepted business model based on risk sharing that promotes shared prosperity. Governments have always played a pivotal role in creating a conducive legal and regulatory framework. They must recognize that *takāful* is markedly different than insurance. Unlike insurance, *takāful* is a unilateral agreement that is based on the principles of mutual cooperation (*ta'awun*) of the participants and donation (*tabarru'*).

Bahrain, Malaysia, and Pakistan have comprehensive *takāful* regulations in place that take into account the unique requirements of the industry. The Saudi Arabian Monetary Authority (SAMA) now requires all *takāful* businesses to be aligned with the cooperative insurance model rather than *wakālah* and *qard* concepts. Several regulatory changes have been introduced recently in many countries; while they are positive in nature, there is concern about the increased inconsistencies across jurisdictions, such as differences in accounting standards. Inconsistencies in *takāful* regulations make it difficult for multinational *takāful* operators to function across regions and also lead to confusion for customers (Ernst & Young 2012).

The global *takāful* industry is small in comparison with the conventional insurance industry. Thus the market needs to gain worldwide brand recognition and exceed performance. *Takāful* can build up public confidence. Once it has, the public can be expected to voluntarily opt for the various *takāful* options in their individual and collective interests. Financing for small and medium enterprises (SMEs) and microfinancing are high on the agenda of the Group of Twenty (G-20). This will have a positive influence on *takāful*, especially for Muslim start-ups and SMEs. Micro*takāful* can be a mechanism to mitigate financial risk for the poor by safeguarding and ensuring the productive use of their savings and credit facilities, and can also be effective in reducing their vulnerability to the impact of disease, theft, disability, and other perils.

Regulators need to be cohesive in their approach to regulation of the industry; regulations should not hamper the growth and stability of the *takāful* market. Industry practitioners and regulators must attempt to discover an approach to implement the conceptual requirements of *takāful* as defined by *shari'ah* scholars in a way that is commercially viable for shareholders and considerate of participants' interests. In the marketplace, the attraction of *takāful* business should be not just for the fact that it is based on *shari'ah* law, but because it is better, rational, and equitable. This aspect should be attractive to everyone, irrespective of any religious foundation upon which the system stands initially.

The dual *takāful*/insurance regulatory system, as in Malaysia, may be a good alternative to adopt and can stand as a worldwide benchmark for *takāful* services in terms of customer satisfaction, quality of services, and transparency of its operations. However, regulators need to watch for any operators taking advantage of the situation and working to converge its operations along the lines of conventional insurance. *Takāful* operators have tended to choose this as their preferred form and have modeled a *takāful* operation around them or have feigned a *shari'ah* wrap over these contracts, just to be compliant. New operators, especially, have taken a businesslike perspective on *takāful*. Although this is correct, there is a risk that the spirit of *takāful* may be lost or severely diluted in the process. Box 5.2 highlights the approach Nigeria has taken to regulation and the challenges the country faces in implementing *takāful*.

Developing a best practice charter as a benchmark for *takāful* operations worldwide is valuable but has proved to be challenging, mainly because of diverse legal frameworks, the varying kind of markets and their level of maturity, and the differences in interpretations on matters related to *shari'ah*. Table 5.3 is an attempt to provide elements of such a charter.

BOX 5.2 Country Case: Regulation and Challenges in Nigeria

With a population of 177.2 million people, Nigeria has about one-sixth of the population of Africa and is the eighth most populous country in the world. Fifty percent of the population is Muslim (U.S. CIA 2015). Nigeria currently has no social security system, and only 1 percent of the total adult population is insured, according to the Nigerian Insurance Regulator (NAICOM). The reasons for the low rate of penetration include low income levels and limited awareness of insurance products and their benefits, as well as a lack of transparency regarding the operating practices of some companies.

To increase the penetration of insurance among the Muslim population, NAICOM has issued landmark guidelines to support the *takāful* operations in Nigeria.[a] The guidelines provide the framework for *takāful* operations. The approved models to operate *takāful* include *muḍārabah* (profit sharing), *wakālah* (agency), and hybrid *wakālah-muḍārabah* (agency–profit sharing).

The guidelines recommend that each *takāful* operation have in place an Advisory Council of Experts (ACE) to ensure that the operations are in line with best practice. The ACE is responsible and accountable for all *shari'ah* decisions, opinions, and views provided by them. As having their own *shari'ah* advisers and experts can be challenging in the initial stages, operators can refer *shari'ah* matters to a *Takāful* Advisory Council, which resides with NAICOM.

NAICOM had two main objectives in introducing the guidelines. The first was to make *takāful* a better platform for financial inclusion, especially for Muslims, but also for Christians and others with ethical inclinations and beliefs. The second was to make *takāful* a better means to intensify the penetration rate of insurance in Nigeria. As Muslims are a big majority, intensifying insurance penetration in the Muslim population can contribute to the nation's gross domestic product (GDP).

The main challenge for both insurance and the *takāful* industry is poverty. Micro*takāful* can play a role in overcoming this challenge; as discussed, micro*takāful* is not social welfare or social assistance but a complementary market solution. For the low-income market to access micro*takāful*, it needs to be affordable and appropriate to the target market's needs and be convenient.

Another major challenge is customers' awareness of *takāful*. For a long time, many Nigerian Muslims believed that insurance is contrary to Islamic principles, particularly with regard to life insurance (Fadun 2014). *Takāful* intermediaries such as the *takāful* agents must be properly trained and committed, as they are usually the operators' first point of contact and primary source of information about *takāful*.

Another important pillar for successful *takāful* operation is the presence of sustainable investment portfolios that comply with *shari'ah* requirements. The lack of Islamic financial instruments poses enormous challenges to *takāful* operators in Nigeria because *takāful* funds cannot be invested in conventional bonds and interest-based financial assets. It is also essential that the regulatory regime does not treat *takāful* less favorably than conventional insurance in Nigeria. This is necessary to promote prudent *takāful* practices.

a. Information collected by the authors and Operational Guidelines 2013, *Takāful* Insurance Operators Guidelines, http://naicom.gov.ng/payload?id=964fc42e-4025-43f3-8b34-97e82b2c50f7.

TABLE 5.3 Best Practice Charter for *Takāful* Operations Worldwide

Takāful core principles	Description	Best practice
Regulations	Clear and transparent regulation and supervisory procedures that are appropriate for *takāful* are needed.	A separate *takāful* law is recommended, but supplementary regulation is needed, at minimum. Micro*takāful* should be regulated differently from *takāful*.
Licensing requirements	A legal entity that intends to engage in *takāful* activities must be licensed before it can operate. The *takāful* legislation must set out the procedure and form of establishment under which companies will be allowed to conduct *takāful* activities within a jurisdiction.	A full-fledged operation with some minimum initial capital for a single license is preferred. A "window" operation may be permissible under special conditions, provided it is only a temporary arrangement.
Takāful model	*Takāful* operators should establish an operational model that outlines the key policies, procedures, and management responsibilities in carrying out the *takāful* operations. The operational model should be based on fair and equitable agreements and approved by the *shari'ah* committee.	The *wakālah* model is preferred, with sharing of investment returns. *wakālah* fees should be limited to 40 percent of *tabarru'*. The profit-sharing ratio to the company should be restricted to 30 percent. Surplus-sharing to the operator is not allowed. Where the law permits, *takāful* funds should be ring-fenced as a *waqf*.
Shari'ah compliance and corporate governance	Regulations must ensure that the *takāful* entity demonstrates the essential features of *takāful* and that they are consistent with *shari'ah* principles. Operators must also establish and implement a corporate governance framework that provides for sound and prudent management and oversight of the business and adequately recognizes and protects the interests of participants.	A proper *shari'ah* governance framework should be followed. A *shari'ah* board should be established and consist of no fewer than three fit and proper members. Members should serve on no more than three committees. The board and *shari'ah* committee will be liable for non-*shari'ah* compliance. A *shari'ah* audit should be conducted annually. A report by the chairman of the *shari'ah* committee should be included in its annual report. Various committees of the board, such as risk management, audit, and investment, must be established.
Risk management and internal control	As part of its overall corporate governance framework, the operator must have effective systems of risk management and internal controls, including effective functions for risk management, compliance, actuarial matters, and internal audit.	Because *takāful* operators derived their income mainly from fees and performance incentives, they must establish effective policies and procedures to manage operating costs. Guidelines on controlling operational cost can be introduced. All operators must acquire their own actuarial expertise.
Conduct of business	Requirements should be established for the conduct of the business of *takāful* to ensure that customers are treated fairly, both before a contract is entered into and through to the point at which all obligations under a contract have been satisfied. These requirements are expected to enhance market discipline in the area of marketing and business development.	To strengthen public trust and consumer confidence in the *takāful* sector, staff must be properly and adequately trained, particularly with respect to operational and *shari'ah* aspects of the business. A minimum levy (for example, 5 percent of total salaries) should be imposed if staff training is deficient.

table continues next page

TABLE 5.3 Best Practice Charter for *Takāful* Operations Worldwide *(continued)*

Takāful core principles	Description	Best practice
		Customers must be treated fairly. • Products should be developed and marketed with due regard for customers. • Customers should be provided with clear information before, during, and after the point of sale. Any advice given should be high quality. • The privacy of information obtained from customers should be protected. • The reasonable expectations of customers should be met.
Capital adequacy and solvency	Capital adequacy requirements (CAR) should be established for solvency purposes so that operators can absorb significant unforeseen losses.	A risk-based capital (RBC) framework should be established. The supervisory CAR should be set at appropriate levels to recognize the different level of maturity of the market.
Investments	Requirements should be set for solvency purposes on the investment activities of *takāful* in order to address the risks faced by the operators.	The concept of "admitted assets" should no longer apply. Risk charges applicable for different asset classes under the RBC framework will ensure the right investment discipline. *Shari'ah*-compliant assets that are back by real assets should have lower risk charges.
Consumer protection	The interest of the participants must be given priority by the operator, especially if there is a conflict of interest.	• The law must require the separation of the *takāful* funds from the shareholder's fund and explicitly stipulate that *takāful* funds do not belong to the operators. • *Takāful* contracts and certificates must be written in a language that is easily understood by the participants and other stakeholders. • The law must stipulate that *takāful* intermediaries have ostensible authority and will bind the operator. • A cooling-off period must be provided to the participants.
Public disclosure	Operators should disclose relevant, comprehensive, and adequate information on a timely basis to enable participants, stakeholders, and the public to better understand the underlying *takāful* operations and to give participants and the public a clear view of their business activities, performance, and financial position.	In addition to their annual reports, *takāful* operators should publish a special report on the fund's investment performance. To further promote transparency, *takāful* operators should publish on their website details of their operational model, together with the underlying *shari'ah* principles, and details of products, fees, and charges.

Notes

1. For more on the Iranian market, see the *World Islamic Banking Competitiveness Report 2014–15* (Ernst & Young 2015).
2. Re*takāful* is a transaction whereby one company (typically, the re*takāful* operator) agrees to indemnify another *takāful* company (the ceding company, or cedant) against all or part of the loss. For this service, the ceding company transfers or shares part of the contribution it receives with the re*takāful* operator.
3. Estimated by Vasilis Katsipis, Dubai-based general manager for market development at insurance rating agency A.M. Best, quoted in "Islamic Reinsurance Moves to Displace Use of Conventional Finance," http://uk.reuters.com/article/2015/04/26/islam-reinsurance-idUKL5N0XJ11Z20150426.
4. Microinsurance Network website, http://www.microinsurancenetwork.org.

References

Akhter, Waheed. 2010. "Takaful Models and Global Practices." *Journal of Islamic Banking and Finance* 27 (1): 30–44.

Brugnoni, A. 2013. "Micro*Takaful*." In *Takaful and Mutual Insurance: Alternative Approaches to Managing Risks*, edited by Serap O. Gonulal. Directions in Development Series. Washington, DC: World Bank.

Central Bank of Bahrain. *Rulebook. Volume 3—Insurance*. 2011. Central Bank of Bahrain.

Cofie, Patience, Manuela De Allegri, Bocar Kouyaté, and Rainer Sauerborn. 2013. "Effects of Information, Education, and Communication Campaign on a Community-Based Health Insurance Scheme in Burkina Faso." *Global Health Action* (6): 20791.

Ernst & Young. 2012. *The World Takaful Report*. London: Ernst & Young.

———. 2014. *Global Takaful Insights 2014: Market Updates*. London: Ernst & Young.

———. 2015. *World Islamic Banking Competitiveness Report 2014–15*. http://www.ey.com/Publication/vwLUAssets/EY-world-islamic-banking-competitiveness-report-2014-15/$FILE/EY-world-islamic-banking-competitiveness-report-2014-15.pdf.

Fadun, Olajide Solomon. 2014. "*Takaful* (Islamic Insurance) Practices: Challenges and Prospects in Nigeria." *Journal of Insurance Law & Practice* 4 (2): 12.

Frenz, Tobias, and Younes Soualhi. 2010. *Takaful and ReTakaful: Advanced Principles and Practices*. 2nd ed. Kuala Lumpur: IBFIM.

Gaurav, Sarthak, Shawn Cole, and Jeremy Tobacman. 2011. "Marketing Complex Financial Products in Emerging Markets: Evidence from Rainfall Insurance in India." *Journal of Marketing Research* 48 SPL (November): S150–62.

Noubiap, Jean Jacques, Walburga Yvonne Joko, Joel Marie Obama, Jean Joel Bigna, and Valery Nzima Nzima. 2013. "Community-based Health Insurance Knowledge, Concern, Preferences, and Financial Planning for Health Care among Informal Sector Workers in a Health District of Douala, Cameroon." *Pan African Medical Journal* 16: 17. doi:10.11604/pamj.2013.16.17.2279.

Panda, Pradeep, Arpita Chakraborty, and David M. Dror. 2015. "Building Awareness to Health Insurance among the Target Population of Community-based Health Insurance Schemes in Rural India." *Tropical Medicine & International Health* 20 (8): 1093–107

Panda, Pradeep, Arpita Chakraborty, Wameq Raza, and Arjun Bedi. 2015. "Renewing Membership in Three Community-based Health Insurance Schemes in Rural India." *International Institute of Social Studies Working Paper Series* 608: 1–28. http://hdl.handle.net/1765/77965.

U.S. CIA (United States Central Intelligence Agency). 2015. *CIA World Fact Book*. Washington, DC: U.S. Central Intelligence Agency.

Yusof, Mohd Fadzli. 2001. "An Overview of the *Takaful* Industry." *New Horizon* 107: 9–11.

6

Nonbank Financial Institutions

Whereas banks are the dominant form of financial intermediaries in most economies, nonbank financial institutions (NBFIs) complement the activities of banks by providing various services that banks typically do not provide. NBFIs provide diversity in the financial sector and perform various functions essential for growth and development of the economy (Carmichael and Pomerleano 2002). A diversified financial sector that includes banks and NBFIs provide a basis for a sound and stable financial system (Bakker and Gross 2004). NBFIs can also act as backup institutions that may help stabilize the financial sector when negative shocks adversely affect the dominant financial institutions, notably banks.

A comprehensive Islamic financial system reflects the broader goals of Islam, which aim not only to achieve economic goals but also to address social needs. The eradication of poverty, socioeconomic justice, and the equitable distribution of income are core features of an Islamic economic system (Chapra 1985). The Islamic financial system should be able to fulfill these general economic goals and include institutions that aim to meet these objectives. Accordingly, Islamic financial institutions should give prominence to risk-sharing modes of financing that promote growth and cater to the social needs of all segments of the society. While Islamic banks modeled as commercial banks do not reflect these features completely (see chapter 3), NBFIs may be able to provide services that fulfill the broader goals of Islam and promote shared prosperity more effectively. Similar to banking and capital markets, for a robust Islamic NBFI sector that enhances shared prosperity, the requirements include supportive institutions and public policy, responsible governance and leadership, and a robust regulatory framework that promotes risk sharing and entrepreneurship.

Recent Developments and Current Status

Broadly speaking, NBFIs cover all financial institutions other than commercial banks. However, for the purpose of this Report,

NBFIs include all those institutions that are not subject to the supervision of the central bank but can act like banking institutions: that is, accepting funds and investing those funds, whether in the capital market or through direct placement. Specifically, this chapter focuses on Islamic asset management, housing finance, and some specialized NBFIs such as *muḍārabah*[1] and *ijārah* (Islamic leasing) financing companies.

The NBFIs operating in the field of Islamic finance can be classified according to the nature of the service they provide to their clients and the segment of their clients. From this perspective, Islamic NBFIs provide four basic financial services for their clients from five different segments (table 6.1):

- Islamic asset management, venture capital, and private equity companies provide investment-related services for their institutional and corporate clients.
- Corporate foundations provide philanthropic services such as *awqaf* (Islamic foundations, endowments, and trusts).
- Asset financing and *mudārabah* companies provide financing and investment services either to their private customers or to customers from various segments of the mass market.
- Microfinance and microsavings institutions provide small amounts of funding, typically to the underbanked (those not served by formal financial institutions).
- Through *ḥajj* funds, Muslims from different income groups can save to finance travel and accommodations for pilgrimages at various stages of their lives.

The composition of the NBFI sector differs from country to country, depending on the legal environment and the organizations that exist. With the exception of a few countries, the nonbank financial sector is relatively underdeveloped in most emerging economies in general and in member-countries of the Islamic Development Bank (IDB) in particular. For example, whereas the banking systems in the Middle East and North Africa (MENA) are generally large relative to other regions, the NBFIs are mostly undeveloped (Rocha, Arvai, and Farazi 2011). The average development index for the nonbank financial sector in the MENA Region (3.3) is much lower than the index for the banking sector (5.5) (Creane and others 2006). Indonesia, however, has a vibrant nonbank financial sector, with a wide array of financial institutions providing a diversity of financial products. In a survey of 3,360 households in Indonesia, 51 percent of the respondents disclosed that they saved in a nonbank financial institution, compared to 41 percent who had bank accounts. Moreover, 52 percent took loans from informal sources, compared

TABLE 6.1 Classification of Nonbank Islamic Finance Institutions

Type of client	Financing	Investment	Pilgrimage	Philanthropy
Institutional	Investment banks and funds	Asset management (fund managers, venture capital, private equity)		
Corporate				Corporate foundations
Affluent	Financing companies	Brokerage, fund managers, *muḍārabah* companies	*Ḥajj* funds	
Mass market	Financing companies, leasing companies, credit unions, and cooperatives			
Underbanked	Microfinance pawn shops, microfinance institutions	Microsavings		

Source: Adapted from IDB, IRTI, and IFSB 2014.

to 25 percent who had formal loans (Cole, Sampson, and Zia 2011).

Not only is the NBFI sector small in most IDB member countries, but the bulk of the NBFIs are still conventional. For example, in Pakistan, the total asset size of the NBFI sector was 747.07 billion Pakistan rupees (PRs) ($7.34 billion) in April 2015, and only 21 percent of the total assets were *shari'ah* compliant (SECP 2015). However, the sector has been moving toward greater *shari'ah* compliance over time. In Pakistan, the Islamic NBFI sectors grew about 224 percent from June 2010 to April 2015, while the conventional sector grew 74 percent; as a result, the share of *shari'ah*-compliant NBFI assets grew from 12.3 percent to 21 percent of all NBFI assets (SECP 2015).

The discussion that follows describes the status and development of different types of NBFIs in IDB members. Unfortunately, the data and information on NBFIs in general and Islamic NBFIs in particular are scattered and are not available in an organized manner. Given these constraints, the discussion that follows summarizes recent developments in Islamic asset management, SME finance, housing finance, and other NBFIs such as *muḍārabah* and *ijārah* companies.

Asset Management

The overall size of the mutual funds industry is relatively small in most IDB member-countries. As table 6.2 shows, the stock market in the MENA Region is relatively large, amounting to 23.37 percent of GDP; however, there are no comparative data available on mutual fund assets for the region (Rocha, Arvai, and Farazi 2011).

Islamic mutual funds grew rapidly in the 1990s, following the ruling by the Islamic *Fiqh* Academy (IFA) on the legitimacy of investment in stocks. The recent growth trends in numbers and assets under management (AUM) of global Islamic funds and mutual funds are shown in figure 6.1. The Islamic asset management industry has gained remarkable momentum since the global financial crisis. The total amount of AUM has more than doubled from $28.35 billion in 2008 to $60.65 billion as of 2014, with a cumulative average growth rate around 13.5 percent. Despite the dramatic growth, the sector still has a market share that is below 1 percent of the total global asset management industry and around 3 percent of all Islamic financial assets worldwide. Nevertheless, during the same period, the number of funds has increased from 756 to 1,181,

TABLE 6.2 Size of Capital Markets and Mutual Fund Assets in Selected World Regions, 2012

Regions	Mutual fund assets to GDP (%)	Stock market capitalization to GDP (%)
Income group		
World	10.91	30.76
High-income	18.75	53.01
Middle-income	2.01	20.14
Low-income	..	19.37
Developing countries only		
Sub-Saharan Africa	19.01	22.19
East Asia and Pacific	4.04	44.07
Europe and Central Asia	1.37	11.66
Latin America and the Caribbean	3.35	24.58
Middle East and North Africa	..	23.37
South Asia	3.76	20.09

Source: World Bank Global Financial Development Database.
Note: .. = negligible.

FIGURE 6.1 Global Islamic Asset Management Industry, 2008–14

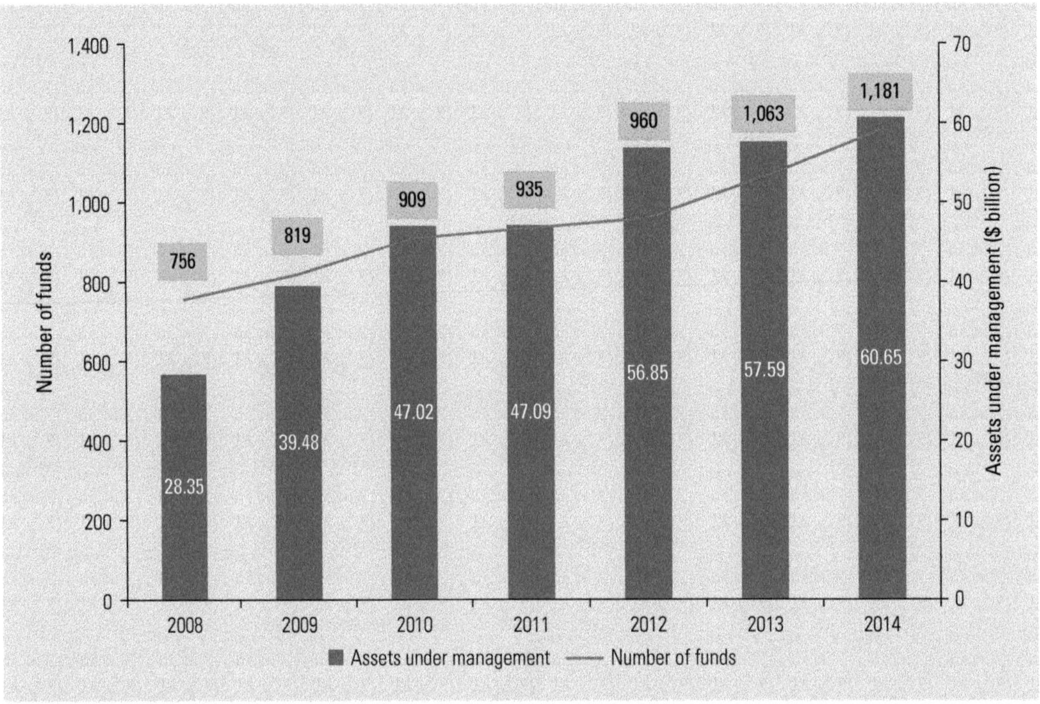

Source: Thomson Reuters 2015.

corresponding to a cumulative average growth rate of around 8 percent per year.

The traditional assets classes include *shari'ah*-compliant stocks, *sukūk*, and money market instruments. Alternative Islamic investment assets comprise real estate/infrastructure, commodities, private equity funds, and some newly established hedge funds. Table 6.3 shows the asset type of the Islamic funds that were launched over the five years from 2009 to 2013. The bulk of the funds (41.8 percent) were equity based, followed by *sukūk* (24.1 percent). Mixed funds were 14.3 percent of the new funds during the period, followed by money market funds (12.8 percent) and real estate funds (4.6 percent).

The global Islamic asset management industry is dominated by mutual funds. As of 2014, mutual funds accounted for almost 88 percent of all assets managed by the global Islamic asset management industry and 80 percent of the total number of Islamic funds. The AUM of Islamic mutual funds rose from $25.71 billion to $53.17 between 2008 and 2014 (figure 6.2), while the number increased from 568 to 953. With a cumulative average annual growth of around 13 percent in terms of AUM and 9 percent in terms of number of funds, the mutual fund segment is the flagship of the global Islamic asset management industry.

A promising segment of the Islamic asset management sector is exchange traded funds (ETFs). From 2008 to 2014, the segment experienced a remarkable rate of growth of around 20 percent on a cumulative average basis. Total AUM by Islamic ETFs grew from $2.17 billion in 2008 to $10.75 billion in 2012. After a sharp decline in 2013 to $5.77 billion, the Islamic ETF sector recovered in 2014, with AUM rising by around 10 percent to $6.33 billion, which accounted for more than 10 percent of total assets managed by the Islamic funds industry.

The share of pension, insurance, and equity funds is around 2 percent of the total AUM (figure 6.2). The share of these three categories of funds did not change significantly from

TABLE 6.3 **Funds Launched and Asset Type, 2009–13**

Year	Total number of funds launched	Bonds (*sukūk*)	Equity	Mixed	Money market	Real estate	Other
2013 (through September)	82	24	30	19	8	1	—
2012	54	9	23	9	6	3	4
2011	62	9	32	4	10	6	1
2010	77	19	34	12	7	4	1
2009	53	18	18	3	11	1	2
Total	328	79	137	47	42	15	8
Percentage	100.00	24.09	41.77	14.33	12.80	4.57	2.44

Source: Thomson Reuters 2014.
Note: — = not available.

FIGURE 6.2 **Assets under Management by Fund Type, 2008–14**

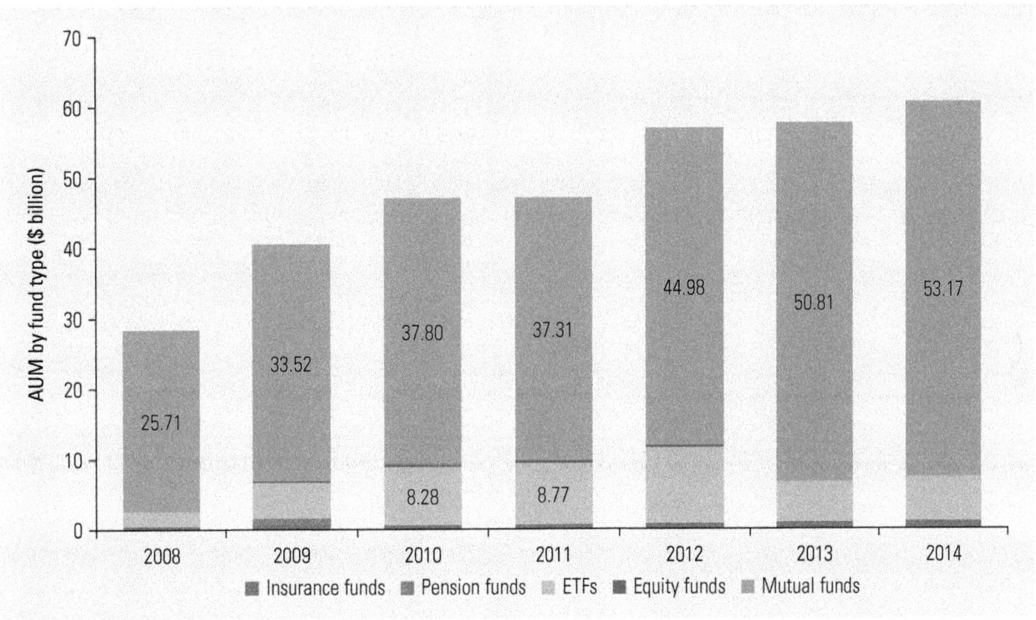

Source: Thomson Reuters 2015.
Note: AUM = assets under management; ETF = exchange traded funds.

2008 to 2013, reflecting the general trends within the industry. This indicates that there is scope for diversification and expansion of these types of funds in the future.

Figure 6.3 shows the distribution of outstanding Islamic funds by geographic area. Islamic funds are concentrated in the Gulf Cooperation Council (GCC) Region (37 percent), followed by Southeast Asia (31 percent). Globally focused Islamic funds make up 17 percent of the total, while 7 percent target North America, and 4 percent are directed toward other Asian countries, notably Japan and China.

As of end-2014, funds invested in equities dominated the Islamic asset management sector, with around 40 percent of the total AUM (see figure 6.4). Money market funds were also popular, accounting for 36 percent of the total. While there was a move away from commodity

FIGURE 6.3 Global Islamic Funds Outstanding by Geographic Area, End-2014

Percentage of assets under management

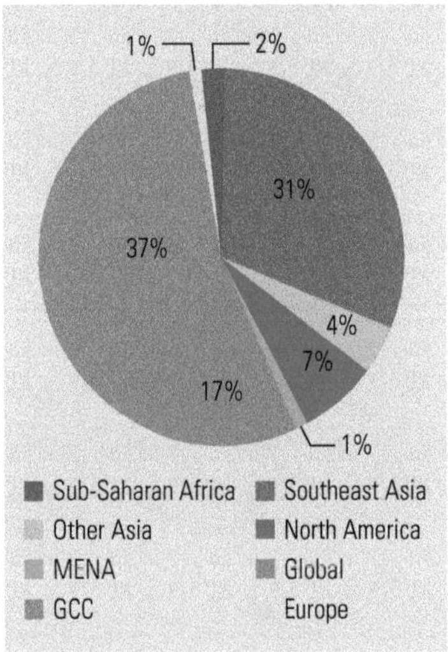

Source: Thomson Reuters 2015.
Note: GCC = Gulf Cooperation Council; MENA = Middle East and North Africa.

FIGURE 6.4 Global Islamic Asset Management Funds by Asset Class, End-2014

Percentage of assets under management

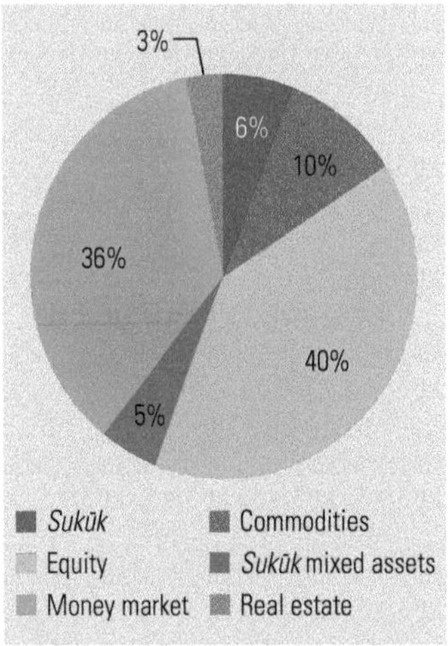

Source: Thomson Reuters 2015.

funds from 2009 to 2014 because of commodity price volatility, these funds still accounted for 10 percent of the total at the end of 2014. *Sukūk* funds constituted 6 percent of the total assets, mixed assets funds made up 5 percent of Islamic funds, and real estate funds accounted for around 3 percent.

Whereas most of the Organisation of Islamic Cooperation (OIC) member-countries have public pension schemes for government employees, the number of private pension schemes is very small. Nevertheless, several *shari'ah*-compliant pension schemes are being established by Islamic financial institutions, which will enhance provision in the private sector. For example, in Pakistan, Meezan Bank has established a voluntary pension scheme called the Meezan Tahafuzz Pension Fund, and MCB-Arif Habib Savings, an asset management firm, launched the Pakistan Islamic Pension Fund. In some countries, such as Turkey, the government has initiated regulatory reforms that promote expansion of pension schemes under public-private partnerships. Under the new regime that became effective in January 2013 in Turkey, the government matches 25 percent of the contributions of participants (KPMG Turkey 2013). The reform has boosted the fund management industry in general and the private pension market in particular in the country (Sezer 2013).

The majority of the asset management products are targeted toward people who are well-off. For example, in the MENA Region, while public pension funds target government employees, private pension funds are targeted toward a small number of privileged professionals (Rocha, Arvai, and Farzi 2011). As a result, people with lower income levels are unable to benefit.

Achieving the goal of shared prosperity will require coming up with products that serve the needs of the poor and low-income groups. One way for asset management products to be more accessible to lower-income groups is to make them more affordable by, for example, lowering the minimum subscription rates. The Meezan Islamic Fund is an example of a fund that has a low minimum subscription—only PRs 5,000 (approximately $50)—to open an account, with subsequent investments of PRs 1,000 (approximately $10), which are very affordable amounts for small investors. Similarly, the Amana Mutual Funds in the United States has a minimum subscription of only $250.[2]

BOX 6.1 Case 1. Green *Sukūk* and the Rising Trend in Responsible Investment

The area of socially responsible investment (SRI) has great potential for the Islamic asset management industry to increase its contribution to shared prosperity. The notions underlying the SRI concept have a lot in common with the broad goals of Islamic finance. The strong emphasis on adhering to the values related to social and environmental development inherent in Islamic theology and jurisprudence has important implications for the investment behavior of investors in Islamic finance. Therefore, relating the Islamic finance products such as *sukūk* to the concept of SRI and building a product structure that complies with the fundamentals of the SRI concept will not only increase the number of products in which both Muslim and non-Muslim investors may invest but also increase the contribution of Islamic asset management to shared prosperity.

One recent example of relating Islamic finance to SRI can be found in Malaysia. The Securities Commission of Malaysia launched a new framework for SRI *sukūk* in August 2014 to facilitate the financing of sustainable and responsible investment initiatives (Securities Commission Malaysia 2014). As an extension of existing *sukūk* regulations, the new framework has refined the conditions for the issuance of SRI *sukūk*, defining the utilization of the proceeds; eligible SRI projects in areas such as education, health, and renewable energy that will contribute to the quality of life within society; disclosure requirements; and the appointment of independent auditors to provide detailed financial reporting.

Following this new legislation, Malaysia's sovereign wealth fund, Khazanah Nasional, issued Malaysia's first social impact *sukūk* under the *Sukūk* Ihsan Programme (Reuters 2015). The aim is to raise 1 billion Malaysian ringgit (RM) ($282 million) and use the proceeds on educational projects. The first tranche of the *sukūk* worth RM 100 million was issued in 2015. The issue received a AAA rating by a local rating agency. The Ihsan *sukūk* has several unique features, including a reduction in the principle amount invested whenever the projects to be financed meet specified performance indicators. Given this feature, the main driver for the demand for the *sukūk* is expected to be the annual distributions investors may collect and the buy-back guarantee provided by Khazanah for a nominal consideration. In addition to local investors, the *sukūk* is expected to attract a wide range of corporate investors with social responsibility agendas.

Along with Malaysia's efforts in terms of SRI *sukūk*, the Gulf countries are working to develop green *sukūk* that will finance renewable and clean energy projects. The Dubai Supreme Council of Energy has announced a partnership with the World Bank to develop a green energy strategy, which also includes *sukūk* financing tool. The United Arab Emirates Securities and Commodities Authority has recently developed reforms to incorporate green *sukūk* into its *sukūk* regulation framework. The Saudi Arabian government also has ambitious intentions in the area of green energy. Given the fact that the Gulf Cooperation Council (GCC) Region is one of the fastest growing regions in the world, with a population expected to exceed 53 million by 2020, the need for sustainable and responsible investments in energy, water, transport, and urban development is also predicted to grow. This need increases the potential for the development of SRI *sukūk* investments within the region.

Sources: Islamic Finance News 2015a, 2015b.

Although still at the idea stage, a recent opportunity in the Islamic finance realm that can contribute to the well-being of a society is the socially responsible investment (SRI) *sukūk*, which provides the investors opportunities to invest in assets and projects that are targeted to produce environmentally sustainable and socially responsible outcomes. Box 6.1 describes a promising new market for sustainable and responsible investment *sukūk*.

SME Finance

Small and medium enterprises (SMEs) contribute significantly to employment in developing countries. SMEs employing 5–250 workers contribute two-thirds (66.4 percent) of the average total permanent full-time employment in 99 countries, Ayyagari, Demirgüç-Kunt, and Maksimovic (2011) estimate. While they find that SMEs contribute greatly to employment and GDP, they do not find a robust relationship between the SME sector and productivity growth.

Despite this remarkable contribution of SMEs to GDP, in a survey of micro and small enterprises from 13 countries, the World Bank (2014, 107) found that limited access to finance was the key obstacle to operations identified most frequently (by 36 percent of the firms). SMEs worldwide face huge financing gaps. Table 6.4 shows the number of formal and informal SMEs that are unserved and underserved and the estimated amounts of the financing gap in different regions.

Although the financing gap for the SME sector is huge in developing countries, traditional banks do not have incentives or appetite to provide financing to these enterprises because they are considered risky and costly (World Bank 2008). Specifically, banks are not willing to finance SMEs due to the various obstacles they face, including not only high risk but also limited specialization, high operating costs, and poorly developed legal systems (IFC 2014b).

This reluctance is also reflected in the financing practices of Islamic banks, as displayed in table 6.5. In a survey of 160 conventional banks from nine countries, the International Finance Corporation (IFC) found that although 47 percent had adequate SME product offerings, the overall SME portfolio penetration rate was only 37 percent (IFC 2014b). The corresponding figures were much lower for Islamic banks: 16 percent had SME product offerings, but the portfolio penetration rate was only 11 percent (IFC 2014a).

In the same study of nine countries, IFC (2014b) estimates that about one-third (32.2 percent) of the SMEs would prefer *shari'ah*-compliant financing. That suggests a potential gap of $8.63 billion to $13.29 billion for Islamic SME financing in these countries. While there is a large demand for Islamic finance from SMEs (as table 6.5 indicates), Islamic banks have been unable or unwilling to meet this demand.

An alternative to provide financing to SMEs would be NBFIs. A survey of 36 providers of Islamic microfinance to SMEs revealed that only 15 percent of the institutions were banks (Sanabel 2012). Nearly half of the providers (49 percent) were nongovernmental organizations (NGOs), followed by NBFIs (24 percent). While 6 percent of the providers were microfinance banks, government organizations and cooperatives constituted 3 percent each. The substantial demand for SME financing

TABLE 6.4 Gaps in Enterprise Financing

Region	Total number of SMEs (million)	Unserved or underserved SMEs (million)	Total formal SMEs (million)	Unserved or underserved formal SMEs (million)	Formal SME credit gap ($ billion)
East Asia and Pacific	188	92	12	8	$150–$180
Europe and Central Asia	20	10	3	2	$150–$190
Latin America and the Caribbean	52	27	3	2	$210–$250
Middle East and North Africa	21	10	2	1	$260–$320
South Asia	78	36	2	1	$10–$20
Sub-Saharan Africa	40	22	4	3	$70–$90

Source: Stein, Pinar Ardic, and Hommes 2013.
Note: SMEs = small and medium enterprises.

TABLE 6.5 Financing Penetration for SME Financing and Preference for *Shari'ah*-Compliant Products

Countries	SME penetration (percent of lending)	Preference for *shari'ah*-compliant products (percent of SMEs)
Egypt, Arab Rep.	8.0	20
Iraq	5.0	35
Jordan	12.5	25
Lebanon	16.1	4
Morocco	24.0	54
Pakistan	7.3	25
Saudi Arabia	2.0	90
Tunisia	15.0	18
Yemen, Rep.	20.3	37

Source: IFC 2014b.
Note: SMEs = small and medium enterprises.

and the low penetration by banks indicate that there is a role that NBFIs can play to fill the gap. The gap can be filled by various types of NBFIs, such as private equity funds, rural cooperatives, and leasing companies. An example of an innovative NBFI using crowdfunding is given in box 6.2.

Housing Finance

The use of Islamic finance has significant implications with respect to enhancing shared prosperity and risk sharing in housing finance. Indeed, the deployment of Islamic finance tools for home financing has the potential to prevent some of the problems that led to the recent global financial crisis. One of the main reasons underlying the global financial crisis was the housing market bubble in the United States, which was fueled by excessive household debt

BOX 6.2 Case 2. Liwwa: A *Shari'ah*-Compliant Peer-to-Peer Lending Platform

Liwwa is an electronic platform that aims to tackle the chronic unemployment and underdevelopment problems of the Middle East. Developed in 2012 by two Palestinian entrepreneurs at Harvard University, it was launched in September 2013. Specifically, the new company's mission is to deliver job and income growth in the markets it serves. Liwwa is operating in Amman, Jordan, for borrowers and across the MENA Region for those who seek to lend to SMEs. The platform provides investors a return on a regular basis through a *shari'ah*-compliant mechanism with no equity or interest in the equation (figure B6.2.1).

The platform focuses particularly on the finance of small businesses in compliance with *shari'ah*. Using the crowdfunding model offered by Liwwa, SMEs that need working capital and physical capital can raise funds from crowds of investors, who pool their assets through the Internet platform in return for the principal amount raised and part of the profit in the form of monthly payments. After the full payment, the borrower becomes the whole owner of the assets acquired through raised funds. Working along the lines of an *ijārah*-like lease-to-own basis, the transactions taking place through the platform are recognized as *shari'ah* compliant. Since investors know what they are going to get in returns and at which date, the model offered is more like a bond than an equity investment. The platform takes services fees from the monthly repayments made by the borrowers to cover administrative expenses and the funding of a reserve to underwrite the payments to the investors.

The services are available to the small businesses in Jordan, and to investors from countries such as Algeria, the Arab Republic of Egypt, Jordan, Lebanon, Saudi Arabia, Sudan, Tunisia, the United Arab Emirates, and the United Kingdom. As of March 2015, the target loan of the company was 10,000–15,000 Jordanian dinars (around $14,100–$21,100). Up to that time, Liwwa had provided 34 loans, some of which were still at the funding stage, for a total of $260,000.

box continues next page

BOX 6.2 Case 2. Liwwa: A *Shari'ah*-Compliant Peer-to-Peer Lending Platform *(continued)*

FIGURE B6.2.1 Liwwa's Operating Framework

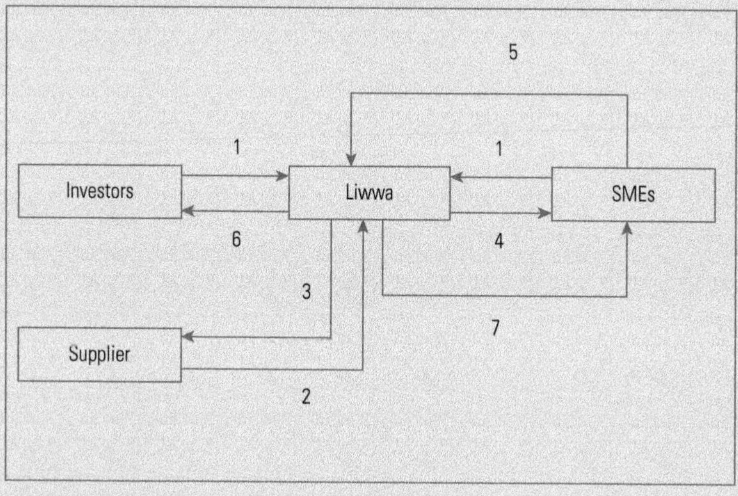

1. Investors and SMEs subscribe to the website.
2. Liwwa buys needed capital goods from suppliers.
3. Liwwa pays the cost from the proceeds collected from investors.
4. The capital is delivered to the SME.
5. The SME repays the capital with regular monthly payments and a final lump sum payment.
6. Payments are delivered to investors after fees are deducted.
7. The ownership is delivered after final payment.

Source: https://www.liwwa.com/.
Note: SMEs = small and medium enterprises.

Although these amounts are rather small, the company has grown by 400 percent since March 2015, when the initial $500,000 of seed capital was paid in. Moreover, the model presents a good example of how Islamic finance tools can be used by people who have excess funds to share prosperity with SMEs so that added value is created. The crowdfunding model of Liwwa, which is based on a lease-to-own structure, has attracted not only investors with an Islamic orientation, but also a diversified set of investors from various parts of the world. This is promising in light of the momentum in the peer-to-peer finance sector worldwide.

Source: https://www.liwwa.com/.

(Mian and Sufi 2014; Turner 2015). Turner (2015) contends that the financial sector has tendencies to create excessive debt and proposes introducing regulations that restrict the growth of credit to the household sector. Mian and Sufi (2014) assert that debt-based contracts used to purchase houses leave the household sector vulnerable when the bubble eventually bursts. For example, equity of a household putting a 10 percent down payment on a mortgage can become negative with a drop in the house price of more than 10 percent in a housing market downturn. While this decreases household wealth and reduces consumption and aggregate demand—which can further aggravate the recession—it leaves the debt owed to the bank intact. They suggest that one way of solving this problem is to use risk-sharing contracts that not only protect households but also can prevent housing bubbles from emerging. In this regard, properly implementing Islamic finance solutions, such as a diminishing *mushārakah* (partnership) structure,[3] in-home financing can serve as a stabilizing factor for both the financial and housing sectors and protect households during recessions.

Housing finance in most IDB member-countries is at a nascent stage. Considerable housing financing is needed to meet housing finance requirements. While the bulk of housing finance is provided by banks, governments in some countries have established specialized home financing institutions. Some 8.2 million units are needed each year in the urban areas of IDB member countries, according to estimates based on the growth rates of population and urbanization (Shirazi, Zulkhibri, and Ali 2012). Providing for these units is estimated to cost $15.6 billion a year. The distribution of the housing units and the corresponding financing costs for different regions are shown in table 6.6.

As an illustration, table 6.7 presents the features of the housing finance market in Pakistan, which has a mortgage-to-GDP ratio of 0.46 percent. The total size of gross outstanding housing financing in the country on December 31, 2014, was PRs 53.7 billion ($5.35 million), advanced to 74,147 clients.[4] Thirty-six percent of the financing was supplied by private banks, 24 percent by the House Building Finance Corporation Limited (HBFCL), 28 percent by Islamic banks, and 11 percent by public sector banks (SBP 2015).

TABLE 6.6 Demand for Housing Units by Region, 2010–20

Regions (number of countries)	No. of units/year (million)	Amount of financing/ year ($billion)
Middle East and North Africa (19)	3.2	6.0
Asia (8)	2.7	5.2
Sub-Saharan Africa (22)	1.9	3.7
Countries in transition (7)	0.4	0.7
Total (56)	8.2	15.5

Source: Shirazi, Zulkhibri, and Ali 2012.

Outreach to the poorer sections of the population can be gauged by examining the average size of financing. Private financial institutions averaged PRs 5 million or more, compared to PRs 3 million for public financial institutions, with HBFCL extending the smallest amount, PRs 2.5 million. Microfinance banks provided PRs 216.07 million to 2,154 borrowers as of December 2014, according to SBP (2015). With an average of PRs 0.1003 million outstanding per borrower, the number of people served appears to be very small compared to the poor and low-income population in the country.

The case of Pakistan shows that most of the housing finance comes from banks and specialized financial institutions that serve the relatively well-off. Some housing financing to the bottom 40 percent of the population is provided by specialized banks such as HBFCL and by microfinance banks. Other NBFIs have a role to play in providing house financing to the unserved. An example of an NBFI that provides home financing is given in box 6.3.

TABLE 6.7 Housing Finance in Pakistan, End-2014

Financial institutions	Gross outstanding (PRs billion)	Outstanding disbursed (percent of total)	Number of borrowers	Average financing size (PRs million)
Public banks	6.0	11	4,991	3.0
Private banks	19.2	36	10,613	5.8
Foreign banks	0.3	1	129	5.0
Islamic banks	15.3	28	3,277	5.1
DFIs	0.1	0	53	—
HBFCL	12.7	24	55,084	2.5
Total	53.7	100	74,147	3.8

Source: State Bank of Pakistan (SBP) 2015.
Note: — = not available; DFIs=development financial institutions; HBFCL = House Building Finance Corporation Limited; PRs = Pakistan rupees.

BOX 6.3 Case 3. NBFI *Shari'ah*-Compliant Home Financing in Canada

Ansar & Islamic Cooperative Housing Corporation Ltd. (ACHC) was established in Toronto in 1981 to provide *shari'ah*-compliant home financing for Canadian Muslims using the diminishing *musharākah* model. ACHC has two kinds of shares. Common shares are shares in the equity of the cooperative. Preferred shares are attached to the individual members' own houses. The price of both common and preferred shares is fixed at Can$100 each. Initially, every member is an investor or common shareholder providing equity to the cooperative. Everyone who wishes to participate in the cooperative must become a member by paying a one-time membership fee of Can$75 and must invest a minimum of Can$600 by buying six common shares. Those members who wish to buy a house through the cooperative must buy and accumulate a certain minimum number of common shares, depending on the cost of the house. This minimum investment must remain in the cooperative for at least six months before the member can qualify to apply for housing finance.

Once a member becomes eligible to buy a house, he/she submits an application to the cooperative. If approved, the member is authorized to locate a suitable house anywhere in Canada, negotiate the price, and obtain a closing date from the cooperative for the full payment and possession of the house. At the time of the purchase of the house, members surrender their common shares and are issued preferred shares to reflect their total contribution, including any deposits they gave to the vendor when they signed the contract to buy the house. The concept of diminishing *musharākah* (partnership) is used to finance the housing. The diminishing partnership model was chosen because of its practical features and flexibility. There is no fixed term in the contract. A rental value for the house is determined, and the members pay a proportionate rent to the cooperative every month. The members are free to buy any number of preferred shares at any time. When they do, their proportionate rent is adjusted for the following month. When members complete 100 percent purchase of the required preferred shares, they surrender those shares to the cooperative and the legal title of their house is transferred to them after sharing any gain or loss in the value of the house. The members are entitled to share 90 percent of any gain or loss, and the cooperative shares 10 percent. At this point, the partnership in that house between the member and the cooperative is terminated. The membership in the cooperative, however, continues and members are expected to continue to invest their savings in the cooperative so that the other members can be helped the same way. The cooperative pays dividends annually to all common shareholders from the rental income according to the ratio of their quarterly ownership of the shares.

Sources: Nasim 2003; http://www.ansarhousing.com/.

Other NBFIs (*Muḍārabah* and *Ijārah* Companies)

A unique example of Islamic NBFIs are the *muḍārabah* companies. *Muḍārabah* companies operate on the principle of "profit sharing and loss bearing," wherein entrepreneurs share the profit with the financier but losses are fully borne by financiers. *Muḍārabah* companies started their operations in Pakistan after the enactment of the *Muḍārabah* Companies and *Muḍārabah* Floatation and Control Ordinance in 1980. After the launch of the first *muḍārabah* company in 1980, the number increased to 56 in the mid-1990s and then declined to 24 as of December 2014 (NMAP 2013; SECP 2014). The value of total assets held by the *muḍārabah* companies was PRs 30.19 billion ($296.8 million) as of December 2014.[5] While the bulk of the funds of *muḍārabah* companies are in the form of equity, some of them also raise funds by issuing *mushārakah* Certificates of Investment and Terms Finance Certificates (NMAP 2013).[6] The total amount of funds raised from different categories of clients is shown in table 6.8. More than two-thirds of the funds raised by *muḍārabah* companies come from individuals, followed by corporations and trusts.

The scope of operations of *muḍārabah* companies is wide ranging. In addition to providing financing using a variety of methods, *muḍārabah* companies are also involved in trading, manufacturing, investment in equities, portfolio management, financing of private equity/venture capital, housing finance, and providing investment finance services (NMAP 2013). Given the range of activities that *muḍārabah* companies can engage in, they can potentially make a positive contribution to economic growth. However, they account for only a very small part of the financial sector, representing only 0.12 percent of Pakistan's GDP as of December 2014.

Another important type of NBFIs are *ijārah* companies. *Ijārah* is similar to the concept of leasing in conventional finance. One of the important features of leasing is the financing of assets without any collateral. Leasing companies are better able to assess credit risk due to their ability to understand the cash flows associated with the assets. Thus leasing can be a better financing mode for SMEs that do not have a sound credit history (Rocha, Arvai, and Farazi 2011). The leasing sector in most of the IDB member-countries, however, is small. Box 6.4 illustrates an example in Tajikistan.

TABLE 6.8 Deposit Raising by *Muḍārabah* Companies, End-2104

Categories	Amount (million PRs)	Percentage of total
Individuals	4,226.84	67.4
Corporates	970.27	15.5
Trusts	840.34	13.4
Financial institutions	229.45	3.7
Total	6,266.90	100

Source: SECP 2014.
Note: PRs = Pakistan rupees.

Islamic NBFIs and Shared Prosperity: Key Challenges and Policy Recommendations

Sectoral Challenges: Supply-Side Issues

The achievement of shared prosperity requires expansion of the NBFI sector to facilitate the provision of financial services to

BOX 6.4 Case 4. ASR Leasing in Tajikistan

The leasing industry in Tajikistan is relatively small. Before the establishment of ASR Leasing as the first *ijārah* company in 2013, the country had seven other conventional leasing companies. ASR Leasing was established by Ansar Leasing of Azerbaijan along with two local partners with initial paid-in capital of only $200,000. The paid-in capital was later increased to $4 million with additional shareholders' funds that include Islamic Corporation for the Development of the Private Sector (ICD) of the Islamic Development Bank Group.

ASR Leasing typically leases fixed assets to small and medium enterprises (SMEs) and corporations up to a maximum of $200,000 per contract, for a tenure that can range from 1 to 4 years. The conditions of the leasing contract include paying a 20 percent minimum security deposit/advance payment and insuring the leased asset for the duration of the tenure. The lease contract can be structured in either the local currency or U.S. dollars. Repayments must be made using the prevailing exchange rate announced by the National Bank of Tajikistan. The expected rate of return on leasing is in the range of 20–23 percent, depending on the length of the tenure. Given that 90 percent of the country's population is Muslim and that SMEs account for more than 80 percent of the trading sector, the demand for Islamic leasing is expected to increase in the future.

Source: Presentation by the managing director of ASR Leasing, http://idbgbf.org/assets/2013/7/9/pdf/23edbe7c-6b56-49a6-9e80-237804c5b058.pdf.

more segments of the population. Specific challenges in expanding the NBFI sector are discussed next.

Increasing the Number and Diversity of Islamic NBFIs

The key constraint on the supply side is the limited number of NBFIs in most Muslim countries. The development of the range of Islamic NBFIs can take place in two ways. The first approach is to create new institutions that do not have counterparts in the conventional financial world. Examples of these are *Tabung Haji* in Malaysia and the *muḍārabah* companies developed in Pakistan. These institutions have unique institutional features serving different purposes in the economy. The second approach is to adopt and adapt conventional financial institutions to encourage them to provide Islamic finance services. Adaptations involve eliminating undesirable elements (like *ribā* and *gharar*) from transactions. In this process, the functions performed by the Islamic NBFIs will be similar to their conventional counterparts, but the operations would be within the bounds prescribed by *sharī'ah*. In response to demand, some conventional NBFIs are offering Islamic financial alternatives to their clients. Examples include the ORIX Leasing Company in Pakistan and the Peoples Leasing and Finance Company in Sri Lanka.[7]

Another key role of Islamic NBFIs is to provide Islamic financial services in countries where establishing Islamic banks is not possible due to legal and regulatory restrictions. As laws related to NBFIs are less stringent than those governing Islamic banks, Islamic NBFIs can provide Islamic financial services under existing laws and regulations. For example, finance companies in the United States and cooperatives in Canada are offering Islamic housing products to Muslims residing in these countries. An indigenous institution providing funds to small-scale enterprises and businesses is the pawning institution in Malaysia (Ahmed 2011). By combining contracts of *wadī'ah* (deposit) and *rahn* (pledge or mortgage), the pawning services provide short-term cash advances, including working capital for businesses.

The financial sector requires specific knowledge and skill sets that analysts, bankers, accountants, and lawyers often lack in developing countries. The growth of the financial sector in general and the NBFI sector in particular can be constrained by the availability of adequate and relevant human capital (Carmichael and Pomerleano 2002, 199). The risks arising in providing financial services to the bottom 40 percent of the population are considerable and need to be dealt with prudently. For example, information asymmetry is more acute in the case of financing SMEs relative to larger firms and would require different types of skills and approaches for mitigation.

Sector-Specific Supply-Side Issues

The limited number of service providers is constraining the asset management industry (Rocha, Arvai, and Farazi 2011). Many countries lack the critical mass of fund managers to serve different segments of the population. Furthermore, there is a lack of suitable instruments and products. Thus there is a need to expand the products geared toward lower-income groups.

SME financing has relatively high risks, as is evident from the proportion of nonperforming loans (IFC 2014a, 33). NBFIs may have limited specialization in SME financing. Their capabilities to serve the SME sector must be improved to deal with the specific risks involved in SME financing (IFC 2014b). Enhancing the skills to manage the risks arising in SME financing is thus important. In coming up with a strategy, a distinction should be made between the different market segments: well-served, unserved, and underserved enterprises. While the former are being funded adequately, the latter two segments are not. In this regard, a classification of SMEs according to sectors would be useful.

The bulk of SME financing is short term and is used to finance working capital. There appears to be a gap in the provision of long-term financing for SMEs. Furthermore, the product offerings for SMEs are very limited. There is a need to come up with new product offerings that meet the needs of SMEs (IFC 2014a). Currently, debt-based products dominate the assets side of the balance sheet. Other modes of financing such as *istiḍnā'*, *muḍārabah*, and *mushārakah* also need to be used. However, the risks associated with these products need to be mitigated.

Since most leasing companies use financial leases in most of the developing markets, there is a need to expand the number of leasing companies that also use operating leases to fulfill the *shari'ah* requirements. An enabling environment that can provide support to these kinds of companies is needed.

Demand-Side and Investor Issues

Consumer demand determines the financial services that are provided. In the case of NBFIs, individuals and entities use the sector to obtain capital and also supply the funds as investors. The expansion of Islamic NBFIs will largely be driven by demand for their services, which in turn depend on several factors, discussed next.

Low Levels of Financial Literacy

Research shows a positive relationship between financial literacy and financial inclusion (Atkinson and Messy 2013). A survey of 301 microfinance institutions revealed limited financial literacy to be the main obstacle in providing financing (Gardeva and Rhyne 2011). This is particularly true for Islamic financial products, which are not only new for many people, but also may be more complex. There is a need to come up with schemes to educate people and raise awareness of Islamic financial products.

Cultural, Social, and Physical Barriers

Many Muslims will not engage with the conventional interest-based financial institutions due to religious convictions. Furthermore, the lack of language and technological skills may prevent people from using modern technology such as the Internet to access financial services. A large percentage of the population living in rural areas in developing countries face physical barriers because of poor physical infrastructure (Atkinson and Messy 2013). One way to overcome the physical barrier is to have local NBFIs that can provide financial services to the poor. Another option is to use modern information and communications technology to deliver basic financial services at a very low cost.

Consumer Protection

One of the key determinants of the growth of the financial sector is the protection of the rights of the investors. Expanding the investor base requires not only products and instruments that are appropriate, but also systems to ensure the protection of clients and investors. Because the NBFI sector is less stringently regulated, cases might emerge where institutions have been mismanaged and have resulted in the loss of investors' assets. After the financial crisis of 2008, some NBFIs, including a few that were Islamic, became insolvent or declared bankruptcy.[8] These failures highlighted the need for sound disclosure of relevant information related to the terms and conditions of the contracts, with the relation to returns and risks. This needs detailed disclosure. In countries that have weak investor rights, funds with longer-term investment horizons will not be forthcoming. Thus leasing companies that depend on long-term funding will face funding constraints that will hamper their growth (Nasr 2004, 9).

Reputation and Credibility

Provision of funds to financial institutions by investors also depends on their perceptions of risks and rights. As a significant percentage of customers use Islamic financial institutions for religious reasons, there is a need to ensure that the products and activities of NBFIs comply with *shari'ah*. Furthermore, perceptions about and trust in the integrity and efficient management of the operations are important determinants of the growth of the Islamic financial industry. There have been a few cases of mismanagement and fraud that have hurt the reputation and credibility of the industry. For example, UM Financial, an Islamic NBFI in Canada, filed for bankruptcy in December 2011 because of mismanagement (Pasha and French 2011).

Legal and Regulatory Challenges

An enabling environment to promote Islamic finance in general entails the presence of a favorable political, economic, and regulatory environment (IFC 2014b). The legal and regulatory framework not only determines the specific NBFIs that can be established in a country, but also the activities they can engage in. There is a need to have not only laws that support Islamic NBFIs, but also a legal infrastructure to support contract enforcement. A sound contract enforcement regime is essential for the development of the financial sector because it not only reduces the transaction costs (Nasr 2004) but also instills trust among investors and financial institutions.

A balanced regulatory framework can play an important role in the healthy growth of the NBFI sector. The key objectives of regulations are to deal with anticompetitive behavior, market misconduct, asymmetric information, and systemic instability (Carmichael and Pomerleano 2002, 33). The nature of an NBFI in terms of its association with these areas of concern and the risks involved will determine the regulatory parameters that would govern the specific institution.

Sector-Specific Legal and Regulatory Issues

In addition to general laws that support economic and financial activities, such as property rights and contractual enforcement, the legal framework is a key determinant of the strength and soundness of the NBFI sector (Carmichael and Pomerleano 2002). Given the diversity of NBFIs, there is a need to come up with laws that can deal with the specific issues arising from the different areas and the ways in which NBFIs operate. While the existing laws on NBFIs can be extended with minor adjustments for Islamic NBFIs, such as Islamic leasing companies and mutual funds, there may be a need to enact new laws to accommodate unique Islamic NBFIs, such as the *Mudārabah* Companies and *Mudārabah* Floatation and Control Ordinance in Pakistan.

The specific issues related to the establishment and operations of Islamic NBFIs, such as licensing, minimum capital requirements, and disclosure requirements, can be covered under regulations for the supervision of specific NBFIs. The nature of regulatory measures applied to different NBFIs will depend on the extent to which they are exposed to and generate anticompetitive behavior, market misconduct, asymmetric information, and systemic instability (Carmichael and Pomerleano 2002, 33). The regulatory measures to deal with these problems can be broadly categorized as competition regulation, market conduct regulation, prudential regulation, and systemic stability regulation.

Because mutual funds are less exposed to systemic risks, investor protection regulations and standards, such as licensing, disclosure, and good governance, would be required (Carmichael and Pomerleano 2002, 111). The regulation of pension funds, however, would depend on their type and the risks involved. For example, whereas a defined contribution scheme managed by competitive private sector entities would have the same regulatory requirements as mutual funds, the regulation of a defined benefits scheme would require more regulatory oversight, which may include periodic actuarial reviews.

A sound legal and regulatory framework for leasing companies is necessary for the growth of the leasing industry in general and for Islamic leasing companies in particular. For leasing companies, the World Bank (2008) asserts that the leasing law should clarify the lessor's effective ownership and repossession rights and acknowledge the lessee's responsibility as the custodian of the asset. For leasing to succeed, it requires a sound legal framework that defines the rights and obligations of the lessor and lessee in general, and in case of bankruptcy in particular. The law needs to recognize that some features of Islamic leasing are different from financial leases. Most countries lack registries for leased assets, which limits leasing financing.

One of the key financial infrastructure institutions that reduces asymmetric information are credit bureaus (Nasr 2004).

Financing to SMEs could be expanded by different NBFIs if credit registries exist that enable financiers to reduce adverse selection problems.

Housing sector financing for construction or acquisition would also require a facilitating legal environment. The lack of efficient laws related to land registration, land division, mortgage laws, laws related to collateral, and precise legal titles can be challenging (Shirazi, Zulkhibri, and Ali 2012).

Notes

1. *Muḍārabah* is a partnership whereby one party (the capital owner) provides capital to an entrepreneur to undertake a business activity. Profits are shared between them as agreed, but any financial loss is borne only by the capital owner because the loss is the capital owner's unrewarded effort put into the business activity.
2. See http://www.almeezangroup.com/MutualFunds/OpenEndFunds/MeezanIslamicFund/tabid/75/Default.aspx for the Meezan Islamic Fund, and http://www.saturna.com/pdf/amana/Amana-application.pdf for the Amana Mutual Funds.
3. Under a diminishing *mushārakah* structure, an investor's equity share diminishes, while a homeowner's share increases over time.
4. The U.S. dollar figure was calculated at the exchange rate of $1.00 to PRs 00.30 as of December 31, 2014.
5. Calculated with an exchange rate of $1 = PRs 101.7 (on June 24, 2015)
6. *Mushārakah* is a partnership whereby all the partners contribute capital for a business venture. The partners share profits on a pre-agreed ratio, while losses are shared according to each partner's capital contribution.
7. See http://www.orixpakistan.com/islamic-financing.aspx for ORIX Leasing Company, and http://www.plc.lk/inpages/products_and_services/islamic_finance.php for the Peoples Leasing and Finance Company.
8. The failures in the GCC, in particular, caused reputational damage to the industry. The institutions affected included Aayan Leasing and Investment Company (2011), Investment Dar (2010), Noor Financial Investment Company (2011), and Arcapita Bank (2012) (Raghu, Pattherwala, and Tulysan 2013).

References

Ahmed, Habib. 2011. *Product Development in Islamic Banking*. Edinburgh: Edinburgh University Press.

Atkinson, A., and F. Messy. 2013. "Promoting Financial Inclusion through Financial Education: OECD/INFE Evidence, Policies and Practice." Organisation for Economic Co-operation and Development (OECD) Working Papers on Finance, Insurance and Private Pensions, No. 34, OECD Publishing, Paris. http://dx.doi.org/10.1787/5k3xz6m88smp-en.

Ayyagari, Meghana, Asli Demirgüç-Kunt, and Vojislav Maksimovic. 2011. "Small vs. Young Firms across the World: Contribution to Employment, Job Creation, and Growth." Policy Research Working Paper 5631, World Bank, Washington, DC.

Bakker, M. R., and A. Gross. 2004. "Development of Non-bank Financial Institutions and Capital Markets in European Union Accession Countries." Working Paper 28404, World Bank, Washington, DC.

Carmichael, Jeffrey, and Michael Pomerleano. 2002. *The Development and Regulation of Non-bank Financial Institutions*. Washington, DC: World Bank.

Chapra, M. Umer. 1985. *Towards a Just Monetary System*. Leicester, U.K.: The Islamic Foundation.

Cole, Shawn, Thomas Sampson, and Bilal Zia. 2011. "Prices or Knowledge? What Drives Demand for Financial Services in Emerging Markets." Harvard Business School Working Paper 09–117. http://www.ifmrlead.org/cmf/wp-content/uploads/2011/08/09-117.pdf.

Creane, Susan, Rishi Goyal, A. Mushfiq Mobarak, and Randa Sab. 2006. "Measuring Financial Development in the Middle East and North Africa: A New Database." *IMF Staff Papers* 53 (3): 479–511.

Gardeva, A., and E. Rhyne. 2011. *Opportunities and Obstacles to Financial Inclusion*. Survey Report. Center for Financial Inclusion at ACCION International. http://centerforfinancialinclusionblog.files.wordpress.com/2011/07/opportunities-and-obstaclesto-financial-inclusion_110708_final.pdf.

IDB, IRTI, and IFSB (Islamic Development Bank, Islamic Research and Training Institute, and Islamic Financial Services Board). 2014. *Islamic Financial Services Industry Development*

Report: Ten-Year Framework and Strategies: A Mid-Term Review. Jeddah, Saudi Arabia: IDB, IRTI, and IFSB.

IFC (International Finance Corporation). 2014a. *Islamic Banking Opportunities across Small and Medium Enterprises in Pakistan*. Washington, DC: IFC.

———. 2014b. *Islamic Banking Opportunities Across Small and Medium Enterprises in MENA*. Washington, DC: IFC.

Islamic Finance News. 2015a. *Environmentally-conscious and Socially Responsible Investment: A Growth Opportunity for Islamic Finance*. Kuala Lumpur.

———. 2015b. *The Grass Is Always Greener? Environmental Sukuk Take the Stage*. Kuala Lumpur. http://www.simmons-simmons.com/~/media/Files/Corporate/External%20publications%20pdfs/Samir%20Safar%20%20Green%20Sukuk%20Article.ashx.

KPMG Turkey. 2013. *Turkish Pension System Amendments: What Is Ahead?* http://www.kpmgvergi.com/PDF/Yayinlar/KPMG-Global-Yayinlar/Turkish-Pension-System-Amendments.pdf.

Mian, Atif, and Amir Sufi. 2014. *House of Debt: How They (and You) Caused the Great Recession, and How We Can Prevent It from Happening Again*. Chicago, IL: University of Chicago Press.

Nasim, Pervez. 2003. "The Experience of Islamic Cooperative Housing Corporation, Ltd." Paper presented at International Seminar on Non-Bank Financial Institutions: Islamic Alternatives, organized by Islamic Research and Training Institute and Islamic Banking and Finance Institute, Kuala Lumpur, May 5–7.

Nasr, Sahar. 2004. "Financial Leasing in MENA Regions: An Analysis of Financial, Legal and Institutional Aspects." Working Paper 0424, Economic Research Forum, Egypt. http://www.erf.org.eg/CMS/uploads/pdf/0424_final.pdf.

NMAP (NBFI and Modaraba Association of Pakistan). 2013. "*Modaraba* Sector of Pakistan." http://www.nbfi-modaraba.com.pk/Data/Sites/1/skins/nbfi/sector_report.pdf.

Pasha, Shaheen, and Cameron French. 2011. "Canada Bankruptcy May Hurt Islamic Finance in North America." *Reuters*, December 5. http://ca.reuters.com/article/businessNews/idCATRE7B40I820111205.

Raghu, M. R., Murtaza Pattherwala, and Animesh Tulsyan. 2013. *Dealing with Bankruptcy in the GCC: A Key Missing Block in the Reform Agenda*. Kuwait: Kuwait Financial Centre Markaz Research.

Reuters. 2015. *Khazanah to Launch Malaysia's First Social Impact Bond*. http://www.reuters.com/article/2015/04/29/asia-bonds-idUSL4N0XQ2A420150429.

Rocha, Roberto R., Zsofia Arvai, and Subika Farazi. 2011. *Financial Access and Stability: A Road Map for the Middle East and North Africa*. Washington, DC: World Bank.

Sanabel. 2012. *Islamic Micro and Small Medium Enterprise (MSME) Finance Survey*. New Cairo, Egypt: Sanabel.

SBP (State Bank of Pakistan). 2015. *Quarterly Housing Finance Review (for the Quarter ending December 31, 2014)*. http://www.sbp.org.pk/departments/ihfd/QR/Housing/2014/Dec-14.pdf.

SECP (Securities & Exchange Commission of Pakistan). 2014. *Summary of NBFCs, NEs and Modorabas Sector, December 2014*. http://www.secp.gov.pk/SCD/pub_scd/sector-summary/mss_dec2014.pdf.

———. 2015. *Summary of NBFCs, NEs and Modorabas Sector, April*. http://www.secp.gov.pk/SCD/pub_scd/sector-summary/mss_April2015.pdf.

Securities Commission Malaysia. 2014. "SC Introduces Sustainable and Responsible Investment Sukuk Framework." http://www.sc.com.my/post_archive/sc-introduces-sustainable-and-responsible-investment-sukuk-framework.

Sezer, Seda. 2013. "Pension Reform Set to Unlock Turkey's Fund Management Industry." *Reuters*, March 6. http://uk.reuters.com/article/2013/03/06/turkey-pensions-idUKL6N0BWA1B20130306.

Shirazi, Nasim Shah, Muhammad Zulkhibri, and Salman Syed Ali. 2012. *Challenges of Affordable Housing Finance in IDB Member Countries Using Islamic Modes*. Jeddah, Saudi Arabia: Islamic Research and Training Institute, Islamic Development Bank Group.

Stein, Peer, Oya Pinar Ardic, and Martin Hommes. 2013. *Closing the Credit Gap for Formal and Informal Micro, Small, and Medium Enterprises*. Washington, DC: International Finance Corporation.

Thomson Reuters. 2014. *Global Islamic Asset Management Outlook 2014*. Thomson Reuters.

———. 2015. *Global Islamic Asset Management Outlook 2015*. Thomson Reuters.

Turner, Adair. 2015. *Between Debt and the Devil: Money, Credit, and Fixing Global Finance*. Princeton, NJ: Princeton University Press.

World Bank. 2008. "Leasing in Developing Countries: IFC Experience and Lessons Learned." *Access Finance*, Issue 23, World Bank Group, Washington, DC.

———. 2014. *Global Financial Development Report 2014*. Washington, DC: World Bank.

———. n.d. Global Financial Development Database. http://databank.worldbank.org/data/reports.aspx?source=global-financial-development.

7

Alternative Asset Classes

Islamic financial institutions have endeavored to provide as wide a range of facilities for their clients as their conventional counterparts. This includes not only banking services and mainstream capital market products, but also alternative investments. Asset diversification is desirable not just for investors seeking *shari'ah*-compliant assets; it also opens up wider possibilities for those seeking financing. The pricing of alternative assets is often uncorrelated with equity prices and those of fixed income instruments, including *sukūk* (Islamic certificates of investment). Hence such assets provide investors a degree of hedging from the inevitable business cycles.

Overview of Alternative Asset Classes

There is a very wide variety of Islamic alternative assets, which in essence comprise all financial investments apart from listed equity and fixed income securities (Schneeweis, Kazemi, and Martin 2003). The major categories include private equity, hedge funds, real estate investment trusts (REITs), the *ḥalāl* food industry, trade financing instruments, and infrastructure investments through project finance (Terhaar, Staub, and Singer 2003). All of these serve very different purposes and share few common characteristics apart from usually being less liquid than mainstream investments. Most are relatively new from an Islamic finance perspective, as the industry has been focused mainly on banking and capital market instruments for most of the half century since its development. It is only in the last decade, and especially since the global financial crisis of 2007–08, that interest in Islamic alternative investments has increased, partly reflecting disillusionment with returns on *shari'ah*-compliant equities and *sukūk* securities.

When considering the merits of alternative asset classes from an Islamic perspective, the principles of risk sharing and participatory finance should be taken into account. How much do the alternative asset classes adhere to these principles, which justify the returns earned by investors? Islamic finance is not about earning windfall gains, but rather implies an active involvement in what is being funded, usually by sharing in risk rather than playing a managerial role in a project (Archer and Karim 2006).

The wide variety of alternative asset classes means that *shari'ah* concerns vary according to the particular asset being considered as an investment vehicle; it is difficult to generalize across alternative assets as a whole. Some of the assets, such as private equity holdings, are inherently more *shari'ah* compliant than others, such as hedge funds. The detail matters from a *shari'ah* perspective, and it is important to understand the workings of the financial arrangements and how returns are generated for the investors. *Shari'ah*-compliant capital is often deployed alongside conventional finance in alternative asset categories. Although such combinations may be quite legitimate, it is necessary to understand the nature of the interactions.

Islamic alternative asset classes are managed by a wide range of financial institutions, including Islamic and conventional banks, Islamic funds, *takāful* providers, pension funds, and other institutional investors. As a consequence, there are no aggregate data enabling comparisons to be made of the size of different asset categories, such as private equity or hedge funds. It is likely that real estate dominates, given the preference of many Muslim investors for tangible assets. This is especially the case with high-net-worth individuals in many Muslim countries, including family offices in the Gulf Cooperation Council (GCC) states, which tend to value investment in commercial and residential real estate more than investment in financial instruments.

Investors in alternative assets, especially those seeking superior returns, typically have a greater appetite for risk than those investing in bonds and traded equities. One motivation for investment in alternative investments is to seek higher returns, especially for investors in private equity and hedge funds. Often investments in alternative assets are less liquid than bonds and listed equities that can be sold at any time (Siegel 2008). Once funds are locked in, there is little that investors can do if there are market downturns as the economic outlook deteriorates. Because alternative assets are so diverse, however, their price movements are not necessarily correlated with those of listed equity or bonds. Some, such as hedge funds, can be regarded as countercyclical. Real estate valuations are subject to different business cycles than those for equity markets. In short, alternative assets may be more risky, but they also serve to diversify risk.

Alternative investments are usually less transparent than those in stock markets, as private equity purchase and sales prices are subject to negotiation, and in the case of real estate, valuations may differ widely. Hedge funds are often opaque, with limited information provided on their investments or the contracts used to generate profits (Agarwal and Naik 2004). This lack of transparency adds to risk, with most investors in alternative asset classes largely relying on their previous performance for information about them, rather than the fundamentals regarding the underlying assets and the disaggregated sources of income and capital gains.

Islamic Private Equity

Shari'ah-compliant private equity investment is subject to the same screens as investment in listed companies, which exclude companies that are heavily leveraged or are engaged in *ḥarām* activities, such as production or distribution of alcohol and pork (Chatti and Yous 2010). Companies that derive a significant proportion of their income from *ribā'* (interest) are also excluded, including conventional banks and many other financial institutions. In practice, as the dominant financial institutions are large listed companies, private equity plays no role in their financing. Rather, it is usually small to medium enterprises (SMEs) that seek private equity, especially in fields such as pharmaceuticals, alternative energy, or information technology, which are inherently *shari'ah* compliant. Injections of private equity into such companies can reduce their debt burdens, resulting in their being more suitable for Islamic investment.

Venture capital represents a subset of private equity finance, as it is sought by recently established companies that are insufficiently mature to be listed on the market but that can use private equity not only to fund development directly but also to gain additional debt finance. In the case of *shari'ah*-compliant venture capital, this can include trade and project financing from Islamic banks, often under *murābaḥah* (trade finance) and *istiṣnā'* (project finance) contracts. *Mushārakah* (joint ventures) and *muḍārabah* partnership finance can also be used for private equity. *Mushārakah* is more suitable for proactive investors who wish to be more involved in the management of the venture that is seeking capital (Choudhury 2001). *Shari'ah*-compliant private equity and venture capital finance should not be seen as an alternative to debt finance, but rather as a facilitator of such financing, while keeping the use of leverage within limits that are acceptable from an Islamic perspective.

Islamic private equity finance has emerged only since the 1990s, with most of the activity confined to Malaysia and the GCC states (Karake-Shalhoub 2008). While much of the financing in Malaysia has been in domestic enterprises, in the GCC the financing has largely been directed toward European and U.S. companies. This is starting to change, however, as opportunities for private equity increase, especially in Saudi Arabia and the United Arab Emirates. Family businesses are becoming more interested in raising private equity finance to fund expansion. In the case of pious owners, Islamic private equity seems the obvious choice, especially as their businesses are already *shari'ah* compliant (Wilson 2006). The institutions providing Islamic private equity finance are mostly investment companies rather than Islamic banks, which are much more constrained as regulated deposit takers.

Case Study: Alkhabeer

Typical of these companies is Alkhabeer Capital, an investment company based in Jeddah, which is playing a major role in the provision of private equity finance in Saudi Arabia.[1] The company was established in 2004 as an investment advisory business focused on the development of *shari'ah*-compliant products, but has since increased its own proprietary capital base, as well as managing investments on behalf of its clients. It employs a staff of 80 professionals, including investment analysts. As table 7.1 shows, its assets under management have grown rapidly. As it has gained more experience with the businesses financed, the return on assets has increased impressively.

Two initiatives sponsored by Alkhabeer in 2014 illustrate its business priorities. The first aims to assist the SME sector in playing an increasing role in the economy of Saudi Arabia. SMEs, while considered to be the engine of growth and stability in developed economies, often suffer from a lack of access to capital in emerging markets. As a result, Alkhabeer decided to support this subsector by providing SMEs with growth capital.

TABLE 7.1 **Alkhabeer Financial Highlights**

	2010	2011	2012	2013	2014
Assets under management (SRls million)	535.84	1,442.87	1,641.87	2,498.18	3,335.07
Total revenue (SRls million)	54.81	64.63	107.35	125.70	158.18
Operating expenses (SRls million)	43.81	45.49	76.31	83.19	100.88
Net income (SRls million)	11.00	19.15	31.04	43.32	57.30
Return on assets (percent)	2.74	3.23	3.89	5.25	6.32

Source: Alkhabeer Annual Report 2014.
Note: SRls = Saudi Arabian riyals.

Second, Alkhabeer decided to invest further in the small but expanding venture capital sector in Saudi Arabia. Whereas the Kingdom is the largest economy in the region, it has lagged regional centers such as Dubai in providing the ecosystem required for venture capital companies to succeed. Despite significant amounts of resources invested in this sector, the landscape is still mostly void of serious participants. No authorized person[2] has yet moved into this arena. Alkhabeer has therefore launched a venture capital initiative to plug the gap in the marketplace.

Alkhabeer Private Equity is closely involved with the senior management of its portfolio companies to realize both operational and financial value for all parties, including co-investors. It invests in potential targets through opportunity-specific funds. Target companies are primarily selected with on the basis of the following investment strategies:

- Acquisition of majority stakes in noncore operating companies owned by family groups
- Acquisition of significant minority stakes in blue chip companies with prospects for initial public offerings (IPOs)
- Involvement in partnerships with international companies
- Investments in small and medium enterprises.

In 2014, Alkhabeer launched two *shari'ah*-compliant closed-end private placement health care funds. The first, Alkhabeer Health Care Private Equity Fund I (AHPEF I closed fund), acquired a majority stake in Eed Group, a Saudi-based health care company based in Jeddah. Established in 2001, Eed Group is one of the leading vertically integrated health care groups in Saudi Arabia. The group initially operated as an independent health care provider focusing on cosmetic surgery and outpatient specialty primary care services, but in 2013 it expanded into additional services such as a pharmacy business, medical equipment supply, and third-party management and operations.

The second initiative, the Alkhabeer SME Fund I, is a private placement closed-end fund launched in December 2014 to manage the acquisition of the majority stake in the Ajaji Medical Group, based in Riyadh. Established in 1995, the group owns and operates four polyclinics and five pharmacies in Riyadh, providing health care services primarily to resident expatriates in the Kingdom. This new fund heralds the implementation of Alkhabeer's private equity SME strategy, which targets *shari'ah*-compliant small and medium enterprises in Saudi Arabia and the United Arab Emirates.

Hedge Funds

The term *hedge* implies an investment strategy that seeks to minimize risk, often by transferring it to another party. Islamic finance involves risk sharing, rather than risk transfers. As sharing is what justifies the returns to investors, hedging activity would appear at first glance to be off limits to investors seeking *shari'ah* compliance. In reality, however, hedge funds represent a very heterogeneous class of assets, and the distinction between risk sharing and risk transfers often becomes somewhat blurred. Hedge funds are relatively safe investments most of the time, but when they fail, the results for the investors can be catastrophic, wiping out all their capital. Some investors are willing to be exposed to hedge funds with such a risk profile, either because they expect vastly superior returns when markets are rising or positive returns in falling markets.

Managers of hedge funds usually have a less restrictive mandate than those managing equity or bond portfolios, as they can invest in derivative instruments such as futures and option contracts to hedge their positions (Ackermann, McEnally, and Ravenscraft 1999). Instead of diversifying by holding a wide range of investments in equities and bonds to reduce risk, they often concentrate on acquiring major holdings in a few companies, while limiting the risks through derivatives trading. The aim is not to attain market returns as with tracker funds or exchange traded funds, but to obtain high absolute returns.

While direct investing in equities is seen as socially useful, as it contributes to business expansion and job creation, the link between derivatives and the real economy is much less clear. Derivatives trading can either destabilize or stabilize financial markets. Although it may be justified in commodity markets, where hedging can be helpful for companies and their clients,[3] its merits in equity or bond markets are more questionable. In particular, short selling, which is widely used by hedge funds, can be viewed as exploitative of counterparties, whose losses accrue to the hedge fund as gains in what amounts to a zero-sum game.

One type of short selling to profit from falling markets is where an investor lends stock to a hedge fund manager under a repurchase contract. The hedge fund manager then proceeds to sell the stock at the prevailing spot price, while simultaneously purchasing a future contract to buy back the stock at a lower price, given some market participants' anticipation of price falls. The hedge fund manager gains from the price difference, while ensuring that the transaction can be closed with the return of the stock to the original investor (Agarwal and Naik 2004).

From a *shari'ah* perspective, short selling activity is highly dubious, as it is regarded as speculative and involves *gharar* (contractual uncertainty or legal ambiguity), which is explicitly condemned in Islamic teaching (Dusuki 2008). Moreover, disposing of stock that is not owned by the seller is viewed as potentially deceptive. Although there is a future contract to buy back the stock, the trades are always in danger of unwinding before the stock is returned to the original supplier. There is also concern that the pricing of the contracts is potentially unfair, especially if the hedge fund manager is in a monopoly position and the transactions are not conducted in an open market. The lack of transparency with hedge fund transactions is often criticized by financial commentators, no matter their religious beliefs (if any).

More fundamentally, simply making money by trading financial instruments that have little connection with real business is not viewed as productive, as it amounts to a zero-sum game similar to gambling, which is designated as *maysir*, a practice also condemned in Islamic teaching. *Maysir* is derived from *yusr,* in Arabic, meaning "ease." Gambling both fails to qualify as work and provides an opportunity to gain a pecuniary advantage at the expense of others. On the same basis, an investment entered into for purely speculative reasons would be deemed unacceptable (Mohamad and Tabatabaei 2008).

Existing Islamic hedge funds claim to use contracts that were accepted in traditional *fiqh* (Islamic jurisprudence), notably *arboun*, which is a type of option contract, and *salam*, a contract under which a financier pays in full, up front, for a commodity to be delivered at a future date. *Arboun* involves paying a deposit for a commodity for delivery at a future date, rather than paying in full. There is a revocation option akin to a call option in the conventional sense. However, the contract is about a sale of a good for which the deposit is part of the price, while the option is about the right to purchase, and the price for this right is lost if the contract is allowed to lapse without being exercised. In classical *fiqh, arboun* is controversial, but it is accepted by the Hanbali School of Islamic jurisprudence (Dali and Ahmad 2005).

Case Study: *Shari'ah* Capital

New York–based *Shari'ah* Capital has a long-short Islamic commodities hedge fund that has been operating since 2007.[4] Sheikh Yusuf Talal DeLorenzo, the firm's chief *shari'ah* adviser, is well known and respected in the Islamic finance industry. The chief executive officer is Eric Meyer, who has long been involved in hedge funds and Islamic finance. Although the fund mainly generates income from commodity trading, transportation and manufacturing have been identified as sectors that can accommodate Islamic hedge funds.

Just over $250 million is invested in *Shari'ah* Capital's fund, with institutional investors from Saudi Arabia, the GCC, and Malaysia among the participants. *Shari'ah* Capital's hedge fund trades in commodities such as oil, as well as in energy, mining, and natural resource stocks.

Investors in the fund buy securities instead of borrowing them, using *arboun* contracts to short the market to comply with the *shari'ah* rule that one must own an asset to sell it. Using *arboun,* the fund manager pays a deposit, which forms part of the purchase price, to buy assets at a later date. In the unlikely event that the sale does not proceed, the seller keeps the deposit and gets back the assets.

Shari'ah Capital's Commodity Fund gained 41 percent in its first year, compared with the Lipper Global Hedge/Long/Short equity index, which had a one-year return that same year of 31 percent. Since then, returns have been more modest, reflecting the poor performance of hedge funds generally, rather than *shari'ah* constraints on trading activity. As the U.S. economy rebounded after the global financial crisis, mutual funds often outperformed hedge funds. However, the low level of investment in *Shari'ah* Capital also reflected the uncertainty over the legitimacy of *arboun* by many *shari'ah* scholars. Islamic institutional investors tend to be conservative and concerned about their reputations and client perceptions. Given this context, it is not surprising that there was a reluctance to invest in structures as controversial as Islamic hedge funds. Nevertheless, major shareholders include the Dubai Multi Commodities Centre Authority (DMCCA), an agency of the Dubai government, which has a 5 percent stake in the fund.

In 2007, *Shari'ah* Capital jointly announced with Barclays Capital the development of the Al Safi Trust, a comprehensive *shari'ah*-compliant platform for alternative investments. Designed as a "one-stop" platform primarily for single strategy hedge funds, Al Safi provides *shari'ah* screening and *arboun* sale solutions, along with prime brokerage, administration, and trustee oversight within a pre-established Cayman trust framework. The Al Safi Trust was named Best Islamic Alternative Product at the Hedge Funds World Middle East Conference in 2009.

In 2008, *Shari'ah* Capital formed a joint venture, Dubai *Shari'ah* Asset Management (DSAM), with Dubai Commodity Asset Management (DCAM), a wholly owned division of DMCCA. DCAM, an investment company licensed by the United Arab Emirates central bank, develops and distributes *shari'ah*-compliant, commodity-linked investment products in the United Arab Emirates. The first four hedge funds were funded by DMCCA in 2008 and registered on the Al Safi Trust platform. Two funds are marketed under the DSAM Kauthar brand name as the DSAM Kauthar Gold Fund and the DSAM Kauthar Global Resources & Mining Fund.

The DSAM Kauthar funds have received numerous performance awards:

- Barclay Hedge, an independent hedge fund research organization with a database of over 5,800 hedge funds, consistently ranked the DSAM Kauthar Gold Fund, Ltd. in its Top Ten Metals and Mining hedge funds, based on its monthly performance results throughout 2009, 2010, and 2011. In both 2010 and 2011, the DSAM Kauthar Gold Fund received the MENA Fund Manager Award for outstanding performance and innovation.
- The DSAM Kauthar Energy Fund was ranked among the Barclay Hedge Top Ten Energy Funds for its performance in February 2011.

Real Estate Investments

Exposure to real estate markets is correctly viewed as a real alternative to equities and bonds, but it should be seen as a very long-term investment with a payback over decades rather than months or even years (Faishal and Eng 2008). Such investments are well suited to the time horizon of pension funds, insurance companies, and other institutional investors seeking rental yields, as well as long-term capital gains, or at least inflation proofing. In the case of Muslim-majority countries, most pensions are paid by the state rather than private providers, and are often financed from current revenues rather than long-term funding. Family *takāful*, the *shari'ah*-compliant alternative to life insurance, remains in its infancy (see chapter 5). Hence institutional investors are much less important than in developed markets. The main potential institutional sources for Islamic real estate investment are the semiautonomous sovereign wealth funds, none of which is managed on a *shari'ah*-compliant basis (Jen 2009).

The means of obtaining exposure to real estate markets are also diverse, with direct investment in commercial and residential property and indirect exposure through investment in construction and real estate development companies. REITs are an increasingly popular asset class, including Islamic REITs, which have been pioneered in Malaysia (Newell and Osmadi 2009). Malaysia has 14 REITs, of which 3 are *shari'ah* compliant. Each specializes in a different asset subclass. For example, Al Hadharah specializes in oil palm plantations. Another, specializing in office buildings and industrial properties, was formed by the conversion of a conventional REIT. Real estate investments are inherently illiquid, but the attraction of REITs is that the funds can be redeemed at any time, as they are listed in a market. Therefore, they represent financial vehicles rather than investments in buildings. The disadvantage is that the prices are more correlated with other market instruments, especially equities, than direct investments in commercial and residential property, because when stock markets are performing well, investors have more spare cash to invest in REITs.

In Malaysia, guidelines for Islamic REITs were issued by the *Shari'ah* Advisory Council of the Securities Commission in November 2005.[5] To ensure *shari'ah* compliance, there are restrictions on the purposes for which investment properties can be used. The rentals cannot be derived from *ḥarām* activities. Prohibited tenancies include *ribā*-based banks; conventional insurance offices; betting shops and casinos; manufacture or sale of non-*ḥalāl* beverages and foodstuffs, such as alcohol or pork products; tobacconists; and entertainment venues of a morally dubious nature.

Where real estate with existing tenants is acquired by the Islamic REIT manager, it is recognized that some of the activities of the tenants may be *ḥarām*. Such activities do not preclude the acquisition of the property, provided they do not account for more than 20 percent of the rental income. However, as tenancies are renewed, only *shari'ah*-compliant activities are permissible, with tenancies such as betting shops or alcohol retailers obliged to close or move elsewhere. The properties should be insured with a *takāful* operator; existing conventional building insurance contracts should not be renewed when they expire. Cash holdings of Islamic REITs should be deposited in an Islamic bank.

Case Study: Al Salam REIT

Malaysia's Johor Corporation, a state investment firm, launched the Al-Salam REIT in June 2015. It has subsequently been listed on the Kuala Lumpur stock exchange.[6] Its mandate is to focus on *shari'ah*-compliant diversified assets, including, but not limited to, commercial retail, office, and industrial assets. It raised RM 900 million ($253.24 million), which is funding real estate projects in Johor, the port city and development zone on the Malay Peninsula across the straits from Singapore. The REIT already owns 31 assets, including a chain of Kentucky Fried Chicken and Pizza Hut restaurants, as well as industrial assets. The REIT manager, Damansara Sdn. Berhad (DRMSB), a Malaysian-based company, was founded in 2005 and has considerable experience, including management of the Al-'Aqar Healthcare REIT, which was listed on the Main Board of Bursa Malaysia on August 10, 2006. By 2014, the Al-'Aqar Healthcare REIT had total assets under management amounting to RM 1.5 billion ($339 million).

Demand for Malaysian Islamic REITs has withstood a sluggish property market, as their steady rental income is popular with pension funds amid a shortage of *shari'ah*-compliant assets. Returns for 2016 are projected to be 6.3 percent, an attractive rental yield. Islamic lenders in Malaysia are facing a shortage of investing options, with worldwide *sukūk* issuance down 28 percent in 2015. The Southeast Asian nation's $1.5 billion global Islamic bond sale in August 2015 drew more than $9 billion of bids and was priced below the initial target, reflecting demand for *shari'ah*-compliant instruments.

There are only 3 listed Islamic REITs in Asia, compared with 128 non-Islamic vehicles, according to data compiled by Bloomberg. Al-Salam REIT is targeted at investors or fund managers with long-term investment objectives who seek regular stable income distribution and long-term capital appreciation. Malaysia's two *shari'ah* REITs outperformed *sukūk* in 2014. The Al-'Aqar Healthcare REIT, majority owned by Johor Corp., returned 11.7 sen a unit to shareholders, equivalent to a dividend yield of 8.4 percent based on its year-end closing price. Axis REIT paid out a quarterly average dividend of 4.94 sen a unit last year, or an annual yield of 5.5 percent. The third Islamic REIT in Asia, Singapore's Sabana *Shari'ah*-compliant Industrial REIT, was less successful. It declined 10 percent in 2015, while the city-state's benchmark stock index rose 2.2 percent.

The falling prices are unlikely to dent the popularity of Islamic REITs due to the amount of funds that need to be invested in a *shari'ah*-compliant manner. Malaysian Islamic banking assets climbed 12 percent to RM 625.2 billion ($141.4 billion) in 2014, central bank data show. That represents almost half of the $300 billion of outstanding *sukūk* worldwide, according to figures from the Malaysia International Islamic Financial Centre.[7]

Investment in *Ḥalāl* Foodstuff

An obvious destination for *shari'ah*-compliant alternative investment is the *ḥalāl* foodstuff industry. This industry has grown worldwide as the global Muslim population has increased and become more prosperous. Although *ḥalāl* foodstuff is traditionally associated with meat production, it extends to other sectors, including pharmaceuticals, and niche areas such as alcohol-free mouthwash. In the past, most *ḥalāl* foodstuff production was undertaken by small family businesses, which did not seek external funding. This is changing as major multinational corporations get involved and as *ḥalāl* products are increasingly marketed and sold by supermarket groups, including those based in North America, Europe, and Japan. This brings new investment opportunities, although there is debate over whether mixed businesses are legitimate destinations for *shari'ah*-compliant investment, or such investment should be channeled solely to enterprises that are exclusively *ḥalāl*.

Until recently, *ḥalāl* production was very fragmented; there were no industry associations and no attempt to use the term *ḥalāl* as a trademark or brand. The United Kingdom–based Muslim Food Board, which was established in 1992, was a pioneer in *ḥalāl* certification.[8] Approved producers can use their registered logo for advertising purposes. The organization provides ongoing monitoring after certification to reassure Muslim consumers, as well as training for those employed in the industry. Similar organizations providing certification are found in Australia and North America, but their absence in most Muslim-majority countries largely reflects the inadequate legal environment for trademark protection. Such protection is as important for investors as for consumers.

Malaysia has had more initiatives in *ḥalāl* activities than most Muslim-majority countries. In 2014, the SME Bank announced it was allocating another RM 200 million ($45.4 million) under its *Ḥalāl* Industry Fund, which is available for SMEs to add value or improve their *ḥalāl* products.[9] The initiative was made in collaboration with strategic partners, including the Islamic Development Bank (IDB), the Malaysia External Trade

Development Corporation, and the *Ḥalāl* Industry Development Corporation, as well as the Young Entrepreneur Fund (YEF), which helps youths ages 18–30 years venture into entrepreneurship. The SME Bank is open for investment from GCC countries, and the involvement of the Jeddah-based IDB gives assurance to these investors. Most of the SMEs are involved in the distribution and sale of *ḥalāl* produce rather than production, apart from fields such as poultry production, where there is a local industry. Much of the cattle and mutton originates in Australia and New Zealand, where *ḥalāl* producers welcome investment from consuming nations.

Case Study: *Ḥalāl* Cluster in Dubai Industrial City

To cater to the growing demand for *ḥalāl* produce, the United Arab Emirates government has established a *ḥalāl* cluster on a site comprising 6.7 million square feet in Dubai Industrial City.[10] The cluster is designated for firms dealing in *ḥalāl* food, cosmetics, and personal care items. An emerging industry of *ḥalāl* certification has been created to attempt to verify any issues that may arise when considering the true definition of "*ḥalāl*" products. The methods for discovering *ḥarām* impurities in products are rapidly improving. These days, the types of animals that the raw materials are derived from can be identified using polymerase chain reaction (PCR), which greatly improves the potential for *ḥalāl* integrity, allowing the development of *ḥalāl* supply chains and product tracking.

The *ḥalāl* cluster has been promoted at the annual *Ḥalāl* Expo held in Dubai, now a well-established business-to-business event.[11] The seventh Expo was held in Dubai in September 2015, with the promoters stressing the huge potential that the global $2.3 trillion *ḥalāl* market has to offer. The Expo has proved to be a high-impact business platform to canvass the lucrative business opportunities that the global *ḥalāl* market presents and cater to the needs of the *ḥalāl* producers, traders, and business leaders looking to expand their business in the Middle East. The value of the *ḥalāl* food sector is almost V700 billion annually. The nonfood sector is even bigger and includes chemicals, health care, cosmetics, personal care, and pharmaceuticals. The Expo also stressed the *shari'ah*-compliant services available in the *ḥalāl* cluster, which include banking and finance, logistics, warehousing, and distribution.

Investment in Traded Commodities

Despite the dramatic fall in commodity prices in 2014 and 2015 with the slowing in China's economic growth, commodities are still regarded as a potentially worthwhile alternative investment asset (Tang and Xiong 2012). From an Islamic finance perspective, commodities are regarded as tangible assets rather than simply as financial instruments. The buying, holding, and selling of commodities are viewed as useful service activities that justify the earning of profits. Historically, many of the great capitals of the Islamic world thrived as trading centers, with the buying and selling of metals and agricultural commodities handled by specialist brokers on behalf of wealthy investors (Kathirithamby-Wells 1986).

As modern Islamic banking emerged in the 1970s, *murābahah* transactions took off, with the Islamic financial institution purchasing commodities on behalf of clients who agree to repay the institution with a deferred lump sum or through installments (Dusuki 2007). The Islamic bank charges a markup for this service, which clients are willing to pay, as they have insufficient funds to buy the commodity until they arrange their financial affairs or receive payments from business partners. Islamic banks can also arrange commodity financing through *salam* and *arboun* contracts. With *salam*, the bank pays in advance the full amount for a commodity to be delivered at a future date. The bank will not be speculating on the future price, as it will usually have a client or clients lined up who have already agreed to purchase the commodity from the bank at a slightly higher price, to cover the bank's financing costs.

These clients prefer to purchase from the bank for a known fixed price, rather than purchasing through a commodity market at a future unknown spot price.

Similar considerations arise with *arboun*, but under these contracts the Islamic financial institutions pay only a deposit for a commodity that is to be delivered at a future date for a fixed price, rather than paying the full amount in advance. As discussed, an *arboun* agreement resembles an option contract, but it is usually exercised, rather than left simply to expire as with derivatives contracts, which are used for gambles on spot and futures prices.

Case Study: Jadwa Saudi Riyal *Murābahah* Fund

Riyadh-based Jadwa was incorporated on August 21, 2006, with paid-in capital of SRl 500 million ($133 million), when the Capital Markets Authority (CMA) of Saudi Arabia granted the company all five licenses to operate as a full service *shari'ah*-compliant investment bank in the Kingdom under license number 37-6034. Jadwa offers wide-ranging investment services that support both individual and institutional clients. Jadwa is a comprehensive financial services firm with a proven track record in asset management, financial advisory, and mergers and acquisitions, as well as researched brokerage.[12]

Designed for low-risk investment in local currency, the Jadwa Saudi Riyal *Murābahah* Fund mirrors certificates of deposits in terms of investment strategy and easy liquidity, but in compliance with *shari'ah* guidelines. Jadwa places the trades with banks in a *shari'ah*-compliant manner in short-term *murābahah* contracts, usually for 30 or 90 days. The fund aims to attract retail investors with a minimum initial subscription of SRl 50,000 ($13,332) and a minimum additional subscription or redemption of SR1 25,000. The fund is valued on a daily basis and charges a management fee of 0.5 percent annually. The fund was first established on June 30, 2007, and has a track record of yielding modest returns while maintaining the value of investors' capital.[13]

Project Finance

Alternative financing can contribute to project finance. Although such financing used to be largely undertaken by governments, there have been many initiatives to encourage private sector involvement since the 1980s (Brealey, Cooper, and Habib 1996). Most of these initiatives have been aimed at diversifying the sources for long-term project finance rather than changing the methods, as the financing largely involved syndicating debt rather than alternative financing such as private equity (Kleimeier and Megginson 2000). Islamic financial institutions can also participate in syndicated funding with the money raised by issuing *sukūk,* rather than bonds paying interest. The IDB, for example, has regular *sukūk* issuances to fund its project financing, and given its Aaa rating by Moody's, the cost of its capital is very low (Moody's Investors Services 2014).

Istiṣnā' is regarded as a particularly useful method for providing project finance, as it is widely favored by Islamic scholars as suitable for paying for manufacturing supplies (Zarqa 1997). Most Islamic finance is used to pay for assets that already exist, but with projects, it often takes several years for facilities to be constructed. For investors, *istiṣnā'* provides a steady long-term income stream once the project is completed, but they may have to wait two years or longer until the first income is received. Such assets are attractive for managers of pension funds and *takāful* providers, especially for family *takāful*, the *shari'ah*-compliant alternative to conventional life insurance. There is an element of risk sharing in *istiṣnā'* contracts, as the completion of projects is often delayed; hence it is important to spell out clearly the protection for investors, while allowing some flexibility for contingencies.

Case Study: The Islamic Development Bank's Funding for Electricity in Rural Mozambique

The Cahora Bassa dam generates most of Mozambique's electricity, but the northern province of Cabo Delgardo had no

TABLE 7.2 **Funding of Phase III Electricity Project in Rural Mozambique**

Agency	Finance ($ million)	Percentage of total funding	Purpose
IDB	9.49	32	248 km subtransmission lines
Arab Bank for Economic Development in Africa (BADEA)	9.00	31	95 km transmission line
European Union	5.99	20	194 km subtransmission line
Government of Mozambique	4.85	17	Joint financing with each donor

Source: IDB Success Story Series, No. 22, June 2015.
Note: km = kilometers.

distribution network. The construction of the network was a long-term project scheduled as three phases from 1999 to 2013. The IDB has been involved since the start. The third phase, implemented from 2009 to 2013, is an especially successful example of syndicated funding involving the IDB and other international agencies, as table 7.2 shows.

The benefits from the Cabo Delgado electrification were not only to households but also to businesses and the wider economy. The former diesel generators were unreliable and expensive to maintain. With reliable electricity supplies, businesses can stay open longer and use modern equipment, including air conditioners, computers, photocopiers, refrigerators, and freezers. Employment opportunities have been enhanced, as businesses have flourished and the local inhabitants have been more willing to stay in the region than move. Many regard being able to recharge mobile phones cheaply and easily as a significant benefit.

Alternative Assets and Economic Development

Although project finance directly contributes to economic development, the link with other alternative investments is less robust. For example, the link between hedge fund investments involving financial speculation and wider development is doubtful. Such investments often benefit the rich and contribute to income inequalities, with so-called trickle-down effects to the less affluent arguably weak—if they exist at all. Private equity finance is more positive from a developmental perspective, but it tends to be concentrated in higher-income countries, as opportunities in low-income economies are less easy to identify and support. The World Bank vision of shared prosperity is commendable, but the challenge of building the physical infrastructure and developing human resources to achieve this goal is enormous (Badré 2015). There is a question of causation: What comes first? Does the accumulation of alternative assets facilitate economic development, or vice versa?

When alternative investment is undertaken using *shari'ah*-compliant contracts, this helps ensure that there are outcomes that contribute to shared prosperity. From an Islamic perspective, economic development should be socially inclusive, which all too often is not the case in practice. Islamic alternative investment contracts should be transparent. It is the responsibility of the religious scholars vetting the contracts to ensure there is no element of *gharar*, defined in classical Islamic jurisprudence as contractual uncertainty or ambiguity that favors one party at the expense of the other (El-Gamal 2001). The prohibition of *gharar* is more important today than ever, especially given the complexity of the contracts for alternative investments. There is considerable potential for fund managers to exploit investors who are locked in (Al-Suwailem 1999).

Regulatory Implications and Policy Responses for Alternative Investments

As alternative investments are a diverse asset class, there are no all-embracing regulations or guidelines that can be simply applied. Usually alternative investments are under the remit of securities or capital market regulators where such institutions exist, rather than being the responsibility of central banks. Within the Islamic world, the Malaysian Securities Commission and the CMA of Saudi Arabia have played leading roles in identifying the issues that arise with alternative investments. The Kuala Lumpur–based Islamic Financial Services Board (IFSB) has not yet issued any standards specifically on alternative investments, as it focuses more on Islamic banking and *takāful*, although it has published Guiding Principles for Islamic Collective Investment Schemes.[14] There is clearly a case for more comprehensive guidance on alternative investments by the IFSB, as it is the institution that includes regulatory authorities from the Organisation for Islamic Cooperation (OIC) States as its members.

At the same time, it must be recognized that those involved in alternative investments are normally sophisticated investors who do not need protection in the same way as retail investors. Many analysts urge so-called "light touch" regulation for alternative investments, as this reduces transaction costs, which ultimately get passed on to the investors. The European Union and the United Kingdom have relatively liberal directives on alternative investments.[15] Nevertheless, in the case of Islamic investment, the *shari'ah* oversight should not be light touch; otherwise this might undermine the credibility of the investments for the pious. There would be reputational risks to the financial institutions offering such investments, and potential reputational damage to the scholars involved in approving the investments.

Shari'ah scholars working on Islamic finance need to address the issue of the permissibility of alternative asset classes more comprehensively. At the international level, this includes the OIC Islamic *Fiqh* Academy (IFA), which has issued *fatāwá* on many Islamic financing contracts, but not specifically on alternative investments.[16] The *shari'ah* scholars advising securities regulators also have a role to play—although at present only the Securities Commission in Kuala Lumpur has a formal *shari'ah* board. It has produced a joint report on Islamic capital markets in collaboration with another institution based in Kuala Lumpur, the International *Shari'ah* Research Academy (ISRA).[17] A similar joint initiative in the field of Islamic alternative asset classes would be welcomed by the Islamic finance community around the world.

Notes

1. http://www.alkhabeer.com/.
2. Authorized person is a registered fund, regulated by the Capital Markets Authority of Saudi Arabia.
3. Many airlines, for example, hedge their fuel purchases so that they can control their costs.
4. http://www.shariahcap.com/.
5. http://www.sc.com.my/guidelines-for-islamic-real-estate-investment-trusts/.
6. http://www.jcorp.com.my/reit-sector-107.aspx; http://www.bloomberg.com/profiles/companies/SALAM:MK-al-salam-real-estate-investment-trust.
7. http://www.mifc.com/.
8. http://www.tmfb.net/about.
9. http://www.freemalaysiatoday.com/category/business/2013/03/22/halal-industry-fund-for-smes-to-improve-halal-products/.
10. http://www.gulfood.com/Content/Dubai-gears-up-for-67million-sqft-Halal-Cluster.
11. http://www.worldhalalexpos.com/.
12. http://www.jadwa.com/en/article/about-jadwa/who-we-are.html.
13. http://www.jadwa.com/en/fund/asset-management-products-and-services/mutual-funds/jadwa-saudi-riyal-murabaha-fund-1.html.
14. http://www.ifsb.org/standard/ifsb6.pdf.
15. http://ec.europa.eu/finance/investment/alternative_investments/index_en.htm#maincontentSec2; http://www.fca.org.uk/firms/markets/international-markets/aifmd.
16. http://www.fiqhacademy.org.sa/.
17. http://www.sc.com.my/highlight/isra-and-sc-launch-joint-publication-on-islamic-capital-markets-principles-and-practices-2/.

References

Ackermann, Carl, Richard McEnally, and David Ravenscraft. 1999. "The Performance of Hedge Funds: Risk, Return, and Incentives." *Journal of Finance* 54 (3): 833–74.

Agarwal, Vikas, and Narayan Y. Naik. 2004. "Risks and Portfolio Decisions Involving Hedge Funds." *Review of Financial Studies* 17 (1): 63–98.

Al-Suwailem, Sami. 1999. "Towards an Objective Measure of *Gharar* in Exchange." *Journal of Islamic Economic Studies* 7: 61–102.

Archer, Simon, and Rifaat Ahmed Abdel Karim. 2006. "On Capital Structure, Risk Sharing and Capital Adequacy in Islamic Banks." *International Journal of Theoretical and Applied Finance* 9 (03): 269–80.

Badré, Bertrand. 2015. *Long-Term Finance for Infrastructure Essential to Ending Poverty*. Washington, DC: World Bank. https://www.linkedin.com/pulse/long-term-finance-infrastructure-essential-ending-poverty-badr%C3%A9.

Brealey, Richard A., Ian A. Cooper, and Michel A. Habib. 1996. "Using Project Finance to Fund Infrastructure Investments." *Journal of Applied Corporate Finance* 9 (3): 25–39.

Chatti, Mohamed Ali, and Ouidad Yous. 2010. "Islamic Private Equity." Munich Personal RePEc Archive Paper 28705. http://mpra.ub.uni-muenchen.de/28705/.

Choudhury, Masudul Alam. 2001. "Islamic Venture Capital–A Critical Examination." *Journal of Economic Studies* 28 (1): 14–33.

Dali, Nuradli Ridzwan Shah Mohd, and Sanep Ahmad. 2005. "A Review of Forward, Futures, and Options from the *Shari'ah* Perspective: From Complexity to Simplicity." Paper presented at the Conference on Ekonomi and Kewangan Islam Bangi, Malaysia, August 29–30.

Dusuki, Asyraf Wajdi. 2007. "Commodity *Murābaḥah* Programme (CMP): An Innovative Approach to Liquidity Management." *Journal of Islamic Economics, Banking and Finance* 3 (1): 1–23.

———. 2008. "*Fiqh* Issues in Short Selling as Implemented in the Islamic Capital Market in Malaysia." *Islamic Economics* 21 (2): 63–78.

El-Gamal, Mahmoud A. 2001. "An Economic Explication of the Prohibition of *Gharar* in Classical Islamic Jurisprudence." *Islamic Economic Studies* 8 (2): 29–58.

Faishal, Muhammad, and Seow Eng. 2008. "*Shari'ah* Compliance in Real Estate Investment." *Journal of Real Estate Portfolio Management* 14 (4): 401–14.

Jen, Stephen L. 2009. "How Big Could Sovereign Wealth Funds Be by 2015?" *Revue d'Economie Financière* (English edition) 9 (1): 195–98.

Karake-Shalhoub, Zeinab. 2008. "Private Equity, Islamic Finance, and Sovereign Wealth Funds in the MENA Region." *Thunderbird International Business Review* 50 (6): 359–68.

Kathirithamby-Wells, Jeyamalar. 1986. "The Islamic City: Melaka to Jogjakarta, c. 1500–1800." *Modern Asian Studies* 20 (02): 333–51.

Kleimeier, Stefanie, and William L. Megginson. 2000. "Are Project Finance Loans Different from Other Syndicated Credits?" *Journal of Applied Corporate Finance* 13 (1): 75–87.

Mohamad, Saadiah, and Ali Tabatabaei. 2008. "Islamic Hedging: Gambling or Risk Management?" Paper presented at the 21st Australasian Finance and Banking Conference. Islamic Law and Law of the Muslim World Paper No. 08-47, Sydney, December 16–18.

Moody's Investors Services. 2014. "Credit Analysis: Islamic Development Bank." October 12. http://www.isdb.org/irj/go/km/docs/documents/IDBDevelopments/Attachments/Capital%20Market/RatingReportsMoodys14.pdf.

Newell, Graeme, and Atasya Osmadi. 2009. "The Development and Preliminary Performance Analysis of Islamic REITs in Malaysia." *Journal of Property Research* 26 (4): 329–47.

Schneeweis, Thomas, C. F. A. Hossein Kazemi, and George Martin. 2003. "Alternative Investments." *Journal of Alternative Investments* 5 (4): 8–30.

Siegel, Laurence B. 2008. "Alternatives and Liquidity: Will Spending and Capital Calls Eat Your 'Modern' Portfolio?" *The Journal of Portfolio Management* 35 (1): 103–14.

Tang, Ke, and Wei Xiong. 2012. "Index Investment and the Financialization of Commodities." *Financial Analysts Journal* 68 (5): 54–74.

Terhaar, Kevin, Renato Staub, and Brian D. Singer. 2003. "Appropriate Policy Allocation for Alternative Investments." *The Journal of Portfolio Management* 29 (3): 101–10.

Wilson, Rodney. 2006. "Islam and Business." *Thunderbird International Business Review* 48 (1): 109–23.

Zarqa, Muhammad Anas. 1997. "*Istisna'a* Financing of Infrastructure Projects." *Islamic Economic Studies* 4 (2): 69–70.

8

Islamic Social Finance

Poverty and financial exclusion go hand in hand. Any attempt to enhance shared prosperity and curb poverty must therefore address the issue of financial exclusion. The task may be more daunting in Muslim societies, where the poor may be excluding themselves from the financial system because of their faith and beliefs. As a 2007 survey for the Consultative Group to Assist the Poor (CGAP) concluded, "Islamic microfinance has the potential to combine the Islamic social principle of caring for the less fortunate with microfinance's power to provide financial access to the poor. Unlocking this potential could be the key to providing financial access to millions of Muslim poor who currently reject microfinance products that do not comply with Islamic law" (Nimrah, Tarazi, and Reille 2008, 1). Islamic social finance that includes the provision of microfinance along with safety nets and social goods could be a powerful tool to fight financial exclusion and poverty and enhance shared prosperity.

Philanthropy and benevolence occupy a central position in the Islamic scheme of poverty alleviation and redistributive justice. Islamic social finance comprises instruments and institutional structures that are rooted in philanthropy. Their integration with for-profit risk-sharing instruments may provide some key success factors while addressing some critical challenges. The broad instrument of Islamic philanthropy is *ṣadaqāt*. When made compulsory on well-to-do Muslims, *ṣadaqāt* is called *zakāt*. When *ṣadaqāt* results in flows of benefits that are expected to be stable and permanent (such as through endowment of a physical property), it is called *ṣadaqāt jāriyah* or *waqf*. Contemporary Islamic economists emphasize that a philanthropy-based intervention inherent in the institutions of *zakāt* and *ṣadaqāt* could potentially take care of the basic needs of the extremely poor and the destitute and create a social safety net (Chapra 2008). A recent study that estimates the potential *zakāt* collection in member-countries of the Organisation of Islamic

Cooperation (OIC) finds supporting evidence that 20 out of 39 OIC countries could actually lift the extreme poor (those living on less than $1.25 per day) above the poverty line simply through the collection and distribution of *zakāt* from domestic sources and remittances (Moheildin and others 2012).

The other institution of philanthropy—*waqf*, or Islamic endowment—is ideal for the creation and preservation of assets that can ensure flows of resources to provide education, health care, and other social goods. *Waqf* may also direct resources toward improving skills and developing human resources through technical assistance and capacity building. The social safety net, technical assistance, and capacity building may then be linked to financial assistance by helping to develop microenterprises. Thus these Islamic financial institutions, by improving access to and the quality of education, health, and other social goods, can play a critical role in achieving the global goals of generating sufficient income-earning opportunities and investing in people's development. These Islamic institutions can also serve to protect the poor and vulnerable against sudden risks of unemployment, hunger, illness, drought, and other calamities. These measures would greatly boost shared prosperity, improving the welfare of the least well-off.

The Islamic approach to poverty alleviation is more inclusive than the conventional interventions based on microcredit. It provides for the basic conditions of sustainable and successful microfinance, blending wealth creation with empathy for the poorest of the poor. It favors models based on equity and cooperation, in contrast to mechanisms that tend to perpetuate debt (Obaidullah and Khan 2007). The discussion that follows briefly describes *zakāt* and *waqf* as the key instruments of Islamic social finance that help reduce extreme poverty and boost shared prosperity. It presents brief case studies to highlight alternative models of intervention that utilize Islamic social finance.

The Redistributive Role of *Zakāt*

Zakāt is a compulsory annual levy on the wealth of the rich that is directed by the *shari'ah*, to flow to the poor and the needy. By definition, it is a tool of redistribution of wealth, transferring wealth from the rich to the poor. Every Muslim individual who possesses wealth beyond a prescribed minimum threshold is liable to contribute from his or her wealth. *Zakāt* is levied on savings that account for part of the wealth of an individual. It is also levied on forms of wealth that are characterized as stocks, such as gold, silver, trade inventory, and livestock. *Zakāt* is not levied on income that is used for consumption, and items of wealth that are for personal and family use, such as a house or a car. It is also not levied on wealth that is categorized as the means of production, or capital goods. Thus the levy of *zakāt* results in the transfer of wealth from the rich without adversely affecting their consumption or productive investments.[1]

Islam stipulates conditions on the use of *zakāt* funds and requires that funds must clearly flow only to specified categories of beneficiaries.[2] *Zakāt* is primarily targeted to the underprivileged and the excluded sections in the society, such as the poorest of the poor, the needy, the destitute, and those in bondage or overburdened with debt. These include individuals with no means of livelihood or inadequate income to meet basic necessities, such as orphans, the sick, the disabled, and the homeless. *Zakāt* is thus rightly seen as a safety net to take care of the basic necessities of life of those who cannot afford them.

Zakāt funds must be clearly distinguished from funds in a treasury of an Islamic country that are pooled through taxes and State revenues. *Zakāt* cannot be used to finance infrastructure projects, public utilities, and services beneficial to all Muslims—the poor and the rich—or to meet the administrative expenditures of the State. *Zakāt* funds may, however, be used to defray the operational costs of managing a *zakāt* organization, in the form of wages and salaries of *zakāt* personnel. This provision aims to maintain the integrity and independence of collection and disbursement of *zakāt* funds (Obaidullah 2012).

The primary objective of *zakāt* is to provide a safety net for all Muslims by providing for basic needs. Basic needs by definition are recurring in nature. Some Islamic scholars thus argue that *zakāt* proceeds should be used for economic empowerment and not simply to meet immediate consumption needs—which could encourage dependence and make the poor permanently dependent on *zakāt*. In their zeal to bring about economic empowerment, proponents often tend to undertake large investments in education, health care, and other social welfare projects (which benefit the poor, the not-so-poor, and even the well-to-do) or engage in financing of microenterprises. Although worthy, such expenditures may result in a drying up of funds to meet the immediate consumption needs of the poorest of the poor.

Economic empowerment and meeting basic consumption needs should not be mutually exclusive. In any program of economic empowerment through *zakāt*, satisfying the immediate basic needs of the poorest of the poor must always be accorded top priority. In a subsequent phase, *zakāt* funds can finance education and training so the poor can gain the skills and human capital to be more self-sufficient. *Zakāt* funds may also be provided as start-up capital for the poor for their business activities, accepted either in the form of outright grants or loans (*qarḍ ḥasan*) or micro-equity without expectation of returns, depending upon the degree of their vulnerability. This would enable the poor to generate a sustainable means of livelihood and transform them from *zakāt* recipients into *zakāt* payers. Such ambitious poverty alleviation and economic empowerment projects, through efficient collection and distribution of *zakāt*, can be undertaken by the State or a not-for-profit organization funded with *zakāt*. At the same time, the use of *zakāt* funds for the provision of microfinance raises several important issues.

Low-Cost Microcredit with *Ṣadaqāt* and *Zakāt*

A critical issue for conventional microcredit and its Islamic equivalent relates to the pricing of the finance. In general, microcredit—whether *shari'ah* compliant or otherwise—remains unaffordable to the poorest of the poor. The cost of microcredit remains high because of the high operational costs involved. Even where the Islamic microfinance provider seeks to recover only the actual cost of financing from the borrower without any profit element, in conformity with *shari'ah*, the very poor are likely to find it unaffordable. The extreme vulnerability of this segment of society makes them reluctant to opt for such loans. As a solution, a model combining *zakāt* and *ṣadaqāt* funds may be used to cover part of the operational costs in a sustainable manner and make the credit affordable to the poor.

The model envisages provision of revolving credit through *qarḍ ḥasan* loans out of pooled *ṣadaqāt* and *zakāt* proceeds. It is a departure from the traditional approach of making grants out of *zakāt* funds to the poor. Creating a credit pool ensures that the fund is automatically replenished every time loans are repaid. The outcome is a sustainable *shari'ah*-compliant financial service provider for the poor.

An excellent example of this model is the Akhuwat scheme, based in Pakistan (box 8.1). The key elements of the Akhuwat strategy are as follows. The first is to bring down the operational cost of providing microcredit to the poor by drawing on volunteers and other means (such as use of places of worship for credit delivery). The second is to mobilize charitable funds on a sustained basis to absorb the operational costs, which are now much lower. As a result, the costs of loans have not just been brought down—they have been brought down to zero.

The model is not without its critics, who feel that the poor should be provided grants and not loans. The provision of microcredit may violate the very essence of *zakāt*: of pulling an individual out of indebtedness. Proponents defend the Akhuwat model on the grounds that the amount of *zakāt* funds mobilized in contemporary Muslim societies may be grossly inadequate if given as grants. As loans from a revolving pool, a given amount of *zakāt* can serve a much larger number of beneficiaries.

BOX 8.1 Case 1. Revolving Credit out of Pooled *Sadaqāt and Zakāt* Proceeds: Akhuwat, Pakistan

From modest beginnings in 2001 (with an initial transaction of PRs 10,000 funded through a single donation), Akhuwat has steadily expanded and now has 350 branches in 250 cities and towns in Pakistan. With a beneficiary-to-staff ratio of 475 to 1, Akhuwat serves 953,933 beneficiaries with a total staff of 2,007 as of June 30, 2015. It had about PRs 4.8 billion in outstanding loans as of June 30, 2015, with total disbursements of about PRs 16.3 billion to date, and an impressive recovery rate of 99.9 percent in the same period.

Drawing on a credit pool established through philanthropic donations, Akhuwat makes small loans (*qarḍ ḥasan*) to the poor. The credit pool is in the nature of a revolving fund that is continuously depleted with the disbursal of loans, and replenished and enhanced as they are repaid and new donations are received. Akhuwat uses a simple loan product that is free from any element of profit. Loans are made to start or expand businesses or to meet social needs that are ultimately aimed at increasing the income of poor and improving the quality of their lives. The loan size is small and is based on the borrower's need and repayment performance. The loan amount may be increased in subsequent cycles, but only up to a predetermined maximum. Akhuwat actively discourages the perpetuation of debt, unlike conventional microcredit. More than 90 percent of Akhuwat borrowers have incomes of less than $70 a month, thus belonging to the poorest of the poor. Akhuwat also provides a small percentage of loans to the moderately poor who are economically active as microentrepreneurs. Akhuwat provides family loans targeting entire households instead of individuals.

Initially, Akhuwat worked on cost recovery basis, with 5 percent of the loan amount termed as the administrative fee, without charging any markup or fee to microenterprises. The sustained growth in charitable contributions and special donations from borrowers has enabled Akhuwat to absorb all costs and make all loans entirely costless. Akhuwat has also consistently worked to minimize its operational costs so that these could be easily absorbed by charitable contributions from its donors. To cut costs, Akhuwat delivers credit and manages the process at places of worship, and draws on volunteers, including for its top staff. The CEO and the top management and about one-third of Akhuwat staff work voluntarily without any remuneration. Akhuwat also seeks to minimize its personnel costs by recruiting staff from the same communities as their borrowers, and not hiring highly qualified professionals. The organization has made minimal investments in office assets. It owns no vehicles. Its staff sits on the floor, as do its clients. It has found a way to do business with the poor that keeps costs to bare minimum. As a result, its operating costs as a percentage of loan amount disbursed have consistently been in the range of 8–12 percent of amount disbursed, and they fell to 5 percent in 2015.

Akhuwat seeks to mitigate credit risk using an innovative combination of credit delivery at places of worship and personal guarantees. Using places of worship for loan disbursement significantly reduces the probability that borrowers will break their commitment to repay their loans on time. In addition, borrowers need to bring two other guarantors to cosign their loans. The guarantors may not be from the borrower's household, and may not have high net worth, but should have high moral character, displaying piety and trustworthiness and willingness to assist the borrower in times of adversity. This mechanism effectively replaces the group guarantee. Extending the loan to the entire family, rather than the individual, also ensures that the entire family is the guarantor and the beneficiary.

The transformation of borrowers into donors has become an important component of Akhuwat's strategy for the future. Past borrowers have increasingly sought to donate to Akhuwat. Such donations now are a significant pool and cover over one-third of Akhuwat's total operating costs.

Source: Personal interviews and information collected from the organization by the authors.

Community-Driven Development with *Ṣadaqāt and Zakāt*

An alternative approach to poverty alleviation that is of more recent origin than the mainstream microfinance models is the community-driven development (CDD) approach. CDD is a grant-based intervention. It approaches the poor as partners in the development process, rather than as mere recipients, and builds on their institutions and resources. Its key elements include the following:

- Focus on communities and/or community groups
- Inclusive and participatory decision-making processes
- Direct transfer of resources to the community
- Community involvement in implementing subprojects
- Community involvement in monitoring and oversight.

While CDD has been quite effective as an intervention, its fundamental weakness has been the absence of a sustained grant-funding mechanism. Even in the most effective of CDD programs, participating poor communities may expect to receive from one to three grants in support of community-identified activities over the course of a CDD program—yet the full development of the community will require much more than these few grants. To sustain local initiatives, an ongoing grant funding mechanism is needed. A *zakāt*-funded CDD program can meet this need, since *zakāt*, by definition, involves recurring annual flows.

However, any arrangement that pools *zakāt* funds to be used for a common good or collective benefit must resolve ownership issues. A key principle of *shari'ah* relating to disbursement of *zakāt* is *tamleek,* which translates as the "transfer of ownership" of *zakāt*. The norm requires the poor and the needy (eligible beneficiaries) to be made owners of *zakāt* or *zakāt*-funded assets. As such, *zakāt*-funded collective enterprises are allowed only when these are fully owned only by the poor. *Shari'ah* scholars rule out the possibility of financing broad development projects with *zakāt* funds that may benefit both the well-to-do and the poor. While this restriction on development projects in the nature of social goods, such as schools and hospitals, appears to be severe, a novel experiment by the Indonesian nongovernmental organization (NGO) Dompet Duafa Republika seems to be providing a solution that is both sustainable and practical (box 8.2).

BOX 8.2 Case 2. Community-Driven Development: Dompet Dhuafa Republika, Indonesia

Dompet Dhuafa Republika (DDR) is a philanthropic institution that helps the poor using donated assets, including *zakāt, ṣadaqāt,* and *waqf,* from individuals, groups, companies, or institutions. The funds dedicated to economic empowerment programs average around 10 percent of total *zakāt* resources available. The low dedication is attributable to apparent *shari'ah* objections by some scholars, who emphasize the utilization of *zakāt* for consumption alone in the short term. In the face of a growing realization that an emphasis on meeting short-term needs may lead to a dependency syndrome among the poor, and that the long-term need of the poor is economic and social self-reliance, DDR seeks to enhance the utilization of *zakāt* for community empowerment programs.

These programs focus on promoting self-reliant communities, enhancing health, and encouraging organic farming and livestock development. Like Akhuwat in Pakistan (box 8.1), DDR extends interest-free loan financing to groups from a pool created out of *zakāt* funds. The distinguishing feature of this model is the phased building of self-reliant communities and the creation of a community

box continues next page

BOX 8.2 Case 2. Community-Driven Development: Dompet Dhuafa Republika, Indonesia *(continued)*

organization that will continue to provide financing to the members.

To ensure full *shari'ah* compliance as well as the efficiency and effectiveness of the intervention, the model follows clearly defined criteria to identify its target region and beneficiaries. A rural region targeted for the program should have comparative advantages in specific commodities or produce; natural resources that can be accessed by the poor; and available human resources in both quality and quantity. It also should not be experiencing or exposed to conflicts or have a high potential for conflict.

The program has the following key components:

- *Awareness building.* It helps the community identify its problems and its potential under the assumption that the community itself has the ability to solve its problems.
- *Organization.* It generates self-help groups as the way to give voice and authority to those groups and helps form a local organization through community initiative.
- *Building of local support.* It prepares a local cadre that will develop local self-help and will take over the "hand-holding" role once the program ends.
- *Technical support.* It provides technical training based on locally available and appropriate technology.
- *Partnership.* The local community figures out what can be implemented and what support will be needed from the program. The community establishes cooperation based on specific roles for each stakeholder, based on mutual trust and transparency.

The program provides the following services to its beneficiaries:

- Developing human resources through training programs, workshops, and meetings among members.
- Developing institutions with proper documentation of standard operating procedures, so each organization or group can be commonly monitored.
- Providing capital to local businesses through group-based credit and self-help savings.
- Providing business development services to improve production methods.
- Developing markets by sharing information about business opportunities, and building networks and synergies.

The program has a clear termination and exit strategy. It withdraws from the region and the program comes to an end as soon as the community cadres are ready to take part in maintaining the program's financial and institutional sustainability. It ensures that a community-based organization is a legal entity with adequate capacity to sustain cooperation among all stakeholders. From a *shari'ah* perspective, this ensures that the *tamleek* condition of *zakāt* is complied with, since the poor beneficiaries ultimately become the owners of the local organization in a collective sense, with the transfer of assets from the program to the local organization. Thus the fact that they are borrowers in the first instance does not appear to violate the *tamleek* requirement.

Source: Personal interviews and information collected from the organization by the authors.

Guarantee Fund with *Zakāt*

As some scholars point out, there is a large gap between the potential and actual realization of *zakāt*—for many reasons. Thus there is a need to leverage the use of such funds. A *zakāt* fund can be used to provide a guarantee for microfinance, while other for-profit Islamic financial institutions can undertake the direct financing. The guarantee can encourage institutions that have been reluctant to finance microenterprises because of the high perceived default risk to extend financing, backed by the guarantee. Given that the observed default rate in

BOX 8.3 Case 3. A *Zakāt* Fund: Al-Aman Microfinance Fund, Sudan

The microfinance program (IRADA) of the Bank of Khartoum (BoK) was established in 2009 with the support and assistance from the Jeddah-based Islamic Development Bank. IRADA was given the mandate to implement the SD 200 million Al-Aman Fund for Microfinance. The fund was formed in a strategic partnership between the apex body of *zakāt* management in Sudan, Diwan *Zakāt,* and 32 Sudanese commercial banks.

In perhaps the first documented example of utilization of *zakāt* for *al-ghārimīn* (the indebted) in an organized manner, a security portfolio of SD 200 million was created. Diwan *Zakāt* contributed 25 percent, and the banks contributed the rest. The portfolio covers all productive sectors (commercial, agricultural, and vocational) across Sudan. It provides insurance to the program against genuine defaults by clients at the second level. At the first level, the default is covered by individual personal guarantor(s) brought in by the client.

Source: Personal interviews and information collected from the organization by the authors.

many microfinance operations is 3–5 percent, the fund may back 20–30 times as many microentrepreneurs. The 3–5 percent of microentrepreneurs facing default will be able to avoid insolvency with the help of *zakāt* funds. A guarantee fund could cover all those who are indebted, both poor and not-so-poor. A pioneer of this model of intervention is the Al-Aman Microfinance Fund in Sudan (box 8.3).

Sustainable Provision of Social Goods through *Waqf*

Waqf is an important institution in the Islamic economy. It is a perpetual endowment. Certain physical assets are held or set aside by the donor and preserved so that benefits flow continuously to a specified group of beneficiaries or a community.[3] By providing a flow of benefits on a sustained basis, *waqf* can thus serve as a mechanism to create and support robust charitable institutions. It has a legal identity separate from its manager and therefore is most suitable for creation of a sustainable entity, governed by the fundamental principles of perpetuity, inalienability, and irrevocability. By creating community assets, it has the potential to address the education, health care, and other social needs in Muslim societies.

Yet the potential of *waqf* remains largely untapped. Thus there is an urgent need to revise the existing inefficient laws to create an enabling legal and regulatory framework. The welcome developments in knowledge pertaining to *waqf* (including reinterpretations of *fiqh* rules based on contemporary conditions) can yield very positive results in developing the *waqf* sector if national laws change to convert the possibilities into realities. Contemporary developments in the Islamic financial sector have also opened up many possibilities in terms of new structures for financing the development of *waqf* assets.

Role of *Waqf* in Establishing Fair and Affordable Prices

The integration of *waqf* with the market has yielded positive results in terms of providing microfinance, education, and health care at affordable prices to the poor and excluded. A case in point is provision of health care by the Waqaf al-Noor, an innovative corporate *waqf* that was structured by the Johor Corporation of Malaysia (box 8.4).

Waqf may also directly contribute to the success of Islamic microfinance experiments to improve the economic lot of the poor. Islamic economists have often sought to make

BOX 8.4 Case 4. Corporate *Waqf*: Johor Corporation's Waqaf Al-Noor, Malaysia

Johor Corporation (JCorp) was established as a State investment corporation in 1968 in the state of Johor, Malaysia. It is one of the country's largest conglomerates, with core business sectors encompassing palm oils, foods and quick service restaurants, specialist health care services, hospitality, property, and logistic services.

As part of its corporate social responsibility (CSR) initiatives, JCorp has created nonprofit entities under its umbrella, called Amal Business Organizations (ABOs). They function as a medium for JCorp to contribute to the development of the society through various aspects of charity, well-being, and recreation, as well as entrepreneurship. In 2011, 27 ABOs were operating in four areas: social and public welfare development, entrepreneurship development, sports and recreation development, and staff welfare.

The innovative element of these initiatives is the establishment of a corporate *waqf* in the form of Waqaf An-Nur Corporation Berhad (WANCorp), a limited liability company set up to guarantee proper management of Johor Corporation and Waqaf An-Nur and the stocks and assets in the endowment. WANCorp has entered into a memorandum of agreement with the Johor Islamic Council, recognizing its role in making a success of JCorp's corporate *waqf*. WANCorp has consequently been endowed with powers of trusteeship and with the duty and obligation to manage JCorp's corporate *waqf*.

JCorp's corporate *waqf* took off in 2006 when JCorp transferred RM 200 million (on a net asset value basis) in public listed shares to WANCorp. WANCorp's main income is derived from the annual dividend payout by the public listed companies (PLCs), part of whose equity is now endowed and transferred to its ownership. These payouts are allocated for reinvestment, as well as to fund Islamic CSR programs that are not restricted to Muslims as beneficiaries. For instance, in 2009, WANCorp received RM 4.9 million as dividends; of this, it allocated 70 percent for reinvestment. It spent another 25 percent of the dividends on various Islamic CSR initiatives, including the nationwide chain of charity Waqaf An-Nur clinics and hospitals to serve the health care needs of the poor of all ethnic groups. Johor Islamic Religious Council is the beneficiary of the remaining 5 percent.

A flagship initiative of WANCorp is to provide health care and dialysis services to the less fortunate segments of the society through a full-fledged hospital, Waqaf An-Nur Hospital, and 16 Waqaf An-Nur Clinics that it owns and manages. The clinics provide health services not only in Johor, but also in nearby states, including Negeri Sembilan, Selangor, Perak, and Sarawak, in cooperation with the respective State Islamic Councils. The number of beneficiaries from these services has steadily increased from 0.56 million in 2009 to 0.77 million in 2011. About 6 percent of the treatments are provided to non-Muslim patients. Patients of Waqaf An-Nur clinics pay only RM 5 for treatment by a qualified doctor, plus the cost of medicine prescribed.

Another program with high impact is the provision of treatment for kidney ailments through dialysis centers that operate alongside these clinics. These centers offer subsidized dialysis treatments. For many patients, the cost is reduced to almost zero with further financial support from other charities (such as the *Bayt al-māl* Funds of state religious councils) that are part of the support network.

Source: Personal interviews and information collected from the organization by the authors.

microfinance more affordable by suggesting an integration of *zakāt* and/or *waqf* with microfinance. A cash *waqf* with returns dedicated to fully or partly absorb the cost of financial and nonfinancial services may be able to ensure that loans are offered at zero or low cost, making them interest-free as well as affordable for the poorest of the poor. Nowhere is this phenomenon better documented than in Bangladesh, which is often referred to as the "university of microfinance." Fa'el Khair *Waqf* offers a real-life example of this exciting solution to poverty and destitution (box 8.5).

BOX 8.5 Case 5. Using *Waqf* to Fund Microfinance: The Fa'el Khair Program, Bangladesh

The Fa'el Khair Program of the Islamic Development Bank was motivated by the urgent need to help the victims of the Sidr cyclone, which devastated the southwestern coast of Bangladesh in November 2007, resulting in loss of life and considerable damage in 30 of the 64 districts of the country. Since cyclones are a recurring phenomenon in the country, long-term rehabilitation solutions were needed, as well as an immediate emergency response. The program has two main components:

- The Fa'el Khair project, initially funded at $110 million, supports the construction of several hundred schools that also serve as cyclone shelters in the coastal belt of Bangladesh.
- The Fa'el Khair microfinance program, initially funded at $20 million, provides urgent relief and support steps to restore the livelihoods of affected farmers, fishermen, and small businesses. It was registered as the Fa'el Khair *Waqf* under the provisions of *Waqf* Ordinance 1962.

The second component initially aimed at providing urgent relief to the victims of the Sidr cyclone in the form of agricultural inputs and support for small businesses. To implement the program, the Islamic Development Bank signed three-year (extendable) agreements with several nongovernmental organizations (NGOs). The microfinance intervention provides interest-free (*qarḍ*) microloans as well as training to the cyclone victims in order to help them recover their losses and regain their livelihoods. When the agreement period of three years is over, NGOs are to return the funds by depositing them into the Fa'el Khair *Waqf* account. The Committee of *Mutawallīs* will then decide whether to renew agreements with the partner NGOs.

The NGOs together recruited and trained some 774 staff and are operating through 80 field offices in the areas most impacted by the cyclone. As of January 2014, *qarḍ* amounting to Tk 8 billion (roughly $105 million) has been disbursed to 192,821 beneficiaries. This implies that the original funding (amounting to $20 million) has been leveraged more than five times. The *qarḍ* repayment rate was as high as 99.75 percent. In addition, 196,710 beneficiaries were trained through 6,338 training courses on agriculture, cattle rearing, and fishing and fish farming.

In 2012, the NGOs were instructed to start implementing their exit plan by returning one-third of the program funds to the Fa'el Khair *Waqf*. It was then up to the Committee of *Mutawallīs* to decide how to use the funds that were returned. They have been placed in Islamic investments that have generated returns in the range of 10 percent a year. These proceeds are being used to cover the administrative costs of the Fa'el Khair Program.

The Fa'el Khair project provides an excellent example of how a benevolent cash donation can be used to engineer a *waqf*. It is also a rare example of how the high administrative costs of a poverty alleviation program (with finance as well as skill enhancement inputs) may be absorbed by returns generated by a *waqf* dedicated to poverty alleviation.

Source: Personal interviews and information collected from the organization by the authors.

Hybrid Models of Islamic Microfinance

Both *zakāt* and *waqf* funds may be used to support microfinance. While the *zakāt* funds can be used immediately and on a one-to-one basis,[4] the establishment of a portfolio with *waqf* funds requires a larger initial amount of resources because only the returns from investing such resources may be used for microfinance.

Zakāt and *waqf* funds should be an integral part of any poverty alleviation initiative. First, they provide for the immediate basic consumption needs of the poorest of the poor, such as food, clothing, and shelter. As discussed, such safety nets can be funded only through charity. Second, they support ways to impart or strengthen appropriate skills so that the poor are able to generate income on a sustained basis without being dependent on charity. *Zakāt* and charity funds can also fund initiatives to impart these technical and entrepreneurial skills.

So that the same individuals may move through several stages, from poverty to self-sufficiency, it is important to link safety nets with microfinance programs. While for-profit microfinance institutions (MFIs) are reluctant to invest in start-up equity, *zakāt* and *waqf* could fill the gap by providing micro-equity to enterprises set up by the poor.

Often, individuals borrow funds from MFIs to meet emergency needs relating to health, education, and social obligations such as weddings and funerals. Further, the gains people may achieve through a growing business could easily be set back by a catastrophe such as a tsunami or even smaller risks at a household or personal level. What is needed is a way to finance productive activities as well as to meet contingencies and emergencies. While a revolving *qarḍ al-ḥasan* fund based on *zakāt* may not be an ideal solution for developing microenterprises, it may be ideal to provide emergency credit. Since individuals burdened with debt constitute eligible recipients of *zakāt*, it may also be used to create guarantee funds that leverage its use for provision of finance to greater numbers of people who suddenly must take on debt. Finally, *zakāt* along with *ṣadaqāt* and *waqf* may be used to establish micro*takāful* projects for the poor and the vulnerable (see chapter 6).

Given these considerations, a hybrid model of Islamic microfinance is presented that can lead to economic empowerment in a comprehensive manner. *Zakāt* plays an important role in the model and is integrated with *ṣadaqāt*, *waqf*, and various nonprofit and for-profit modes of Islamic finance. The model encompasses 11 activities:

1. A *zakāt* fund is created with contributions from the *zakāt* payer (*muzakkī*).
2. A program is established to facilitate *waqf* of physical as well as monetary assets. The physical assets are used to support education and skills training. The monetary assets may be in the form of a cash *waqf* or simply as ordinary *ṣadaqāt*.
3. The program carefully identifies the poorest of the poor and the destitute who are economically inactive and directs a part of the *zakāt* funds as a safety net to meeting their basic needs. A revolving *qarḍ* fund is created to provide emergency credit.
4. Skills training is provided to the economically inactive, using the revenue from community-held physical assets under *waqf*.
5. Beneficiaries graduate with improved skills and managerial acumen. The recurring costs of the training programs are borne by the *zakāt* fund.
6. Beneficiaries are formed into groups with mutual guarantees under the concept of *kafālah*.[5]
7. Financing is provided using a combination of for-profit debt-based modes, such as *bayʿ mu'ajjal*, *ijārah*, *salam*, *istiṣnāʿ*, and *istijrār*, or equity-based modes, such as *muḍārabah*, *mushārakah*, or diminishing *mushārakah* (see the glossary for definitions).
8. Group members pay back their debt or meet the expectations of equity providers and, in turn, are provided with greater amounts of financing.
9. Guarantee against default by the group is provided by the *zakāt* fund, and actual defaulting accounts are paid off with *zakāt* funds; this is the distinct feature of this model.
10. Group members are encouraged to save under appropriate microsavings schemes.
11. Group members are encouraged to form a *takāful* fund to provide microinsurance against unforeseen risks and uncertainties resulting from loss of livelihood or illness (see chapter 5).

A few recent experiments in Islamic microfinance in Sudan use hybrid models of intervention with components that are rooted in benevolence, which may easily be replaced with *zakāt* or *waqf*. A good example is the Abu Halima *Muḍārabah* Greenhouse Project in Sudan, discussed in chapter 3 (box 3.1).

The various case studies clearly demonstrate that the institutions of *zakāt* and *waqf* can be used to provide finances to the deprived and underprivileged, provide for their education and health care, and create livelihood opportunities by enhancing skills and extending financial services. These have been made possible despite the many challenges and constraints, notably the absence of an enabling environment and supportive infrastructure. The sections that follow highlight some good practices at the macro, meso, and micro levels in several countries across the globe. If replicated, these will go a long way toward strengthening the institutions of *zakāt* and *waqf*, enabling them to address the key problems they are meant to tackle, such as poverty, exclusion, and denial of opportunities, in a sustainable manner.

Meeting the Resources Gap for Poverty Alleviation

While poverty and deprivation is a global phenomenon, the plight of Muslim societies is particularly bad. The role of Islamic philanthropy-driven funds, or what are called Islamic social funds, assumes great significance in countries with high levels of exclusion and deprivation. This section seeks to estimate to what extent Islamic social funds may meet the resource requirements to alleviate deprivation for a sample of countries in South and Southeast Asia and Sub-Saharan Africa.[6] It proceeds first by estimating the resource gap and then discusses the potential Islamic social funds that could be tapped to meet the resource gap.

Estimating the Resource Gap

The resource gap has been estimated by using the poverty gap index, which is defined as the mean shortfall below the poverty line, expressed as a percentage of the poverty line. The World Bank has used the recently updated poverty lines of $1.25 a day in 2005 purchasing power parity (PPP) terms for the extreme poor and $2.00 a day for the relatively poor, which represents the mean of poverty lines found in the poorest 10–20 countries ranked by per capita consumption.[7] This reflects the depth of poverty, as well as its incidence. The poverty gap index does not explicitly provide the total income (consumption) shortfall. For this purpose, the estimated poverty gap indexes based on international poverty lines of $1.25 a day and $2.00 a day, respectively, have been converted into percentages of gross domestic product (GDP) for selected countries. Table 8.1 shows the resource gap for sampled countries. The resource gap is highest in Bangladesh, Tanzania, India, and Pakistan and lowest in Malaysia and South Africa.

Estimating the Potential Resources from *Zakāt*

The estimates for the *zakāt* potential of the countries under study are based on three different opinions of jurists regarding *zakāt* and the method of calculating *zakāt* liability, denoted as Z1, Z2, and Z3. Z1 is estimated in accordance with the majority traditional view—according to which *zakāt* is levied

TABLE 8.1 **Gap in Resources Needed to Alleviate Poverty**

Country	Resource gap at $1.25 a day (percentage of GDP)	Resource gap at $2.00 a day (percentage of GDP)
Bangladesh	7.570	33.360
India, total population	2.390	12.590
India, Muslim population	0.344	1.813
Indonesia	0.350	2.740
Malaysia	None	0.020
Pakistan	1.620	13.350
Kenya	0.320	0.960
Nigeria	1.470	3.500
South Africa	0.001	0.010
Sudan	0.490	2.200
Tanzania	3.020	8.170

Sources: Global Islamic Finance Development Center calculations, based on Obaidullah and others 2014; Obaidullah and Shirazi 2015.

on agriculture, livestock, stock-in-trade, gold, silver, and money. Z2 is based on the view of some contemporary Muslim scholars that *zakāt* is payable on net returns of manufacturing concerns, rentals of building, and net savings out of salaries. Z3 is based on views of the Maliki School, in which the *zakāt* base includes buildings and other fixed assets, except those assigned for personal and family use.

Zakāt is collected from the rich Muslims only, and non-Muslim citizens are exempt from the payment of *zakāt*. Thus the GDP of each country under study has been adjusted by taking into account per capita income and the proportion of Muslim population in each country. The average score of Zs 1–3 has been applied as a proxy to estimate potential *zakāt* collection for the countries.

Table 8.2 shows that *zakāt* potential under Z1 varies from about 1.00 percent of GDP to 1.74 percent of GDP in the five predominantly Muslim countries. Under Z2, potential *zakāt* ranges from 2.00 percent of GDP to 3.71 percent of GDP, while under Z3 it ranges from 2.25 to 4.18 percent of GDP. Potential *zakāt* is much lower for the Muslim minorities in India (0.26 percent) and Singapore (0.65 percent of GDP). The potential is low for South Africa, as well, reflecting its small Muslim population.

TABLE 8.2 Estimates of the Potential of *Zakāt*

Percentage of GDP

Country	Z1	Z2	Z3
Bangladesh	1.63	3.48	3.92
India	0.26	0.55	0.63
Indonesia	1.59	3.39	3.82
Malaysia	1.11	2.36	2.66
Pakistan	1.74	3.71	4.18
Kenya	0.13	0.27	0.30
Nigeria	0.86	1.84	2.08
South Africa	0.03	0.06	0.07
Sudan	1.44	3.08	3.47
Tanzania	0.54	1.15	1.30

Sources: Global Islamic Finance Development Center calculations, based on Obaidullah and others 2014; Obaidullah and Shirazi 2015.

Note: Z1 is estimated in accordance with the majority traditional view. Z2 is based on the view of some contemporary Muslim scholars that *zakāt* is payable on net returns of manufacturing concerns, rentals of buildings, and net savings out of salaries. Z3 is based on views of the Maliki School. See text.

Juxtaposing tables 8.1 and 8.2 provides a comprehensive picture of whether and to what extent the resource shortfall required for poverty alleviation may be met by potential *zakāt* collection. The resource shortfall in Bangladesh is much higher than its potential *zakāt* collection. However, in some other countries, resources needed for poverty alleviation can easily be provided by the potential *zakāt* collection. Indian Muslims can generate enough resources (0.630 percent of GDP) to provide for the resource shortfall (0.344 percent of GDP) for lifting their extreme poor out of poverty. Countries like Nigeria, South Africa, and Sudan can easily generate resources for poverty alleviation. In some countries with Muslim minorities, the gap between resource required and potential *zakāt* collection is minimal. In Kenya, for instance, the resource gap for extreme poverty is 0.32 percent of GDP, whereas corresponding potential *zakāt* collection is 0.30 percent of GDP, using the Z3 measure. However, Tanzania would be unable to bridge the resource gap with potential *zakāt* collection.

Based on the evidence from sampled countries, it appears that the potential resources from *zakāt* collection alone can meet the shortfall in resources required for poverty alleviation in most countries in the sample.

Estimation of Potential Resources from *Waqf*

The process of estimating potential resources from *waqf* is more challenging due to the absence of data in most countries. However, based on limited data available for two countries, India and Indonesia,[8] the potential resources that may flow from the *waqf* assets can be estimated.

Estimates of the economic potential of *waqf* assets in India indicate that there are about 490,000 registered *waqf* assets in India, with a total area of about 600,000 acres and with a book value of about Rs 60 billion. Many of the *waqf* properties are located in city centers, and the current market value is many times more than the book value. The authors of the *Islamic Social Finance Report 2014* argue, "as the book values of the properties are about half a century old, the current value can safely be estimated to be several times more and the market value of the properties can be put at Rs 1,200 billion (about $24 billion). If these properties are put to efficient and marketable use they can generate at least a minimum return of 10 percent, which is about Rs 120 billion (about $2.4 billion) per annum. Wherever the *waqf* lands have been put to efficient use, they have generated an average return of about 20 per cent" (Obaidullah and others 2014, 75). At Rs 120 billion, the annual return is about 0.3 percent of India's GDP as of 2005. The resource shortfall of the Muslim poor is 0.344 percent, as indicated in table 8.1. By combining *zakāt* and *waqf*, a surplus could be generated, which would be enough to lift the poor Muslims in India out of grinding poverty.

Zakāt and *waqf* could also wipe out extreme poverty in Indonesia. According to data obtained from the Ministry of Religious Affairs, the market value of registered *waqf* land is about Rp 590 trillion ($60 billion). At a similar minimum rate of return of 10 percent, these assets may generate an annual cash flow of $6 billion, which is 0.849 percent of Indonesia's GDP. This compares favorably against a resource shortfall of 0.350 percent needed to lift Indonesia's poor above the $1.25-a-day poverty level.

Estimation of Potential Resources from a Social Tax (Equivalent to *Zakāt*)

A recent study extended the analysis of *zakāt* and *waqf* to a scenario where a social tax equivalent to *zakāt* potential is levied and collected.[9] This study found the expected impact of social tax collection to be at least 2.93 percent of GDP (equivalent to the median for *zakāt* collection under three different definitions of *zakāt*: Z1, Z2, and Z3). This includes transfers to reduce the poverty gap and headcount ratio and improve the income distribution of the lowest 40 percent of population for a sample of 104 low-income and middle-income countries. It finds that if countries choose to levy 2.93 percent of the GDP as social tax, then as many as 66 countries could entirely cover the resource gap measured at the $1.25-a-day level, and the rest of the countries would be able to bridge the poverty gap partially.

Toward the Optimal Mobilization of *Zakāt and Waqf* Resources

The previous sections clearly demonstrate how *zakāt* can potentially meet the resource gap for poverty alleviation in all the countries under study. However, the potential remains unrealized, as actual *zakāt* mobilized falls far short of its potential in most countries. For instance, in Indonesia, the actual *zakāt* collected according to the latest figures available is just 0.03 percent of GDP against a potential of 1.59 percent, while the estimated resource shortfall is 0.41 percent of GDP. In Pakistan, actual *zakāt* collected is just 0.06 percent of GDP, against a potential of 1.74 percent, while the estimated resource shortfall is 0.71 percent of GDP. In Sudan, the situation is better; the actual *zakāt* collected is 0.33 percent of GDP against a potential of 1.44 percent and an estimated resource shortfall of 0.49 percent. In Malaysia, the actual *zakāt* collected is 0.24 percent of GDP, against the potential of 1.11 percent with an estimated resource shortfall of 0.01 percent of GDP.

Similarly, while potential returns from existing *waqf* could meet the resource gap to eradicate extreme poverty, the actual returns are dismal. Studies show widespread usurpation of *waqf* assets by both State and non-State actors, as well as leasing of *waqf* assets at rates that are grossly below market.[10]

Trends in Mobilizing *Zakāt* and *Waqf* Resources

Mobilization of *zakāt* has generally been increasing in the countries under study, as shown according to the latest data available:

- Brunei Darussalam increased mobilization by 55 percent over 10 years ($13.8 million in 2010).
- Indonesia increased mobilization by over

32 times over 10 years ($231.6 million in 2012).

- Malaysia increased mobilization by 7 times over the past 12 years and by 37 times over 22 years ($628.6 million in 2013).
- Nigeria collected total *zakāt* of $3 million in 2013, but it has fluctuated greatly.
- Pakistan increased mobilization by 40 percent[11] over 3 years ($105 million in 2011).
- Singapore increased mobilization by 20.2 percent over 3 years ($20.4 million in 2012).
- Sudan increased mobilization by 4.8 times over the past 9 years ($220 million in 2013).

In Indonesia and Pakistan, where private institutional *zakāt* collection is permitted, several nongovernment actors perform exceedingly well. In Indonesia, private institutional collectors together mobilize about 38 percent of total national collection (Islamic Social Finance Report 2014). Interestingly, just three institutions account for 17 percent, or one-sixth, of the total national collection. Similarly, in Pakistan, just one NGO—the Edhi Foundation—collects about 16 percent of all *zakāt* mobilized, according to unofficial estimates.

With respect to mobilization of *waqf* resources, data indicate a near-freeze in the creation of new social *waqf*, though religious *waqf* continue to be created. Places of worship (*masjids)* and seminaries (*madrasas*) have increased in numbers, especially where new Muslim communities have emerged. There has been some rejuvenation of social *waqf* in the form of cash *waqf* in Indonesia, Malaysia, and Singapore. Some development of *waqf* assets and their prudent investment to generate returns has also occurred in these countries, as well as in Sudan, which is also known for its successful family *waqf*.

What factors have contributed most to success in mobilization of *zakāt* and *waqf*? What factors constitute major obstacles and challenges? What should be the strategic response of policy makers? Some policy recommendations follow.

Evidence and Policy Recommendations to Better Mobilize *Zakāt* Resources

1. Contrary to commonly held perceptions regarding the lack of dependability in the flow of donations, *zakāt* is dependable and sustainable, and could be a growing source of funds for institutions that acquire the necessary professionalism in fundraising and seek continued improvement in their social credibility through actions to promote integrity, transparency, and good governance. This is the evidence in Southeast Asian countries. The evidence is more mixed in the agrarian economies of Sub-Saharan Africa, where there is greater volatility in *zakāt* collections because of the changing fortunes in the farming sector.
2. There is a clear upward trend in the mobilization of *zakāt* in South Asia and Southeast Asia. *Zakāt* mobilization has grown steadily in Indonesia and Malaysia, under two distinct *zakāt* management systems. While *zakāt* collection is mandatory in Malaysia, it is voluntary in Indonesia. The pattern of growth is more varied in other countries in those regions, such as Bangladesh, India, and Pakistan, as well as in Sub-Saharan Africa. While *zakāt* is mandatory in Sudan and four states in Nigeria, it is voluntary in other states of Nigeria, as well as in the other countries under study. In Sudan, *zakāt* has been steadily increasing at an annual average growth rate of 19 percent. In absolute terms, *zakāt* collected in Sudan is impressive. At around $200 million per year, it ranks lower than Saudi Arabia, Malaysia, and Indonesia. However, in terms of per capita *zakāt* collected, it fares better than Indonesia. Annual *zakāt* collection in all Nigerian states together is much smaller—around $3 million—particularly considering the much larger size of the Muslim community. This is perhaps explainable because these bodies are relatively new, and the per capita income of the Nigerian

people has fallen greatly since the country became independent.

3. Malaysia and Sudan provide supporting evidence for compulsory *zakāt*. The Nigerian states that have both compulsory and voluntary *zakāt* provide modest supporting evidence in favor of compulsory *zakāt*, with relatively better performance in states like Jigawa and Zamfara. However, the policy in these states may not have paid off well in view of lack of enforcement mechanisms, unlike in Sudan. The voluntary nature of *zakāt* may not itself have contributed to the poor performance of other states. A more important factor may be the absence of a vibrant network of organizations at different levels. In Indonesia, Pakistan, and South Africa, the performance of voluntary *zakāt* organizations has been excellent. Irrespective of whether *zakāt* is compulsory or voluntary, a policy of decentralization seems to work. The presence of a network of healthy institutions at multiple levels—in the public, not-for-profit, and private domains—seems to lead to increased public awareness and greater participation in the process of poverty alleviation through *zakāt*.
4. The issue of incentivizing *zakāt* payment is crucial. Where *zakāt* payment is made compulsory and noncompliance leads to penalties and punishment, weak enforcement can lead to low *zakāt* collection, as in the case of some Nigerian states. With reasonably strong enforcement mechanisms, as in Sudan, incentives in the form of benefits for compliance (such as tax incentives for levies of *zakāt* on salaries), as well as costs for noncompliance (such as making *zakāt* payment a precondition to other commercial transactions), work well. At the same time, where *zakāt* payment is voluntary, its mobilization has not been any less impressive.
5. Where *zakāt* collection and distribution is entrusted entirely to the State, *zakāt* may be seen as a component to the aggregate resources available to the State. In this sense, *zakāt* payment may function as a perfect substitute for the direct taxes to the State and may be allowed as deductions to taxes payable. However, there must be absolute clarity on the issue, as well as coordination between *zakāt* and tax authorities. The absence of clarity seems to have adversely affected *zakāt* collection in Sudan in the initial stages of operation of the Diwan, but it was sorted out later with a tax incentive that was made available only on *zakāt* paid on salaries. In the Nigerian states, on the other hand, the incentive was withdrawn because of difficulties in coordination among agencies, creating further confusion. Where private agencies are permitted to collect *zakāt*, there seems to be merit in allowing *zakāt* payment as a deduction to taxable income only, on a par with various kinds of charity flows. Treating *zakāt* payment on a par with taxes to the State when the payment is made to private collecting bodies might seriously erode State revenues.
6. There does not seem to be a strong case for having standardized and globally acceptable definitions of assets liable to *zakāt* and methods of estimating *zakāt* liability. Since Islamic societies are typically characterized by a multitude of *madhabs* and schools of thought, the *zakāt* laws must retain enough flexibility to accommodate alternative views. The diversity in legal opinions should be respected. However, in societies like Sudan, where there is great homogeneity in *shari'ah* legal positions, and where *zakāt* is compulsory, the clarity provided by law in the definitions and methods seems to have imparted greater stability and added to enforceability. Where *zakāt* is voluntary, it is more practical to ensure that *zakāt* estimation is an outcome of a consultative process between the *muzakki* (*zakāt* payer) and the institutions that collect *zakāt*.
7. The success or failure of an institution as *zakāt* collector and distributor depends not so much on whether it is

in government or private hands, but on the credibility and trust it enjoys among the *muzakki* population—which in turn depends on the integrity, transparency, and good governance reflected in its practices and as perceived by the stakeholders. For example, the national *zakāt* body in Indonesia is highly regarded, while the national body in Pakistan seems to suffer from a severe deficit in trust.

8. The coexistence of public and private players as *zakāt* collectors raises certain issues. Competition among a multitude of *zakāt* institutions brings efficiency and gives more choice to the *muzakki*. However, competition also presupposes a level playing field for the players. Where the public agency also assumes the role of the regulator of the *zakāt* sector, it should restrict itself only to regulation, leaving *zakāt* collection to private agencies. Alternatively, the entire process of *zakāt* management could be undertaken by the public agency, through its own decentralized network. Such a scenario does not preclude the involvement of private players as agents of the public body, as is the case with Malaysian states.
9. Using a large network of private institutional collectors to mobilize *zakāt* is far more efficient than having a large number of unconnected private individual collectors. How to remunerate the private collector, however, is a tricky issue under *shari'ah* and calls for putting in place adequate and transparent mechanisms to ensure that a minimal percentage of *zakāt* collected is used in this manner. Use of private entities should not be pushed too far. For example, private agencies should not be allowed to offer *zakāt* investment services, as this might involve a misalignment of objectives of such private agencies with those of other stakeholders.
10. In the context of in-kind *zakāt* involving crops and livestock, some specific policy recommendations may be made. Due to the vast expanse of agricultural areas and given the hugeness of the monitoring task, the *zakāt* collection efforts may be timed to allow for the seasonality of crops. *Zakāt* mobilization should actively involve local committees as a way to build social capital and enhance community solidarity. Local participation should be sought in the collection of *zakāt* on agricultural products of smallholdings, inventory merchandise, and leased property in the locality.

Policy Recommendations to Better Mobilize *Waqf* Resources

1. The legal framework must not put undue restriction on creation of new *waqf*. A case in point is the restriction on the creation of new *waqf* in Zanzibar. Legal requirements that make the process more difficult, such as the approval of the head of State, are both unnecessary and undesirable. A simple process of registration with the regulatory body is both desirable and adequate. The legal framework should actually encourage creation of new *waqf* by minimizing financial and nonfinancial costs of creating and managing *waqf*. Sudan, for instance encourages the creation of *waqf*; by law, the major objectives of the Diwan are to conduct scientific studies and research on *waqf*, carry out training and capacity building and institutional development in the field of *waqf*, and encourage citizens to establish *waqf*. The case of Zamfara state in Nigeria is quite interesting: government agencies and contractors are encouraged to endow a certain percentage of their total revenues as *waqf*, thereby ensuring the continuous enhancement of *waqf*.
2. *Waqf*, in general, have fallen behind common trusts and other forms that are organizing charitable and nonprofit activities in response to evolving social needs. Creation and management of *waqf* is a relatively more complex and demanding process and involves

additional financial and nonfinancial costs. Incentivizing *waqf* in a manner similar to secular trusts and other forms of nonprofit organizations, such as through tax rebates on contributions for the donor/endower, would make the system both efficient and fair.

3. The legal framework should make it possible for all segments of the society to establish *waqf*. Currently, some laws restrict making a *waqf* only to Muslim individuals. Laws should permit both non-Muslims and institutions to establish *waqf* as long as the purpose of *waqf* is religious or charitable.
4. The legal framework should not restrict the definition of the endowed asset to immovable tangible assets, such as real estate, but should also explicitly recognize movable, financial, and intangible assets, such as cash, equities, bonds and financial securities, transportation vehicles, rights on land and buildings, leasing rights, and intellectual property rights.
5. Most observers and scholars of *waqf* believe that the institution of family *waqf* must be revived. Sudan and Mauritius provide some excellent examples of family *waqf*. The law in Mauritius explicitly provides for family *waqf*. Interesting features include the possibility of restricting the benefits to one or two generations; the need for concurrence of a wife before a husband may make a *waqf;* a list of relatives who may benefit from *waqf* and the order of priority among them; the definition of a child and a descendant; how *waqf* benefits should be apportioned between children and descendants and other possible beneficiaries across generations and between males and females; and the conditions under which the benefits will lapse.

Toward Better Management of *Zakāt* and *Waqf* Resources

Zakāt management essentially involves its safe deposit and its timely distribution among the *asnaf*, or the eligible categories of beneficiaries within the annual cycle. Related considerations include prioritizing among the categories of beneficiaries and among regions. Prudent *zakāt* management requires completely and effectively transferring resources to beneficiaries and meeting their pressing needs as soon as possible.

Prudent *waqf* management, on the other hand, requires preservation and development of the *waqf* assets, investment and generation of returns, and ensuring that the returns/benefits flow to the beneficiaries as intended by the *waqif*.

Trends in Use of *Zakāt and Waqf*

Distribution of *zakāt* has kept pace with its mobilization and is growing in almost all sampled countries that have a *zakāt* management system in place. The trends in *zakāt* distribution in the sampled countries reveal that the poor receive the following:

- More than 90 percent of *zakāt* distributed in Bangladesh, Indonesia, India, and Pakistan
- More than 80 percent of *zakāt* distributed in Brunei Darussalam
- About two-thirds of *zakāt* distributed in Sudan
- About 35–40 percent of *zakāt* distributed in Malaysia and Singapore.

As a percentage of total *zakāt* distributed, the following are distributions *to fi-sabilillah* (those in the path of Allah):

- Less than 5 percent in Indonesia and Sudan
- About 40 percent in Singapore and Malaysia.

Within the poor category, education, health, and social safety nets receive priority; around 10 percent is allocated for economic empowerment programs in Indonesia.

As much *zakāt* is collected as is distributed in Malaysia and Singapore, over time. In Brunei Darussalam, the relative proportion varies widely, from 50 percent to 500 percent, indicating symptoms of *zakāt* "holding" or accumulation of surplus.

The proportion of administrative costs to *zakāt* collected varies from zero to 10 percent for most countries. The exception is India, where anecdotal evidence suggests that the percentage could be more than 30 percent. In countries with in-kind *zakāt* such as crops and livestock, such as Nigeria and Sudan, the costs are higher due to costs of storage and transportation. Sudan considers 20 percent as the cap for the proportion of administrative costs.

Some policy recommendations are discussed next, in the light of findings pertaining to the countries under study.

Policy Recommendations to Improve the Use of *Zakāt*

1. Considering various legal opinions relating to the distribution of *zakāt* among eligible beneficiaries, there is a case in favor of a scheme of prioritization among different types of beneficiaries, with highest priority being given to the needs of the extreme poor.
2. Basic consumption needs are, by definition, more urgent than needs that may be deferred to a future date. In this sense, *zakāt* is traditionally viewed as a solution to the consumption needs of the poor. However, there is also merit in using *zakāt* to enhance the wealth-creating capacity of the poor so that they are able to get out of the vicious circle of poverty and find lasting solutions to their needs. Complete neglect of the empowerment dimension is likely to perpetuate the dependency syndrome among the poor.
3. The term *tamleek* implies a process of imparting ownership. In the context of *zakāt*, *tamleek* is seen as a requirement that essentially entails making the *mustahiq* the owner of the donated funds. This clearly rules out the possibility of giving *zakāt* as a loan to be repaid later. The question of ownership, however, opens up two further issues. Should the poor beneficiary have absolute right to decide how he or she will use the funds? Where there is a genuine possibility that the poor may not use the donated cash in an optimal way, can the institution distributing *zakāt* insist on conditionality for the possible use of *zakāt*, such as *zakāt* payment in the form of scholarships to poor students to cover tuition fees? Given the recent evidence in the development literature in favor of unconditional cash transfers (UCTs) over alternative methods of financial assistance to beneficiaries (Haushofery and Shapiro 2013), the case in favor of interpreting *tamleek* as UCTs appears to be a sound one. However, it is perhaps a good idea to treat the issue more as related to efficiency than as a matter of *shari'ah* compliance.
4. Traditionally, scholars have frowned upon the prospect of giving *zakāt* as loans, since *zakāt* is supposed to make the *mustahiq* the owner of donated funds and not a borrower of funds. The objections seem to lose weight in light of the leveraging possibility that loans offer. Arguably, a professionally managed *zakāt*-financed microfinance program could potentially serve a much larger population of the poor as compared to the prospect of grant-making to a small number of beneficiaries. Further, a scenario where the poor are also made the sole owner of the revolving fund is on far stronger grounds. The first scenario (an independent *zakāt*-funded microfinance institution) appears to involve efficiency-related gains while raising concerns about *shari'ah* compliance. The second scenario (the microfinance institution being owned by the poor) is clearly superior, as it simultaneously takes care of the *tamleek* requirement.
5. *Zakāt* payment is an act of worship (*ibada*) for the *zakāt* payer or *muzakki*. It is a matter of grave concern for the *muzakki* to ensure that *zakāt* is not only paid, but also distributed in compliance with the norms of the *shari'ah*. A *zakāt* institution essentially acts as an agent of the *zakāt* payer or *muzakki*. As the

principal, the *zakāt* payer or *muzakki* would like its agent to ensure that the *zakāt* funds flow to eligible beneficiaries according to *shari'ah*. Therefore, fulfillment of the conditions relating to collection and distribution of *zakāt* is the most fundamental requirement for a *zakāt* institution to earn the trust of the *zakāt* payers and enhance its credibility.

6. Separation of *zakāt* funds from other forms of donations is a primary concern for a *zakāt* institution acting as an agent of the *zakāt* payer or *muzakki* for distribution of *zakāt*. Since the conditions relating to eligibility apply only to *zakāt* and not to other forms of donor funds, it becomes extremely important to ensure separation between *zakāt* and other types of funds. To ensure this is the case, *zakāt* institutions must put in place appropriate standard operating procedures and accounting and governance practices.
7. The *shari'ah* identifies *zakāt* officials as one of the eight eligible categories of beneficiaries. Therefore, part of the *zakāt* mobilized by the institution may be used to cover the administrative and operational costs of the *zakāt* institution. While some would like to place a legal cap of one-eighth on the percentage of *zakāt* that may be used for this purpose, others would like to treat the matter as one of good governance. As good practice, a *zakāt* institution that typically collects other forms of donations should cover its administrative and operational costs from such "free" funds as much as possible.
8. Within the overall eligibility framework stipulated by *shari'ah*, a *zakāt* payer or *muzakki* may have a unique preference or priority scheme in favor of specific regions, beneficiaries, or projects. In the interest of good governance, a *zakāt* institution should ensure compliance with such "revealed preferences." While there may be practical hurdles that impede such compliance for some *zakāt* institutions, an increasing use of information technology in *zakāt* management may make a payer-to-beneficiary (*muzakki-to-mustahiq*, or M2M) flow a reality as well as a good practice to replicate.
9. There is a case in favor of using *zakāt* to cover genuine credit defaults by the poor, since such borrowers qualify as eligible beneficiaries in the teachings of *shari'ah*. There is, however, need for caution while designing an institutional mechanism for this purpose. It is not easy for any microfinance institution operating with inadequate and imperfect information to differentiate between genuine and willful defaulters. The simultaneous functioning of a microcredit initiative and a *zakāt*-based initiative to cover credit defaults by poor borrowers under the same organizational umbrella may involve serious conflicts of culture and moral hazard issues. The Sudanese experiment of using *zakāt* only as a third-level institutional guarantee to microfinance providers (after postdated checks and personal guarantors) is a step in the right direction for a *zakāt*-based credit default mechanism to evolve.
10. There is a need to revisit the *fiqh* of Muslim minorities, as it relates to *zakāt*. The interpretations of "eligible" beneficiaries (*asnaf*), the definition of assets liable to *zakāt*, and the legal and institutional infrastructure for *zakāt* are largely influenced by whether Muslims are a majority or minority in the population.
11. *Zakāt* management in Sub-Saharan Africa in general seems to have suffered a great deal due to absence of mid-level organizations, such as networks, training and education providers, consultancy and standard-setting bodies, and advocacy organizations. As a result, public awareness about *zakāt* obligations is extremely low in many parts of this region. Data are very scarce. Capacity building is extremely important, but neglected. Arguably, a large percent of *zakāt* should go to this. A major change in the mind-sets of all stakeholders is needed. There is a lot to

be done in the matter of improving the administration, governance, and disclosures. Transparency and accountability are preconditions for credibility and successful fund-raising.

12. In the context of in-kind *zakāt* such as crops and livestock, some specific policy recommendations may be made. *Zakāt* should be distributed in the neighborhood in order to enhance community solidarity. A large proportion of cattle collected as *zakāt* should be distributed at the collection area itself to save on costs of transportation and storage. The workers engaged in the collection of *zakāt* for cattle may be given a special in-kind incentive to devise livelihood projects for rural poor owners of livestock. *Zakāt* bodies should set up their own storage facilities and warehouses to save the crops and livestock.
13. Because management of in-kind *zakāt* entails huge collection costs, a more flexible approach is called for in relation to the cap on operational costs, which is traditionally one-eighth of *zakāt* funds collected. Further, once *zakāt* are collected, the transportation and storage of in-kind *zakāt* involves substantial costs. This justifies the strategy of on-the-spot distribution.

Policy Recommendations to Improve the Management of *Waqf*

1. Preservation of *waqf* is the most important concern in *waqf* management. The legal framework must clearly articulate the permanent nature of *waqf* arising from the principle of "Once a *waqf*, always a *waqf*." In case old laws fail to ensure protection, they must be replaced with new provisions that enable recovery of lost *waqf* assets. A good example is the Sudanese law that empowers the Diwan to recover all the endowed money that is possessed by other individuals, institutions, companies, or governmental authorities or to receive just and equitable compensation from them.[12]
2. While preservation is important, the law must clearly recognize the importance of sustaining and enhancing the benefits that result from the *waqf*—this being the ultimate purpose of the act of *waqf*. This is possible only when the importance of development of *waqf* is clearly recognized. An undue emphasis on preservation (such as constraints on leasing) would lead to neglect of developmental possibilities with private participation. Similarly, an undue emphasis on development, to the extent that it results in loss of full or partial ownership of assets to private developers, would dilute and vitiate the concept of *waqf*. The regulatory framework must seek to strike a balance between concerns about preservation and development. A good example is the Sudanese law that seeks to strike a balance between preservation and development aspects of investment by requiring the Diwan to undertake the maintenance and improvement of endowed funds and the evaluation, construction, and reconstruction of endowed assets. Further, the issue of sale and replacement (*istabdal*) of endowed assets is explicitly dealt with by the law. The Diwan is empowered to sell an endowed asset to replace it with better ones "only to the extent deemed absolutely necessary."
3. *Waqf* is an institution originally and always meant to be in the voluntary sector, with management of *waqf* entrusted to private parties. However, the State has often sought to play a role in the ownership and management of *waqf* assets, at times governed by motives to expropriate, and at other times, by the need to curb the corrupt practices of private trustee-managers. There is no clear answer to the question of whether ownership and management of *waqf* assets should be in private hands or with the State. There seems to be some positive evidence that the State can play the role of an efficient manager of *waqf* assets. Contrary to general belief, State control may not necessarily hamper creativity

and innovation in *waqf* development. Positive examples include corporate *waqf* as well as cash *waqf* in Malaysia, and large-scale development of existing *waqf* assets in the public-private mode in Malaysia, Singapore, and Sudan.

4. Where *waqf* management is in private hands, the State agency as regulator should clearly stipulate elaborate and clear eligibility criteria for a *mutawallī* or *nazir*, or trustee-manager, not only covering aspects of integrity and trustworthiness but also professional competence. If the individual or institution so nominated meets the criteria, the regulator must respect the expressed intention of the *waqif* or endower. Laws must clearly articulate the responsibility of *waqf* management to emphasize not only preservation and protection of *waqf* assets, but also their development. The responsibility should also include transparent and honest reporting of financial assets and transactions. Laws must clearly stipulate the method of determining remuneration of managers, sufficiently incentivizing sound and professional management of *waqf* assets. The laws in Indonesia and Mauritius provide good examples related to these matters. The law stipulates that the remuneration to which a *mutawallī* is entitled shall not exceed one-tenth of the income of the *waqf*.
5. There is every reason for the State to take punitive action against *mutawallīs* who are negligent or lack integrity and transparency. The measures must act as effective deterrents against further acts of carelessness, neglect, and misappropriation. At the same time, the State should not be allowed to wield absolute power to engage in irrational or whimsical action against the *mutawallī*. Instances of unfair and unlawful action by the State are numerous, as are cases of corrupt *mutawallīs*. There is need for effective checks and balances in the law against wrongful acts by both the State and private *mutawallīs*. Power has a tendency to corrupt, and the possibility of such action can significantly increase the nonfinancial cost of creating new *waqf*. Endowers are likely to seek alternative forms of organizing their charitable activities if there is a possibility of undue State interference in the management of the endowed assets or outright usurpation of the endowed assets by the State.
6. The law must explicitly prohibit the *waqf* asset from being used as a mortgage, confiscated, given away, sold, inherited, exchanged, or being alienated into any form of right. The *waqf* asset, however, may be exchanged as an exception to the above general rule, when this is deemed to be in the public interest. Such exchange requires prior permission from the regulator, with additional conditions that the exchange is necessary or beneficial to the *waqf*; consistent with the objects of the *waqf*; made against another asset of equal or higher value; and made with due respect to the inalienability of religious *waqf*. Laws are quite explicit in preventing the *waqif, or mutawallī,* from selling, exchanging, or using the *waqf* assets as collateral for mortgages. They can, however, permit leasing for varying periods. Caps on leases range from 1 year in Zanzibar to 3 years in Mauritius to 99 years in Singapore. In India, caps were 3 years, subsequently increased to 30 years. However, the rules could be less explicit in preventing similar actions by State agencies. Laws often permit sale and replacement (*istibdal*) by State agencies to the extent considered necessary and even in some cases sale of the property where the intentions of the endower cannot be reasonably carried out.
7. *Waqf* development must be a mandatory obligation of the *waqf* management. Innovative financing methods may be employed that bring in new *waqf* capital to develop existing *waqf*. Innovative methods may also be employed that facilitate private-public partnerships that involve the transfer of rights to

lease, as distinct from ownership rights to private financing entities for a finite, yet sufficiently long period to provide a fair return on investment capital. Legal constraints motivated by preservation concerns, such as on long-term leasing of *waqf* assets, should be removed. The Singaporean and Sudanese cases of partnership between the State *waqf* body and private Islamic financial institutions are worth replicating in other countries.

8. Financial penalties, especially when these are expressed in absolute amounts, tend to lose their effectiveness as deterrents over time. These should either be subjected to continuous revision or be linked to the extent of misappropriation.
9. It is compulsory to invest *waqf* assets, whether they are real estate or movable assets like cash. Investment can generate returns, which may then be applied to the purpose for which the *waqf* has been created. The assets purchased using the *waqf* investment returns do not form part of the *waqf*, and therefore may be resold, unlike the original assets that have been given as *waqf*. Further, the conditions given by the endower or *waqif* with regard to the investment of the *waqf* or conditions that the returns from investment are to be spent on specific areas are also binding. It would be rational to try to minimize risks through diversification or avoidance of high-risk investment activities. Risk minimization, however, may not be sought if the purpose of the *waqf* itself is to engage in specific risky ventures.

Policy Recommendations to Integrate *Zakāt* and *Waqf* with Microfinance

1. There are sound economic reasons why conventional microfinance and especially microcredit may not be appropriate for the chronically poor and the destitute. Loans to the destitute may make the poor poorer if they lack opportunities to earn the cash flow necessary to repay the loans. A destitute person may or may not be reluctant to incur debt and start a microenterprise because of risk and uncertainty about cash flows. Profit-maximizing and risk-minimizing behavior on the part of the microfinance institution would lead to exclusion of such clients. Usually, such clients do not possess the entrepreneurial and technical skills needed to create wealth. Such an economically inactive individual would find it difficult to obtain financing from for-profit MFIs. Indeed, more than financial services, these individuals must be provided their basic needs, such as food, shelter, or guaranteed employment. Such safety nets may be funded through charity. Such individuals also need training to develop skills before they can make good use of microfinance. Thus, safety nets may be linked with microfinance programs, so that the same individuals may move through several stages: from extreme poverty to a stage where they are able to meet their consumption needs, then to a stage where they acquire the necessary technical and entrepreneurial skills to set up microenterprises, and then to a stage where they are able to obtain required funds from MFIs and get the microenterprises up and running. Fighting poverty in this way requires an integrated finance-plus approach, or the provision of financial services along with business development services that are linked to social safety nets. This is possible only by bringing philanthropy and cooperation into the model of microfinance. With the institutionalization of philanthropy and its integration with for-profit microfinance, Islamic MFIs would perhaps be better placed to address the needs of the extreme poor.
2. There are also sound economic reasons why high-cost microfinance may push beneficiaries into a spiral of debt. Microfinance entails high administrative charges, monitoring costs, and of course, high portfolio risk. Thus it is invariably costlier than the traditional

sources of finance. At the same time, both the microfinance institution and its clients may find this an attractive option if they believe that the expected return on the microenterprise is higher than the cost of debt. Such expectations may indeed materialize for the successful projects during "good times." However, the same may not be true for all projects at all times. Debt-related liability can compound and accentuate the financial problems of a project experiencing bad times and hasten its failure. The pace, frequency, and intensity of such failure is directly related to the levels of cost of debt. In contrast to debt, profit- and risk-sharing mechanisms provide a clear alignment between the profitability of the project and cost of capital. The latter rises and falls in line with the realized profits of the venture. Islamic MFIs, as compared to conventional MFIs, are more inclined to use profit- and risk-sharing modes. Even when they use financing methods that create debt such as *murābaḥah*, the amount of debt once created cannot be increased through restructuring if the client fails to repay the debt on time. Further, given the Islamic emphasis on avoidance of debt, an Islamic MFI should refrain from seeking to entrap a client in ever-rising levels of debt.

3. Charity and philanthropy occupy a central position in the Islamic scheme of poverty alleviation. The *shari'ah* clearly identifies eight categories of beneficiaries who may benefit from *zakāt*. Out of these, the potential beneficiaries relevant from the standpoint of poverty alleviation programs are the poor (*fuqara*), the destitute (*masakeen*), the indebted (*ghārimīn*), and the *zakāt* administrators (*amileen*). Scholars generally agree that *zakāt* may be disbursed in the form of a grant or may be used to form a revolving credit pool from which microloans may be provided. *Zakāt* could thus form the basis of designing a range of programs for the poor, including safety net programs to meet basic consumption needs, and improve health and education; economic empowerment programs involving skill enhancement and business development services; programs to provide emergency grants or credit; programs to provide micro*takāful*; and programs to provide guarantees against credit default. The administrative costs related to *zakāt* management may partially be recovered from the *zakāt* collected, thus paving the way for a self-sustained *zakāt* management institutional infrastructure.

   There is total flexibility with respect to beneficiaries of voluntary *ṣadaqāt*. In the case of *ṣadaqāt jāriyah* or *waqf*, perpetuity of endowed assets is an essential condition that ensures that benefits from the assets flow to the beneficiaries on a sustainable basis. *Waqf* similar to *zakāt* may form the basis of various poverty alleviation initiatives, as discussed. While the major requirement in the case of *zakāt* is that benefits flow to the poor, in the case of *waqf*, benefits must flow to beneficiaries as intended by the donor. However, if the intention of the donor is not explicit, the proceeds may be used for general-purpose community welfare projects, including poverty alleviation initiatives. *Waqf* therefore provides a definitive mechanism with added elements of sustainability and flexibility. The issue of high-cost microfinance can be addressed by creating *waqf*s whose benefits can be dedicated to absorbing specific cost elements so as to make microfinance affordable to the extreme poor.

   In an Islamic system, far greater priority is given to the needs of the chronically poor than those of the poor or the moderately poor or the not-so-poor. Therefore, an Islamic microfinance institution, unlike its conventional counterpart, is expected to aggressively integrate the various forms of Islamic philanthropy with for-profit microfinance to address the multiple issues related to poverty alleviation programs.

4. *Murābaḥah* remains overwhelmingly popular among Islamic MFIs for two main reasons. First, *murābaḥah* is simple. The straightforward calculation of the installments for repayment is easier for the beneficiary to comprehend. In contrast, the payments under a partnership-based mode are uncertain, and therefore are less favored. Second, *murābaḥah* is familiar. For conventional MFIs venturing into Islamic microfinance and using *murābaḥah*, the transition is less demanding. Among all Islamic products, *murābaḥah* comes closest to interest-bearing microloans.

   For Islamic modes of finance involving multiple contracts such as *murābaḥah*, *shari'ah* compliance often requires careful sequencing of contracts to ensure that profits are associated with risk bearing. However, in the context of microfinance involving a large number of repetitive contracts for small amounts, adherence to desired sequencing becomes practically impossible. Creative *fiqhi* solutions such as *istijrār* may have significant advantages over *murābaḥah*, as *istijrār* is tailor-made for repetitive transactions.

   Partnership-based modes place demands on beneficiaries by the need for proper bookkeeping and the reporting of the financial results of the business. Financial illiteracy acts as a constraint. Further, the beneficiaries may be justifiably reluctant to share information relating to all aspects of their business with the MFI. Output-sharing modes or revenue-sharing modes[13] may work better in such situations due to the "revealed" nature of the benefits to be shared between the parties and the difficulties and uncertainties associated with cost calculation.
5. For-profit *shari'ah*-compliant methods of financing offer no built-in protection against exploitation and abuse through overpricing. Enhancing the financial literacy of poor clients is perhaps the only effective bulwark against such exploitation. The following examples clearly highlight the possibility of exploitation, and therefore the need for financial literacy:

   a. Returns on micro-*murābaḥah* and micro-*ijārah* financing are deemed *shari'ah* compliant, while interest rates are not. However, both can be, and often are, high to the point of exploitation.
   b. In case of participatory modes of finance such as *muḍārabah, mushārakah,* and *mudharaa,* the sharing ratio could be unfairly biased against the poor beneficiary because of their low bargaining power. Similarly, in case of fee-based financing through *wakālah* and *ḥawālah*, the agent-microfinance institution may charge an exorbitant fee for the same reasons.
   c. The permissibility of *salam* (sale of nonexistent produce) is linked to the economic benefits it confers on poor farmers who need financing before they can cultivate their crops or produce their agricultural goods. However, *salam* can involve exploitation when the advance price paid to the poor farmer is artificially pegged at low levels due to his or her weak bargaining power.

   An Islamic economy promotes free pricing and allows intervention by the regulator only when natural forces of demand and supply are manipulated to result in an artificial price. By implication, price ceilings or administered prices are frowned upon in a market where there is free and fair play of competitive forces in the determination of prices. However, in the case of financing methods where the regulator is in a position to determine a fair estimate of the costs for the MFI, it may seek to regulate the profit margin so that prices charged by MFIs ensure full cost recovery and a fair amount of returns in the interest of sustainability.

   At times, identifying an appropriate organizational structure may offer a bulwark against possible exploitation.

For example, in the case of *salam*, a farmer's cooperative may replace the vendor and thus prevent exploitation of individual farmers by the latter.

6. There is no consensus on how to estimate the actual cost of operations chargeable to the beneficiary under not-for-profit modes, such as *qard* and *kafālah*. There is a need to develop accounting standards to estimate the actual cost of operations and clear guidelines on what should ideally be passed on to the beneficiary. Vigilance by *shari'ah* scholars to prevent disguised *ribā* may also ensure that actual administrative costs recoverable from the beneficiary in *qard* or *kafālah* are not overstated.
7. A conventional MFI seeking to transform into an Islamic MFI is confronted with a range of issues at various levels. An enabling environment and a regulatory and policy framework are needed that permit the MFI to engage in trade, leasing, and investment in real projects. This is usually not permitted for a conventional MFI, which is viewed as a financial intermediary. The law must recognize the special status of Islamic MFIs, which are financial intermediaries as well as players in the real economy at the same time. Fiscal constraints in the form of taxes on real transactions must be removed.
8. Islam gives utmost importance to the family as the core social institution that plays a major role in shaping the future of humankind. It also sees a balanced role for men and women in ensuring the economic and social well-being of the family. Islam promotes the concept of "family empowerment" by exhorting men and women to play their respective roles in seeking economic and social well-being of all members of the family. Indeed, the "women only" approach to conventional microenterprise development and poverty alleviation is less favored than family empowerment. Nevertheless, there are successful examples of women's empowerment through affordable Islamic microfinance (see box 8.6). Further, there is the possibility that in underdeveloped countries, women may be exploited instead of being empowered, wherein they are made to take the loan-related liability while the

BOX 8.6 The Role of Islamic Finance in Empowering Women: The Islami Bank Bangladesh Limited Microfinance Program

Women in developing countries face barriers in access to trade, industry, educational services, health care, and politics, leading to a lower well-being of their families and less progress for their countries. Furthermore, because gender inequality remains an issue, women encounter many problems in the economy, such as narrower occupational choices and lower earnings compared to men.

In Bangladesh, microcredit programs aiming to reduce poverty have been developed and have generated employment for women who live in marginal areas, where a majority of them can engage in activities such as management of crops, livestock, fisheries, and energy. However, because these institutions provide interest-based credit, many of the poor are excluded from the benefits of these loans due to religious reasons.

With the aim of alleviating rural poverty by providing *shari'ah*-based microfinance, Islami Bank Bangladesh Limited (IBBL) launched a Rural Development Scheme (RDS) in 1995. It focuses on the agricultural and rural sector, and seeks to generate

box continues next page

BOX 8.6 The Role of Islamic Finance in Empowering Women: The Islami Bank Bangladesh Limited Microfinance Program *(continued)*

employment and raise the income of the poor. The scheme has 650,000 participants, of whom 90 percent are women. Women who participate in the RDS program can supplement their household's income, help increase household expenditures, diversify income sources, and provide insurance in the face of risk in the form of their extra earnings and saving.

As a result of the RDS, women's income and assets have increased, which has played an important role in enhancing women's economic independence and self-confidence. Furthermore, the program has helped break the cycle of poverty women live in and has allowed them to have more control over their lives and economic decisions. Most importantly, the health and hygiene of women's families has improved through investments in pure drinking water and sanitation funded by the microfinance loans. Recipients' children have also increased their years of schooling.

IBBL's RDS illustrates the role that Islamic finance can play in empowering women and providing opportunity to share growth and prosperity. With the aspiration of promoting distributive justice to maximize social welfare and reduce poverty, Islamic financial institutions can play an active role in including women in economic activities, thus strengthening both their families and their countries.

Source: Rahman 2015.

male member in the family manages to pocket the cash. Therefore, there is merit in the argument that Islamic MFIs should aim to empower families and not women alone.

9. The institutionalization of charity as well as voluntarism is a creative strategy that has the effect of drastically cutting down operational costs. Under this arrangement, microfinance can be provided at low or zero costs, making it affordable to the poorest of the poor.
10. Combining Islamic charity, especially *zakāt* collection and application, with for-profit financing involves serious transparency and governance issues concerning the commingling of funds. A major condition in raising *zakāt* funds requires such funds to be directly channeled into the hands of the eligible beneficiaries or the poor; they cannot simply be credited to the organization capital. In the absence of relevant and adequate accounting standards and regulatory norms, *shari'ah* scholars have generally discouraged the use of *zakāt* funds in economic empowerment initiatives, preferring the direct channels of distribution for consumption purposes instead. Therefore, better accounting standards and regulatory norms are needed. Further, the law relating to charities must clearly address governance issues related to the commingling of funds.

Notes

1. Islamic Law provides elaborate rules relating to estimation of the *zakāt* base (the amount of wealth on which *zakāt* is levied) and the rates of levy that vary with forms of wealth. With most forms of financial assets, the rate is 2.5 percent.
2. The eight eligible categories of beneficiaries of *zakāt*, according to *shari'ah*, include *fuqara* (the poorest of the poor); *masakeen* (the needy and the destitute); *ameleen-a-alaiha* (*zakāt* personnel); *muallafat-ul-quloob* (people whose hearts are inclined toward Islam); *fir-riqaab* (those in bondage); *ghārimīn* (the indebted); *ibn al-sabīl* (travellers); and *fi-sabilillah* (those in the path of Allah).

3. The nature of the expected benefit or purpose of the *waqf* is clearly stated in the *waqf* deed or articles of association created for that purpose by the donor. The donor also specifies the trustee-manager(s), who ensure that the intended benefits materialize and flow to the community. The trustee-manager is variously described as *mutawallī* or *nazir*. The *waqf* deed provides for the method of compensation of the trustee-manager, usually a part of the earnings or benefits from the assets under *waqf*.
4. That is, a dollar (or its equivalent, in local currency) in the fund can support a dollar (or its equivalent) in microfinance lending.
5. *Kafālah* and other *fiqhi* terms used for various modes of Islamic finance are explained in the glossary.
6. The data are drawn from Obaidullah and others (2014) and Obaidullah and Shirazi (2015).
7. For more precise estimates, national poverty lines and microdata of each country are required, which are not available. Therefore, international poverty lines and the corresponding poverty gap indexes are used for estimation.
8. See chapter 2 of Obaidullah and others (2014).
9. This section is based on Shirazi and Zarka (2015).
10. See, for example, chapter 11 of Government of India (2006).
11. Based on figures available for *zakāt* collected by the government of Pakistan; excludes *zakāt* collected by private institutions and individuals.
12. The law excludes endowments from application of any superseding law, and the law also applies the provisions of the Evacuation of Public Buildings Act concerning expropriation to endowments.
13. Unlike profit and loss–sharing modes known in mainstream Islamic finance, output or revenue sharing is simpler. A landowner and a landless farmer can come together and jointly undertake farming; the postharvest output is shared between them as per an agreed ratio.

References

Chapra, M. U. 2008. *The Islamic Vision of Development*. Jeddah, Saudi Arabia: Islamic Research and Training Institute, Islamic Development Bank.

Government of India. 2006. *Social, Economic and Educational Status of the Muslim Community of India: A Report* (Sachar Committee Report). New Delhi: Government of India.

Haushofery, J., and J. Shapiro. 2013. "Household Response to Income Changes: Evidence from an Unconditional Cash Transfer Program in Kenya." https://www.princeton.edu/~joha/publications/Haushofer_Shapiro_UCT_2013.pdf, accessed on January 19, 2016.

Moheildin, M., Z. Iqbal, A. Rostom, and X. Fu. 2012. "The Role of Islamic Finance in Enhancing Financial Inclusion in OIC Member Countries." *Islamic Economic Studies* 20 (2): 55–120.

Nimrah, Karim, Michael Tarazi, and Xavier Reille. 2008. *Islamic Microfinance: An Emerging Market Niche*. Washington, DC: Consultative Group to Assist the Poor (CGAP).

Obaidullah, M. 2012. *Zakāt Management for Poverty Alleviation*. Jeddah, Saudi Arabia: Islamic Research and Training Institute, Islamic Development Bank.

Obaidullah, M., and T. Khan. 2007. *Islamic Microfinance Development: Challenges and Initiatives*. Jeddah, Saudi Arabia: Islamic Research and Training Institute, Islamic Development Bank.

Obaidullah, M., and N. S. Shirazi. 2015. *Islamic Social Finance Report 2015*. Jeddah, Saudi Arabia: Islamic Research and Training Institute, Islamic Development Bank.

Obaidullah, Mohammed, Nasim Shah Shirazi, Dadang Muljawan, and Hylmun Izhar. 2014. *Islamic Social Finance Report 2014*. Jeddah, Saudi Arabia: Islamic Research and Training Institute, Islamic Development Bank.

Rahman, Md. Mizanur. 2015. "Women's Participation in Islamic Microfinance in Bangladesh and Their Role in Sharing Prosperity: An Empirical Study." Paper presented at the inaugural World Bank-IDB-Guidance Financial Symposium on Islamic Finance, Istanbul, September 8–9.

Shirazi, Nasim Shah, and Muhammad Anas Zarka. 2015. "Social Tax and Transfers for Reducing Income Inequality and Poverty: A Case for Low- and Middle-Income Countries." Paper presented at the Financial Management Association Annual Meeting, Atlanta, Georgia, October 14–17.

9

Public Policy Measures to Enhance Shared Prosperity

If the world is to succeed in meeting its targets for the transformative and sustainable new development agenda, all possible resources must be mobilized. Building on the basic principles of Islamic finance that support socially inclusive activities that promote development, the Islamic financial sector has great potential to help achieve the Sustainable Development Goals (SDGs). Financing for development focuses on four pillars: domestic resource mobilization, better and smarter aid, domestic private finance, and external private finance. Islamic finance has the potential to play a major role in supporting all four of these pillars (Ahmed and others 2015).

Given the magnitude of the task of promoting shared prosperity and achieving the SDGs, the important role that Islamic finance can play in supporting implementation of the goals and ensuring more robust and inclusive growth cannot be missed. Islamic finance could support efforts to achieve the SDGs and thus shared prosperity through five tracks: financial stability; financial inclusion; reducing vulnerability; social and environmental activities; and infrastructure finance, according to Ahmed and others (2015). Table 9.1 summarizes the interventions and potential contributions of Islamic financial institutions, capital markets, and social finance.

Mobilization of Islamic financial institutions, capital markets, and the social sector in promoting strong growth, enhanced financial inclusion, and intermediation; reducing risks and the vulnerability of the poor; and more broadly contributing to financial stability and development will be pivotal in achieving SDGs in countries with a serious commitment to Islamic finance. However, an effective role for Islamic finance would require the supply of an innovative mix of products, adequate governance of Islamic finance intermediaries,

TABLE 9.1 Potential of Various Channels of Islamic Finance to Meet the SDGs and Enhance Shared Prosperity

	Financial institutions	Capital markets	Social sector
Financial stability	• Organizational diversity (venture capital, private equity firms, *muḍārabah* companies) • Equity-based financing • New equity-based financial firms	• Expansion of equity-based capital markets • Listing opportunities for medium and smaller firms • Public and private risk-sharing *sukūk*	
Financial inclusion	• Special units to provide microfinance in Islamic banks • Organizational diversity (cooperatives, nonprofits) • Use of ICT to expand provision of services	• Social *sukūk* to raise funds • Retail *sukūk*	• Integration with microfinance • *Waqf/zakāt*-based MFIs • Subsidize MFIs
Reducing vulnerability	• Savings opportunities for the poor • Expansion of micro-*takāful*		• Using *zakāt* and *waqf* as safety nets • Use waqf/*zakāt* to pay contributions for *takāful*
Social and environmental factors	• Incorporation of macro-*maqāṣid* perspective in operations • Financing development of social sector	• Positive screening (along with negative screening) • Social *sukūk* • *Sukūk* to develop *waqf*	• Expand *zakāt* and *waqf* base • Increase the efficiency and effectiveness of *zakāt* and *waqf*
Infrastructure development	• Syndicated finance	• Private/public sector *sukūk* for infrastructures • Retail *sukūk*	

Source: Ahmed and others 2015.
Note: ICT = information and communications technology; MFIs = microfinance institutions. For definitions of Arabic terms, see glossary.

and a supportive legal and regulatory framework. In addition, based on the experience with the Millennium Development Goals (MDGs) that preceded the SDGs, and given the requirements of Islamic finance instruments for better ex ante and ex post understanding and scrutiny of transactions, the need for high-quality data cannot be overemphasized.

The Islamic financial sector cannot reach its full potential in terms of the expected socioeconomic benefits without supportive public policy, conducive financial regulations, and strong institutions. While this assertion is true for any financial system, the significance of the proper public policy initiatives and legal and business environment, and the need for strong political will to overcome the obstacles, are much higher for Islamic finance. The policies needed to spur economic activity are also important to the growth of the Islamic financial sector. Similarly, the obstacles that constrain the business environment and create legal uncertainties not only hamper economic growth but also are detrimental to Islamic finance.

It is imperative to note that the existing legal and regulatory environment is not attuned to the requirements of Islamic finance. There is a need for reforms not only in financial sector regulations to comply with the Islamic financial principles but also in the legal system to provide necessary protection for new types of institutions, help in contract enforcement, and provide favorable tax treatment. Implementing these changes is not within the power of individual Islamic financial institutions or in the hands of the users of finance, who are the source of the demand for Islamic finance. Here the role of regulatory bodies, development agencies, taxation authorities, legislatures, and governments becomes crucial to move Islamic finance forward. Coordination among various stakeholders and strong political will are needed to bring about the change.

The recommendations contained in the previous chapters underscore the point that interlinked and coordinated policy responses across various dimensions will be required. Some key recommendations for the development of an Islamic financial sector aligned with shared prosperity include strengthening the enabling regulatory environment, enhancing the scale of and access to Islamic finance, improving liquidity management and ensuring stability of the financial sector, bolstering human capital, increasing Islamic finance literacy, promoting risk sharing, promoting project-specific *sukūk*,[1] broadening the investor base by introducing retail *sukūk*, developing capital markets, and enhancing the small and medium enterprise (SME) sector. These and other recommendations require coordination among various stakeholders and organizations nationally as well as internationally.

At present, the Islamic financial infrastructure at the international level consists of various support institutions that are responsible for setting standards concerning regulatory, *shari'ah* (Islamic Law), and accounting aspects, as well as institutions that are facilitating market development, credit rating, and arbitration of commercial and financing disputes. These support institutions offer services to all Islamic financial institutions and to the country-level regulators.

Each of these Islamic financial infrastructure institutions has a different and well-defined scope for its work. The Accounting and Auditing Organization for Islamic Financial Institutions (AAOIFI) sets accounting, auditing, and the related *shari'ah* standards for Islamic financial services institutions (IFSIs). The Islamic Financial Services Board (IFSB) is tasked with designing regulatory and supervisory standards for Islamic banks; it has also started issuing standards or guidance notes for other nonbanking institutions, as well. The International Islamic Financial Markets (IIFM) promotes development of Islamic capital markets. The IIFM has focused on developing standardized documents for various Islamic capital market products, including *sukūk*. The International Islamic Rating Agency (IIRA) provides credit rating services, taking into consideration the *shari'ah* compliance of the financial institutions and their products and services. The International Islamic Center for Reconciliation and Arbitration (IICRA) handles resolution of financial and commercial disputes among the Islamic financial institutions, their customers, or other third parties through arbitration and reconciliation. It thus addresses the uncertainty and ambiguity faced by Islamic financial institutions regarding *shari'ah* compliance of the decisions issued by conventional law courts.

These infrastructure organizations not only help avoid multiplicity of efforts and costs, but also significantly contribute to better regulation, convergence/harmonization of rules, and improved *shari'ah* compliance—the factors that enhance shared prosperity through financial sector stability and its compliance with *shari'ah*.

At the country level, central banks, security market commissions, and the respective regulatory bodies contribute to the regulation and development of the Islamic financial sector. The contributions of taxation authorities, legal and judicial institutions, and other support organizations are also important.

The discussion that follows surveys recent initiatives to develop the Islamic financial sector and related regulatory policies and evaluates them in terms of their alignment toward meeting the goal of promoting shared prosperity. This evaluation is done in relation to the Ten-Year Framework and Strategies document (10YF) for the development of the Islamic financial sector. Many other regulatory measures and financial sector policies that affect shared prosperity only indirectly are not discussed.

The Status of the Ten-Year Framework and Mid-Term Review

The Ten-Year Framework document was jointly produced by the Islamic Research and Training Institute (IRTI), the Islamic Development Bank (IDB), and the IFSB in 2007 in consultation with a large number of IFSIs and central banks. The document was created to have a strategic framework to systematically study, discuss, and propose policy measures to promote the orderly development of the Islamic financial services industry. It aimed to provide a general blueprint for new and existing Islamic finance jurisdictions in designing and developing their national plans and major initiatives as part of their financial sector development policies.

The 13 framework recommendations proposed have stood the test of time. Nonetheless, in order to reflect the current status of the Islamic finance industry more accurately, three recommendations have been added. The updated set of recommendations is based on three pillars:

1. Enablement: Fostering conditions for the industry to thrive
2. Performance: Enhancing the effectiveness of institutions active in the industry
3. Reach: Expanding the set of potential beneficiaries of the industry.

The Mid-Term Review (MTR) was launched in 2014 in conjunction with the 11th IFSB Summit, hosted by the Bank of Mauritius. It discussed proposed measures to address the gaps or challenges in meeting the objectives of the Ten-Year Framework, as well as the roles of the public and private sectors and other stakeholders of the IFSIs in carrying out the 16 recommendations, taking into account the state of development of the IFSIs in the respective jurisdictions (IRTI, IDB, and IFSB 2014).

How Did the Ten-Year Framework Document Come About?

The idea of preparing such a strategic framework document was first considered during the Seminar on Challenges Facing the Islamic Financial Industry, held on April 1, 2004, in Bali, Indonesia. The seminar, which was jointly organized by IRTI and IFSB, was held in conjunction with the meeting of the IFSB Council hosted by Bank Indonesia. To follow up on the issues discussed in the seminar, IRTI and IFSB undertook a joint initiative to address the challenges in a systematic manner and began preparing the Ten-Year Framework and Strategies document.

As a first step, a number of leading specialists and practitioners were asked to prepare technical papers on various themes. These were presented in a technical workshop jointly organized by IRTI and IFSB, held from May 31 to June 1, 2005, in Dubai, and hosted by the Dubai Financial Services Authority. IRTI and IFSB jointly held a policy dialogue on the same theme on June 22, 2005, in Putrajaya, Malaysia, which was facilitated by Bank Negara Malaysia. A drafting committee was formed as a result, which held three meetings and finalized a draft document. The draft document was distributed by IFSB to solicit feedback from its members and other interested parties. It was also discussed at the Islamic Bankers' Forum on May 28, 2006, in Kuwait, which was jointly organized by IRTI, IFSB, and the General Council for Islamic Banks and Financial Institutions (CIBAFI). At its final meeting on August 17, 2006, in Kuala Lumpur, Malaysia, the drafting committee reviewed all the comments, received feedback, and reached a consensus on the revised document.

Why Was a Mid-Term Review Conducted?

In 2013, IRTI and IFSB initiated a Mid-Term Review of the Ten-Year Framework, as more than half the period has passed since its publication in 2007. The MTR was aimed at assessing the impact of macroeconomic events, monitoring progress in implementing the recommendations, and proposing additions or modifications to the recommendations to guide the industry. The effort was considered crucial due to the increasingly challenging economic and financial environments, as well as the significant developments taking place in the international financial landscape, particularly after the 2008 global financial crisis. Even more important was to ensure that the Ten-Year Framework document remained relevant as a platform for various Islamic finance jurisdictions to assist them in orchestrating the future direction of the industry. The Mid-Term Review was guided by the following objectives:

- To assess the impact of developments in the global financial system following the global financial crisis on various segments of the Islamic finance industry
- To examine the progress and current status of the priorities and initiatives suggested in the Ten-Year Framework and Strategies
- To identify gaps in implementing the priorities and initiatives
- To assess the need for a reorientation of such priorities and initiatives.

The Mid-Term Review thus sought to assess progress made by the industry in implementing the 2007 recommendations of the Ten-Year Framework and to amend it in light of developments since its publication.

In conducting the Mid-Term Review, IRTI and IFSB were supported by a number of prominent research institutions and have engaged with leading regulators, market players, academicians, and *shari'ah* scholars. Intensive discussions took place in roundtables held in Qatar, Malaysia, and Turkey, where IRTI and IFSB had an opportunity to obtain further insights from key stakeholders and the entire Review Committee.

What Were the MTR's Key Findings?

Following in-depth research and engagement with key stakeholders in the industry, the MTR document generated three main findings:

1. The industry has shown growth and resilience. Market share and profitability are growing, the number of institutions has expanded, and numerous industry-level initiatives are under way, reflecting customer confidence in the sector, whose concept has been proved in many markets.
2. Macroeconomic events and external factors have brought both challenges and opportunities to the sector, which has been affected by the global financial crisis directly and indirectly, via the economic impact, the approach to financial regulation, the strength of partners and counterparties, and the value of assets and investments. As the global economy has stumbled, some member-countries of the IDB have acted as important centers of growth. Political developments in recent years have also made several countries more open to Islamic financial services. Technological innovations such as branchless financial services are now available, which can allow the industry to broaden its reach.
3. The development of the industry has varied by sector. Islamic banking remains the most developed subsector of the industry. Estimates of its total asset size and growth rate vary significantly (from nearly $1 trillion to well above that level). To cite a notable example, Islamic microfinance has made the transition from a concept with isolated case studies to a fledgling sector in multiple markets. Moreover, the breadth and sophistication of *shari'ah*-compliant instruments (shares and *sukūk*) in capital markets have improved. However the performance of certain instruments in terms of market value has been mixed due to overall capital market challenges. Challenges related to the *shari'ah* compliance remain.

What Are the Distinct Features of the MTR?

Three additional recommendations were made (in addition to the 13 recommendations in the original document):

- Recommendation no. 14. Develop an understanding of the linkages and dependencies between different components of Islamic financial services to enable more informed strategic planning to be undertaken.

- Recommendation no. 15. Foster and embrace innovative business models, including new technologies and delivery channels, in offering Islamic financial services.
- Recommendation no. 16. Strengthen contributions to the global dialogue on financial services, offering principles and perspectives to enhance the global financial system.

The three-pillar framework was introduced. While the original document categorized the recommendations into two groups (institutional and infrastructural), the new categorization (enablement, performance, and reach) places greater emphasis on the outcome desired from the framework. The first pillar (enablement) centers on fostering conditions for the industry to thrive. The second pillar (performance) supports efforts to enhance the effectiveness of institutions active in the industry. The third pillar (reach) seeks to substantially increase the commitment to expand the set of potential beneficiaries in the industry.

Key performance indicators (KPIs) were developed to help address weaknesses and monitor progress in a more focused manner. As noted, the progress made on the original recommendations has been mixed. While many countries have adopted international standards specific to Islamic financial services, those have not gone far enough and more work is needed.

Metrics for tracking progress, which initially were not specified, are now considered crucial for assessing progress. Thus the MTR proposes a set of KPIs, and countries are urged to set national targets to meet them.

A stronger implementation plan was established for a range of stakeholders. The role of central banks and governments will be especially important in driving implementation.

Twenty Key Initiatives were identified and prioritized, based on their potential impact and the feasibility of implementation (see table 9.2).

Distinctive features of the MTR are illustrated in figure 9.1. As the figure shows, the framework is dynamic. The three main pillars (enablement, performance, and reach) support the 16 core recommendations, implementation plans, and key initiatives, but all those elements strengthen one another and strengthen the entire system.

Why Does the MTR Matter?

The recommendations of the MTR must be implemented in a diverse group of nations that vary in terms of region, culture, stages of economic development, and types of law (Islamic Law, common law, and civil law). Thus the MTR recognizes that diverse views are particularly salient with respect to whether

- Countries should have specific laws for Islamic financial services or fit Islamic structures into a single set of financial services laws.
- Countries should adopt national-level *shari'ah* boards or retain *shari'ah* governance solely at the institutional level.
- Central banks should allow conventional institutions to offer Islamic financial services.
- Adopting international standards specific to Islamic finance is essential or not.
- Product standardization should be a policy objective or not.

Against this diverse backdrop, an underlying theme is that a supportive public policy stance is essential to enable the industry to reach its full potential. Different countries have been successful under various models; each choice has benefits and drawbacks. In all models, a strong and supportive public policy stance can help contribute to greater confidence, which energizes the private sector.

The MTR therefore does not seek to prescribe specific approaches to the choices above. It does, however, urge various jurisdictions to deliberate carefully on these matters and form well-considered strategies. The MTR also encourages Islamic financial services to offer benefits to the wider economy and the public at large, and advocates thoughtful strategies on how best to bring about these benefits.

TABLE 9.2 **Twenty Key Initiatives under the Mid-Term Review**

Pillar	Initiative
Enablement	Integrate Islamic finance in national development plans.
	Introduce national Islamic financial services master plans.
	Enhance regulatory implementation and enforcement.
	Harmonize, where possible, regulation and regulatory frameworks across borders.
	Adopt and strengthen national *shari'ah* governance frameworks.
	Where mandates overlap, align the positions of industry bodies.
	Link Islamic financial markets across borders.
	Form a "Technical Assistance and Linkage Network."
	Form regional working groups.
	Foster information-providing institutions that support the provision of Islamic finance.
	Incorporate Islamic finance data in statistical and official reporting.
Performance	Institute centralized R&D for Islamic financial products in addition to the decentralized R&D.
	Establish diversified financial institutions.
	Demonstrate the industry's distinctive value proposition.
	Fund public infrastructure projects to build Islamic capital markets.
Reach	Revitalize *zakāt* and *awqāf* for greater financial inclusion and make them an integrated part of the Islamic financial system.
	Ensure that regulations allow for the use of new technology to provide affordable services.
	Engage with newly opened markets.
	Foster the financing of a wider set of economic sectors.
	Brand Islamic financial services for wider markets.

Source: IRTI, IDB, and IFSB 2014.
Note: R&D = research and development.

FIGURE 9.1 **Distinctive Features of the Mid-Term Review**

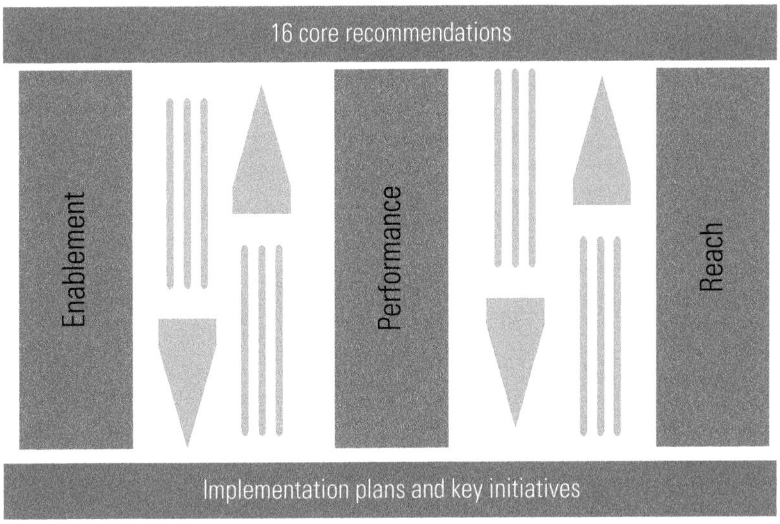

As a result, the framework recognizes the need to uplift the underprivileged in society so they can also benefit from the economic growth. The framework also recognizes that the "financialization" of economies has considerably worsened the linkage between the real sector and the financial sector and has failed to ensure that the least privileged benefit from economic growth.[2]

The third pillar of the MTR addresses such issues. It shares this focus with the World Bank Group, which has recently revised its mission to make "shared prosperity" the second of its twin goals (see chapter 1). The MTR and the World Bank Group are committed to this goal; however, the mechanisms of attaining a society based on shared prosperity under each approach might differ.

As discussed in chapter 1, achieving shared prosperity from the perspective of Islamic economics and finance is based on four fundamental pillars: an institutional framework and public policy in line with the objectives of Islam; prudent governance and accountable leadership; promotion of an economy based on risk sharing and entrepreneurship; and financial and social inclusion for all.

Enacting and Implementing Policies to Promote Shared Prosperity: A Three-Nation Case Study

This section examines whether policy objectives in selected jurisdictions are in line with the notion of shared prosperity by seeing how they have adopted the MTR's Key Initiatives. The analysis compares the strategic plan or road map established in selected jurisdictions, and related efforts, with the Key Initiatives. Indonesia, Malaysia, and Pakistan were selected because these countries have comprehensive road maps or strategic plans.

The objective of the comparison is to figure out whether the MTR and the selected strategic plans and road maps are moving in the same or similar directions. In addition to content analysis, feedback was also gathered from regulators in Indonesia (Financial Services Authority, Otoritas Jasa Keuangan) and Malaysia (Bank Negara Malaysia).

Over the course of the Mid-Term Review process, over 70 initiatives were suggested to help implement the recommendations. These initiatives included ideas from sector specialists, input from expert reviewers, and guidance from various review committees. An analysis of how Indonesia, Malaysia, and Pakistan have adopted these initiatives follows.

Integrate Islamic Finance in National Development Plans and Introduce National Islamic Financial Services Master Plans

This initiative is of the utmost importance since it is the basis for the institutional building and policy formulation to bring about shared prosperity. Some recent developments in selected jurisdictions have been promising. The fact that a strategic plan or a road map on a national level is in place in jurisdictions such as Indonesia, Malaysia, and Pakistan shows that the governments in those countries are no longer taking Islamic finance lightly.

The Indonesian government committed to taking the initiative to the next level by establishing the National Committee in Islamic Finance, chaired directly by the president of Indonesia, Joko Widodo (box 9.1). Indonesia recently introduced a revised version of its 2002 road map. In addition, the Financial Services Authority (OJK), has come up with a road map for Islamic capital market development and a road map for sustainable finance in Indonesia for 2015–19 (Indonesia OJK 2015a, 2015b, 2015c). Although the road map for sustainable finance does not address Islamic finance directly, the objectives of promoting economic sectors such as agriculture, manufacturing, infrastructure, SMEs, and energy, which contribute to sustainable development and have a high multiplier effect for the Indonesian economy, are aligned with the norms of Islamic finance. A key step forward would be if the country could promote Islamic modes of financing to mobilize funds and investment for these sectors.

BOX 9.1 Indonesia's Initiative to Take Islamic Finance to the Next Level of Development

Indonesia has become one of the main engines for growth in the world of Islamic finance. However, compared to the country's huge potential and its large Muslim population, the development of Islamic finance in Indonesia remains modest. Penetration of Islamic finance has been surprisingly low: only 3.7 percent of the total banking sector, according to the latest data in the *World Islamic Banking Competitiveness Report 2016* (Ernst & Young 2015).

It has become evident that the traditional bottom-up approach in Indonesia can no longer be relied upon. Thus the Financial Services Authority (Otoritas Jasa Keuangan, OJK) felt the need to provide further clarity on how the Islamic finance industry should move forward. Hence it undertook a revision of the first blueprint for the development of Islamic banking development, first published in 2002. A revision is vital to align future steps with the long-term development plan for the Indonesian economy and to anticipate the commencement of the South East Asia Economic Society in early 2016. In early 2015, OJK published the road map for the development of Islamic banking development (OJK 2015a), followed by the road map for the development of the Islamic capital market (OJK 2015b) and a road map for sustainable finance (OJK 2015c) in Indonesia.

Sustainable finance from OJK's viewpoint is defined as comprehensive support from the financial services industry to achieve sustainable development resulting from a harmonious relationship between economic, social, institutional-governance, and environmental interests.

The road map for sustainable finance sets forth a detailed work plan on the sustainable finance program for the banking, capital market, and nonbank sectors of the financial services industry as governed by OJK. The road map is also aligned with the Master Plan for Indonesia's Financial Services Sector, which will serve as a reference for other stakeholders in the sustainable finance program.

The goals of the sustainable finance program in Indonesia include the following:

1. Improving the resilience and competitiveness of the financial services industry so it can grow and develop in a sustainable manner. Resilience, in this respect, is associated with improved risk management, while competitiveness is associated with the ability to innovate and produce environmentally friendly products and services.
2. Providing financing resources required by the public by using the pro-growth, pro-job, pro-poor, and pro-environment approach.
3. Contributing to the national commitment to address the challenge of global warming by supporting businesses' efforts to mitigate and adapt to climate change, in a move toward a competitive low-carbon economy.

Sources. Indonesia OJK 2015a, 2015b, 2015c

The Malaysian government amended its Islamic Financial Services Act in 2013 (Bank Negara Malaysia 2013). The following are among the major changes:

- It consolidated various pieces of legislation, acts, and regulations issued at different points in time for various financial subsectors. The consolidated act helps remove ambiguities across subsectors.
- It provided legal recognition and standing for *shari'ah* governance and the *shari'ah* governance framework. Such governance had been in practice previously but had not had legal cover.
- Most significantly, it required financial institutions to properly differentiate between Islamic deposits (which are principal-guaranteed *shari'ah* contracts) and investment accounts (which are principal-nonguaranteed *shari'ah* contracts) in their business processes and clearly communicate the differences to stakeholders. This implies putting into place appropriate processes to utilize such funds, calculate their profits, maintain transparency, and communicate this information.

Pakistan's central bank has set out its strategic plan for 2014–18 regarding the Islamic banking industry (SBP 2014). This is an effort to reach an industry-wide consensus on the future direction of the industry in the country. The four key elements of this strategy are well aligned with the recommendations of the MTR:

1. *Enabling of the policy environment.* Enabling the legal, regulatory, supervisory, and liquidity management frameworks, the taxation regime, and the financial accounting and reporting framework
2. *Shari'ah governance and compliance.* Standardization and harmonization of *shari'ah* practices, as well as creation of distinct Islamic banking products and services
3. *Awareness and capacity building.* Increasing coordination and collaboration among internal and external stakeholders to enhance awareness of Islamic finance and build stakeholders' capacity
4. *Market development.* Initiatives for product diversification and financial inclusion, with the collaboration of stakeholders.

Harmonize, Where Possible, Regulation and Regulatory Frameworks across Borders

Harmonization of regulations is necessary to increase cross-border market activity and to encourage more collaboration between market players. In the context of Islamic finance, the importance of harmonization of *shari'ah* through *fiqh* interpretations cannot be understated. *Shari'ah* scholars in Indonesia and Malaysia regularly conduct symposiums on these matters. Although both countries follow the same school of thought, in practice there are differences that cannot be overlooked. A similar effort to resolve differences in understanding may be considered in the Indian subcontinent.

Adopt and Strengthen the National *Shari'ah* Governance Framework

Prudent governance and accountable leadership are required to bring about shared prosperity and are needed to support the development of Islamic finance. The *shari'ah* governance framework is advanced in all three countries, particularly Malaysia. All three countries have introduced a comprehensive two-tiered *shari'ah* governance framework whereby *shari'ah* boards are in place not only at the national level but also at the institutional level. In all three countries, no *shari'ah* scholar may serve in more than two Islamic financial institutions. This limitation is in place to ensure the credibility and accountability of not only the products and the institutions, but more importantly the industry as a whole.

Where Mandates Overlap, Align the Position of Industry Bodies

A strong commitment to create synergies among regulators across sectors is needed. The banking sector has been the dominant sector in the Islamic financial services industry. Harmonization of regulations is needed to enable other sectors to flourish as well. The governments of Indonesia and Pakistan have clearly stated that effective coordination and collaboration among key stakeholders are vital for sustaining the momentum for growth of Islamic finance.

The principles set out by standard-setting bodies in the Islamic financial services industry, such as the IFSB and AAOIFI, also need to be synchronized with one another. All three countries have made a strong commitment to continuously align their regulations with the principles of these bodies.

Establish Diversified Financial Institutions

Achieving an economy based on shared prosperity cannot be attained by depending solely on the banking sector, given its risk tolerance, costs, and business model. It is thus very important to support the development of other segments of the sector to achieve balanced growth of a stable and inclusive industry that covers the full spectrum of financial services. Indonesia and Pakistan are excellent examples; their respective road maps

BOX 9.2 Diversified Institutions and Efforts toward Financial Inclusion: Highlights of Some Policy Initiatives of the State Bank of Pakistan

- The State Bank of Pakistan (SBP) has developed a National Financial Inclusion Strategy (NFIS) that encompasses many of the areas needed to develop the Islamic financial sector (SBP 2015a). The Strategy covers Islamic finance, along with other areas such as branchless banking, SME finance, infrastructure finance, microfinance, rural and agricultural finance, housing finance, digital payment systems, consumer protection and financial literacy, insurance, and pensions.
- Pakistan has a well-recognized legal and regulatory framework for microfinance. In 2015, ten microfinance banks (MFBs) were operating in Pakistan. All are privately owned and have a diversity of ownership and approaches.
- Three leading microfinance institutions (MFIs) have been transformed into MFBs. They are now among the top five MFBs in the country.
- Pakistan is one of the few countries in the world that has a national microfinance credit information bureau.
- A microfinance credit guarantee facility provides MFBs and MFIs with the access to commercial funding sources such as banks and the domestic capital market.
- Branchless banking has become a promising way to deliver financial services at low cost. Pakistan has built up the retail capacity of financial institutions through an agent network that reduces service delivery costs. The use of such services is growing quickly. For example, during the last quarter of 2014, around 72 million transactions worth PRs 372 billion ($3.55 billion) were processed, with an average size of PRs 5,181 (about $50).[a] A Secured Transaction Law will facilitate establishment of a registry office in the country to use movable assets as collateral.
- SBP has issued a separate regulatory framework for housing finance.[b]
- SBP is encouraging the development of agricultural financing based on warehouse receipts and *salam* concepts. It has issued a consultative paper on the "Framework of Warehouse Receipt Financing in Pakistan" (SBP 2015b).

Source: Compiled from various sources available at the SBP website, http://www.sbp.org.pk/.
a. Speech by Riaz Riazudding, deputy governor, State Bank of Pakistan, July 6, 2015. http://www.sbp.org.pk/DG-Speeches/DGSpeech-06-Jul-2015.pdf.
b. Speech by Ashraf Mahmood Wathra, governor, State Bank of Pakistan, May 28, 2015, delivered at the International Conference on Affordable Housing Finance. http://www.sbp.org.pk/about/speech/Governors/Mr.Ashraf.Mahmood.Wathra/2015/Affordable-Housing-28-May-15.pdf.

explicitly state the need for diversification at the level of both products and institutions. More importantly, the road maps also address the need to move away from products that create debt and toward greater use of products based on risk sharing.

Diversified financial services increase financial inclusion. Further improvement is possible through policies that target the adoption of new technologies to lower the cost of delivery of finance, incorporate regulatory changes to increase the use of the new delivery channels, and enhance financial literacy to increase its acceptance by the population. This route has been followed in the National Financial Inclusion Strategy recently embraced by Pakistan (SBP 2015a) (box 9.2).

Revitalize *Zakāt* and *Awqāf* for Greater Financial Inclusion and Make Them an Integrated Part of Islamic Financial System

The potential of *zakāt* and *awqāf* in alleviating poverty and improving financial inclusion is high. However, use of this potential requires not only initiatives from the contributors but also a concrete support from the authority at the national level, as it involves working with *zakāt* organizations, financial institutions, and the *zakāt* beneficiaries. In Indonesia, for instance, *zakāt* is a tax-deductible instrument; such a policy is expected to encourage more people to pay the annual *zakāt* obligation. This practice has a legal standing based on the Indonesian National Act on *Zakāt* Management (Act No. 38/1999).[3] Following registration at the *Zakāt* National Authority (BAZNAS), the *muzakki* (*zakāt* payer) will receive a *zakāt* ID card along with a *zakāt* ID number (NPWZ).[4] Once the payer completes the *zakāt* payment at the bank or via an automated teller machine (ATM), as a proof of *zakāt* payment, the payer will automatically receive a notification from BAZNAS stating that the *zakāt* payment has been received. The proof is then factored in when paying the tax. The initiative indicates the government's commitment to make this sector part of the Islamic financial system. Indonesia and Pakistan are perhaps the strongest proponents of incorporating financial inclusion as a policy objective.

Foster the Financing of a Wider Set of Economic Sectors

Islamic finance is often known for serving the "haves" rather than the "have nots," which may be contrary to the fundamental principles of ideal Islamic finance and the rationale for institutionalizing Islamic finance. Current evidence may reinforce such a contention. However, some recent efforts may be widening the economic base for Islamic finance somewhat. For instance, the introduction of retail *sukūk*[5] in Indonesia is an indication that Islamic finance can also be designed to cater to segments of society with lower net worth. It will facilitate greater retail participation in the *sukūk* market by making *sukūk* available in smaller denominations that can be bought directly by retail investors. This not only meets the retail investors' demand for access to a wider range of investment products, but increases the diversity of the investor base to the issuers and makes the market more liquid. Access for retail investors to *sukūk* was previously available only through *sukūk* unit trust funds (mutual funds) and exchange traded funds. Retail investors buy for their own investment; they are the direct opposite of institutional investors, who buy on behalf of their clients and have the capacity to hold until maturity.

Pakistan clearly makes financial inclusion a goal in its road map of Islamic banking development and Islamic capital market development for the 2014–18 period. Pakistan also places greater importance on channeling financing to the agriculture sector and to SMEs.

Incorporate Islamic Finance Data in Statistical and Official Reporting

Some jurisdictions have started to compile Islamic finance data as an official reporting requirement for their regulatory purposes. About 16 jurisdictions are now collecting and reporting aggregated prudential indicators data proposed by the IFSB. Indonesia, Malaysia, and Pakistan are among the countries that are collecting and compiling such data and regularly contributing to the IFSB database on prudential indicators for Islamic banking. Data for 2013 and all quarters of 2014 are available now on the IFSB website.[6]

Develop the Required Pool of Specialized, Competent, and High-Caliber Human Capital

The development of a pool of competent, skilled, and high-caliber human capital is also important for developing Islamic finance and using it to enhance shared prosperity. Pakistan has been developing education and research infrastructure to promote Islamic finance in partnership with leading higher education institutions. It aims to develop the industry's human capital base in the form of Islamic finance professionals, specialists including *shari'ah* scholars, economists, and researchers to meet the growing demands for compliant products and services in Pakistan. Through a nationwide competition, three universities have been selected to establish Centers of Excellence in Islamic Finance in three provinces. The impact of these centers will be felt in a few years.

Malaysia has established the International *Shari'ah* Research Academy (ISRA) as part of the International Centre for Education in Islamic Finance (INCEIF) at the national level, as well as several other smaller institutions affiliated with educational institutions or professional bodies, to meet the human capital needs of this growing sector. Along similar lines, Indonesia has also created centers of learning and training at the national and regional levels.

Islamic finance has been a priority area in Malaysia for more than three decades. Because of strong policy commitment, legal, institutional, and regulatory frameworks and infrastructure have evolved and are in place. However, despite such support and commitment, Islamic finance's share of the market is still below potential. The reason why is related to the fact that every system develops its own culture, and the culture it develops help perpetuate the system. The financial institutions, supporting rules, and methods that were created for Islamic finance were not radical departures from the existing debt-based institutions. However, with the introduction of the Financial Services Act in 2013, it is expected that the public will be able to distinguish between an Islamic and conventional financial institution in terms of product offering, and it is hoped that this will lead to higher penetration of Islamic finance in Malaysia.

Table 9.3 depicts the key initiatives set out by MTR's three pillars against the progress of Islamic finance development in Indonesia, Malaysia, and Pakistan.

TABLE 9.3 Progress in Developing Islamic Finance in Indonesia, Malaysia, and Pakistan

MTR's three pillars	Twenty key initiatives	Country analysis			Remarks
		Indonesia	Malaysia	Pakistan	
Enablement	Integrate Islamic finance in national development plans.				Well established in all three countries.
	Introduce national Islamic financial services master plans.				Well formulated in all three countries.
	Enhance implementation and enforcement of regulations.				May require further development.
	Harmonize, where possible, regulation and regulatory frameworks across borders.				Harmonization does not take place across jurisdictions. Furthermore, although Indonesia and Malaysia share the same *fiqh* school of thought, in practice there are variations of financial products offered in the market.
	Adopt and strengthen national *shari'ah* governance frameworks.				Malaysia may be most advanced.
	Where mandates overlap, align the positions of industry bodies.				Adaptation and adoption are promising.
	Link Islamic financial markets across borders.				Needs a boost.
	Form a Technical Assistance and Linkage Network.				Further synergy needed.
	Form regional working groups.				

table continues next page

TABLE 9.3 Progress in Developing Islamic Finance in Indonesia, Malaysia, and Pakistan *(continued)*

MTR's three pillars	Twenty key initiatives	Country analysis			Remarks
		Indonesia	Malaysia	Pakistan	
	Foster institutions that support the provision of information about Islamic finance.				
	Incorporate Islamic finance data in statistical and official reporting.				Efforts established by central banks in each country.
Performance	Institute centralized R&D for Islamic financial products in addition to the decentralized R&D.				This is a vital initiative that remains largely unmet.
	Establish diversified financial institutions.				
	Demonstrate the industry's distinctive value proposition.				Indonesia stands out, as it has introduced the concept of sustainable finance that also fosters a harmonious relationship with economic, social, and environmental interests.[a]
	Fund public infrastructure projects to build Islamic capital markets.				
Reach	Revitalize *zakāt* and *awqāf* for greater financial inclusion and make them an integrated part of the Islamic financial system.				
	Ensure that regulations allow for the use of new technology to provide affordable services.				The act and regulations are rather silent on this matter. Pakistan has issued a National Financial Inclusion Strategy and made some progress in exploiting new technology in delivering financial services to a wider population at lower cost.
	Engage with newly opened markets.				
	Foster the financing of a wider set of economic sectors.				
	Brand Islamic financial services for wider markets.				

Source: Compiled from the Mid-Term Review of the Ten-Year Framework and Strategies.
a. Road map for Sustainable Finance in Indonesia 2015–2019, 16.

Work is fully implemented. Work is under way. Work has started. Work needs to be initiated or developed.

Challenges and Policy Recommendations

Recognition is growing among policy makers in the financial sector that with its emphasis on risk sharing and asset-based financing, Islamic finance has the potential to foster investment and infrastructure, and thus to support the Group of Twenty (G-20) strategy to raise global economic growth. One recent positive development is the attention that the G-20, under the presidency of Turkey, has given to Islamic finance. The final communique of the G-20 meeting in 2015 made explicit reference to alternative financing, such as asset-based finance, which needs to be developed through capital markets.[7] Such encouraging developments offer significant opportunities to the stakeholders of Islamic finance to take core principles of Islamic finance to the next level and to have Islamic finance compete at a global level through its value proposition of risk-sharing, asset-based, and ethical finance.

A joint G-20 draft note prepared by the World Bank and International Monetary Fund (2015), in consultation with the IDB and other stakeholders, highlights the need for integrating Islamic finance in the global financial system (see box 9.3). The note calls for the full adoption of IFSB and AAOIFI standards to manage the risks arising from exposure to equity, complexity of products, and uncertainties over resolution of insolvency.

In addition to these efforts, creating supportive infrastructure in the form of business information bureaus that can collect and share information about business worthiness (as opposed to creditworthiness) of firms seeking finance will greatly help Islamic banks as well as other nonbank institutions scale up financing to SMEs and microenterprises.

Finally, in its developmental stage, the Islamic financial services industry needs strong public policy support from the governments and stakeholders to realize the full potential of Islamic finance in achieving sustainable development and becoming a beacon of shared prosperity.

Long-term sustainability of Islamic finance can be achieved if Islamic financial

BOX 9.3 Integrating Islamic Finance into Global Finance: IMF–World Bank Joint G-20 Note

For countries that wish to further develop Islamic finance, **national policies** should aim to build an enabling environment and level the playing field with conventional finance. Actions could include the following:

- Further opening up to Islamic financial services, including by considering granting licenses to new Islamic financial institutions, and adapting regulatory and supervisory frameworks to take into account the industry's specific features (national regulators) where deemed appropriate
- Exploring means for enhancing liquidity management of Islamic banks (central banks)
- Adapting tax systems to avoid Islamic finance instruments being at a disadvantage (ministries of finance)
- Tapping into *sukūk* markets to finance investment through asset-pooling schemes that could allow for regular issuance of tradable instruments while strengthening public investment frameworks (ministries of finance)
- Providing the right incentives to ease access to asset-based and equity-like financing, particularly for SMEs (ministries of finance and regulators).

At the **global level**, actions could include the following:

- Increasing the G-20 membership in the Islamic finance standard setters
- Leveraging these institutions to further cooperation and experience sharing among the G-20 members, and advance standardization, notably of *sukūk*
- Granting membership to Islamic finance standard setters in the consultative groups of global standard setters with the view to strengthen the emerging cooperation between these institutions
- Systematically incorporating the industry's features in global standards and guidance, and developing accounting and statistics standards for *sukūk*
- Stepping up the engagement of international financial institutions and multilateral development banks (MDBs) in Islamic finance through analytical work, policy advice, and capacity development
- Expanding MDBs' operations to include Islamic finance instruments.

Sources: http://www.g20.org.tr/wp-content/uploads/2015/09/IMF-WBG-Note-on-Integrating-Islamic-Finance-into-Global-Finance.docx. Also see: http://g20.org.tr/resources/current-presidency/?stream%5B%5D&wpv_column_sort_id=post_date&wpv_column_sort_dir=desc&wpv_post_id=4472&wpv_view_count=4475-CPID4472&wpv_paged=1.

services have a positive impact on the lives of a broader spectrum of people. Islamic finance holds the promise of sharing risk, sharing prosperity, promoting social and economic justice and ethical finance, strengthening linkages with real economic activity, increasing the stability of financial systems, and supporting the pursuit of mutual gains with social responsibility. To realize these benefits, policy makers need to address the challenges and issues that are constraining the proper development of Islamic finance. The policy stance must be clear, firm, and openly made in coordination with various stakeholders.

Development of sustainable legal and economic institutions—as envisioned by the principles of Islamic economics and articulated in chapter 1—should be the first priority. Development of institutions cannot be done overnight; it takes time and requires strong commitment and efforts by policy makers. A long-term view and vision is required to achieve the full potential of such institutions. Issues can be prioritized as part of the strategy by the national and supranational authorities, instead of avoiding them because they are difficult. Some recent developments are highlighted in box 9.4.

Many of the problems in the current direction the Islamic finance industry is taking and its deficiencies in achieving the goals of risk sharing and shared prosperity can be traced to the tendency to avoid addressing these systemic challenges. When faced with bottlenecks, which the individual financial institutions cannot correct by themselves, the players in the industry tend to seek out suboptimal short-term solutions. These devices or strategies provide them a way out of the difficulty, but they do not necessarily generate long-term solutions or foster institutional development. This short-term, self-interested approach also dilutes the spirit and objectives of Islamic finance. Hence intervention by the authorities and coordination of efforts by all stakeholders to create an enabling environment for Islamic financial sector is very important.

As discussed in this Report, Islamic finance emphasizes financing economic transactions through trade finance, leasing, partnership, and securitization through asset-backed *sukūk*. Hence it can directly contribute to economic growth and shared prosperity. This approach entails commercial and economic risk taking and managing of those risks. However, the financial sector supervisory

BOX 9.4 Regulatory Developments at the International Level: Supporting Shared Prosperity

In the regulatory arena, a recent development is the issuance of core principles of the regulation of Islamic finance by the Islamic Financial Services Board (Standard No. IFSB-17) (IFSB 2015). One of the stated objectives of IFSB-17 is to link the financial sector with the real economic sector (see para. 8 of IFSB-17). Such a linkage is one of the key features of Islamic finance to promote the sharing of economic and enterprise risks among investors and financiers.

In the area of Islamic capital markets, the advocacy organization for the Islamic financial services industry, International Islamic Financial Markets (IIFM), has come up with two initiatives. The first is standardization of documents for various hedging and capital market products. The second is its work toward creating bankruptcy resolution regimes for *sukūk*. This second initiative is conducive to promotion of shared prosperity by streamlining *shari'ah* compliance and quick resolution in case of default and bankruptcy.

Source: Standard No. IFSB 17 is available at http://www.ifsb.org/standard/.
Note: More information about IIFM activities can be found at http://www.iifm.net/.

frameworks that exist in many countries focus only on financial risk management and thus hinder the growth of Islamic finance. For Islamic finance to flourish, key reforms are needed in the areas of financial sector regulations, liquidity management, taxation, bankruptcy resolution, and infrastructure to support asset-backed financing. Sector-specific policy recommendations are presented in table 9.4.

TABLE 9.4 Recommendations and Policy Interventions by Sector

	Institutional framework and public policy	Governance and leadership	Risk sharing and entrepreneurships	Financial and social inclusion
Banking	• Create an enabling regulatory environment by supporting consistent regulations and ensuring consistent implementation of the Basel III and Islamic Financial Services Board (IFSB) framework. • Ensure that systemic risks in dual banking systems (conventional and Islamic) are addressed. • Implement cross-border supervision. • Improve liquidity. • Ensure stability.	• Harmonize *shari'ah* governance through efforts to unify cross-country *shari'ah* rulings about Islamic finance.	• Introduce innovative risk-sharing products and services, rather than replicating conventional risk-transfer products.	• Enhance the scale of and access to Islamic finance to include low-income earners. • Bolster human capital. • Increase Islamic finance literacy.
Capital markets	• Create a level playing field for debt and equity instruments by o Eliminating the tax shelter on interest expense. o Allowing tax-free transfer of assets in asset-backed *sukūk* or at least treat the transfer fee as a tax-deductible expense.	• Incorporate higher ethical standards through a transparent governance mechanism and robust regulatory framework. • Improve *shari'ah* governance: o Align *shari'ah* screening standards for equities across jurisdictions o Publish *shari'ah* screening standards, and list compliant equities for the convenience of investors on a periodic basis. • Provide disclosures relevant to *shari'ah* compliance, especially events that may trigger noncompliance in the regular reporting of firms. • Strengthen resolution frameworks and investor protection mechanisms.	• Encourage investment in equities, which is the purest form of risk sharing that not only distributes wealth more equitably but also creates more jobs and enhances shared prosperity. • Improve the scalability and liquidity of *sukūk* by providing an enabling environment for trading *sukūk* in secondary markets. • Provide incentives for issuing long-term *sukūk* based on more equity-like structures such as *muḍārabah* and *mushārakah*.	• Introduce retail *sukūk* for smaller investors. • Relax the condition for listing of companies in order to provide a larger universe of equities for investment.

table continues next page

TABLE 9.4 Recommendations and Policy Interventions by Sector *(continued)*

	Institutional framework and public policy	Governance and leadership	Risk sharing and entrepreneurships	Financial and social inclusion
Takāful	• Adopt a holistic approach while formulating the policy guidelines for the industry that takes into consideration both the industry and consumer in a *shari'ah*-compliant manner. • Design policies that balance the protections for participants' rights with the need for effective pricing, greater solvency, operators' financial sustainability, good business conduct, and relevant disclosures. • To avoid confusion among Muslims, set up a board consisting of *shari'ah* scholars at the national level to provide guidance as to how to implement *takāful*. • Expand investment through the Islamic capital market to provide flexibility in the implementation of the risk-based capital regime.	• Establish clear and transparent corporate governance and a regulatory framework for the formal as well as informal *takāful* operations. • Regulate the *takāful* industry based on its risk characteristics. A risk-based approach may be desirable; however, this should take into consideration the difference between conventional insurance and *takāful*. • Set requirements for solvency purposes on the investment activities of *takāful* in order to address the risks faced by the operators.	• Introduce *takāful* and micro*takāful* as a mode for pooling risk and assets. • Recognize that the long-term *shari'ah*-compliant investment from the savings and investments in *takāful* funds can be a critical source for economic development. • Encourage investment in capital market instruments.	• Allow participants to use micro*takāful* for savings and investment. • Allow micro*takāful* for family, health, crop, livestock and property based on cooperative (*wakālah*-partner) model.
Nonbank financial institutions (NBFIs)	• Develop policies that require strong investor protection and stringent disclosure requirements as far as the investment is concerned. • Ensure that the products and activities of NBFIs comply with *shari'ah*.	• Develop legal infrastructure to support contract enforcement. This is a prerequisite for the development of the financial sector, as it not only reduces transaction costs but also enhances investor confidence. • Clearly define regulatory requirements such as licensing, disclosure, and corporate governance.	• Enhance diversification by directing more financing to small and medium enterprises relative to larger firms. • Develop skills and alternative approaches to mitigate risks (moral hazard) through proper monitoring and evaluation.	• Increase the number and diversity of Islamic NBFIs. • Encourage Islamic NBFIs to provide Islamic financial services in countries where establishing Islamic banks is not possible due to legal and regulatory restrictions.

table continues next page

TABLE 9.4 Recommendations and Policy Interventions by Sector *(continued)*

	Institutional framework and public policy	Governance and leadership	Risk sharing and entrepreneurships	Financial and social inclusion
Islamic social finance	• Recognize the diversity in *zakāt* management practices around the world and create an adequately flexible and enabling regulatory environment. • Introduce/reform the *waqf* regulatory framework in order to establish *waqf* as an institution in the voluntary sector. • Recognize Islamic social finance as a sustainable means of absorbing operational cost and provide "affordable" financing to the poor.	• Create a network of supporting infrastructure institutions, including research, training, and advocacy for the sound and orderly function of Islamic social finance institutions. • Develop a sound governance system that recognizes the significance of trust and credibility as key drivers underlying Islamic social finance. • Harmonize the financial reporting of the Islamic social finance institution to enhance transparency.	• Mitigate and absorb high risks with financing to the poor through mechanisms rooted in philanthropy and benevolence. • Make innovative use of *zakāt* and *waqf* to create risk management tools (credit enhancement/ guarantees and micro*takāful*).	• Recognize self-exclusion as a key problem due to religious, cultural, and ethical beliefs of the poor. • Enhance social and human capital through community empowerment initiatives funded through the sustainable Islamic social funding instrument.

Notes

1. Project-specific *sukūk* are the *sukūk* that are issued for financing a specific project (or a well-defined set of projects), and they generate returns for *sukūk* holders from the same project(s). For a general definition of *sukūk*, see the glossary.
2. See Palley (2007), who notes that the principal impacts of financialization are to elevate the significance of the financial sector relative to the real sector, transfer income from the real sector to the financial sector, and increase income inequality and contribute to wage stagnation.
3. http://kemenag.go.id/file/dokumen/UU3899.pdf.
4. NPWZ stands for Nomor Pokok Wajib *Zakāt*, or *zakāt* ID number.
5. Retail *sukūk* in Indonesia are available to individual investors, as opposed to only institutional investors. The minimum investment requirement is Rp 5 million (about $350).
6. For the Prudential and Structural Islamic Financial Indicators (PSIFIs) data, see http://ifsb.org/psifi_01.php.
7. http://www.g20.org/English/Documents/PastPresidency/201512/t20151201_1661.html.

References

Ahmed, Habib, Mahmoud Mohieldin, Jos Verbeek, and Farida Wael Aboulmagd. 2015. "On the Sustainable Development Goals and the Role of Islamic Finance." Policy Research Working Paper 7266, World Bank, Washington, DC.

Bank Negara Malaysia. 2013. "Islamic Financial Services Act 2013." http://www.bnm.gov.my/documents/act/en_ifsa.pdf.

Ernst & Young. 2015. *World Islamic Banking Competitiveness Report 2016.* http://www.ey.com/Publication/vwLUAssets/ey-world-islamic-banking-competitiveness-report-2016/$FILE/ey-world-islamic-banking-competitiveness-report-2016.pdf.

IFSB (Islamic Financial Services Board). 2015. *IFSB 17 Core Principles for Islamic Finance Regulation (Banking Segment).* http://www.ifsb.org/standard/IFSB17-%20Core%20Principles%20for%20Islamic%20Finance%20Regulation%20(Banking%20Segment)-April%202015_final.pdf.

IRTI, IDB, and IFSB (Islamic Research and Training Institute, Islamic Development Bank, and Islamic Financial Services Board). 2014. *Islamic Financial Services Industry Development: Ten-Year Framework and Strategies.*

A Mid-Term Review. http://www.ifsb.org/docs/2014-05-12A%20MID-TERM%20REVIEW%20FINAL.pdf.

OJK (Indonesia's Financial Services Authority). 2015a. "Roadmap for the Development of Islamic Banking." http://www.ojk.go.id/id/kanal/syariah/berita-dan-kegiatan/publikasi/Documents/roadmap-pbs_2015-2019.pdf.

———. 2015b. "Roadmap for Islamic Capital Market Development." http://www.ojk.go.id/Files/box/roadmap-pms_2015-2019.pdf.

———. 2015c. "Roadmap for Sustainable Finance in Indonesia 2015–2019." http://www.ojk.go.id/id/berita-dan-kegiatan/publikasi/Pages/Roadmap-Keuangan-Berkelanjutan-Sarana-Berinovasi-LJK.aspx.

Palley, Thomas I. 2007. "Financialization: What It Is and Why It Matters." Working Paper 153, Political Economy Research Institute, University of Massachusetts, Amherst. http://www.peri.umass.edu/fileadmin/pdf/working_papers/working_papers_151-200/WP153.pdf.

SBP (State Bank of Pakistan). Various years. "Various Speeches of the Governor and Deputy Governors." http://www.sbp.org.pk.

———. 2014. *Strategic Plan Islamic Banking Industry of Pakistan 2014–2018*. http://www.sbp.org.pk/departments/pdf/StrategicPlanPDF/Strategy%20Paper-Final.pdf.

———. 2015a. *National Financial Inclusion Strategy*. http://www.sbp.org.pk/AC&MFD/Events/National-Financial-Inclusion-Strategy-Pakistan.pdf.

———. 2015b. "Framework of Warehouse Receipt Financing in Pakistan." A Consultative Paper. http://www.sbp.org.pk/acd/Guidelines/2014/Draft-Frmwork-Warehouse-Receipt-Financing.pdf.

World Bank and IMF (International Monetary Fund). 2015. "Integrating Islamic Finance into Global Finance." Draft Note for the G-20. http://www.g20.org.tr/wp-content/uploads/2015/09/IMF-WBG-Note-on-Integrating-Islamic-Finance-into-Global-Finance.docx.

Chapter Attributions

Team Leads

Mohamed Azmi Omar, Director General, Islamic Research and Training Institute, Islamic Development Bank Group (IDBG)

Zamir Iqbal, Lead Financial Sector Specialist, Finance and Markets (F&M) Global Practice, World Bank

Team Coordinators

Dawood Ashraf, Senior Researcher–Islamic Finance, IDBG

Nihat Gumus, Financial Sector Specialist, World Bank

Authors by chapter

Chapter number	Chapter title	Author(s)
	Overview	Dawood Ashraf (IDBG) World Bank staff
1	Islamic Finance and Shared Prosperity	World Bank staff
2	The State of Development and Shared Prosperity in OIC Countries	World Bank staff
3	The Islamic Banking Sector	Ousmane Seck (IDBG) Muhamed Zulkhibri (IDBG) Tamsir Cham (IDBG) Anis Ben Khedher (IDBG) World Bank staff
4	Islamic Capital Markets	Syed Salman Ali (IDBG) Dawood Ashraf (IDBG) Anis Ben Khedher (IDBG) World Bank staff
5	*Takāful* (Islamic Insurance), Re*takāful*, and Micro*takāful*	Ezamshah Ismail (INCEIF) World Bank staff
6	Nonbank Financial Institutions	Habib Ahmed (Durham University) World Bank staff
7	Alternative Asset Classes	Rodney Wilson (INCEIF) Dawood Ashraf (IDBG)
8	Islamic Social Finance	Mohammed Obaidullah (IDBG) Nasim Shah Shirazi (IDBG)
9	Public Policy Measures to Enhance Shared Prosperity	Salman Syed Ali (IDBG) Hylmun Izhar (IDBG) World Bank staff

Note: IDBG = Islamic Development Bank Group; INCEIF = International Centre for Education in Islamic Finance.

Index

Boxes, figures, notes, and tables are indicated by "b," "f," "n," and "t" respectively.

E

F

Z

ECO-AUDIT

Environmental Benefits Statement

The World Bank Group is committed to reducing its environmental footprint. In support of this commitment, we leverage electronic publishing options and print-on-demand technology, which is located in regional hubs worldwide. Together, these initiatives enable print runs to be lowered and shipping distances decreased, resulting in reduced paper consumption, chemical use, greenhouse gas emissions, and waste.

We follow the recommended standards for paper use set by the Green Press Initiative. The majority of our books are printed on Forest Stewardship Council (FSC)–certified paper, with nearly all containing 50–100 percent recycled content. The recycled fiber in our book paper is either unbleached or bleached using totally chlorine-free (TCF), processed chlorine–free (PCF), or enhanced elemental chlorine–free (EECF) processes.

More information about the Bank's environmental philosophy can be found at http://www.worldbank.org/corporateresponsibility.

green press INITIATIVE